Christianity and Homosexuality

Christianity and Homosexuality
Some Seventh-day Adventist Perspectives

Edited by David Ferguson, Fritz Guy, and David R. Larson

Adventist Forum
Roseville, California

Adventist Forum
P.O. Box 619047
Roseville, California 95661-9047

© 2008 by Adventist Forum

All rights reserved. Published 2008

Library of Congress Cataloging-in-Publication Data
[TO BE REQUESTED from Library of Congress]

ISBN 09673694-2-8

Table of Contents

Dedication	vii
Preface	xi

Part One
    Autobiographical   P1-1

Learning to Spin the Coin of Truth
    By Sherri Babcock   P1-3
A Pastor's Perspective: Growing Up Adventist and Gay
    By Leif T. Lind   P1-15
Homosexuality and Seventh-day Adventist Families
    By Carrol Grady   P1-31
Response: Whose Choice? Which Closet?
    By Bonnie Dwyer   P1-53

Part Two
    Biomedical Perspectives   P2-1

Biological Determinants of Homosexual Orientation
    By Ben Kemena   P2-3
Psychiatry, Antihomosexual Bias, and Challenges
    for Gay and Lesbian Youth
    By Harry C. Wang   P2-29
Response: Science and Sexual Orientation
    By Aubyn Fulton   P2-45

Part Three
    Behavioral Science Perspectives   P3-1

Interaction and Angst: The Social Experiences of
    Gay and Lesbian Seventh-day Adventists
    By René D. Drumm   P3-3
The Caring, Welcoming Church? The Seventh-day Adventist
    Church and Its Homosexual Members
    By Ronald Lawson   P3-29
Response: Social Experiences in the "Caring Church"
    By Catherine Taylor   P3-75

Part Four
    Scriptural and Theological Perspectives   P4-1

"In Christ There Is Neither…":
    Toward the Unity of the Body of Christ
    By John R. Jones   P4-3
Same-sex Love: Theological Considerations
    By Fritz Guy   P4-43
Same-sex Love in the "Body of Christ"?
    By Roy E. Gane   P4-63
Is the Church Ready for Same-sex Sex?
    By Richard Rice   P4-73

Part Five
    Christian Social Perspectives   P5-1

Christian Sexual Norms Today: Some Proposals
    By David R. Larson   P5-3
Ministering to Gays within the Church Community:
    A Pastoral Perspective
    By Mitchell F. Henson   P5-23
Public Policy Issues Involving Homosexuality
    By Mitchell A. Tyner   P5-35
Love, Subsidiarity, Equality, and Inclusiveness
    By Gary Chartier   P5-51

Contributors   B-1
Scripture Index   B-4
Judicial Index   B-6
Subject Index   B-7

Dedication

In Memory of Mitchell Henson

Not many pastors can last for twenty-three years in one congregation, but Mitchell Henson did. He stood on the shoulders of a long list of leaders who have led the dynamic Glendale City Seventh-day Adventist church in Glendale, California, for over a century. He built on the legacy of these great preachers and innovative leaders. His ministry provided a challenge to other pastors to develop congregations that meet the great Advent message to bring the Gospel to every nation, kindred, tongue and people.

His congregation became a beacon of what it means to have an inclusive congregation, but this development was not without difficulties (examples of which are touched upon in Chapter 16, Mitch's contribution to this volume). However, through the years, every time a challenge has come, it has resulted in the congregation becoming more solid in its support of a welcoming ministry—including the establishment of special programs and official policies. All of this was the result of Mitch's preaching and the living model of warmth and caring he provided.

This book is therefore dedicated to Mitch's memory in gratitude—and in the hope that other pastors and individual members will, through a reading of this material, choose to address the challenge of creating more welcoming, inclusive congregations.

Preface

Preface

This is an important book. It is the result of a comprehensive, collective Seventh-day Adventist effort to come to terms with the tension between traditional Adventist understandings of human sexuality and the realities of homosexual orientation, experience, and relationships.

Like many other Christian communities of faith, we Adventists take seriously the contents of the Bible *as a whole* as "the infallible revelation of [God's] will"; and the Bible nowhere has anything good to say about same-sex relationships.[1] Yet within our fellowship is a significant number of persons who are dedicated, active members of Adventist congregations and at the same time partners in committed, long-term homosexual relationships—persons who are, in effect, incurably Adventist *and* incurably gay. In the 1970s, some of these Adventists formed Seventh-day Adventist Kinship International, which was incorporated as a not-for-profit organization in 1981 and now has more than one thousand members in twenty countries on five continents.[2] One of the Kinship officers serves as liaison with the General Conference of Seventh-day Adventists. In 1980, the first general membership meeting—the first annual Kinship Kampmeeting—convened at Payton, Arizona. In 2000, Kinship invited a dozen heterosexual Adventists—pastors, teachers, administrators, and health care professionals—to become members of a Kinship Advisory Council and thus to help Kinship increase the general Adventist understanding of homosexuality. In January 2006, with the support of the Adventist Forum and a grant from the E. Rhodes and Leona B. Carpenter Foundation, the Advisory Council sponsored a conference in Ontario, California, which provided a first reading of most of the papers that constitute this book.

Part One offers three personal accounts of homosexuality within Adventism—the stories of the daughter of a respected educator, of a pastor who served the Church on three continents, and of the mother of a gay man—with a response by a journalist and editor. Part Two gives the biomedical perspectives of two experienced physicians, one an academic clinician and the other a child psychiatrist in private practice; the response is by a psychologist. Part Three addresses individual and collective issues in the Adventist experience of homosexuality, with reports by a professor of social work and a sociologist, and a response by a licensed clinical social worker. Part Four contains an extensive examination of the relevant biblical materials by a New Testament scholar and a reflection by a theologian, with responses by an Old Testament scholar and another theologian. Part Five address issues of

Preface

personal ethics, pastoral ministry, and public policy, with a response by a scholar in business ethics and law.

Each chapter stands on its own. As a result, the book has two prominent characteristics—diversity and reiteration—that we regard as assets rather than liabilities. We have made no attempt to homogenize the contents, perspectives, or literary styles of the various chapters, nor have we endeavored to eliminate the repetition of facts and ideas as the authors developed their own independent contributions to the discussion.

We hope that *Christianity and Homosexuality: Some Seventh-day Adventist Perspectives* will stimulate conversation and enhance understanding among Adventists around the world—hence the responses and the questions at the end of each chapter. The word *some* in the subtitle reflects our awareness of other, quite different Adventist points of view; we expect to learn from them as they are expressed in critical reviews of the book and of its individual chapters. Thus we intend the book to be an expansion and not the end of the ongoing conversation.

We also hope that the book will benefit those in other communities interested in the realities of sexual orientation and relationships. The chapters provide information and insights not readily available elsewhere, and some of them break new interpretive and conceptual ground.

We are profoundly grateful for the generous investment of time and effort by the authors of the chapters and the responses. We are also grateful for the initiative and encouragement of the Kinship Advisory Council; the moral support of the publisher, the Adventist Forum; the financial support of SDA Kinship International; and the technical expertise of Leigh Johnsen as copyeditor and Steve Smith as layout designer.

David Ferguson
Fritz Guy
David R. Larson

Notes and References

1. The quotation comes from the Seventh-day Adventist Statement of Fundamental Beliefs, article 1, accessible online at <www.adventist.org/beliefs/fundamental/index.html>.
2. For a brief history, see the Kinship Web site at <www.sdakinship.org/history.htm>.

Part One
Autobiographical

Part 1-2

Learning to Spin the Coin of Truth

By Sherri Babcock

I need to start with a disclaimer. My story does not come close to the heart-wrenching tales that many homosexual people have. Many young Adventist homosexuals have been thrown out of their homes and estranged from their families, but that is not my story. Both Jill, my partner, and I have been blessed with parents who believe in unconditionally loving their children, and our family is treated no differently than the families of our siblings.

Many Adventist homosexuals have been refused baptism, removed from personal ministry positions, or disfellowshipped, leaving them without a spiritual community. But that is not my story. Jill and I are actively engaged in our local Adventist church.

Many Adventist homosexuals have lost jobs, careers, and the credibility of their entire life work when their orientation has become known, but that is not my story. In our places of employment, Jill and I have been able to be open about our family, and we have experienced very little harassment and discrimination.

So why listen to my story over the hundreds of others that could be told? Maybe my story needs to be told specifically *because* it is less heart wrenching. In spite of periods where I have struggled and been in pain, my story provides generous glimpses into what a Christian attitude toward homosexuality might look like.

Sherri Babcock

Early Years

My story starts within the context provided by my Adventist ancestors. My great-great-grandfather, D. A. Robinson, cofounded Atlantic Union College in 1881 along with Adventist pioneer Stephen Haskell. He later became the first male Adventist missionary to India, following behind nurse Georgia Burrus. My great-grandparents *and* my grandparents were missionaries to Africa. My parents are both Adventist educators, my father being the current president of Atlantic Union College, and they were missionaries in Pakistan when my conscious childhood memories began.

With this rich family heritage, my childhood was filled with stories of church history, miraculous mission stories, Bible stories, Pathfinder activities, and relationships with student missionaries. I experienced firsthand the thrill, adventure, and responsibility related to serving God and God's remnant church. I assumed that God's plan for my life included attending Seventh-day Adventist schools through college, taking a year off to be a student missionary, getting married, working for the Adventist Church, becoming a fully credentialed missionary, and spreading the "truth" throughout the world so Jesus could return.

In Sabbath School and Bible classes, I was taught both sides of the truth coin. On one side, I learned the importance of "absolute truth": how possession of the truth defined the Seventh-day Adventist Church and qualified it as remnant. I learned the importance of knowing right from wrong, along with what things were right and what things were wrong.

On the other side, I learned about the importance of "present truth": how early Adventists redefined their beliefs through Bible study, prayer, and divine revelation; how they were led by the Holy Spirit to cast their message in the light of what was important for the present day. I was taught that Adventists were expected to study for themselves and know why they believed the way they did. I learned that God held people accountable only for living up to the amount of light they had been given, and that God took an individual's history, culture, and abilities into consideration.

In the midst of all this traditional Adventism, I was discovering that parts of me did not fit the traditional Adventist ideals. My father was constantly reminding me to "act like a lady." I preferred playing with my brother's cars, trucks, and Legos, rather than with my own dollhouse and Barbies. I wanted to climb trees, excel in school, wrestle, and fly kites, rather than read *Little Women* and learn how to sew.

Learning to Spin the Coin of Truth

By the age of eight, I had completely claimed the "Tomboy" label already given to me. I often wondered why God had made me a girl, when boys had so much more fun, freedom, and adventure. I frequently asked God to make me into a boy.

In spite of my tomboy identity, I was flattered when a missionary kid from another town, who was four years older than me, asked me to be his "girlfriend." Little did I know that his idea of having a girlfriend meant having sex. When I realized what he wanted and tried to back out, he overpowered me.

Confused and ashamed, I was afraid to tell my parents, so the sexual abuse continued until he went away to boarding academy two years later. At that point, I segmented my short life and promptly erased my memory of almost everything from the previous two years. I needed a clean start.

As I entered my preteen years and the boys I considered my best friends started to show an interest in dating me, I began to feel that I was someone else living inside a girl's body. That someone else was eventually given the name Sandy Smith. Sandy represented someone totally androgynous (which perfectly described how I felt) and Smith was totally anonymous (not the college president's daughter).

I would spend long hours in the evenings pacing the parapets around our flat-roofed house, talking to God and pretending to be Sandy, someone who was strong and independent and didn't fit a traditional label. Although I couldn't name it, I knew something was wrong with me. The emotional isolation and loneliness were unbearable, and I felt I would never be able to be my true self.

One night, while in the persona of Sandy Smith, I came perilously close to committing suicide by jumping off the parapet. Just as my center of gravity went over the edge of the roof, a college girl, whom I considered to be my adopted big sister, appeared on the sidewalk below. Not wanting to land on her or for her to witness my death, I twisted around, caught the parapet, and scrambled back to safety. That suicide intervention was so providential that it stopped me from ever seriously considering suicide again.

Teenage Years

My circle of friends expanded in the eighth grade, when my parents returned to the United States. My unique accent and life perspective made me intriguing to the American boys. I suddenly realized that I could date any boy I wanted, and my girlfriends all thought I was crazy for not taking advantage of it. So my first few years in the United States were marked by dating the most sought-after boys and enjoying the attention it brought me from the girlfriends that I had crushes on.

During my junior year in academy, my roommate had a falling-out with her boyfriend of four years. She was heartbroken and would cry herself to sleep every night. One night, she asked me to come down to the bottom bunk and hold her until she fell asleep. During the next week, I would hold her spoon fashion until she drifted off. Then, I would climb back up to my bunk and go to sleep.

The second week, I started to I realize that I didn't want to go back to my bunk. I wanted to shelter her from the pain and be there for her on a more long-term basis. I didn't understand my feelings, but I had a sense that they would get me into trouble. I prayed that the feelings would go away, and I spent a lot of time trying to figure out what was going on with me.

One day, while I was agonizing on the way to clarinet practice, I silently cried out, "God, what is WRONG with me?" I immediately got my only audible response, as I heard a voice booming through the hallway, "Sherri, you are a homosexual." I spun around to see who had spoken, and if anyone else had heard, but the hall was empty.

I started to cry and ran out of the building screaming "No, God, anything but that! I'd rather die!" After running through the woods and fields around the school for an hour, I ended up on a large rock in the middle of a pond. I was exhausted and still crying as it began to rain.

After regaining my composure, I reminded myself of what I had learned about "absolute truth." Since I was clearly taught that homosexuality was wrong, I decided that this must be my cross to bear. I had to overcome this temptation and allow God to change me. Although I was already the junior class pastorette, I spent even more time leading out in spiritual activities.

I buried myself in schoolwork, and I started to date boys who were not necessarily the most popular, but who were good solid Christians and my close friends. I graduated from academy as senior class president and valedictorian.

Young Adult Years

During my sophomore year in college, I realized that spontaneous attractions to women were still occurring, in spite of my dedication to

Learning to Spin the Coin of Truth

change. Dreaded and unbidden, those feelings would pop up at the most startling moments. I was trying everything to bury myself in studies, church activities, and other distractions, but it wasn't enough. Thinking that I must need to dedicate my life to God more deeply, I continued the original life plan and took a year off to be a student missionary.

Although being a student missionary was definitely an enriching, life-changing experience, I realized during that year that even while I was living a life totally dedicated to God's service, my feelings were not changing. In desperation, I came out to my parents and asked for help. Although my parents assured me of their unconditional love and support, they obviously could not make my decisions.

By the end of that year, I started to understand that for some unknown reason, this was not something that God was going to change. In spite of that realization, I still could not accept being a homosexual.

After returning to college, I decided either to live a single, celibate life or to see again if I could fall in love with boys I was friends with. I dated sporadically, but the struggle, isolation, and loneliness almost resulted in an emotional breakdown. At that point, I finally threw my salvation on God's mercy and started trying to find another woman to develop a relationship with. I had to find out if I really was a homosexual. If I were, I figured I could be of more use to God as a "less-than-perfect" woman than as an insane one.

By mid-year, I had discovered my first love. The comfort level and lack of emotional angst that I felt when with her were liberating. I experienced for the first time being totally myself. I felt whole and realized that several facets of my life had finally become integrated. Along with this wonderful new experience came the constant fear of being publicly exposed and getting kicked out of school.

At the end of the year, I transferred to Walla Walla College to finish my engineering degree. It soon became clear that the distance and social pressures to "get married and have children" were more than our relationship could bear. Heartbroken, I started dating men again, but I felt like I was lying to them at best and driving myself insane at worst.

I worried that if I got married, I would ultimately end up breaking a good man's heart and ruining both of our lives. I got severely depressed and decided to drop out of school, even though I only had one quarter left and I had just been selected Outstanding Engineering Student of the Year. I needed to find out who I was and locate people with whom I could be myself. I decided to go to San Francisco and start a new life.

Sherri Babcock

Coming Out and Healing Years

When I called my educator parents to tell them of my decision, they were adamantly against the idea of me not finishing my degree. On discovering that I was serious about pursuing such a disastrous course, they promised to find me a contact number for SDA Kinship if I would promise to stay in school and graduate.

I gave them my promise and contacted Kinship the week before spring break, asking if I could meet some of its women members in southern California during the break. They not only welcomed my impromptu visit, but let me stay in their homes, took me out to eat, spent long hours sharing their own life stories, and introduced me to the gay and lesbian community.

One night after telling them my life story, I asked, "But, how can God love me if I am a homosexual?"

Marge didn't miss a beat. She said, "Sherri, if someone had just told you their life story, and it was similar to the one you have just told us, would you be judgmental or offer them your love and understanding?"

I replied, "I'd understand, of course, I know the struggle they've been going through."

Then Marge looked me right in the eye and said, "Sherri, do you honestly believe that you are more loving than God?" At that moment, I realized that God's grace was big enough to love me, even if I had turned out to be a lesbian.

On the long drive back to school, I processed everything I had learned and the people I had met in California. I realized that, like any community, the gay and lesbian contains both healthy and unhealthy people, activities, and social scenes. I determined to sift out the bad and keep the good. I was finally ready to start looking at the other side of the truth coin: to study and find out what my "present truth" was, and why I believed it.

During my final quarter at Walla Walla, I connected with more Kinship members and the local gay community. Out of loneliness, I quickly fell into a mismatched relationship with an Adventist woman, and then stayed in it out of a sense of obligation. She then moved to Ohio with me after I graduated and both of us got jobs at Worthington Foods.

Living with her, I soon discovered that she was definitely not my type of Adventist. She didn't like to attend church, and she drank,

Learning to Spin the Coin of Truth

smoked, and liked to go to bars regularly. During our two-year relationship, we attended church only sporadically, and I discovered that our relationship frequently cut me off from my hobbies, interests, and support networks.

Since we worked different shifts, I frequently had free time, but she jealously forbade me to go out with friends. As a result, I spent a good part of those two years cross-stitching, serving on the SDA Kinship Board, and continuing my study of the Bible references used against homosexuality. I learned to understand the context and original language translations. I finally came to believe that God expected me to live my life according to biblical ideals, but within the context of my sexual orientation.

When our relationship fell apart, I started processing the childhood sexual abuse. As I let my inner child tell her story, I relived the experiences mentally and emotionally. For several months, it was all I could do to keep going to work every day. Many areas of my life went on hold as I dealt with this new crisis. Through counseling and education, I learned how to nurture and protect my inner child. I joined a twelve-step program for abuse survivors and gained healing from sharing stories with others.

As I became more open about both the abuse and my sexuality, I discovered that many people tried to link these two aspects of my life in a cause-and-effect relationship. It became frustrating for me to explain repeatedly that sexual abuse does not necessarily affect sexual orientation, as evidenced by the multitudes of straight women who survive abuse. I eventually realized that people who need a reason for homosexuality will find one regardless of its relevance. As for myself, I believe I would have been a lesbian with or without a history of sexual abuse.

As my healing progressed, I entered a handful of brief relationships. Although some of those lasted a couple months, most never got past the initial dating stage. I discovered that I didn't trust my own emotions and judgment. Even though I wanted someone to share my life with, I was not emotionally ready. So I chose to be celibate for one year. I took that year to rediscover who I was as a person, to broaden my base of friends, and to develop a basic comfort level with myself.

Sherri Babcock

Growth and Family Years

Halfway through my year of celibacy, I met Jill through mutual friends at a gay-friendly ecumenical church. She respected my celibacy commitment, and we started a slow-moving friendship that eventually transitioned to dating. Early on, I invited Jill to visit the Adventist church, and she readily accepted.

The first Sabbath I took her to church, I could tell it was not going to be a normal service. The chairs were arranged in a circle two rows deep. We selected some chairs on the second row on the right side and the service started. I soon discovered that the guest speaker was the assistant to the president from the General Conference. I was familiar with him, since I had worked at the General Conference several summers during college.

I remembered my parents mentioning that the appearance of my picture and name in *Kinship Connection* had recently caused quite a stir over the General Conference grapevine. However, since I had never worked closely with him and had not even seen him in several years, I doubted he would remember me by sight.

As the sermon started, he settled into several stories of how the Seventh-day Adventist Church in Russia was growing by leaps and bounds. He was a virtual encyclopedia of miraculous opened doors and opportunities to spread the gospel. In the middle of this grandiose presentation, he suddenly remembered who I was, stopped talking about Russia in mid-thought, walked over to stand in front of Jill and me, and launched into a diatribe about the evils of homosexuality

I was shocked and humiliated. How could this happen the first time that I brought Jill to my beloved church? I don't know how long it continued, but at some point, he turned around and continued his sermon on Russia as though he had never stopped. On the way home, I stumbled all over myself apologizing to Jill.

In spite of that introductory experience, Jill agreed to attend church with me again. As our relationship deepened, I struggled with the idea of being "unequally yoked" with a non-Adventist. But God pointed out with some humor that being yoked with a spiritually equal Methodist was a whole lot better than being yoked with a spiritually unequal Adventist! So, after my year of celibacy was over, I asked Jill to enter into a long-term relationship with me.

We solidified our relationship two years later at a Celebration of Covenant, held at a local metropolitan park. We decided to tap into an

Learning to Spin the Coin of Truth

old Quaker tradition and selected six couples to serve as our sponsors. Our sponsors were people with experience who could mentor us in relationship building. We were both incredibly blessed to have our parents serving as two of those six couples. The wedding weekend was perfect, and more than eighty friends and family members from across the country attended. As a helicopter whisked us away from the reception, I knew that I had never been happier in my life.

About three years after our wedding, Jill let me know that she really wanted to have a child. I, on the other hand, was quite content with our life and didn't even want to imagine the challenges presented to gay parents. Because of my reluctance, our discussions about parenting continued for another two years. When I finally realized how deeply ingrained her feelings were, I agreed to coparent. We selected a donor that the child would be able to meet at the age of eighteen, and Jill got pregnant on the first try.

Grace was born on her due date exactly nine months later. We chose the name *Grace* not only because it was the name of my great-grandmother, but also because we had recently finished reading *What's So Amazing about Grace?* by Philip Yancy. We felt that this little gift of a baby perfectly symbolized the undeserved and unexpected ways that God moved in our lives.

It didn't take me long to fall in love. As I learned to care for this little girl, I began to get surprising insights into the meaning behind biblical parenting metaphors for God. My spiritual relationship was incredibly enriched by becoming a parent myself. I became more loving toward those around me as I experienced the fragility and worth of such a tiny human life. As Grace gets older, I am continually challenged to find new and creative ways to explain God and how God works in the world. I am constantly amazed at the strength of her childlike faith and her own uncomplicated relationship with God.

Shortly before Grace was born, my twelve years of employment with Worthington Foods came to an end. Due to the acquisition by Kellogg, my plant engineer position overseeing the Worthington and Zanesville facilities was eliminated. Kellogg generously offered me the only available engineering manager position—a transfer to their headquarters in Battle Creek, Michigan.

After interviewing with my new employer, I realized that Kellogg required seventy to eight hours of work each week, mandatory committee meetings on Sabbath, and three weeks of travel every month. So, after much prayer, I declined the transfer offer and decided to start my own consulting practice in the Columbus area. It was a huge leap of faith to go from a regular paycheck to what turned out to be very little income for the next nine months.

Just as Jill's maternity leave came to an end, I finally landed a long-term project management contract. The work was steady enough, so Jill was able to make the choice to stay home and parent Grace on a full-time basis. For five years, we have been extremely well cared for. Now that contract is ending, and the future is again unclear as I approach the birth of our second child. However, if there is one thing I learned from my previous experience, it is that God's timing is far superior to anything I might plan, even if I *did* have complete foreknowledge.

Church Involvement

During the first eight years of our relationship, Jill and I attended an assortment of churches in the Columbus area: the Abundant Life Fellowship of Seventh-day Adventists, where I was a member; Spirit of the Rivers Ecumenical Church, where we had met; the Dublin Seventh-day Adventist Church; and the First Baptist Church of Granville, where we learned about social justice, built a Habitat for Humanity House, and had our daughter, Grace, dedicated.

Shortly after Grace's dedication, we decided to attend another Seventh-day Adventist church because of the wonderful children's program and because I deeply missed worshipping on Sabbath. Although we have never officially joined the church, we have been attending there for five years now.

We try to attend church quietly, avoid confrontations, and testify to God's working in our lives as a family. We are constantly amazed by the grace, love, and acceptance we have received from many of the members. The other parents in cradle roll and kindergarten treat us as a family. The church school staff has approached Jill and me to encourage us to send Grace to their school.

Jill is expecting our second child in April, and some of the church members are already asking if they can host a baby shower for us. And I recently accepted an invitation to serve as the chair of the Church Facilities Committee.

In spite of the many wonderful relationships we have at church, we often feel that we have still not found our true spiritual home. We still feel the need to keep our opinions and spiritual insights to ourselves

Learning to Spin the Coin of Truth

during Sabbath School discussions. We still occasionally endure Sabbath School diatribes against the evils and threats to Christianity that homosexuals, homosexual marriages, and homosexual families pose. And we keep waiting for some vigilante to decide that it's time to "clean house" and get rid of us.

Maybe our true spiritual home cannot be experienced this side of heaven, but we occasionally get glimpses of the promise that keeps us seeking new ways to nurture our relationship with God. We feel blessed that for now, that relationship includes being a part of the Worthington church family.

Conclusion

Although my story is far from finished, I currently find myself using both sides of the truth coin to provide guidance in my life. Instead of focusing on one side at a time, I am learning to spin it on its edge.

On one hand, I am constantly trying to identify and distinguish right from wrong, sift out the bad, and cling to the good. On the other side, the varied church communities that we have been involved with have expanded my definition of God's church, God's work, and God's people.

I now understand "truth" as concepts, metaphors, and guiding principles instead of black and white commands and literal stories. I have discovered that truth, understood in this way, is immediately applicable to my daily life, and it calls me to greater commitment, greater faith, and greater action.

Sherri Babcock has enjoyed a loving, stable relationship with her partner, Jill Babcock, for more than thirteen years. They live in a suburb of Columbus, Ohio, with their five-year-old daughter, Grace, and are expecting their second child in April. Sherri is a registered mechanical engineer and supports the family with the proceeds from her own consulting and project management business.

Questions for Discussion

1. Of everything you have been taught about "truth," what percentage have been teachings on "absolute truth"? What percentage have been teachings about how to discern "present truth"?

Sherri Babcock

2. How has your personal understanding about the nature of "truth" changed as you have matured?
3. What have you been taught about "truth" in regards to appropriate expressions of sexuality?
4. What challenges are presented to your current understanding of "truth" by Sherrie's testimony?
5. Read 1 Corinthians 13:11, 12 within the context of the famous "love" chapter. How does this passage reflect Paul's understanding of how our thinking processes mature, especially in how we relate to others?

Notes and References

1. Philip D. Yancey, *What's So Amazing About Grace?* (Grand Rapids: Zondervan, 1997).

A Pastor's Perspective: Growing Up Adventist and Gay

By Leif T. Lind

I worked as a pastor and a missionary for the Seventh-day Adventist Church for twenty years, on three continents. I am the father of two grown-up children who, like me, have lived and worked in several different cultures and countries.

I am gay.

It took me years before I could say the word, even to myself. As a pastor and a married man, I struggled for years in a private hell from which there seemed no escape. As a minister, I felt I had no one to turn to, and, as far as I knew at the time, I was all alone in a frightening and traumatic dilemma.

Third Culture Kid...and Gay

But I'm getting ahead of myself. My growing-up years were basically very happy ones. I came from a loving, two-parent family, and my parents were proud of me. I grew up essentially as a single child, as my two sisters were out of the home by the time I arrived. My parents being Norwegian missionaries in Kenya and Uganda (where I was born), I had wonderful opportunities for experiences that only travel can bring.

Growing up and going to school in eight different countries, although disconcerting at times, was largely a beneficial experience.

Leif T. Lind

My father served in numerous church leadership positions—from mission director to division president—and was a legend in his day.

I was considered a "good" Seventh-day Adventist kid growing up, and my classmates generally liked me. I was straight looking enough that I did not attract the negative attention that sometimes torments gay youths as they grow up. My childhood asthma also provided a convenient excuse for me not to participate in some of the more active school sports, which I did not particularly enjoy and at which I did not excel.

During my adolescence, no one talked much about gays—the word was not even commonly used then. I grew up in remote mission fields in a conservative family in which the topic of sex itself was never discussed. In retrospect, I now realize I can hardly blame myself for being so late in discovering (or admitting) my sexual identity.

I also understand how the mind can play strange tricks in an attempt to deny the obvious—especially when acceptance is too painful or incongruous with one's belief system. I *knew* I couldn't be like those strange homosexuals, with their outlandish behavior and costumes I occasionally read about in the media. That simply wasn't me. (It still isn't!)

So how old was I when I first understood who I was? I don't really know for sure. Looking back today, I realize from early childhood impressions that I considered men attractive long before I had the vaguest notion of sex. But generally for me, it was a gradual, sickening awakening to the fact that I simply wasn't the same as others.

In college, I know some of my friends were concerned about me for not having "enough" girlfriends, or at least not showing enough interest in the one or two that I did have. Again, I assumed I was "doing the right thing" by asking out a girl or two or going steady with them; I was probably unable to distinguish between simple friendship and genuine inner bonding.

What I did understand at some level, though perhaps I did not know why, was that I had a tremendous need for male bonding. Whether intentional or not, it turned out that all of my close male friends were straight. Perhaps this was simply an unconscious attempt to play it safe with feelings I still couldn't understand.

To Everything There Is a Season

Before I knew it, my high-school and college years had passed.

A Pastor's Perspective: Growing Up Adventist and Gay

Hindsight often distorts or changes one's outlook, and it can be hard to remember exactly what one was thinking at the time. I don't believe I knew or fully understood who I was when I made the decision to marry.

I worked at that time as a pastor in Norway while corresponding with my fiancée in Canada. What did I really expect? Perhaps I just hoped everything would turn out all right after getting married. In any case, I was once again making the "right choices" in life.

This quest for doing right (even perfection) is, of course, commonly held within Adventism. I believe it is also common among gays and lesbians, who may try to overcompensate for their perceived inadequacies by showing their church and families that they can be successful, or "make good," in life.

Concerning marriage, I asked myself, Didn't almost every man get married? Despite my sense of humor, I have always taken life seriously. I had never engaged in premarital sex—straight or gay. I had high ideals for marriage (I still do), and wanted to make a happy home for my wife and children. The option of not marrying simply did not occur to me.

Even Paul himself said it was better to "marry than to burn" (1 Cor. 7:9), although some of his ideas on marriage are hardly considered the norm. Scripture also says it is "not good that man should be alone" (Gen. 2:18), a text I consider as relevant today as when it was written.

So my fiancée and I married, and I continued to deny the inevitable. My conservative church upbringing did not prepare me to accept the overwhelming sense of devastation and loneliness I faced when I finally admitted a mental attraction to men that no amount of my praying or fasting would change. Yes, I believed God could do anything, but for some reason, it seemed, he was not answering my pleas.

Return to the Birth Country

The years passed—by and large, happily. We experienced both joys and challenges raising a family in the mission field, where we had been transferred. Some nights I would wake up in a sweat, having dreamt (as a conscientious Adventist!) that I was in a courtroom scene at "the time of the end."

In my dream, somebody asked me if I was gay, and I argued with myself about whether or not to tell a lie. (Yes, I am a poor actor, despite having desperately put on the biggest show for years!) If I admitted that I was gay, I would discredit my faith and the church I loved; if I told a lie, I would be eternally damned. It was a no-win situation.

Sometimes I would dream of being eternally lost for having same-sex desires that I couldn't even explain. Then I would beg God again to forgive me for being what I was. Years passed before I discovered that I was praying the wrong prayer.

Quite apart from the sheer terror of facing my orientation head-on was the overriding concern I had for biblical integrity. For me, this was paramount. How could I possibly understand the handful of scriptural references to homosexuality without seeing in them an outright condemnation of my very being?

Well-meaning relatives later warned me about God's judgment and the danger that I might rationalize away Scripture. How could I disagree? Rationalizing can be a danger for anyone, even the accuser. I was probably more aware of that peril than they realized. But I also knew that growth in understanding can be painful for anyone—straight or gay—and that many are unwilling to look honestly at all aspects of the question.

As Adventists, we all know the so-called problem texts relating to the Sabbath and the state of the dead—yes, on almost any subject—texts that on first reading seem to say one thing, but that we know after careful study say something entirely different.

Part of the reason for this difficulty in understanding is that the Bible's authors wrote in a culture, time, and language foreign to today's world. We strive to understand the principles involved and learn what the writer has tried to tell us. With prayer and careful study we as church members are encouraged to tackle any biblical subject. Why should we treat the topic of homosexuality any differently?

And so I avidly, in secret, studied Scripture and read books on the subject, sometimes disagreeing with both the "traditional" (conservative) and "progressive" (liberal) viewpoints. I had to know in my own mind what I believed and why. Years later, I prepared a thirty-five-page biblical study for myself, summarizing my own understanding on the subject.

Gay…and Adventist?

In the early 1980s, the concept of the existence of other gay Adventists first dawned on me after I read a special issue on the topic in *Spectrum*.

A Pastor's Perspective: Growing Up Adventist and Gay

I read and reread the experiences of other gay church members, hardly daring to believe their stories. It still seemed too remote for me; North America was a world away.

The same issue (as well as an earlier one of *Ministry Magazine*) presented the sad saga of Colin Cook. Former-pastor-turned-counselor Cook, himself a "former" homosexual, claimed the ability to provide counseling to church members struggling to become straight. Although the Church promoted his program as "the answer to homosexuality," I remember being extremely skeptical of his claims at the time and thinking, Either this man was never really gay or he is simply not being honest. Time revealed the danger of his claims after repeated charges and evidence of his sexual abuse of male clients.

Going to America

In 1990, after eight years in the mission field, we returned to North America. My wife's health was not good after repeated bouts with malaria, and we felt it was time for the children to attend church school after having been home schooled for years. We gladly accepted a call to pastor two churches, and for several years we put down new roots, with our children attending local church school and my wife taking nursing studies.

The pressure inside me mounted, however. I began to realize that continually living in fear was draining an enormous amount of energy while I was trying to deny an essential part of my core being.

Out of the Closet

I will never forget the day I finally decided to come out to my wife of almost twenty years. True to form, I had planned months ahead. I had compiled a list of books, tapes, Web sites, and personal phone numbers to help her cope with what I knew would be a traumatic event for her. I would wait until a week after she had graduated from nursing school so that the news would not affect her studies. I planned to tell our two teenagers a few days later.

This was without doubt the hardest thing I have ever done. I was literally sick to my stomach for months beforehand. I kept arguing with myself that I really had no reason to tell her anything. I even got melodramatic, telling myself it would be better for me to die alone with the secret I held. I wasn't even "living the gay lifestyle." But I also knew it was time to be honest; I was living a lie. Although our married life appeared normal, I was experiencing mental torment in an effort to conceal inner longings that my wife could never meet.

I also knew that, at some level, my wife knew all was not well, and that she was hurting. "I sense there's a barrier between us," she said on a couple occasions. I just scoffed at her words, terrified that she might guess the truth. *I* knew what she meant, but I sensed she didn't really understand.

On Friday, February 2, 1996, with our teenagers away on a church campout, I finally told her about the real me. Knowing my tendency to joke, she didn't believe me at first. When it finally hit home, we both sobbed on each others' shoulders for what seemed an eternity. We talked until the early hours of the morning, and then again for most of the next day.

For her, it was the beginning of a nightmare; for me, the weight of the world had been lifted off my shoulders. To her credit, never once (then or since) has she blamed me for being gay, nor has she tried to convince me to change my orientation. Her disappointment in my years of deception was to be expected. Still, we were, at least for several weeks afterward, probably closer than we had ever been before.

In my own planned way, I knew full well what the consequences could be. I knew that our marriage, like the overwhelming majority of "mixed marriages," would probably break up. (This is something we both eventually agreed on, as we worked through anger issues, a normal part of any grieving process.) I knew it would be difficult for our children to accept, although they, too, have been amazingly understanding about the gay issue—far more than I had expected. By their admission, the breakup of the marriage was hardest on them.

After Coming Out:
Facing the Conference and the Future

News of our story did not break for several months after my coming out. All that had changed in my life was that my family now knew who I was. During this whole time, I fully understood that I would probably lose not only my pastoral job, but also my career. I knew the difficulties unemployed pastors face, particularly because they have usually not been trained for other occupations.

Confronting this at midlife would not make things easier. How would I continue to take care of my family? What about medical

A Pastor's Perspective: Growing Up Adventist and Gay

coverage for myself and other family members? What about losing retirement benefits? Would unemployment insurance—assuming I got it—cover me long enough to finish retraining? It was, for me, a frightening scenario.

I had hoped that our family would shortly be able to move and make a graceful transition to nondenominational employment elsewhere, but this did not happen. Understandably enough, my wife needed to talk to others about our crisis, and although she tried to be careful about the people to whom she spoke, one shocked church member felt it their duty to report me immediately to the conference.

When the conference finally found out, I was given what I can only describe as an ultimatum: immediate resignation without the usual severance pay, despite twenty years of church service with a clean record. The ministerial director of the conference, a pastor who had repeatedly insisted that we think of him as our "buddy" rather than merely our boss, never once sought to talk with my wife or me once he knew I was gay. It was as if I had ceased to exist.

Now, most people would describe me as fairly easygoing and agreeable. Those who know me well understand that I can be also quite determined, and I considered the ultimatum of "immediate resignation without severance" unfair. I did not feel like being a doormat.

Not only did the conference's ultimatum go contrary to local government law; it also violated denominational policy. In a phone conversation, the conference president at that time appeared sympathetic, saying that he understood how I could see my treatment as unfair. He also agreed that had the issue been anything other than homosexuality, the decision would probably have been different.

The conference leaders summoned me to appear before them. I showed up, but I did not inform them that I would attend with someone they knew very well: an attorney previously terminated from denominational service for being gay. Although this approach was foreign to me, I felt trapped and was afraid.

I will never forget the expressions on some of the faces the moment we appeared together in the conference committee room. It was a Kodak moment, had I only brought in a camera! On being questioned, I assured them that the attorney was there only as "a friend." Although he said almost nothing during the meeting, I had made my point, and we reached a considerably happier compromise than would have otherwise been possible. One could only wish that the perceived threat of legal action had not been necessary to achieve this result.

Leif T. Lind

I remained unemployed for about two years, retraining while looking for work. During that period, I received unemployment insurance for as long as I was eligible because the government believed my version of the story: that the conference had fired me rather than that I had resigned, as my termination letter from the conference had guardedly stated (for obvious reasons). The conference president even went so as far as to inform me verbally that the denomination might still employ me "if"—and he said it was a big "if"—I were to remain celibate and "if" I could find a local church willing to accept me as a pastor on those terms.

I will never know whether or not he was serious, but he undoubtedly knew that the Church needed to be cautious for legal reasons, and he was perhaps uneasy about the steps I might take. He need not have been concerned.

I was then on my own. The family had separated, my wife relocating thousands of miles away and the children, aged fifteen and seventeen years, going off to church boarding schools. I felt, as I know they did, that the world had fallen apart. I moved a few miles away and started to attend a local Adventist church, where the pastor and his members accepted me warmly, and I was even permitted to teach the adult Sabbath School class regularly.

I found a two-bedroom apartment in town, where I could share the rent with another man. For this, the new conference president criticized me. In my response to a letter from him, I wrote in August 1997:

> If someone who wishes to judge me for my rooming situation would be willing to help pay my rent for a one-bedroom apartment instead, I would gratefully accept such an offer. Since I don't realistically expect such assistance, I don't believe anyone else has much to say either. Would it be better if I chose to share a two-bedroom apartment with a female roommate? This is part of the Catch-22 situation we often find ourselves in: we are censured by others, regardless of the company we keep.

Furthermore, I expressed my desire to remain a church member:

> I personally feel the call and the fulfillment from working within the Church's mission. Should I be restricted from doing what I feel God has given me talents to perform, particularly when I commit myself to Him on a daily basis? I do not personally believe such limitation would come from Him.

A Pastor's Perspective: Growing Up Adventist and Gay

Throughout this process, I was relieved to find that many local church members supported both my wife and me during this difficult process of coming out. A couple months later, however, I received a letter from the new pastor at my former church in which he questioned me regarding my request for church membership transfer:

> As you know, you have many friends in the _____ Church who are deeply concerned with your well-being and your relationship with the church, and who sincerely hope that we will all one day walk the streets of gold together.
>
> In responding to your request we are constrained to uphold the teachings of the church in this regard and therefore find it a necessity to ask you to respond to the following questions before we can decide whether or not we can grant your transfer.
>
> 1. Are you presently practicing the homosexual lifestyle?
> 2. Are you determined by the grace of God to keep yourself from practicing the homosexual lifestyle?
> 3. Is it your understanding that the homosexual lifestyle is not scripturally defendable?
>
> Leif, we are uplifting you in our prayers to God as we await your response to this matter.

I was not "practicing the homosexual lifestyle" and did not at that time have a partner. I still felt the questions unnecessarily intrusive, and wondered how many straight men or women would have such direct questions addressed to them when they asked for membership transfer. Although my request for membership transfer was initially granted, I was later required to drop church membership.

Relative Concerns

Probably the hardest part of the coming-out process—after coming out to my wife and children—was the effect it had on other relatives of mine. I had not anticipated the storm it produced, particularly from the Adventist side of the family. Although I prefer not to divulge some of the intense feelings that emerged (some of which unfortunately remain to this day), I was shocked to hear of my nieces threatening to inform my eighty-six-year-old mother about my sexual orientation unless I told her myself. I wasn't sure at the time about the necessity of doing

Leif T. Lind

so, but I was sure that it wasn't their place to inform her and that, if it were done, I would much rather do so myself.

One of the first missives I received from my family came from a concerned niece who wrote in 1996:

> Dear Leif,
>
> You are my uncle, you're part of my family and I want to love you as I always have. Nothing you do will change that or make me stop praying for you—or hope the best for you. But this love and concern compels me to say that you are making a terrible mistake that will and has affected the lives of so many people—family friends and your congregation....
>
> Are you willing to abandon your responsibility as father and husband to pursue a sexual life style that "makes you happy?" The biggest tool Satan uses is selfishness. When your priorities take precedence over everyone else's, then God cannot speak to you. It is [my husband's] and my opinion that you have bought a lie straight from Satan....
>
> It appears that by your actions which are purely self serving, that you are not serving God—who is COMPLETELY SELFLESS. You can search the scriptures all you want to—Satan knows them better than we—and I am sure that he can persuade you to believe any lie he wants. But from our study of scripture, this life style is completely against God's will (Rom. 1:26, 27, 1 Cor. 6:9, 10) and as such is outside of Christianity—because it destroys family and it will eventually destroy you.
>
> We've prayed and thought about this and in our opinion here are some lies that Satan is telling you:
>
> You were born this way and thus do not have a choice to stop. We all have lusts, anger and frustrations that we can make decisions about every day. Some people are compulsive—that is not an excuse to be an alcoholic. Some have too many hormones—that is not an excuse to cheat on your spouse. We all have choices to make and Satan wants you to believe that you don't have a choice in this matter. That is the biggest lie!... This life style has been condemned by God Himself. As proof—look at the hurt going on around you and in you right now. This has already destroyed your family—that should be enough of a signal from God.
>
> Leif, I have to tell you that this whole situation hurts me

A Pastor's Perspective: Growing Up Adventist and Gay

very much. I can't talk with any of my family without the hurt of your actions coming up in conversation. I have relived my divorce to some degree by this and my heart aches for [your wife] and the kids.

I responded to her letter as best I could, believing her intentions, at least, to be good. Besides commenting on some of the assumptions and stereotypes she believed, and noting what I considered her inappropriate comparison between homosexuality and alcoholic addiction, I noted the following:

> You mention that because of the hurt and pain around our family right now that I should see this as a "signal from God." However, I believe all this is a reminder of the fact that we live in a world of sin. You will remember that Job's friends thought the same about Job's plight (and no, I am *not* comparing my difficulties to his! only making the point that problems are no definite proof of anything except that we live in a world where sin causes problems). His three friends were convinced it was a "signal from God." So were the disciples in Jesus' day (John 9:1-3) who held the common Jewish belief that suffering had to be the result of the individual's sins.
>
> I find it ironic that we as Adventist Christians still fall into some of the same pitfalls as the ancient Israelites!

That was the last I ever heard from this niece, but there was more to come from other family members.

Move to the Washington, D.C. Area

By early 1998, my partner of a few weeks and I had decided to move to the Washington, D.C. area, where we both found work. We had met through a support group for Adventist gays and lesbians, and we both felt a commitment to the church in which we had been raised and worked. We started to attend one of the Adventist churches in the area, and there we heard again, rather indirectly, from one of my relatives.

Although we did not know about this immediately, we later discovered that my brother-in-law, a retired pastor, had felt conscience bound to phone our senior church pastor and "let him know the truth" about my partner and me. Our pastor already knew, because we had been open with him and his staff from the beginning. There were no surprises here.

Leif T. Lind

To his credit, the pastor ignored the phone call and never breathed a word about it to us until just before he left, alluding to it when we invited him and his wife to our house for a farewell Sabbath lunch. We first heard about the incident through other family members.

In 1999, my boss at that time, a church member, decided to inform one of the new pastors at our church about my partner and me. Literally within the hour, the pastor complained to the pastoral staff about us. But again, those in the church office were not surprised, and they dropped the matter despite protests from the new pastor.

The year 2000 saw a flurry of correspondence from another niece (sister of the one who had previously written, and daughter of the brother-in-law who had phoned our church). She was also ostensibly concerned about my spiritual well-being.

> You have proven to me that you are well versed in the Bible and I expected that much. On the other hand because God has blessed you with that knowledge He expects more from you too. If your lifestyle is so OK, why do you have to defend yourself so much from me and the entire world which, as you know, has a hard time getting over that orientation. I do believe that God made Adam and Eve, not Adam and Steve. Why do you have a hard time with the verses that say, "Do not lie with a man as with a woman," or "Do not lie with animals," etc.? I suppose you think it is alright to go lie with an animal then?...
>
> You can try to justify your actions as much as you wish. I am sorry you still think I am being judgmental, but until God brings some of my faults or wrong thinking to my conscience then I have to go with what I know. It is also hard for me to accept your lifestyle when I have had to try to explain to my children that their minister uncle is not a minister anymore because he has chosen to live a gay lifestyle. Your actions, like a ripple in a pool go out and affect a lot more people than just you.... I think you have convinced yourself that you are alright in your thinking because you need to. And since you are a "devout" Christian that makes it right. Why do you keep Sabbath and the other commandments, but do not keep, "Do not fornicate?" What are you going to say when Christ comes back and your kids are not there, the kids that God entrusted to you? You were the head of the family and have NOT set an example."

A Pastor's Perspective: Growing Up Adventist and Gay

I tried to reason, but, as I have since learned, use of logic in this subject is not always helpful! After a few more rounds of communication, I told her there simply wasn't any point in further discussion. It may have seemed harsh, but I could see no other reasonable way to deal with this matter. However, I was still to hear more.

Pastors at our church had come and gone. A few months later, our new senior pastor informed us that my niece had complained to her pastor about my partner and me, and her pastor had written an accusatory letter to our pastor. This time, our pastor talked directly with us, interrogating us about our relationship, posing personal questions that would never have been asked of any straight couple. It was almost the final straw, and we refused to discuss the matter further. The subject was reluctantly dropped.

Worth the Price?

Do I regret the decision to come out and be honest? I regret the considerable pain I have caused both family and friends. I regret having lost my vocation as a pastor with a church that I still love and support. Although I now have a wonderful employer, my current job is not likely to provide a long-term career solution, and I am still unsure what path my professional life will take.

But not for one moment am I sorry that I was honest about myself. I am now at peace with myself and with God, and happier as a result. I have shared almost nine happy years with an Adventist partner who holds the same values and commitment in life. In some ways, I wish I had made the decision earlier in my marriage—had I been able. Doing so would have been easier on my former wife (with whom I still have an amicable relationship), though not on the children, who would have been younger.

To those who ask the question, "What makes a person gay?" I reply, "What makes a person straight?" The truth is, no one knows; no one really understands. "Weak father, domineering mother?" Certainly not in my case. And who would choose to be gay? Who would choose to pit themselves against all odds and make life as difficult as possible if it were really a matter of choice or sexual "preference"? Not too many people I know.

What does it mean to be gay? What does it mean to be straight? Certainly neither orientation is all about sex, as some may believe. As I mentioned earlier about my high school girlfriends, there is an emotional connection or inner bonding that a gay person simply cannot achieve by living a straight life. In addition, an entirely different mindset is involved in which a general sensitivity (often including strong proclivities to music and the arts) makes itself evident.

Clichés perhaps, but still largely true. For a gay man, this often translates into seeing the whole world with gentler, more sensitive eyes than his straight peers. "Feminine virtues," as I have all too often been reminded? Or Christian ideals toward which all of us should strive (Gal. 5:22, 23; Matt. 5:3-12)? But that is another subject.

The current General Conference president—a fellow compatriot, my former professor, and a personal friend of our family—recently gave the following advice about homosexuality in his youth-oriented question-and-answer online forum *Let's Talk*. (His column on homosexuality is filed, ironically, under the heading Pop Culture, rather than the more logical heading Relationships—where the topics of Dating, Family, Marriage, and Sex are listed.) He counsels the Church's youth:

> This means that the biblical expectation is for those who believe they have a homosexual orientation to live a celibate life or to limit sexual activity to within a husband-and-wife marriage situation.

It is precisely this type of advice that leads to the tragedy that our family, as well as many others, has experienced!

One can only pray that the Church will no longer take an ostrich-in-the-sand approach, but face the reality that its gay brothers and sisters are everywhere in the Church: from congregational laity to college faculty, church pastors, and even General Conference workers. We are hurting and isolated, and as much in need of denominational acceptance, support, and the forgiving grace of Christ as anyone else.

Please don't continue to ignore us. I believe Christ can use us all.

Questions for Discussion

1. Why did most of the opposition experienced by the writer come from the more religious members of his family?
2. How do you think the Church's reaction to the author's coming out influenced his wife? His children?

A Pastor's Perspective: Growing Up Adventist and Gay

3. Do you feel it is best to keep "mixed marriages" together at any cost? What price is paid by the gay person and his or her spouse, either by staying together or by deciding to divorce?
4. What is there about Adventist culture that makes members feel responsible for compelling others to accept their idea of what is "strait and narrow"?
5. Does the Church have a right to interrogate its members concerning their personal lives? Why is this often practiced only selectively? Should members consistently be questioned?

Homosexuality and Seventh-day Adventist Families

By Carrol Grady

I believe God loves families! I love my family. I am the descendent of four generations of wonderful Seventh-day Adventist families. The man I love is a Seventh-day Adventist minister, missionary, and church administrator. Together, we have raised three fine sons, whom we love dearly. Today, I am going to tell you about our youngest son, Paul, who is gay. As I share our story, I represent almost six hundred families with whom I have become acquainted through my ministry over the past ten years.

It is my hope that whatever viewpoint you may currently hold, you will be willing to set it aside and respect, listen to, and try to understand the different outlooks presented here. To quote Jewish rabbi and politician Jonathan Sacks, "each of us…must learn to listen and be prepared to be surprised by others. We must make ourselves open to their stories, which may profoundly conflict with ours. We must…be ready to hear of their pain, humiliation and resentment, and discover that their image of us is anything but our image of ourselves."[1] I believe that we need to approach this subject with compassion and humility.

Carrol Grady

Family Background

Let me give you a little family background to begin. My parents were hospital workers, and I spent my elementary school and academy years surrounded by major Adventist institutions in Takoma Park, Maryland. We moved to Paradise Valley, California, and I attended La Sierra College, where I met my husband, a theology student. Our first ten years in the ministry were in Southeastern California, where Bob was the first youth pastor at La Sierra Church, and later we pastored and built a new church in Victorville, California.

Paul, the youngest of our three sons, was born in Hawaii, where Bob was a departmental director for the mission. As a preschooler, Paul was a sunny, outgoing, lovable little guy who instantly made friends with everyone. When he was three, we moved from Hawaii to Singapore, then the headquarters of the Far Eastern Division. Bob spent five years in the Southeast Asia Union and ten years at the division headquarters as director of the Sabbath School Department.

Paul was so excited when he was old enough to start school, but his enthusiasm quickly faded as the older boys in his grades 1–4 classroom started teasing him and calling him a sissy. That was just the beginning of the harassment he faced throughout his school years—most of which we were unaware of at the time.

He started piano lessons when he was seven, and took to music like a duck to water. He was a bookworm who read beyond his years. He also wrote poetry, and showed talent in art class. In the grades 5–8 classroom, every other year the boys took cooking and sewing, whereas the girls took woodworking and auto mechanics. Most of the boys were less than enthusiastic about this, but Paul thoroughly enjoyed learning to cook and bake bread. He made our bread at home, and baked chocolate chip cookies at the drop of a hat! When he entered academy he had the job of baking bread for the cafeteria.

As he neared puberty, he was frequently moody. We later learned that it was in his seventh-grade Bible textbook that he first discovered the name for what he had always sensed was different about himself. From that moment on, he began praying earnestly that God would change him. He was the only student in his class during his seventh- and eighth-grade years at the mission school, but he began laying plans to have a girlfriend as soon as he started academy. He was determined to overcome his unwanted feelings and be "like the other boys."

In academy, he had a lot of friends, but he also seemed to march to

Homosexuality and Seventh-day Adventist Families

the beat of a different drummer. His interests were different from those of his classmates. He often seemed to go his own individualistic way. On a very subconscious level, this stirred a sense of uneasiness in me that I didn't recognize until later. On a conscious level, I chalked it up to him being a teenager. I later learned that several of the academy boys had guessed he was gay and made fun of him. He told us later this was when he first thought of suicide.

All three of our boys graduated from Far Eastern Academy and went on to Pacific Union College. We returned to the United States after Paul finished academy. When he was in college, I noticed little signs of rebellion, such as sometimes staying home from church, and I sensed even more strongly that something was troubling him, but I still didn't know what was wrong. I thought we were talking about all the things that were important to him, but I later realized he was holding a lot back as he began to come to terms with his sexual orientation. While we were at the General Conference, where Bob was in the Church Ministries Department, and while Paul was a junior English major at PUC, we first learned he was gay.

He later told us his number one priority when he went to college was to find a nice girl to marry. He was sure if he did this God would change him. And he did meet a very sweet girl while working at Wawona Junior Camp the summer before school started. Although he told her he was gay, she believed she could help him change. They announced their engagement near the end of his freshman year and planned to get married at Christmas of his senior year. But just when they were ready to order their wedding invitations they broke up, for no apparent reason that we could discover. Bob left on a six-week trip to South America and I was left to puzzle over this huge disappointment by myself.

One by one, little things I had noticed through the years that were different about Paul—things that sometimes made me feel uneasy—began to surface from where I had stuffed them deep into my subconscious. I remembered how he always wanted to be the mommy when he and the little girl next door played house, how he loved to dress up in costumes as a little boy, how he had become infatuated with the idea of being a ballerina after we attended a performance of *Swan Lake* by the Bolshoi Ballet, how he never liked rough-and-tumble games like soccer, how he loved to set the table with my best dishes when we had company.

Although I now realize that these behaviors are stereotypes and not all gay men have them—nor are all men who do have them necessarily gay—at the time these observations and others seemed to point me in an unthinkable direction. Since then, I have read research indicating that engagement in nongender-typical behavior as a child is a strong predictor of adult homosexual orientation in men.[2]

I had to know if my suspicions were true, so finally, in desperation, I decided to call the college church pastor to whom Paul and his fiancée had gone for premarital counseling. I told him what I suspected and asked if he thought I should talk to Paul about it. After a long, tense moment of silence, he said, "Yes." That terrible moment divided my life into "before" and "after."

No One to Talk To

Up to that point, I had scarcely given homosexuality a thought; yet somehow I had absorbed the idea that gay men were perverted and obsessed with sex. I certainly never dreamed that homosexuality was something that could touch me or my family. But when I learned Paul was homosexual, I realized something had to be wrong with my understanding. I *knew* Paul wasn't perverted. He had always been a very spiritually oriented child.

My heart churned with fears, questions, and grief. I desperately needed to talk with someone who could share my sorrow and help me understand. But the great sense of shame, the silence in our church about this subject, made me feel there was no one to whom I could talk. I also felt a terrible burden of guilt. Bob and I were church leaders; how could this happen in our family? I was Paul's mother. It must be my fault. I must have made some awful mistakes in raising him.

I kept everything inside, but I couldn't sleep; all the unanswered questions kept whirling through my mind. The stress was tremendous. I began to have various physical problems. When I went to the doctor, he was concerned because my blood pressure was elevated. Finally, I broke down and told him everything—after several months, he was the first person I had been able to talk to about it. He counseled me to see a therapist. Although there was shame connected with that, too, the need for someone to share my despair was greater than my feeling of humiliation.

After I started my ministry for other families, I learned that fear and shame mark the initial, and often continuing, experience of many

Homosexuality and Seventh-day Adventist Families

Adventist parents. Recently, I talked to parents who had kept their secret hidden for more than thirty years because they were afraid that their church family would condemn and reject them.

Bob and I were overcome with a sense of sadness and loss. We had grown to love Paul's fiancée and had looked forward to having her as a daughter-in-law. We had anticipated a bright future for Paul, with all his talents. His dream was to return to Singapore and teach English at Far Eastern Academy, but that no longer seemed likely. From all we heard—and of course our ears were by then tuned to everything that touched on this issue—Paul was destined for a lonely, unhappy life. This was near the beginning of the AIDS epidemic, so this terrible fear also preyed on our minds. These are feelings that many Adventist parents experience, almost always without support or help from their church.

Eventually, when parents get past their initial feelings of personal devastation, they are often overwhelmed with sorrow as they begin to realize what their child has struggled with alone for many years, and the loneliness and rejection they fear he or she will face in the future.

Harassment in Adventist Schools

Paul had decided to break off his engagement because he realized he still did not feel the physical attraction for his fiancée that he knew she felt for him. He knew it wouldn't be fair to her to marry under those circumstances. Because God had not answered his prayers or rewarded his efforts to change, he finally accepted the fact that he was gay. He was tired of trying to deny and hide from this reality, so he began "coming out" to his friends. For the most part, they were accepting and supportive, but as word began to get around, some of the young men in his dorm started to harass him. One day he went into the bathroom and saw the words, "Paul Grady is a fag!" written on the mirror.

I don't know if you can imagine how that made *him* feel. But perhaps you *can* imagine how *you* would feel if you heard *your* child called a fag. For me, it was like being kicked in the stomach. Another time, several students tied the bathroom door shut when he was in the shower, and when he tried to open it, they shouted, "Get out of here, you dirty queer! We don't want you contaminating our dorm!" Paul went to the men's dean, but nothing was done to stop the abuse.

The last straw came when he found another sign on the bathroom mirror that said, "Death to all fairies! Kill Paul Grady!" That frightened him, and he moved out of the dorm. He was in the middle of student teaching at that time, and the stress and fear made it difficult for him to concentrate. Although he had always been a top student, he was unable to get his teaching credentials.

I have heard many parents tell about similar experiences by their children in Seventh-day Adventist schools. One mother said her son never seemed to fit in and be accepted at school. When he was in fifth grade he came home one day and asked her what "fag" meant. She had no idea. She thought maybe it meant a cigarette. He said he was sure it meant something worse than that, the way the kids said it to him.

So she went to the principal and asked him. He hemmed and hawed around and finally shame-facedly told her it was a slang term for homosexual. She was shocked. "Don't let them call my son that anymore!" she demanded. A couple years later, when she was the Pathfinder leader, their club took a trip to Canada. They stayed overnight in a church school and as they were carrying supplies into the classroom, she found that someone had written "Chris is a fag!" on the blackboard.

Several times, her son asked her plaintively, "Mom, do you think I'm a homosexual?" She carried that secret fear in her heart as he grew up, until her fears were finally confirmed.

Some years later, they met Chris's former principal, who shook his hand and said, "I always knew you'd turn out okay!"

Years of simmering resentment exploded as Chris angrily exclaimed, "You were supposed to protect me back then, but you never did. You let the kids tease me and make my life miserable!"[3]

Don was another young person who experienced harassment. His mother told me that he had problems getting along in the local day academy so she and her husband decided to send him to boarding school. When he came home for his first break, he begged his parents not to send him back, but they thought he was just homesick and insisted that he return. During his next break, he told them with shame that on several occasions the other boys in the dorm had shoved him into a shower stall and urinated on him. Horrified, they called the boys' dean. He suggested that Don needed to learn to stand up for himself. After that, his parents let him stay home and attend public school. There he found other gay students and finally felt accepted. But he also was drawn into the sexually permissive lifestyle of the secular high school students. He eventually contracted AIDS and died.

Homosexuality and Seventh-day Adventist Families

Both of these stories, and thousands of others like them, represent a human tragedy. Young people who feel different, who are struggling to understand themselves, and parents who hear this painful news, should be able to expect understanding and support from their church, their pastor, and their church school teachers. Of all places, our churches and schools should be places where children can feel safe and protected. Instead, those who could be helpful in such situations have never been educated or given information to help them relate in a redemptive way, so they bungle through and usually hurt, alienate, and denigrate those who need their help.

I believe principals and presidents, dormitory deans, campus pastors and chaplains, and others responsible for caring for our students need sensitivity training to make them aware of the needs of gay and lesbian students and of the dangers they face. A well-thought-out set of guidelines for handling harassment situations ought to be formulated. These leaders—and perhaps even school board chairs—should be required to read such books as *My Son, Beloved Stranger,* by Carrol Grady (Tajique, N.M.: Alamo Press, 2005); *Stranger at the Gates: To Be Gay and Christian in America,* by Mel White (New York: Simon and Schuster, 1994); *Prayers for Bobby,* by Leroy Aarons (San Francisco: HarperCollins, 1995); *Pastoral Care of Gays, Lesbians, and Their Families,* by David Switzer (Minneapolis: Augsburg Press, 1999); and *Homosexuality and Christian Faith: Questions of Conscience for the Churches*, edited by Walter Wink (Minneapolis: Fortress Press, 1999).

Will My Child Be Lost?

One of the most urgent and painful questions that troubles Christian parents when they first learn their child is gay is this: What does this mean for my child's salvation? Will my child be lost? Suddenly it becomes very important to know just what the Bible says about homosexuality.

Whether or not they've ever really thought about it before, most Adventist parents start out believing that homosexuality is a sin and homosexuals won't go to heaven. It's not until they discover *their child* is gay that they begin to question that assumption. It doesn't take most parents long to realize that this is not something their child has chosen—in fact, he or she has typically spent many years praying about and trying to overcome it. Almost all gay young people who have grown up in Christian families spend years trying with every fiber of their beings to change, to overcome their innate feelings, to "be normal."

This leads to some very difficult questions. If God says homosexuality is a sin, why didn't he answer my child's many prayers pleading to be changed? Why does God apparently condemn people for something they were born with and that he won't change for them? For both child and parent, these questions can lead to a crisis of faith.

I had to find answers to this challenge to my faith. Since I didn't feel comfortable talking with anyone, I set out to find answers by myself. I read everything I could find on the subject. For a long time, I was careful to read only what I thought supported my belief system, but I didn't find helpful, satisfactory answers to all my questions.

I grew up in a loving, strict, but not fanatical Adventist home, attended only Adventist schools, married an Adventist minister, and lived most of my life in Adventist communities. My worldview was very much the product of Adventism. Although our Adventist pioneers courageously challenged the understandings of the churches out of which they came, I grew up fearing that if I questioned what I had been taught I was opening my mind to Satan's deceptions.

This made it very difficult for me to consider the possibility of other ways of thinking, but eventually I began to read more broadly. I discovered a wide variety of views can be found among theologians about the interpretation of the so-called "clobber texts" (the six biblical references to same-sex behavior that have been used to "clobber" homosexuals[4]).

Without going into detail, after many years I have become convinced that the biblical references to same-sex behavior were written in a situational and cultural context that does not apply to people with a homosexual orientation, and that the Bible does not give specific instruction regarding how homosexuals should live.

I realize that unless theologians and church leaders have come to know and love Christian gays and lesbians as real people and to sympathize with the painful dilemma they face, they are not usually willing to look beyond tradition and study with an open mind. But I believe God understands and sympathizes with his gay and lesbian children with a tender love that surpasses our own.

What Causes Homosexuality?

Another big question that confronts parents when they first learn that

Homosexuality and Seventh-day Adventist Families

their child is gay is this: What really causes some people to be attracted to the same sex instead of the opposite sex? I have tried to keep up with reports in the popular literature about the latest scientific research on this subject. More and more, the research seems to point to a fluctuation in prenatal hormone levels that governs the hardwiring of the brain, which may be influenced by a variety of factors, as the most likely cause.[5]

One study was of special interest to me. It has been observed that gay men frequently have several older brothers. Some scientists theorize that certain mothers may have some sort of reaction against male hormones that becomes successively stronger with each male pregnancy and interferes with their production of male hormones.[6] Since Paul was my fourth male pregnancy, I have wondered if that could be the reason for his homosexual orientation.

Throughout much of the twentieth century, scientific thought was dominated by the theory that environmental influences, or nurture, determine gender identity, one of the aspects of sexual orientation. One of those who propounded this theory was John Money, a researcher at Johns Hopkins University, who pioneered surgical treatment of intersex infants (the approximately 1 percent of all births in which babies have ambiguous genitals or both male and female sex organs). He believed that they could successfully be made anatomically female and raised as girls.

His most famous case involved identical twin boys, one of whom lost his penis through a botched circumcision. Under Money's supervision, this twin was raised as a girl. For decades, this case was quoted in textbooks as proof that gender identity can be changed by environmental factors. This also lent credence to the belief that sexual orientation is determined by environment, and thus can be changed. It was later discovered that the twin supposedly raised successfully as a girl had always felt he was a boy, had many behavioral problems, and, when finally told about his history, insisted on living the rest of his life as a male. Unfortunately, the trauma that both twins endured eventually led each to commit suicide.[7]

Learning about and getting to know people with other sexual variations has helped me understand homosexuality better and to be convinced that there is a biological basis. A few years ago, I saw a couple of documentary films on intersex births that made me think that if so many babies are born with physical differences, which we can see, it would seem reasonable that many can be born with differences in the brain, which we can't see.[8]

Many intersex adults are now coming forward to protest decisions, made when they were infants, to try to change their gender. I know of one woman whose parents assumed she was a girl and raised her as such, only to see her develop male characteristics at puberty. Doctors advised her parents to transform her through surgery into a female and to give her female hormones. This was never mentioned again in the family, but in her thirties she finally discovered that she was chromosomally male, which explained her emotional and sexual attraction to women.

Over the past ten years, at least six or seven transsexual people (those who have the physical characteristics of one sex, but who identify with or feel themselves to be a member of the other sex) have contacted me to talk about their difficulties. I don't think many people really understand the emotional discomfort such people experience, or the relief they feel when they can live in a body that corresponds to the way they perceive themselves.

I was also interested to learn that various homosexual behaviors, such as courtship displays, mating, and raising of young by same-sex couples, have been observed in at least 450 species of mammals, birds, fish, and insects.[9]

Can Homosexuality Be Cured?

During those first desperate weeks, when I needed knowledge so badly but was afraid to talk to anyone, I visited the Family Life office at the General Conference, pretending I was looking for help for a friend. I was given a booklet by Colin Cook that promised homosexuality could be cured.[11] After reading it, I became certain this was the answer! But a short time later, I learned that Colin Cook had been accused of inappropriate sexual behavior toward his counselees. This resulted in much emotional trauma for the vulnerable young men who came to him for help, many of whom I have since talked with.[11]

I have also learned that sexual impropriety by a counselor or another counselee in this type of program is not uncommon.[12] Cook claimed he had become heterosexual. He married and had two children. But a number of years later, when he started his ministry again in Colorado under the auspices of Colorado for Family Values, some of his counselees again accused him of sexual improprieties, and eventually his wife divorced him.[13]

I read several books about "curing homosexuality" by authors such

Homosexuality and Seventh-day Adventist Families

as Leanne Payne, Tim LaHaye, and Elizabeth Moberly.[14] They all subscribe in some way to the theory that homosexuality is the result of dysfunctional parenting and that it can be cured through therapy, prayer, and faith. Of course, this lays a heavy burden of guilt on parents. Bob and I went through years of painful regret and guilt over our perceived role in making Paul a homosexual. We knew we hadn't been perfect parents, but we tried our best to give our boys a good Christian foundation.

I think evangelical Christians believe so strongly in the necessity of change for at least two reasons: (1) They believe that God condemns homosexuality and that he is omnipotent; therefore, he has both the obligation and the power to change a person's sexual orientation. (2) God has promised to answer the sincere prayers of born-again believers; therefore, if a believer has faith and the desire to change, his/her prayers will be answered.

I have read about founders or principle spokesmen of many "change" programs, men who have toured the country telling others they had overcome homosexuality, only to realize after a number of years that, although they had claimed this change by faith, it had never actually taken place in their lives. For a while, they had been able to convince themselves they were seeing evidence of change, but they eventually realized that their attraction to their own sex remained the same as ever. In the meantime, most of them had married and had children. As a result, their whole family suffered a great deal of trauma.[15]

I have listened to the stories of quite a few gay and lesbian Adventists who have spent many years and thousands of dollars trying to change their sexual orientation. They have gone through counseling and "change" programs and tried aversion therapy, drug therapy, and even exorcism—all to no avail. Indeed, I have not yet met anyone who has changed his or her orientation.

I have also heard many troubling stories about people who are scarred emotionally and spiritually as a result of these programs. Being told that they were not cured because they didn't have enough faith, didn't have a true desire to change, or didn't pray hard enough, results in self-condemnation. Many feel rejected by God and believe they cannot be saved, so they turn to a promiscuous lifestyle, and not a few commit suicide.[16]

I have come to believe that the damage these programs do to so many people is an indictment against them and that the harm they inflict more than offsets any good they may do for some people. Recently, groups like Exodus and NARTH have touted one recent, much-publicized study by Robert Spitzer, in which two hundred subjects claim to have changed their sexual orientation.

However, professional organizations consider this study seriously flawed because it lacked controls and independent measurements. It was based entirely on self-reporting in forty-five-minute telephone interviews with people highly motivated to say they had changed because of their affiliation with exgay groups. Spitzer himself says that, despite the active cooperation of NARTH and exgay religious groups, it took more than sixteen months to recruit two hundred people who had undergone treatment. Spitzer expressed dismay because reparative therapists misrepresented his study, using it to claim that reparative therapy works. Instead, he says, change is exceedingly rare.[17]

Another article, which refers to the continuum between totally homosexuality and heterosexuality as perceived by Alfred Kinsey, states,

> [I]f an individual is somewhere in [the middle of the spectrum], environment can be a major influence, especially when the person is young. Because society strongly favors the straight life, in the vast majority of cases the shift will be toward heterosexuality....[I]t is reasonable to assume that most of the people who currently live as homosexuals were probably close to the gay end of the continuum to begin with; in other words, they probably have strong genetic tendencies toward homosexuality.[18]

Our Story Updated

This is probably where Paul's story needs to be brought up to date. After realizing that all his prayers and pleading had not brought about change, he decided he could no longer trust and believe in God. He met Jeff, a young Catholic man a couple years older than himself. Jeff invited Paul to sing in the choir at his large Catholic church, and even though Paul had turned his back on God, his love of music kept him from completely losing contact.

They began living together, but Jeff, a very conservative Catholic who had once entered a monastery, was never completely comfortable being sexually active. Three years later, Paul called to tell us that he

Homosexuality and Seventh-day Adventist Families

and Jeff had decided to be celibate and that he had decided to become a Catholic. He told us later that he had come to the point where he was ready either to plunge completely into the secular gay community or to return to God in the context of Catholicism. Like Jeff, he embraced an extremely conservative religious viewpoint.

They lived together another six years, then parted as good friends. Paul went back east to work for a Catholic foundation. While there, he became acquainted with a Carmelite priest who, with two novices, was starting a monastery. Paul made the decision to enter this new monastery.

Paul's decision to become a Catholic was very difficult, especially for Bob. But his decision to enter the monastery was so much *more* difficult. The Carmelites are a contemplative order; they observe the rule of silence. And they are cloistered, which meant that we would have almost no contact with our son once he took final vows. He told us he would be able to leave the cloister only to attend our funerals.

He stayed in the monastery for about nine months. He later told us it was a very dysfunctional situation. The Prior counseled Paul about his homosexuality, but was extremely manipulative and controlling. Paul came home and stayed with us a few months until he got his feet back on the ground. He had given everything he owned to the monastery when he entered.

From the time he came home, we noticed a big difference in him. There seemed to be a wall between us. Until then, we had been able to talk about everything. I had gone to mass with him a number of times, and he had occasionally gone to church with us. He had been very supportive of the book I had written. But after his experience in the monastery, he was unwilling to discuss homosexuality—or religion—with us. He told us later that the Prior had tried to turn him against us. When he first came home, he was so suspicious that he thought we were trying to *buy* his love because we helped him get new clothes and a car. He was irritable and depressed and seemed to have a lot of internalized anger.

He still harbored a desire for monastic life. A few months after he came home, Paul and Jeff attended a retreat at another Carmelite monastery in Minnesota. He inquired about entering there, but the novice master told him he first needed to overcome his homosexuality. Paul came home determined to change his orientation. It was ironic! He wanted to enter a monastery to help him control his homosexuality, but he couldn't enter the monastery until he had already overcome it.

Part 1-43

Soon after, he moved into his own place. He read some books about how to change, then began trying to find a reparative therapist. The nearest one he could find was in Portland, Oregon. Before he started, I told him I had heard from many people who had tried to change but been unsuccessful, and I hoped he wouldn't be too disappointed if it didn't work for him. But he said he felt it was something that he had to try, so I promised we would support him.

After eight or nine months, he asked me to accompany him to a session. I thought the therapist wanted to hear my story in order to understand Paul better, but I was mistaken. He was curt, almost hostile. If I started to say anything, he turned to me and said, "I'm not your therapist, I'm Paul's. You are here to listen." He kept asking Paul, "How did you feel when this or that happened? I know how I would have felt. I would have been very angry." It felt manipulative and confrontational, as if he were trying to force me to say it was my fault that Paul was gay.

Afterward, I told Paul I couldn't attend any more sessions like that with him. He responded with an angry letter. For almost a year, he had little contact with us. That was such a painful time. We had tried to maintain a loving, respectful relationship with him from the time we found out he was gay. I was upset with his therapist for trying to destroy that relationship.

Paul was in therapy for three years altogether. Gradually, he began to call us more and to visit us, until we were back on a friendly basis again. About a year ago, he bought a house and could not afford his therapy any longer. During this past year, we have become quite close again. He brings his friends over for meals and games at our house and has invited us to his house on a number of occasions.

He thinks he is ready to see if he can have a relationship with a girl, but I don't see any signs of change in his orientation. He joined a Catholic singles Web site, went on an Alaska cruise with a singles group, and has traveled as far as Spokane, Washington, and Vancouver, British Columbia, to meet girls. He tells us about each one, but after one or two dates he'll say, "She was a nice girl, but we decided there just wasn't any spark."

I wish I could tell him, "Honey, there probably never will be a spark," but he has to figure that out himself.

Paul has struggled for many years with depression and is currently taking two antidepressants and anti-anxiety medication. He has rented out rooms to three of his friends. In a way he seems happier now, because he has something like a family situation. He and his roommates eat together in the evenings and on Saturday nights they get together to play games with other friends. He has found, at least temporarily, a substitute for the family he has always wanted.

The Desire for a Companion

Before I continue, I want to ask that you try to put aside all your preconceived ideas and just listen to a mother's heart. Like all parents, we want our children to have rich, fulfilling lives. As we think of the lonely, difficult path our gay sons and daughters face—often shunned and despised by those who don't care to understand them, perhaps persecuted and discriminated against—our hearts ache. We long to make the world a better place for them. That longing may lead to the ultimate question: Why is it wrong or sinful for my child, who is unable to have a successful heterosexual marriage, to want that same kind of relationship with a same-sex partner? Is it possible that lifetime celibacy is not God's requirement for all homosexuals?

True, the Bible indicates that when God created a perfect world, his plan was for marriage between a man and a woman, but does that mean he would not make adjustments in that plan when a fallen world makes such a marriage impossible for some people? It was God who said, in the beginning, "It is not good for man to be alone" (Gen. 2:18).

He also commanded the first couple to "be fruitful and multiply" (Gen. 1:28). The effects of living in a fallen world make that impossible for some people, but don't we encourage infertile couples to make use of modern reproductive science or to adopt children so they can have normal families? Why shouldn't our gay children have as close to normal families as possible?

What is the real meaning and purpose of marriage, anyway? Is it not to help us better understand the kind of relationship God wants to have with us? Is it not to help us learn to submit our will to our partner, as we submit ourselves to Christ? Is it not a school where we learn to love unselfishly and put another's needs before our own? Is it not meant to create a bond that will help us build community and make the world a better place? Do not our gay and lesbian children need the blessings and benefits of marriage as much as our straight children?

The Web site of the Family Research Council lists the many benefits of marriage. Study after study shows that those who are married live longer, have stronger immune systems, have better mental health, are less likely to commit suicide or abuse alcohol and drugs, express greater happiness and satisfaction with their lives, are less exposed to violence, make more money, have more self-respect, and are more likely to be productive, responsible citizens than single persons. What are the ethical implications of Christian groups who actively seek to deny these benefits to gay and lesbian couples?[19]

The October 3, 2005, issue of *Newsweek* carried a cluster of articles concerning Type D (for Distress) personalities. They claim that stress and loneliness are perhaps the most important factors in predicting heart disease. One article by Dean Ornish, in particular, makes a case for the need of each person to have a close and intimate companion. He says:

> Love and intimacy are at the root of what makes us sick and what makes us well. If a new medication had the same impact, failure to prescribe it would be malpractice....
>
> Study after study finds that people who feel lonely are many times more likely to get cardiovascular disease than those who have a strong sense of connection and community. I'm not aware of any other factor in medicine—not diet, not smoking, not exercise, not genetics, not drugs, not surgery—that has a greater impact on our quality of life, incidence of illness and premature death....
>
> In one study at Yale, men and women who felt the most loved and supported had substantially less blockage in their coronary arteries....And when researchers at Duke surveyed men and women with heart disease, those who were single and lacked confidants were three times as likely to have died after five years....
>
> We can see that these relationships are among the most powerful determinants of our well-being and survival. We are hard-wired to help each other. Science is documenting the healing values of love, intimacy, community, compassion, forgiveness, altruism and service.... Rediscovering the wisdom of love and compassion may help us survive.[20]

Might not this passage illustrate the need God places in each of us for a loving, committed, intimate relationship, and the risk of denying fulfillment? It's true that in less-than-optimum conditions this need can be partially filled by a close friendship. But our church has failed to

Homosexuality and Seventh-day Adventist Families

make any effort to help provide this for gay and lesbian people. Though some Adventist churches may tolerate gay or lesbian persons, only in rare circumstances do they offer them a warm, loving supportive community.

Many church members are afraid of being very friendly with a gay person. They don't feel comfortable. If male, they may fear being perceived as homosexual themselves. Yet if a gay person establishes a close friendship with another gay person, this is viewed with suspicion. And it may, indeed, lead to the desire for a committed relationship.

It's easy for me to understand why adultery, promiscuity, incest, rape, and pornography are considered sexual sins, because they hurt those who initiate them as well as the victims. But why should true love and commitment between two people of the same sex be considered sinful, if that is the only way they can bond emotionally and sexually?

I have had the God-given opportunity to know many gay and lesbian people. I have seen the difference between those who have made peace with who they are, found a lifetime partner, and established stable relationships, and those who are involved in the constant struggle of trying to deny who they really are and suppress their natural desires for love and companionship. I think it is too easy for church leaders who are happily married to decide glibly that all homosexuals must endure a lifetime of celibacy.

The Church's Response

Many of the families I know have eventually been able to work through all these questions that confront them and to find helpful answers. The one thing still a problem for most is the response of their church. Almost everyone has a story to tell of hurtful and unkind words or actions from pastors and other church members. I've often heard about a son or daughter coming home to visit and attend church with parents, only to hear someone crack a gay joke, or make a condemning remark. As a result, the son or daughter refuses to go to church with their parents again.

Let me briefly share one of the many stories I have heard. One mother and father told me about their son, married for seventeen years, with two teenage daughters. He and his wife were very active in their church as musicians and Pathfinder leaders, and he was church organist and an elder. From the first, his wife had sensed something amiss in their marriage. A number of times, she asked her husband if he was having an affair, and he assured her that he was faithful to her.

At last, she demanded to know what was wrong and he finally told her he was gay. He had married her in the hope that marriage would change him, but he was unable to be sexually attracted to her. Within a few months, she took their daughters and left him, after telling the pastor and others in the church that her husband was gay. The pastor's response was to disfellowship the husband and tell him he was no longer welcome in their church.

Variations on this experience are, unfortunately, very common. When the Bible tells us to "bear one another's burdens" (Gal. 6:2) and "to love our neighbors as we do ourselves" (Matt. 19:19), why do we see so much coldness, hostility, and rejection in our church? I think much of it can be blamed on a lack of knowledge, on fear of what is different, and on simply not knowing how to react in a loving way. But the fact remains that literally thousands of gay and lesbian people and their families are leaving our church that, although professing compassion, has not shown by its deeds that it really cares about the experiences and needs of this segment of its members.[21]

Harold G. Porter, pastor emeritus of the Mt. Auburn Presbyterian Church of Cincinnati, Ohio, says that the church's problem is not in reconciling homosexuality with the Bible, but in trying to reconcile the continuing abuse and condemnation of gay and lesbian people with the love of Christ.

Unfortunately, this attitude of the church toward homosexuality makes it difficult for parents to respond in the most loving and helpful way to their gay son or daughter from the very beginning. I have seen and heard of far too many cases where parents believe their child has made a sinful choice and they must show their strong disapproval, frequently by disowning their child. Certainly this is not the way God would have us act, but parents need education and support to know the best way to respond. Because of the frequency of such experiences, gay and lesbian young people, as well as those who are older, fear telling their parents and families and try to hide their real selves.

I believe our church *must* do a better job of encouraging parents to demonstrate God's unconditional love for their children. Parents need a network of support. They need to be taught to stand by their children, no matter how judgmental others may be. Our church periodicals ought to be promoting a pastoral, caring attitude toward gays and lesbians

Homosexuality and Seventh-day Adventist Families

and their families, in spite of the criticism of those who don't understand.

Many of our children don't want to leave the church in which they have grown up—the church that has molded their worldview and their goals and aspirations. In spite of the lack of support and understanding they have found in their church, many still want to be a part of it, unless and until they are asked to leave or are disfellowshipped. A fortunate few may find a church that reaches out and shows them Christian love, but sadly, most leave. Even then, they come to the annual Kinship Kampmeeting to listen earnestly to words of hope brought by courageous church leaders, to sing the old hymns and choruses with deep emotion, and to take part in the only communion service many of them attend all year.

I know there are still many church leaders who feel anger at Kinship over the lawsuit of a number of years ago—a lawsuit that the church lost. There are still scars on the hearts of Kinship members, too, because their church fought to keep them from using its name. The fact remains that Kinship is the only place where gay and lesbian Adventists can find help and healing when their church or family rejects them. Many parents I know are thankful for Kinship as a place where their son or daughter still maintains some kind of connection with the Church.

It has broken my heart to watch the vast hemorrhage of gay and lesbian people and their families—people I have come to know and love—as they, reluctantly or in anger, leave their church, in which they have found so much pain and rejection. Although there is little consensus on the percentage of the population that is gay or lesbian, even if we take the lower figure of 3 percent and add to that at least two family members, we can see that perhaps 5 percent of our church members are affected.

At the 2005 General Conference Session in Saint Louis, one of the topics of discussion was membership loss. In his sermon on the last Sabbath of the session, President Jan Paulsen made a plea for our church to have an open door, to be a safe family, open to all—a family that values and welcomes everyone and turns no one away—a church that values justice and compassion. Referring to Solomon's prayer at the dedication of the temple, Paulsen said, "Lord, You love the stranger whom I may think does not belong in this house. Please help me to remember that."[22] I hope with all my heart that what Paulsen said was meant for gay and lesbian people and their families, too!

Our churches need to be reconciling communities of love. How I wish that, whatever our understanding on this issue, we could open our arms, our hearts, and our churches to our gay and lesbian members and reassure them that God loves them. Evangelist H.M.S. Richards's daughter, Virginia Cason, had two gay children. When another mother would ask her what she should do about her gay child, she would answer, "Just keep them and love them!" *We* need to keep them and love them, and leave the convicting to the Holy Spirit and the judging to God.

More than anything else, I long for our church leaders to be willing to study this issue with open minds and to show those who struggle with it that they care and want to help bear their burdens. How can we answer God in the Day of Judgment if we have turned a deaf ear to the cries of our own children?

Questions for Discussion

1. What can pastors and church members do to support parents and family members of gay and lesbian people?
2. Would you tell parents that their gay son or daughter can be delivered from homosexuality and encourage them to send their child to a "change ministry"?
3. Do you think pastors and church members need to develop more sensitivity in the statements they make regarding homosexuality?
4. Do Christians bear any responsibility for hate crimes against homosexuals or for the many thousands of gay and lesbian people and their families who leave the church?
5. Would you like to see the church appoint a broadly represented committee to study the issue of homosexuality in depth?

Notes and References

1. Jonathan Sacks, *The Dignity of Difference* (London: Continuum, 2002), 100–11.
2. Michael Bailey and Kenneth J. Zucker, "Childhood Sex-Typed Behavior and Sexual Orientation: A Conceptual Analysis and Quantitative Review," *Developmental Psychology* 31 no. 1 (Jan. 1995): 43–55.
3. Ella Hammond, "Behind Closed Doors," *Someone to Talk to*, <http://www.someone-to-talk-to.net/new_page_86.htm>.

4. David Balch, ed., *Homosexuality, Science and the "Plain Sense" of Scripture* (Grand Rapids, Mich., Wm. B. Erdmans, 2000); Robert L Brawley, ed., *Biblical Ethics and Homosexuality: Listening to Scripture* (Louisville, Ky.: Westminster John Knox Press, 1996).
5. Anne Moir and David Jessel, *Brain Sex: The Real Difference between Men and Women* (New York: Carol, 1989).
6. R. Blanchard and A. F. Bogaert, "Homosexuality in Men and Number of Older Brothers," *American Journal of Psychiatry* 153 (1996):27–31.
7. John Colopinto, *As Nature Made Him: The Boy Who Was Raised as a Girl* (New York:HarperCollins, 2000).
8. Cheryl Chase, *Hermaphrodites Speak!* (San Francisco: Intersex Society of North America, 1997).
9. Bruce Bagemihl, *Biological Exuberance: Animal Homosexuality and Natural Diversity* (New York: St. Martins, 1999).
10. Colin Cook, *Homosexuality, An Open Door?* (Boise, Idaho: Pacific Press, 1985).
11. Ronald Lawson, "The Troubled Career of an Ex-Gay Healer, Colin Cook: Seventh-day Adventists and the Christian Right," paper presented at the meeting for the Society for the Scientific Study of Religion, San Diego, Calif., Nov. 1997.
12. Wayne Beson, *Anything but Straight: Unmasking the Scandals and Lies behind the Ex-Gay Myth* (New York: Harrington Park, 2003).
13. Lawson, "Troubled Career."
14. Leanne Payne, *The Healing of the Homosexual* (Westchester, Il.: Crossway, 1985).; Tim LaHaye, *What Everyone Should Know about Homosexuality* (Wheaton, Il: Tyndale Press, 1980); Elizabeth Moberly, *Homosexuality, A New Christian Ethic* (Cambridge [Cambridgeshire]: James Clarke, 1983).
15. Beson, *Anything but Straight.*
16. Tony Campolo, *Speaking My Mind* (Nashville, Tenn.: W. Publishing Group, 2004), 61–63.
17. D. A. Robinson, "Analysis of Dr. Spitzer's Study of Reparative Therapy*," ReligiousTolerance.org*, <http://www.religioustolerance.org/hom_spit.htm>.
18. Robert Epstein, "Do Gays Have a Choice?" *Scientific American Mind* (Feb.-Mar., 2006): 51–57.

19. Bridget E Maher, "The Benefits of Marriage," Web site of the Family Research Council <http://www.frc.org/get.cfm?i=IS050B01>.
20. Dean Ornish, "Love is Real Medicine," *Newsweek,* Oct. 3, 2005, 56.
21. Seventh-day Adventist Position Statement on Homosexuality, voted Oct. 3, 1999, during the Annual Council of the General Conference Executive Committee.
22. Jan Paulsen, "If My People," *Adventist Review,* July 14–28, 2005, 19.

Response: Whose Choice? Which Closet?

By Bonnie Dwyer

To Leif, Sherri, and Carrol, I am grateful for their willingness to write about difficult life experiences and particularly appreciative of their stark honesty. That honesty demands the same in response.

As a heterosexual person, I was specifically intrigued by the friends and families in these stories, noting the ripple effect of homosexuality. Rather than asking questions about when and how the gay person concluded he/she was homosexual, I kept wondering about why a friend or family member said this or did that. How does one respond appropriately to the gay people in our lives? What does it really mean to love one another? That wondering reminded me of a couple of personal experiences.

Once I was part of a conversation with the children's Sabbath School teachers at a small church in a politically right-wing county in Northern California. The leader of the Early Teens told the group that he wanted to discuss social issues with his teens, not just tell them familiar Bible stories. "What issues?" I asked. Homosexuality was first on his list. My immediate response was, "Please, don't discuss homosexuality with them, because you will not be able to get it right. If you condemn homosexuals, you will run the risk of emotionally damaging any child there who might have homosexual tendencies. If you don't condemn homosexuals, you will run the risk of angering parents who consider homosexuality sinful. No matter what you do, you will get it wrong."

Afterward, I wondered if I was the one who got it wrong by saying such a thing. Who needs to come out of the closet first? Shouldn't I have simply spoken up for gay people, and thus helped to make our church a safe place for homosexuals? What is the best way for a congregation to handle this topic? Is ignoring it really a good solution?

I know I was inspired by the account a friend told me of his church, also in Northern California, and how they handled the issue of homosexuality. They began by reading the Philip Yancey book *What's So Amazing about Grace?* Then one of the Sabbath School teachers put together a drama on the topic, and an extensive discussion followed. That seemed to me to be an excellent example of one way for a congregation to study, think, and discuss a sensitive topic. What I don't know is whether or not the conversation in that congregation affected the way gay people are treated. That would seem to be the most important consideration.

The second incident concerns the publication of Leif's and Sherri's stories, which took place in *Spectrum* after their original presentation at the Ontario Conference in 2006. Sherri Babcock contacted her pastor to let him know what she had said and to ask if he wanted his congregation identified by name in the journal. In my first conversation with him, he was happy to have his congregation identified. He was proud to have Sherri and her partner, Jill, as regular participants in congregational life, but after he discussed the issue further with Sherri he concluded that perhaps it would be better to leave out the name. The price paid by other Adventist congregations that have been open and accepting of gay people made the cost of openness still seem too steep.

What these stories show me is that the heterosexual members of the Church have much to learn from the homosexual community. Those of us who are heterosexuals sometimes change our congregational membership simply because we like the way one pastor preaches better than another, and we have much to learn about what it means to be a loving community, to be supportive of people whose lives are different from our own.

Sherri's first lesson from the members of Kinship was the realization that she was not more loving than God.

The oft-changing challenge of love comes through in Carrol's account of not only loving her son, but also trying to love or relate to the significant people in his life—first his fiancée, then his

Response: Whose Choice? Which Closet?

conservative Catholic partner, then his therapist. What is expected of love today could be totally different tomorrow. Do we have the courage to make that shift? How do we change our expectations?

Leif shows us the value of simply speaking truth. His response to those who ask what makes a person gay is noteworthy: "What makes a person straight? The truth is no one knows; no one really understands.... And who would choose to be gay? Who would choose to pit themselves against all odds and make life as difficult as possible if it were really a matter of choice or sexual 'preference'?"

In my mind, choice is the basis of Christianity, but the choice is not about sexuality, it is about how we treat other people. That is the choice about which we should be most concerned.

Is our response to another person a loving one, or one of condemnation? Is condemnation ever a loving response? The admonition against judging others in Matthew 7 would seem to indicate that Christ did not think it a wise practice. Thus, I have just as hard a time understanding the judgmental attitude toward homosexuality among some Christians in these stories as I do of the condition itself. How does the state of someone else's life ever justify acting contrary to the Great Commandment?

That text, John 15:17, is one that I keep returning to with questions. What does it really mean to love one another?

When homosexuality is viewed through the lens of these personal experiences—rather than being seen as a social issue—it totally changes the conversation. It can no longer be a debate about causes or choices, it simply is—a part of their life story and ours. The choice we need to address is our own.

Questions for Discussion

1. How have these stories affected your ideas about homosexuality?
2. If you were asked to lead a discussion about homosexuality at your local church, what would you do?
3. If you could sit down with Leif, Sherrie and Carrol, what questions would you want to ask?
4. What questions do you think they would ask of you, if they could sit down with you?

Part 1-56

Part Two
Biomedical Perspectives

Biological Determinants of Homosexual Orientation

By Ben Kemena

Is homosexuality a choice or innate—sin or biology?

    The notion that sexual orientation has a biological basis has moved from speculation to resolution over the past 150 years. Although precise details remain uncertain, the rationale for a biological basis is clear. Yet the politics and rhetoric that surround this issue continue to swirl in a whirlwind of rancor and bigotry. Those who perceive sexual orientation as a moral issue based on human choice cite a lack of absolute proof. This approach is similar to that of people who accurately point out that cigarette smoking is merely associated with cancer—the sequence and moment of causation has not been found. Those who perceive sexual orientation as a biologically determined human trait recognize the disturbing consequences of genetic discovery. For instance, as more gene sequences are discovered that predictably convey sexual orientation, should parents be offered prenatal testing that permits abortion of unwanted gay children? Or should these gay children be carried to full term and born, only to face years of so-called "change therapy" (proven or not), not unlike left-handed children who were beaten or scolded into using their right hand.

    Sexual orientation has a biological basis—but before one examines the issue further, one must ask a different question: What are the hidden agendas that motivate the discussion? Do we want to understand the biological basis because of general intellectual curiosity? Or do we want to use this information to justify our own views? Are we willing to review the research information honestly—and willing to change our opinions—or not? That is the context within which this discussion must begin.

Cultural Background

The concept of sexual orientation had its scientific genesis in the intellectual ferment of the Hapsburg Empire during the 1840s. Until then, only one specific form of heterosexual intimacy (vaginal-penile intercourse practiced only for the possibility of procreation) was viewed as typical or standard, and in European society it was considered legitimate solely within the confines of a marriage sanctioned by the Christian church. Any other form of sexual expression was labeled an "inversion," which included bestiality, prostitution, pedophilia, homosexuality, rape, masturbation, bondage, premarital and extramarital activities, and a variety of other manifestations. Physicians and scientists began to realize in the mid-nineteenth century that the clustered category of sexual inversions was too generalized. They began to believe that there were important differences between various forms of inversion. Thus, inversions were slowly separated into different subcategories and homosexuality was distinguished from other kinds of inversion.

The late-nineteenth century was a period of rapid ideological advance in medicine and human sciences. In 1889, implementation of Munich's sewer system gave credence to a belief in "germ theory"—that "bad germs" lay in sewage and should be avoided. This belief was associated with a huge decrease in illness, even if the reasons were not completely understood. Most large cities in the world began to clean up their water systems after the Munich experience. Similarly, physicians and scientists began to believe more firmly in the biological basis of human functions. They started to see the heart as more than a spiritual soul—it had an actual physiologic action—and illnesses such as cancer and tuberculosis were not seen developing in individuals because of flaws they possessed, but because of biological pathogens. As one might imagine, these notions had a profound effect on the notion of mentation and behavior as well. For the first time in history, mental function and manifest behaviors were linked to cellular biology rather than conscious human choice or providential punishment.

The other contextual consideration revolves around the abrupt

Biological Determinants of Homosexual Orientation

change in the political climate of the nineteenth century. During the eighteenth century, the Enlightenment had struck at the heart of feudalism. Societies were moving away from the notion that governance should be based on blood lineage to the concept that all men are created equal. The political enlightenment slowly began to infiltrate the sciences. It is no surprise that this idea came to nurture researchers like Charles Darwin and Sigmund Freud. Belief in blood nobility was giving way to a more egalitarian view of humanity—but the process was slow. The notion that every man had the same genetic code, the same necessity for blood flow, and the same basic essential organ functions shocked the Western class structure. For Western societies of the nineteenth century, it was one thing to give lip service to the ideal of equality, but quite another to live it, as the American Civil War and its immediate aftermath demonstrated.

At the dawn of the twentieth century, most physicians and scientists still explained homosexuality as a product of social degeneracy, as they had learned during their youth and early training. In 1886, Viennese psychiatrist Richard von Krafft-Ebing's monumental work, *Psychopathis Sexualis*, rationalized the "scientific justification" of degeneracy, labeling homosexuals, Jews, Negroes, rapists, murderers, and incest abusers as the most dangerous of social "degenerates." Those who subscribed to the theories of social degeneracy typically came from the privileged classes. This theory—in its essence—claimed that society valued different "types" of humans differently. White, educated (landowning) Protestant European males had highest standing on the "degeneracy pyramid"; everyone else held lower positions. Social degeneracy was used to justify racism, slavery, and anti-Semitism, and to argue against women's suffrage. Some people also used it to justify indifference to the poor and afflicted. Indeed, degeneracy and societal Calvinism were used together to dehumanize and ignore the poor (consider the Robber Barons of the industrial revolution). Social degeneracy was also employed to justify brutal human experimentation on women, people of color, and homosexuals—for their loss was not considered a burden to society. In addition, it was used to ennoble the roles of white men of European ancestry—and to justify the use of imperial power, including its abuses. For most people, social degeneracy was eventually and supremely discredited with the destruction of Nazi Germany, a nation-state built on the flawed theory of Aryan supremacy, and the necessary illuminations that came with the Nuremberg trials.

As one might imagine, those who spoke against the status quo of social degeneracy in the early twentieth century risked marginalization, ridicule, and personal ruin. When Viennese physician Sigmund Freud dared to state in 1905 that "homosexuals are not sick people," he was immediately ridiculed as a degenerate Jew. Those most likely to speak against the notion of social degeneracy—such as Jews, women, Catholics, and people of color—occupied positions subordinate to the leading classes of white European men, and on that basis they and their arguments were typically discredited.

The death of degeneracy theory is hardly one hundred years old—and vestiges remain—but its indictment is clear. Women have gained the right to vote without the moral collapse of society. The Holocaust repudiated any justification of anti-Semitism. Empires and colonies have collapsed of their own weight, and monarchies have given way to responsible enfranchisement. Civil rights for people of color have not brought chaos and anarchy—indeed, just the opposite. The exposure of human experimentation in Nazi Germany and Tuskegee, Alabama, showed that physicians and scientists worked within the ethic of society rather than above it. But perhaps most importantly, a better understanding of molecular biology fueled the scientific enlightenment of the twentieth century. Degeneracy theory has completely unraveled with the illumination of molecular genetics, which is defined by the double-helix molecule of DNA base pairs (1953) and the completion of the Human Genome Project (2000). Both accomplishments demonstrate a strict molecular basis to humanness that is otherwise morally neutral.

In 1892, when medical literature in the United States first printed the word *homosexual*, social degeneracy had not yet been closely examined or discredited within the human sciences. Homosexuals were placed near the bottom of the degeneracy pyramid—and the consequences of being there have been considerable. In 1895, when British playwright Oscar Wilde was sentenced to prison for homosexual activity, general agreement existed on both sides of the Atlantic Ocean. Homosexual expression was seen at that time as a degenerate activity from which general society must be protected. For homosexuals across the globe, the fact that Oscar Wilde's privileged status offered no protection from a forced prison labor sentence sent a clear and unambiguous message: society would never tolerate the likes of any homosexual, no matter what their merit or the importance of their contributions to society.

Biological Determinants of Homosexual Orientation

One small group of physicians and scientists began to ponder the issue of what normal human expression is, and they realized that understanding that which is "normal" (or typical) is crucial to understanding the "abnormal" (or variant). This realization became increasingly helpful with respect to infectious illness (such as pneumonia, influenza, and tuberculosis) and cancer. But it was much more difficult to assess with respect to human sexuality, in part, because "objective data" was much harder to obtain. Furthermore, because there were potential negative legal consequences to candid conversations about sexual activity, genuine candor—even in research settings—was scarce.

Yet research in the field of human sexuality moved forward in other ways, even though the research was built upon the foundations of degeneracy and feudalism. In 1919, Berlin researcher Magnus Hirshfield published a remarkable paper, which stated that homosexuality was innate and likely influenced by internal gland secretions. He specifically used the term *internal gland* because scores of experiments up to that time had demonstrated that castration did not "cure" homosexual desire. Between 1880 and 1914, American physicians in New York, Texas, Kansas, and Indiana had published numerous studies revealing that castration did not obliterate homosexuality, particularly homosexual desire. Of course, what was never mentioned during the time was the significant number of surgical deaths from the procedures performed in the pre-antibiotic era. Furthermore, in the shadows of the degeneracy pyramid, research that led to significant homosexual deaths was not considered consequential to society. By 1920, medical researchers clearly understood that homosexuality was not a choice. Rather, it had a biological basis more complex than believed at first. The medicalization of human sexuality, which dated back to the 1840s, was in full swing.

In 1871, English researcher Charles Darwin observed a variety of human and animal behaviors and published his findings in the *Descent of Man and Selection in Relation to Sex*. In this published work, Darwin was convinced that certain variations in sexual behavior must be at least "partly inherited." This was a striking notion and resonated with Gregor Mendel's genetic theories of inheritance, which are now known as Mendelian genetics. However, until further elucidation of genes and the discovery of DNA molecular structure in 1953 by James Watson and Francis Crick, most research on homosexuals revolved around observations of activity rather than genetics.

After World War I, an international group of health care professionals argued that a number of sexual behaviors, including private homosexual behavior, should be decriminalized. These scientists argued that the human experience in sexuality was poorly known and should not be legislated. But their arguments were largely discredited because they also condoned broader heterosexual expression (including mixed-class, mixed-race, and mixed-religious marriages)—which society at that time had difficulty accepting. Indeed, until 1966, mixed racial marriages were illegal in many American states.

In 1930, Freud made a strong statement regarding homosexuality. "[P]unishing homosexuality," he wrote, "is an extreme violation of human rights." In 1935, he published his now-famous "Letter to an American Mother," in which he wrote, "homosexuality is nothing to be ashamed of…it is no vice." Freud had come to know homosexuals in Vienna over the course of his professional life. He observed that when homosexuals were not persecuted, they functioned well and actively contributed to society. His findings were ignored—and, eventually, he was forced to flee Nazi Germany.

Thanks to the degeneracy pyramid of human value (or lack thereof), the 1930s saw the beginning of a thirty-year epic of brutal experimentation on homosexuals in pursuit of a "cure." Experiments were conducted with radiation, chemicals, electricity (to the testicles), convulsive shocks (to the head), and emetics (forced vomiting). Many patient subjects died, and the results were decidedly unsatisfactory, even by the standards of the cruelest researchers. Those who told of "cures" reported that they lasted only for "days" or up to "two months," but no long-term "successes" were reported. La Forest Potter, a New York physician, published claims in 1933 that chest radiation reduced homosexual urges, but many of his patients subsequently died. Another New York physician, Louis Max, recommended "high electrical doses" to the testicles for a short-term "cure" that lasted only days. In 1941, Samuel Liebman performed the first published series of lobotomies (partial removals of the brain) on "effeminate negroes," with frustrating results: many of his subjects died; those who lived ended up hypersexual, demented, and incontinent. In 1959, the last major study of lobotomy was published based on studies at Pilgrim State Hospital in New York. Although one hundred lobotomies had been performed on homosexuals, there were no reported cures. In fact, most of the patients had become aggressive and hypersexual, and they

Biological Determinants of Homosexual Orientation

remained in institutional care until death.

In the United States, the bombing of Pearl Harbor precipitated a military crisis regarding homosexuality. In 1941, more than 40 percent of inmates in some military prisons were considered homosexual "deviants." Unwilling to police its crowded jails, the United States military establishment declared homosexuality an "illness," and "sufferers" received dishonorable discharges without trial. Although arguably more humane than imprisonment, homosexuals dishonorably discharged had few options aside from suicide or moving into lives of hiding and anonymity. But prisons were cleared and many of their jailors permitted to serve on the war front. In 1941, the medical profession had not yet defined homosexuality as a mental disorder, the assumption being that it needed no further illumination since it was already considered a criminal activity. However, this unilateral military decision to declare homosexuality an illness would have far-reaching consequences.

After World War II, crude hormone extracts were developed to treat human reproductive disorders, enable contraception, and address hormone deficiency syndromes. In 1949, American researcher George Thompson reported that his electro-convulsive therapy, along with hormone injections, did not obliterate homosexual attraction or desire. The frustration of researchers in the immediate postwar period was obvious. They understood that homosexuals existed and that, despite advances in medicine and science up to that point, this "abnormality" or "illness" defied their attempts to eradicate it. The degeneracy pyramid was giving way to new questions.

In the United States, the McCarthy era ushered in the politicization of homosexuality. In 1950, New York senator Ken Wherry suggested during a U.S. Senate hearing that there was no distinction between a communist and a homosexual. The term *commie-pinko-fag* became a figure of speech. In 1952, the American Psychiatric Association first listed homosexuality as a mental disorder. Thus, homosexuals could either be jailed as communists or placed in asylums without their consent. This development conveyed another chilling message: homosexuals were legitimate subjects of persecution —and the choice was either jail or asylum.

Ben Kemena

Recent Developments

The post-World War II era nurtured some new voices. One of the most influential was Alfred Kinsey, from Indiana. He, like many before him, struggled to understand and define a fuller scope of human sexual activity. He understood that no one had ever actually set themselves to the task of understanding human sexual behavior. No one really understood at that time what it meant to be "normal" or "abnormal," and Kinsey decided to establish a statistical record using a research questionnaire. In 1948 and 1953, he published *Sexual Behavior in the Human Male* and *Sexual Behavior in the Human Female*. Male homosexual behavior was noted in about 10 percent of those interviewed and female homosexual behavior in about 5 percent—both figures much higher than previously suspected. Furthermore, Kinsey's research revealed that many heterosexual couples were engaged in sexual activity outside of marriage or with nonprocreative potential (in other words, sexual activity outside of vaginal-penile intercourse). His observational studies remain a landmark study for a variety of reasons. Most important for homosexuals, it was the first study that offered a confidential voice and eventually moved intellectual discussions away from the dichotomy of "normal versus abnormal" to "illness versus variation." In other words, for 5 to 10 percent of the population, "homosexuality" was "normal." Therefore, the real issue was whether or not this group was "sick."

Meanwhile, psychoanalysts were proposing their own theories in order to understand and treat homosexual degenerates. In 1950, Edmund Berger proposed that psychoanalysis might be able to "cure" homosexuality by identifying "psychic masochism" forces in the life of homosexuals—typically due to domineering mothers and absent fathers. On scrutiny, however, long-term cures were neither reported nor could they be documented independently. In 1962, New York psychoanalyst Irving Bieber stated that maternal domination "demasculinates" male offspring, which thus supposedly led to homosexuality. It was Bieber's belief that "most, if not all, homosexuals would prefer to be heterosexual" and seek "treatment." Given the social situation of New York in 1962, most homosexuals would have probably asked for "treatment" rather than face jail or asylum, but Bieber never published statistics on "cures," nor did he follow up with other questions. Berger and Bieber were instrumental in changing a cultural view about homosexuality that still lingers:

Biological Determinants of Homosexual Orientation

homosexuality is the result of maternal error (and, therefore, blameworthy), and is implicitly linked to the "feminist movement" of the 1960s and 1970s. Yet a substantive review of their theories would eventually expose their false claims. Americans Bieber and Berger were not alone. In 1954, completely without any substantive data, the British Medical Association proclaimed that homosexuality was "curable" through "Christianity, forestry, farm work and market gardening."

Other psychiatric researchers decided to approach sexual orientation from a different perspective. American researcher Evelyn Hooker reviewed Kinsey's data and decided to move the framework of discussion away from whether or not homosexuality is "normal" (or typical or usual)—which appeared to be valid for between 5 and 10 percent of the American population—to whether or not this sexual expression is "pathological" (sick and/or harmful). In other words, should homosexuality be labeled an illness or a variant human trait like left- or right-handedness? This turned out to be a very good question.

In 1957—two years before the last series of one hundred lobotomies was performed—Evelyn Hooker published her results. Her observational conclusions were provocative: in "blinded studies," homosexuals were as healthy mentally as heterosexuals. Indeed, when the two groups were mixed, they could not be separated by expert panels on the basis of psychopathology. Freud's 1905 resounding statement that "homosexuals are not sick" was reaffirmed! It was a startling discovery, one confirmed by many other researchers who used the same blinded techniques. In 1967, Evelyn Hooker was selected to lead the Task Force of Homosexuality for the National Institute of Mental Health, and in 1971 the task force released its report, with the approval of President Richard Nixon, recommending that homosexuality be decriminalized and destigmatized. In the wake of Hooker's task force, many states passed laws that followed this recommendation, and they have lasted to the present time. In 2003, the U.S. Supreme Court overturned previous legal decisions in a landmark Texas case and decriminalized private consensual adult homosexual behavior.

On June 27, 1969, a small group of American homosexuals revolted in New York City—a revolt that became known as the Stonewall Riots. Until June 1969, police had routinely raided bars and clubs that catered to homosexuals. Although otherwise law abiding, the patrons were arrested only because of their suspected homosexuality.

After almost two weeks of nightly riots, the New York City mayor suspended police raids unless illegal activity was reasonably suspected. For the first time in American history, homosexuals in one jurisdiction had won the right to free public assembly. It was a landmark event in the history of homosexual rights, and it is now celebrated around the world as Gay Pride Day.

The Stonewall Riots also marked the beginning of change with respect to medical research. With more societal acceptance of homosexuals, increasingly candid and legitimate cross-sectional population studies began. Early research on behavior had often been tainted by the biased nature of the populations surveyed, which often consisted of patrons of gay bars. More recent behavioral studies that represent a genuine full cross section of homosexuals have dramatically improved. Because objective tests that can identify an individual homosexual have come into use only recently (through plethmysography or secretory measurements of sexual arousal to stimulus), most research is still based on self-reporting, which involves issues of safety, confidentiality, and trust.

In 1973, the American Psychiatric Association unexpectedly reversed its 1952 policy decision regarding homosexuality. Although Hooker's task force findings and the Stonewall Riots clearly provided part of the context for review of the research and the task force's decision, the actual policy vote was organized by members who hoped to continue defining homosexuality as an illness. The confidential vote was startling, especially for the homosexuals themselves. Since then, most other countries have followed suit. In 2000, the Chinese Psychiatric Association also removed homosexuality from its list of illnesses.

However, despite some scientifically enlightened events, draconian approaches could still be found. In 1970, Baltimore physician John Money used high-dose progesterone injections to control sexual behavior in court-convicted sexual offenders (rapists) and posited that this practice might be useful to enforce celibacy for homosexuals. During the cold war, experiments were conducted in East Germany that altered the prenatal hormonal environment in hopes of producing stronger athletes who would win at the Olympic Games. As part of the observational side-effects of these studies, Gunther Dorner noted in 1975 that a linkage might exist between the use of diethylstilbestrol, congenital adrenal hyperplasia (with resulting ambiguous genitalia at

Biological Determinants of Homosexual Orientation

birth), and lesbianism. Dorner concluded that the prenatal hormonal environment may predispose individuals to homosexual orientation, but the exact sequence of hormonal injections, cofactors, and long-term results remain unknown.

In 1980, the first report surfaced of a constellation of symptoms in gay men that eventually became known as Acquired Immunodeficiency Syndrome, or AIDS. Researchers eventually discovered that this syndrome arose from a viral infection (retrovirus) identified as Human Immunodeficiency Virus. This infection affected the world and the gay community profoundly, and research on sexual orientation and homosexuality continued. Many conservative Christians considered AIDS (HIV infection) as God's wrath and as a warning to homosexuals. In response to this accusation, the medical community became increasingly polarized in its approach to human sexuality. On a worldwide basis, AIDS is actually a sexually transmitted disease that has many heterosexual victims, but in Western societies, it will always be viewed as a disease associated mainly with homosexuals.

In 1984 Richard Green began a series of reports that followed a group of boys for more than twelve years. These boys were identified in his study as so-called "sissy-boys"—boys that did not play, explore, or interact as aggressively as other boys their age. Green noted that in his group of "sissy-boys" testosterone levels were lower than in their "non-sissy" peers. Furthermore, during his twelve-year follow-up period, Green eventually identified about two-third of the boys as homosexual. Given societal views regarding homosexuality, many parents of the "sissy-boys" wanted their sons treated for the "condition."

At the insistence of their parents, many of the boys were subjected to behavioral therapies and hormonal injections from a very early age, but whether "treated" or untreated the "sissy-boys" of either group were later identified as homosexual at the same percentage rate. This lent more credence to earlier reports that hormone levels alone did not cause homosexuality. It was also noted that none of the young boys, who ranged in age from three to seven, ever appeared to have made a conscious choice about their sexual orientation, which had been apparent for some since very early childhood. In a follow-up to Green's study, a group of American researchers examined whether hormonal levels across populations might be used to predict sexual orientation. The researchers found that neither testosterone levels nor other endocrine tests could be used to predict sexual orientation reliably. In other words, although most "sissy-boys" matured as homosexuals, most homosexuals were not identifiable in childhood as "sissy-boys."

In 1988 American researcher R. C. Friedman published a large series of family studies. His studies revealed that neither "castrating mothers" nor "detached fathers" are necessary or sufficient causes for homosexual orientation. His studies were a deliberate follow-up on the theories of Berger and Bieber. Friedman strongly suggested that homosexual orientation was much less a matter of "environment" or family nurturing than had been previously proposed.

The research of Green and Friedman initiated a new round of discussions and research strategies. Surveys of gays and lesbians revealed that most felt "different" from their peers at a very early age, often before age five. Childhood follow-up studies such as Green's suggested that sexual orientation was probably established by early childhood. Neither homosexual nor heterosexual research subjects could identify the moment when they made an actual "choice" about their sexual attractions. Neither hormone levels nor hormonal manipulation seemed to change homosexual desire. (Although large doses of progesterone could obliterate libido, the emotional desire remained unchanged.) The ultimate conclusion of this discussion led to the speculation that, although possibly influenced by hormones, homosexuality must have a basis far more complex than previously appreciated. A new strategy was born to investigate the possibility of a genetic basis for sexual orientation. Specifically, new research was directed at genetics (through studies of twins) or body structures (via studies of brains, ears, or hands) with a genetic basis that might offer new clues.

The 1990s heralded the first positive biological outcomes research after years of pertinent negative hormone research. In 1991, British-born California researcher Simon LeVay published research that suggested structural brain differences between homosexual and heterosexual men. Differences in brain structure, which were directed by genetics, lent support to belief in a genetic basis for sexual orientation. In the same year, Michael Bailey and Richard Pillard published a study of gay twins. They found that an identical twin brother was much more likely to be homosexual if his brother was homosexual than if he was a fraternal, or nonidentical, twin. Others have confirmed this research. In 1999, Texas researchers noted that differences in otoacoustic sound emission from lesbian ears were

Biological Determinants of Homosexual Orientation

statistically different from those of heterosexual women. Publications like these continue to link differences between human structure and sexual orientation—and by obvious inference, to the genetics that directs these developments.

In 1993 Dean Hamer investigated homosexual brothers. In thirty-three of forty pairs he examined who were known to have maternal homosexual relatives, five gene markers in the region of Xq28 were shared on the pair's X chromosomes. In other words, they had inherited these from their mother. For many people, this discovery marked the scientific moment of resolution. Homosexuality was more than likely to have a genetic basis rather than being a consequence of conscious sinful choice. Researchers quickly pointed out that human sexuality is an exceedingly complex issue, and that genetics most likely combine with environmental factors to create a spectrum of human sexual desires. Hence, the notion that homosexuality has a *genetic predisposition* has become a useful descriptive term. The nature (genetic) versus nurture (human experiences) arguments are most likely linked. For instance, we know that the sexual behavior changes among people who are raped or subjected to violence. Life experiences clearly have an impact on sexual expression. This insight may help explain why seven of the forty brother pairs did not possess the marker Xq28 genetic factor in Hamer's study. It might also suggest that the eradication of gay people through genetic engineering may be difficult to achieve.

Continuing Controversy

Many Christian organizations immediately vilified Hamer and condemned his work as flawed—because he is homosexual. This development harkens back to the degeneracy pyramid and Hamer's status as a "less-valuable" human being. However, after several years, an independent review exonerated his work and a Dutch research group produced similar results. A small group of medical researchers continues to condemn homosexuality. One of their arguments claims to link homosexual orientation to pedophilia. However, a 1992 prospective study by Carole Jenny at Denver's Children Hospital reviewed more than eight hundred cases of childhood sexual abuse and found only three cases that involved a homosexual offender. When Colorado voters attempted to deny basic civil rights to gay people in Colorado through a state constitutional amendment, the U.S. Supreme

Court overturned it, based partly on findings in the Denver Children's Hospital study. Many Christians have also criticized the practice of permitting gay couples to raise children—children often unwanted by traditional heterosexual couples—but a growing number of studies reveals that such children end up healthy and well-adjusted, and that their sexual orientation is a function of their own individuality rather than being caused by a gay parent. No independently reviewed research study has shown that rearing by a gay parent is detrimental to children. Furthermore, cultures tolerant of homosexuals do not appear to raise more gay and lesbian children than those that tout homosexual oppression.

Although the rhetoric and polarization continue, the medical and scientific community has generally come to accept homosexual orientation as a normal human variant. The small group of health care professionals arguing that homosexual orientation is a conscious and sinful choice has quietly changed tactics. Their attention has increasingly turned to behavior modification through the use of hormone injections, or "chemical castration" agents. Although these agents alter libido and arousal, there is no evidence that they change homosexual desire. Furthermore, the side effects of long-term (presumably lifelong) use are considerable. In addition, members of the group have never answered the question that Evelyn Hooker posed almost fifty years ago: What is the actual pathology of homosexual expression? The group can argue this issue on moral opinions, but it fails to answer the question on reasonable scientific merit.

Therefore, at this time in medical history the American Psychiatric Association, the American Psychological Association, the American Medical Association, the American Academy of Pediatrics, the National Association of Social Workers, and the American Bar Association—along with numerous professional groups from Europe and around the globe—have come to view homosexual orientation as a normal variant of human sexual expression. These organizations have established ethical guidelines for the professional care and inclusion of homosexuals in society as gay men and women who are honest, whole, integrated, and authentic. Furthermore, as a sexual orientation, homosexuality should not and does not carry the stigma of innate pathology; homosexual orientation is not an illness. As with their heterosexual peers, homosexuals often face mental illnesses, but many of these can be linked to the trials, bigotry, and prejudice of society-at-large. Indeed, Gary Remafedi, a Minnesota pediatrician, published a

Biological Determinants of Homosexual Orientation

study in 1991 revealing that a disproportionate number of gay youth attempt or commit suicide as a reflection of social cruelty they face on a daily basis. One of the worst adolescent crime sprees, the Columbine High School incident in 1999, can be linked to homosexual epithets hurled against two teenage boys who subsequently sought revenge.

With the completion in 2000 of the Human Genome Project, which maps the complete genetic DNA sequence for the human body, an entirely new round of molecular based genetic research is underway. This includes explicit research that links genetics to sexual attraction. We await these studies with much anticipation.

In the meantime a small group of fundamentalist Christians still claims success with so-called "reparative therapies," which supposedly convert homosexuals into heterosexuals. Although they tout high rates of success, no reparative therapy group has allowed independent peer review of its data or research subjects. Failures have been notorious and painful, particularly among homosexual leaders in this group such as Colin Cook, whom the Seventh-day Adventist Church previously supported, and John Paulk of Focus on the Family. Furthermore, none of these groups has published its success rates five or ten years after the alleged conversions. New York psychiatrists Arial Shidlo and Michael Schroeder have followed a group of volunteers willing to be studied while undergoing reparative therapy and more than two hundred other people afterward for more than five years. The broad lack of success is obvious. Fewer than 4 percent of the volunteers have been able to maintain celibacy, but all continue to be attracted to the same gender, according to standard criteria. In the complex sexual world, there may certainly be individuals who appear to "change" on occasion, but there are often mitigating factors of abuse, incest, drug use, and violence in such cases that complicate the equation. For the vast majority of people, sexual orientation—whether heterosexual, homosexual, or bisexual—is not a choice, but part of one's inherent being.

As the scientific information is digested, social backlashes and advances will occur simultaneously. Several European nations and Canada allow gays to affirm their relationships through legally recognized mechanisms, including civil marriage. Several American states are debating this issue, and the U.S. Supreme Court has overturned a decision it handed down in 1986 that supported the ongoing criminalization of private consensual adult homosexual behavior. It is interesting to note that allowing homosexuals the full right to marriage —as in Canada, the Netherlands, and Spain—has not led to the anarchy

Ben Kemena

and chaos that many Christian fundamentalists have predicted. Rather, it has allowed homosexual persons to integrate more fully and to contribute to society. The Roman Catholic Church has condemned homosexual orientation and blamed homosexuals for its current predicament of pedophile priests rather than owning its dysfunctional clerical system. This type of approach will continue to permeate research on and discussion about homosexual orientation. But there is no denying that homosexual expression dates back to antiquity, and whether legislated, condemned, tolerated, or accepted, it will continue as a full part of the human condition.

In conclusion, there is still little certainty on the subject except to say that sexual orientation is not a conscious choice. The degeneracy pyramid has been discredited at great human cost and has given way to scientific investigation that has more legitimacy. Studies of childhood suggest that sexual orientation trends can be identified as early as the ages of three or four years, but predictions for each child are far from 100 percent certain. Body structure and studies of twins suggest a strong genetic link with homosexuality, as does direct gene analysis. Furthermore, efforts to alter sexual orientation—no matter how extreme the means—have failed dramatically. Some efforts are currently underway to control libido and arousal with chemicals, and these raise many ethical issues. However, these efforts do not change the basic gender type attraction and desire. Furthermore, hormone levels cannot be used as predictive markers for sexual orientation. Given the lack of demonstrable pathology among loving consensual homosexual adults, most professional medical and scientific organizations currently view homosexual orientation as a human normal variant, similar in nature to right- or left-handedness, and they condemn societal prejudice and bigotry against homosexual persons on the most basic humanitarian grounds. Homosexuals are born as gay individuals, and, to date, we can neither predict nor alter this course. Some people argue that the world would be a better place without homosexuals, but the consequence of eliminating them from society might be catastrophic.

The Seventh-day Adventist Church claims to be committed to a responsible health care message, scientific training, and charitable evangelical mission, but its current policy in regard to homosexuals is antithetical to scientific evidence and ethical conduct. There are now probably more than one million gay and lesbian Adventist "refugees" who are either living dishonest, "closeted" lives or have been purged

Biological Determinants of Homosexual Orientation

from church society. This is a human tragedy of epic proportions. Just as one might imagine God cast as white or black, man or woman, Jew or Gentile, it could also be said that gay children are created in the image of an unfathomable and loving God. May we pray for change in the institutional church, and may we understand that until the Word of God is presented to gays and lesbians in a way recognizably Christlike, the promise of a Second Coming will remain unfulfilled.

Questions for Discussion

1. A large body of scientific evidence suggests that sexual orientation has both genetic and biological determinants. Given Adventist leadership in parent-child health care, if homosexuality can be linked to a specific genetic marker, should all prospective parents at Adventist hospitals (through pre-natal testing) have the right to abort a fetus which carries this chromosomal marker?
2. While not officially supported by written church doctrine, some Adventists believe that all homosexuals must maintain lifelong celibacy as a moral imperative. If so, what systems of cultural and spiritual support should the Adventist church family provide as a daily and lifelong substitute for this lack of intimacy and love so that gays can fully mature in their Christian journey?
3. Neither Jesus in the Gospels nor Ellen White in her writings specifically addressed homosexual orientation (as we know it in the 21st century)—though both extensively addressed sexuality. What reasons can you give for their silence on this issue and the spiritual space it may provide for all Adventists?
4. Many countries and thirty American states allow homosexuals to be fired from jobs, evicted from apartments or denied mortgage loans strictly on the basis of their sexual orientation. These same states and countries may also deny hospital visitation, nursing home placement and burial for the same reasons. How should Adventists approach these issues as a matter of social justice?
5. About 30-50% of Adventists admit to knowing a gay person as a close friend or family member even though current Adventist church policies condemn homosexuals and homosexual orientation. If those policies were to change, what impact might the inclusion of gay Adventists have on the worldwide church?

Appendix 1: Official Seventh-day Adventist Church Position Statement on Homosexuality, 1999 revision

Statement voted and approved by the General Conference of Seventh-day Adventists Executive Committee at the Annual Council Session on Sunday, October 3, 1999—Issued from Silver Spring, Maryland, U.S.A.

The Seventh-day Adventist Church recognizes that every human being is valuable in the sight of God, and we seek to minister to all men and women in the spirit of Jesus. We also believe that by God's grace and through the encouragement of the community of faith, an individual may live in harmony with the principles of God's Word.

Seventh-day Adventists believe that sexual intimacy belongs only within the marital relationship of a man and a woman. This was the design established by God at creation. The Scriptures declare: "For this reason a man will leave his father and mother and be united to his wife, and they will become one flesh" (Gen. 2:24, NIV). Throughout Scripture this heterosexual pattern is affirmed.

The Bible makes no accommodation for homosexual activity or relationships. Sexual acts outside the circle of a heterosexual marriage are forbidden (Lev. 20:7–21; Rom. 1:24–27; 1 Cor. 6:9–11).

Jesus Christ reaffirmed the divine creation intent: "'Haven't you read,' he replied, 'that at the beginning the Creator "made them male and female," and said, "For this reason a man will leave his father and mother and be united to his wife, and the two will become one flesh?" So they are no longer two, but one'" (Matt. 19:4–6, NIV). For these reasons Adventists are opposed to homosexual practices and relationships.

Seventh-day Adventists endeavor to follow the instruction and example of Jesus. He affirmed the dignity of all human beings and reached out compassionately to persons and families suffering the consequences of sin. He offered caring ministry and words of solace to struggling people, while differentiating His love for sinners from His clear teaching about sinful practices.

Appendix 2: What American Health Care Professional Organizations Say about Reparative Therapy Efforts to Eliminate Homosexual Orientation and Desire

The term *reparative therapy* refers to psychotherapy aimed at

Biological Determinants of Homosexual Orientation

eliminating homosexual desires. It is used by people who do not think homosexuality is one variation within human sexual orientation, and still believe that homosexuality is a mental disorder. The most important fact about reparative therapy, also sometimes known as "conversion" therapy, is that it is based on an understanding of homosexuality that has been rejected by all major health and mental health professions. The American Academy of Pediatrics, the American Medical Association, the American Counseling Association, the American Psychiatric Association, the American Psychological Association, the National Association of School Psychologists, and the National Association of Social Workers, have all taken the position that homosexuality is not a mental disorder and thus there is no need for a "cure." Altogether, these organizations represent more than half a million health and mental health professionals.

The Diagnostic and Statistical Manual of Mental Disorders, the defining standard in its field published by the American Psychiatric Association, does not include homosexuality as a mental disorder. All other major health professional organizations have supported the American Psychiatric Association in its declassification of homosexuality as a mental disorder, which occurred in 1973. The idea that homosexuality is a mental disorder or that the emergence of same-gender sexual desires among some adolescents is in any way abnormal or mentally unhealthy has no support among health and mental health professional organizations.

Despite the unanimity of the health and mental health professions on the normality of homosexuality, the idea of "reparative therapy" has recently been adopted by conservative organizations and aggressively promoted in the media. Because of this aggressive promotion, a number of health and mental health professional organizations have recently issued public statements about reparative therapy.

In its policy statement on homosexuality and adolescence, the American Academy of Pediatrics states: "Confusion about sexual orientation is not unusual during adolescence. Counseling may be helpful for young people who are uncertain about their sexual orientation or for those who are uncertain about how to express their sexuality and might profit from an attempt at clarification through a counseling or psychotherapeutic initiative. Therapy directed specifically at changing sexual orientation is contraindicated, since it can provoke guilt and anxiety while having little or no potential for achieving changes in orientation."

The American Medical Association addresses the subject in its policy statement on Health Care Needs of Gay Men and Lesbians in the United States, which asserts that "most of the emotional disturbance experienced by gay men and lesbians around their sexual identity is not based on physiological causes but rather is due more to a sense of alienation in an unaccepting environment. For this reason, aversion therapy (a behavioral or medical intervention which pairs unwanted behavior, in this case, homosexual behavior, with unpleasant sensations or aversive consequences) is no longer recommended for gay men and lesbians. Through psychotherapy, gay men and lesbians can become comfortable with their sexual orientation and understand the societal response to it."

In July 2000, the AMA specifically addressed reparative therapy with the following statement: "[We] oppose any psychiatric treatment, such as 'reparative' or 'conversion' therapy which is based upon the assumption that homosexuality per se is a mental disorder or based upon the a priori assumption that the patient should change his/her homosexual orientation."

The American Counseling Association has adopted a resolution stating that it "opposes portrayals of lesbian, gay, and bisexual youth and adults as mentally ill due to their sexual orientation; and supports the dissemination of accurate information about sexual orientation, mental health, and appropriate interventions in order to counteract bias that is based on ignorance or unfounded beliefs about same-gender sexual orientation." Furthermore, at its 1999 world conference, ACA adopted a position that opposes promotion of "reparative therapy" as a "cure" for individuals who are homosexual.

The American Psychiatric Association in its position statement on Psychiatric Treatment and Sexual Orientation states: "The potential risks of reparative therapy are great, including depression, anxiety and self-destructive behavior, since therapist alignment with societal prejudices against homosexuality may reinforce self-hatred already experienced by the patient. Many patients who have undergone 'reparative therapy' relate that they were inaccurately told that homosexuals are lonely, unhappy individuals who never achieve acceptance or satisfaction. The possibility that the person might achieve happiness and satisfying interpersonal relationships as a gay man or lesbian is not presented, nor are alternative approaches to dealing with the effects of societal stigmatization discussed."

The American Psychological Association in its Resolution on

Biological Determinants of Homosexual Orientation

Appropriate Therapeutic Responses to Sexual Orientation, which the National Association of School Psychologists has also endorsed, asserts that it "opposes portrayals of lesbian, gay and bisexual youth and adults as mentally ill due to their sexual orientation and supports the dissemination of accurate information about sexual orientation, and mental health, and appropriate interventions in order to counteract bias that is based in ignorance or unfounded beliefs about sexual orientation."

The Policy Statement on Lesbian, Gay and Bisexual Issues of the National Association of Social Workers "endorses policies in both the public and private sectors that ensure nondiscrimination; that are sensitive to the health and mental health needs of lesbian, gay and bisexual people; and that promote an understanding of lesbian, gay and bisexual cultures. Social stigmatization of lesbian, gay, and bisexual people is widespread and is a primary motivating factor in leading some people to seek sexual orientation changes. Sexual orientation conversion therapies assume that homosexual orientation is both pathological and freely chosen. No data demonstrate that reparative or conversion therapies are effective, and in fact they may be harmful."

The National Association of Social Workers believes "social workers have the responsibility to clients to explain the prevailing knowledge concerning sexual orientation and the lack of data reporting positive outcomes with reparative therapy. NASW discourages social workers from providing treatments designed to change sexual orientation or from referring practitioners or programs that claim to do so."

As these statements make clear, health and mental health professional organizations do not support efforts to change a person's sexual orientation through reparative therapy and they have raised serious concerns about its potential to do harm. Many of the professional associations are able to provide helpful information and local contacts to assist school administrators, health and mental health professionals, educators, teachers, and parents in dealing with school controversies in their communities.

Appendix 3: Select Timeline the Recognition of Homosexual Orientation

1869   Karoly Maria Kerbeny of Hungary coins the term *homosexual*.

Ben Kemena

1871	Charles Darwin in *The Descent of Man, and Selection in Relation to Sex* seems "quite certain that variations in [sexual] behavior must be at least partly inherited."
1878	N. Emmons Paine of the New York Insane Asylum promotes castration for masturbation and advocates "medicalisation" of homosexuality.
1884	Neurologist George Beard claims that masturbators are typically uninterested in opposite sex.
1886	R. von Krafft-Ebing in *Psychopathis Sexualis* writes that homosexuality is degeneracy, equating degeneracy with homosexuals, Jews, Negroes, rapists, murders, and incest.
1892	J. A. Symonds first uses the term *homosexual* in the United States.
1893	Texan F. C. Daniel asserts that all "degenerates," which include blacks, Jews, homosexuals, the poor, alcoholics, and drug addicts, should be castrated.
1895	In *Sexual Inversion*, authors J. A. Symonds and Havelock Ellis reject "all degeneracy theories," plead for social tolerance of variations from "normal," and argue that such variations might be valuable. Trials of Oscar Wilde end with prison sentence.
1896	In a case report, E. S. Talbot of Chicago claims that castration does not eliminate homosexual desire.
1899	H. C. Sharp of Kansas reports castration of forty-eight homosexual boys, with inconclusive results.
1905	Sigmund Freud asserts that "homosexuals are not sick people."
1907	In Indiana, H. C. Sharp writes about hundreds of vasectomies being performed on sexual deviants, including homosexuals, and claims that the survivors end up with a "more sunny disposition."
1919	German Magnus Hirshfield argues that homosexuality is innate, influenced by internal gland secretions.
1928	World League for Sexual Reform, an international group of health care professionals based in London, argues that private homosexual behavior should be decriminalized.
1930	Sigmund Freud writes that "punishing homosexuality is an extreme violation of human rights."

Biological Determinants of Homosexual Orientation

1933   In New York, La Forest Potter uses chest radiation therapy of the thymus gland in an effort to reduce homosexual urges.

1935   In "Letter to an American Mother," Sigmund Freud writes that homosexuality is "nothing to be ashamed of, no vice."

Czechs J. Srnec and Kurt Freund use chemical aversion therapy with emetics; claim that 7/25 of homosexuals are "cured" after two months.

Louis Max of New York tries electrical aversion therapy using electric shock to the testicles of male homosexuals, but reports no long-term cures; behavior modified only for "days." Still, he recommends "high electrical doses."

1941   United States researcher Samuel Liebman attempts treatment of "effeminate negroes" with hormones and electro-convulsive therapy, neither of which prove effective; performs first lobotomy for homosexual behavior, which leads to hypersexualism, dementia, and incontinence.

United States military declares homosexuality an "illness"; "sufferers" receive dishonorable discharge without trial; in some military prisons, 40 percent of inmates or more have been convicted of sodomy.

1948   In *Sexual Behavior in the Human Male*, Indiana researcher Alfred Kinsey finds male homosexuality much more common than previously suspected (10 percent of population, according to the Kinsey Scale) and evident in every class and geography.

1949   George Thompson uses electro-convulsive therapy with metrazol to address homosexuality, but finds it ineffective.

1950   During McCarthy era, New York senator Ken Wherry suggests that no distinction exists between communism and homosexuality.

Edmund Berger proposes that psychoanalysis can "cure" homosexuality by identifying "psychic masochism"—typically due to a domineering mother and absent father; no long-term cures are independently documented.

1952   American Psychiatric Association lists homosexuality as a mental disorder.

1953   Alfred Kinsey publishes *Sexual Behavior in the Human Female*, finds that female homosexuality is much more common than previously suspected (5 percent of the population).

1954 British Medical Association claims homosexuality is "curable" through "Christianity, forestry, farm work, and market gardening."

1957 Using "blinded studies," U.S. researcher Evelyn Hooker sees homosexuals as mentally healthy as heterosexuals; claims that two groups could not be distinguished by expert panels on the basis of psychopathology.

1959 Pilgrim State Hospital in New York performs one hundred lobotomies on homosexuals, but does not "cure" homosexuality; most lobotomized subjects became "hypersexual" and aggressive.

1962 Irving Bieber of New York claims that maternal domination "demasculinates" male offspring, which leads to homosexuality; writes that "most, if not all, homosexuals would prefer to be heterosexual" and seek "treatment," which implies existence of a "cure"; however, no follow-up is conducted, nor are statistics given.

1967 Evelyn Hooker leads the Task Force on Homosexuality for the National Institute of Mental Health.

Term *homophobia* is coined in popular literature.

U.K. decriminalizes private homosexual acts between consenting adults.

1969 In June, Stonewall Riots in New York inspire gay pride celebrations in later years.

1970 John Money of Baltimore uses medroxyprogesterone acetate hormone injections to control sexual behaviors in court-convicted sexual offenders.

1971 Task Force on Homosexuality releases report recommending that homosexuality be decriminalized and destigmatized.

1973 American Psychiatric Association removes "homosexuality" from DSM-II; no longer considers it an illness (vote is actually organized by those who believe homosexuality is an illness).

1975 In East Germany, Gunther Dorner claims that prenatal hormones may predispose children to homosexual orientation, basing his postulate on studies of diethylstilbestrol (lesbian

Biological Determinants of Homosexual Orientation

linkage) and Congenital Adrenal Hyperplasia (ambiguous genitalia at birth).

1980 First report emerges of what would later be known as Acquired Immunodeficiency Syndrome.

1984 Californian Richard Green claims that, in so-called "sissy-boys," testosterone levels are lower than in "non-sissy" peers.

1985 HIV testing becomes widely available in United States and Europe.

1986 In *Bowers vs. Hardwick*, U.S. Supreme Court rules that Georgia may continue to criminalize private consensual homosexual behavior.

1987 Richard Green's twelve-year follow-up of "sissy-boys" with or without treatment of behavioral therapy and hormones shows no difference in outcome of homosexual orientation.

1988 R. C. Friedman finds that large family studies reveal that "castrating mother" and "detached father" are neither necessary nor sufficient causes for homosexual orientation.

1990 United States researchers L. Goreen, E. Fliers, and K. Courtney find that neither testosterone levels nor other endocrine tests can be used reliably to predict sexual orientation; studies find that most "sissy-boys" mature as homosexuals, but that most homosexuals are not identified in childhood as "sissy-boys."

1991 Gary Remafedi of Minnesota discovers that disproportionate numbers of homosexual youth attempt or commit suicide; identifies risk factors.

United States researcher Simon LeVay finds structural brain differences between homosexual and heterosexual men.

J. Michael Bailey and Richard Pillard claim that homosexual men with identical twin brothers are much more likely to be homosexual than if they have a fraternal twin brother.

1992 Colorado passes Amendment 2, which rescinds all antigay discrimination laws in the state.

1993 In Washington, D.C., Dean Hamer discovers that 33/40 homosexual brother pairs (with maternal homosexual relatives) share five gene markers in the region of Xq28 (maternal X chromosome).

Carole Jenny of Colorado studies eight hundred cases of childhood sexual abuse in Denver Children's Hospital during 1992–93, finds that only three cases involve homosexual offenders.

1996   In Connecticut, Jeffrey Satinover advocates psychiatric medications and/or hormonal modifying agents to "cure" homosexuality.

In *Romer vs. Evans*, U.S. Supreme Court overturns Colorado's Amendment 2 as unconstitutional; sees that gays are often targets for discrimination and that they deserve the potential of antidiscrimination protection

1998   Israelis Ariel Rosler and Eliezer Witztum evaluate "new generation" of chemical castration agents.

1999   Texans Dennis McFadden and Edward Pasanen find that Otoacoustic emissions in lesbians are unique.

2000   Human Genome Project completed.

2001   Arial Shidlo and Michael Schroeder preliminary report on "reparative therapy"; see broad lack of success.

Vermont recognizes gay couples through the mechanism of civil union.

2003   In *Lawrence vs. Texas*, U.S. Supreme Court overturns its 1986 decision and decriminalizes private consensual adult homosexual behavior.

2004   California, Massachusetts, Oregon, and New York debate the civil recognition of gay couples, in accordance with precedents of several European nations and Canadian provinces.

2005   Roman Catholic Church in formal Vatican statements blames worldwide pedophile-priest scandals on homosexuals and bans homosexuals from seminary life.

2007   New Hampshire becomes the fourth state to legalize civil unions of gay couples, effective January 1, 2008.

Psychiatry, Antihomosexual Bias, and Challenges for Gay and Lesbian Youth

By Harry C. Wang

In July 2005, the board of trustees of the American Psychiatric Association (APA) voted to support same-sex marriage. In its statement, the APA reiterated its "longstanding interest in civil rights and legal issues that affect mental health as well as a code of ethics that supports and respects human dignity. Educating the public about lesbian and gay relationships and supporting efforts to establish legal recognition of same-sex civil marriage is consistent with the Association's advocacy for minority groups."[1]

Psychiatrists and psychologists have not always held such an enlightened position. By adhering to unproven theoretical formulations and by classifying homosexuality as a mental disorder for decades, mental health professionals told gay and lesbian individuals that something was wrong with them. Simultaneously, society used the official diagnostic position as a basis to justify its discrimination against them.

In this chapter, I will discuss how psychiatry has viewed homosexuality through the years and offer an intriguing account of how the APA reversed its position. I will also describe how antihomosexual bias affects the development and psychological lives of lesbian and gay youth.

Homosexuality was still considered an illness when I entered Loma Linda University Medical School, but by the time I had graduated in

1974 it had been declassified as an illness. Unfortunately, I didn't know this because there was no discussion about homosexuality during my education.

Definitions

Let's begin with some basic definitions. *Gender identity* is the self-awareness of being male or female, thought to be established by the age of three. This is the core sense of one's gender, most often corresponding with one's anatomical gender. *Gender role* is the observable behavior that society designates as masculine or feminine, usually established between the ages of three and seven. This is what is most easily seen, although often defined in stereotyped ways. *Sexual orientation* is the emotional-erotic attraction that an individual develops toward another person. There is a continuum of attraction that can be solely opposite gender, solely same gender, or in-between.

Heterosexual individuals are attracted to those of the opposite gender. Homosexual individuals are attracted to those of the same gender. Bisexual individuals are attracted to those of both genders. Transgender individuals do not align with their anatomical gender and take an opposite gender role. Their sexual orientation may be either. Lesbian, gay, bisexual, and transgender individuals are often referred to as part of the LGBT community. Most research on LGBT individuals has focused on gay men and lesbians.

Changing Views of Homosexuality

The first scientific views of homosexuality in the 1800s were heavily influenced by the religious traditions of the day, which had long viewed nonprocreative sexuality as a sin or vice. These religious beliefs led to centuries of criminalization of homosexual acts.

By the later part of the nineteenth century, medicine and psychiatry had begun to vie with church and state for authority in the area of sexuality. This led to the definition of homosexuality as an illness or pathology, rather than a sin or crime.

The first clinical, scientific paper on homosexuality was published in 1869 by Carl Westphal, a Berlin psychiatrist. Westphal coined the translated term *sexual inversion*. Basing his conclusions on more than two hundred case histories, he believed that homosexuality was congenital in origin.[2]

Psychiatry, Antihomosexual Bias, and Challenges

Psychiatrist Richard von Krafft-Ebing, in his 1886 book on sexual deviation titled *Psychopathia Sexualis,* labeled homosexuality a "degenerative" condition. He believed it was inherited from a variety of family pathologies such as insanity, epilepsy, and/or alcoholism.[3]

Sigmund Freud

Sigmund Freud, the father of modern psychiatry, is often portrayed as antigay, perhaps unfairly. He did not believe homosexuals were "degenerate" and welcomed homosexuals into psychoanalytic societies. In his famous "Letter to an American Mother," he wrote: "Homosexuality is assuredly no advantage, but it is nothing to be ashamed of, no vice, no degradation, it cannot be classified as an illness; we consider it to be a variation of the sexual function produced by a certain arrest of sexual development."[4]

Freud viewed homosexuality as a phase in the psychosexual development of all children. These early homosexual tendencies remain, he believed, even after one becomes heterosexual. Thus, Freud felt that everyone has a constitutional bisexuality.

He postulated that, for a male, an unresolved oedipal conflict combined with an intense relationship with one's mother leads to an identification with the woman he could not have. Instead of identifying with his father in loving his mother, the homosexual male identifies with his mother and becomes like her in his attraction to males. This represented, in Freud's view, an immature fixation at a state short of heterosexuality.

Homosexuality and "Treatment"

In the 1940s, after Freud's death, psychoanalyst Sandor Rado began to question Freud's views on homosexuality. He rejected Freud's concept of bisexuality as well as the congenital etiology. Rado believed homosexuality was caused by a "phobia" of members of the opposite sex that could be remedied through treatment.[5] Rado's views began a significant shift in thinking that led psychiatrists and other mental health professionals to believe they could change the sexual orientation of homosexuals.

In 1962, Irving Bieber, who agreed with Rado's position, published results from case studies of homosexuals in psychoanalytic treatment. Bieber believed that homosexuality was caused by pathological parent-child relationships. The most common mother-son dyad was said to be "close-binding-intimate." Fathers were described as "detached" and "hostile." Bieber used these conclusions to encourage treatment of homosexuality, with the goal of helping patients overcome their "fear" of heterosexuality.[6]

Other Viewpoints

At the same time that Rado's views were becoming influential, other research emerged. Alfred Kinsey shocked the public through his groundbreaking empirical study on the sexual behavior of American males.[7] Kinsey found that homosexuality was more widespread than commonly believed, with 10 percent of males reporting same-gender sexual behavior for at least three continuous adult years. These findings startled a public who believed that homosexuality was deviant and/or sinful.

Clellan Ford and Frank Beach challenged the public through their cross-cultural and cross-species analysis of sexual behavior. They found that homosexual behavior was present in most societies and common in animals, especially subhuman primates.[8]

Psychologist Evelyn Hooker was the first researcher to study the psychological functioning of nonclinical gay men.[9] Psychiatrists had previously based their findings on homosexuals in treatment. Sponsored by the National Institute of Mental Health, Hooker's study did not find any significant differences on Rorschach and other projective testing between nonclinical gay and heterosexual men. These findings began an important change in the mental health profession's thinking about homosexuality.

Numerous subsequent studies have confirmed Hooker's findings—that being a homosexual does not, by itself, equate with psychopathology.[10]

American Psychiatric Association Position Prior to 1973

I will now turn to the views of organized psychiatry. Homosexuality was listed as a sexual deviation in the first and second versions of the *Diagnostic and Statistical Manual of Mental Disorders*, published by the American Psychiatric Association (DSM-I 1952; DSM-II 1968). In those handbooks, which are used to diagnose mental disorders, homosexuality is grouped with transvestitism, pedophilia, fetishism,

Psychiatry, Antihomosexual Bias, and Challenges

and sexual sadism. Unfortunately, very little scientific data was used to formulate the classification and it is unclear whether Hooker's studies were even considered. As noted by James Krajeski, current editor of *Psychiatric News*: "When this lack of data is combined with the fact that neither DSM nor DSM-II contained a definition of what constituted a mental disorder or normalcy, it is apparent that tradition rather than science was behind the inclusion of homosexuality in the diagnostic nomenclature."[11]

Gay activists challenged this orthodoxy. The success of the civil rights and feminist movements of the 1960s led homosexuals to seek similar societal acceptance and rights. When gay men and lesbians publicly fought the police during the 1969 Stonewall riots in New York City, the modern gay liberation movement was ignited. Part of the gay activist strategy was to challenge publicly institutions that expressed antihomosexual bias. Activists disrupted the 1970 and 1971 meetings of the American Psychiatric Association, forcing removal of an exhibit that displayed aversive conditioning techniques for the treatment of homosexuals.[12]

Simultaneously a group of more progressive psychiatrists (some of whom were closeted homosexuals) began to seek out leadership positions within the APA with plans to address pressing social issues of the day, including homosexuality. At the 1972 APA meeting a gay psychiatrist by the name of John Fryer spoke as part of a panel on homosexuality. Fearful that his employment would be affected, he adopted the persona of "Dr. H. Anonymous," wearing a wig, a mask, and a multicolored oversized tuxedo while speaking with a voice-distorting microphone. Fryer had been fired from two psychiatry residency positions because of his sexual orientation. He informed the audience about what it was like to be gay and a psychiatrist and made an enormous impact at the meeting.[13]

Later that year the nomenclature committee of the APA decided to give serious study to the diagnostic issue. It was responsible for making recommendations about future revisions to the DSM. The committee reviewed scientific studies of non-patient homosexual populations using standardized instruments and/or structured psychiatric interviews. These showed that most gays and lesbians were satisfied with their sexual orientation and were functioning well. This led the committee to embrace a nonpathological view of homosexuality.[14] The committee also learned how the current diagnostic label increased discrimination against gays and lesbians.

Homosexuality as a "mental illness" was being used by the government and private institutions to deprive lesbians and gays of their rights. For example, the Defense Department refused security clearances to homosexuals because of their "mental illness."[15] Furthermore, the committee heard the following testimony regarding the psychological impact of classifying homosexuality as a disease:

> We are told, from the time that we first recognize our homosexual feelings, that our love for other human beings is sick, childish and subject to "cure." We are told that we are emotional cripples forever condemned to an emotional status below that of the "whole" people who run the world. The result of this in many cases is to contribute to a self-image that often lowers the sights we set for ourselves in life, and many of us asked ourselves, "How could anybody love me?" or "How can I love somebody who must be just as sick as I am?"[16]

American Psychiatric Association after 1973

At the 1973 APA meeting in Honolulu there was lively debate among psychiatrists about homosexuality. Activist Ronald Gold was invited to speak on a panel and titled his presentation "Stop It, You're Making Me Sick!" He said: "To be viewed as psychologically disturbed is to be thought of and treated as a second-class citizen; being a second-class citizen is not good for mental health…I think you're prepared to agree that my previous illness was at least in part a direct result of the crimes perpetrated on me by a hostile society. You have been willing accomplices in such crimes."[17] That evening Ronald Gold invited Robert Spitzer, a key member of the DSM nomenclature committee who was beginning to shift his views on homosexuality, to a gathering of the Gay-PA, a group of closeted psychiatrists who informally met at the meetings. He was amazed to recognize prominent psychiatrists there and decided that the next DSM had to change.[18]

Six months later, the APA board removed homosexuality as a diagnosis. The American Psychological Association and the National Association of Social Workers subsequently endorsed this decision. In the subsequent DSM-III (1980), "ego-dystonic homosexuality" replaced "sexual orientation disturbance." This diagnosis applied to individuals who were persistently distressed by their sexual orientation and wanted to change it. The diagnosis was a compromise between

Psychiatry, Antihomosexual Bias, and Challenges

professionals who did not want homosexuality mentioned in the manual at all and those who were still attempting to change sexual orientation through treatment.

The diagnosis of ego-dystonic homosexuality was removed from the DSM in 1987 and in subsequent DSMs published in 1994 and 2000 (DSM-III-R 1987; DSM-IV 1994; DSM-IV-TR 2000). In 1992, the World Health Organization's International Classification of Diseases (ICD-10) also removed the diagnoses of homosexuality.

Adolescent Development

Despite the changes in the official position of organized psychiatry, society continues to hold biases against homosexuals. I will now turn to the challenges that gay and lesbian youth face.

Normative tasks of adolescence include separation-individuation; intensification of peer relations; identity formation, including sexual identity; and formation of plans for the future.

Separation-individuation is the process of attaining psychological separateness from one's parents. This involves a realization of what is liked and disliked about one's parents and what values are accepted or rejected. The end result is an adolescent able to negotiate the world separate from his or her parents and capable of disagreeing with them without feeling unduly distressed.

Peer relationships provide a sense of belonging through the mutual sharing of activities, ideas, and emotions. Friendships for lesbian and gay youth are complicated by feelings of isolation with an awareness of being "different" from peers, often by the age of four.[19] Opportunities to associate with other gay and lesbian youth may be limited and interactions with heterosexual youth may be awkward.

> When I was around 5 or 6 years old, I felt that I was different from others. I didn't have a name for it at first, but around 10 or 12 I realized what these differences meant. It was a very painful experience. It was not something I wanted…I couldn't speak to anyone about my feelings. I was convinced that if anyone knew, I would be subject to prejudice and hatred. I didn't know how common homosexuality was. I thought I was probably the only one in the world. So I lived in an atmosphere in which I always had to hide. (Ron, a pseudonym)[20]

Identity formation is the end result of answering the question "Who am I?" One's beliefs and values are a large part of this, but identity formation also encompasses ethnicity, culture, religious beliefs, and sexual orientation. This process can be compromised if important parts of one's identity (for example, ethnic or religious) reject one's sexual orientation as "wrong," "sinful," or "depraved."

Entrance into puberty brings on an increase in sexual feelings, thoughts, and behaviors. An awareness of same-gender attraction has been reported by the median age of thirteen.[21] Many homosexual youth, however, engage in opposite-gender dating in denial of same-gender feelings and/or to conform to societal expectations. Opportunities to understand and explore same-gender feelings may be limited.

Finally, teens need to set goals and make plans for their future. The support of friends, parents, and mentors can be invaluable if they are available. Homosexual youth often struggle with uncertainty and doubt about their future knowing that they face personal and professional challenges because of their sexual orientation.

Sexual Identity Formation

A number of theorists have described developmental pathways for the sexual identity formation of lesbian and gay individuals.[22] I will describe Troiden's model with the understanding that it serves as a guide only, since development is always fluid and may not be linear.

In the first stage, *sensitization,* gay or lesbian children perceive being different and feel marginalized. They may take an atypical gender role and may not feel that they fit in with their peers. The hallmark of the second stage is *identity confusion*. This occurs when the lesbian or gay adolescent begins to question if they are homosexual. Cognitive dissonance develops because of altered perceptions of self, inaccurate information about homosexuality, and societal antihomosexual bias. In stage three, *identity assumption*, gay or lesbian individuals come to accept their sexual orientation, often by late adolescence or early adulthood. This leads to increasing contact with other homosexuals and explorations of sexuality. *Commitment*, stage four, is the integration of sexual orientation in all aspects of one's life. There may be disclosure to heterosexuals, friends, and close family members. Some may reject heterosexuals as a legitimate

Psychiatry, Antihomosexual Bias, and Challenges

reference group, whereas others may be able to value supportive heterosexuals with less anger and alienation.

Psychosocial Issues for Homosexual Youth

The main internal and external challenge for gay and lesbian youth is coping with biases toward their homosexuality. They may have internalized self-hatred and low self-esteem. At times, these feelings can be acted out behaviorally through high-risk sexual behaviors or the use of drugs and alcohol.[23]

Many teens attempt to hide their feelings and questions because they fear being discovered. Although this may offer some protection from rejection and abuse, isolation results.

Lesbian and gay individuals of color belong to a "double minority" and must also deal with the biases of their ethnic group toward their homosexuality as well as societal bias against their color. Those who are also part of a religious community with antihomosexual bias belong to a "triple minority" and must also face rejection by God and by their church group.

It is no wonder that anxiety and depression is common, occurring three to four times more frequently for gay and lesbian youth than for heterosexual youth.[24] Suicide is the third leading cause of death for all youth aged ten to twenty-four, but it is believed by some to be the leading cause of death for lesbian and gay youth.[25] Many studies have shown that gay and lesbian youth attempt suicide at two to three times the rate of heterosexual youth.[26]

> I wish I could be there. I would love to talk about the serious implications of not being able to acknowledge, often even to one's self, that you have an alternative sexual orientation from the majority…It is, I believe, in the adolescent years of academy life where the greatest harm and pain occur. Out of my own academy class one dear friend committed suicide a number of years ago because of his inability to be accepted as he really was.[27]

> I wouldn't allow myself to have female friends. I cut pictures of boys out of magazines and taped them all over my room. And I would write in my journal every night and talk about how much I hated myself and how I didn't want to be

this way. And it ultimately led to me being very depressed and very suicidal.[28]

HIV Infection

Gay youth continue to be at significant risk of acquiring HIV infection. Recent preliminary findings from the National HIV Behavioral Surveillance system show a HIV prevalence rate of 14 percent for gay men between the ages of eighteen and twenty-four.[29]

It is estimated that one-half of all new HIV infections in the United States occur in young people between the ages of thirteen and twenty-four.[30] In 2002, HIV disease was the eighth leading cause of death for all youth fifteen to twenty-four years of age and was the sixth leading cause of death in males twenty-five to thirty-four years of age.[31]

HIV/sexual health education continues to be an urgent priority for all adolescents, especially for gay youth.

Family Responses

When parents provide support and understanding, lesbian and gay youth experience less stress, have improved self-esteem, and are more accepting of their sexual orientation.[32]

Unfortunately, not all parents are supportive. More than one-third of LGBT youth report verbal abuse by family members and 10 percent report physical abuse.[33] As many as 26 percent of gay youth are forced to leave home because of conflict over their sexual orientation, and it has been estimated that gay youth account for 25 percent of homeless youth.[34] "I got kicked out of my house in July, and at that point there was violence involved," recalled one young homosexual from Massachusetts. "My mother went nuts and came at me with an iron. I ran downstairs and locked the door, she called the police. The police came and asked me what was going on," he continued. "My mother started saying that I'm always in Boston with fags and told me that I should leave....He [the police officer] started cracking all kinds of gay jokes and told me I should leave."[35]

School Experience

The Gay, Lesbian and Straight Education Network recently conducted the first nationwide survey of more than three thousand thirteen to eighteen year-old students and one thousand high school teachers on

Psychiatry, Antihomosexual Bias, and Challenges

the subject of bullying in schools.[36] The most common cause of bullying reported was about one's physical appearance. The second most common cause was about actual or perceived sexual orientation. The survey found that LGBT students were three times more likely then non-LGBT students to feel unsafe at school (22 percent versus 7 percent). Furthermore, 90 percent of LGBT students (versus 62 percent of non-LGBT teens) reported being harassed or assaulted during the previous year.

Gay and lesbian teens develop negative attitudes toward school because of this treatment, and 28 percent of gay students drop out of high school because of discomfort and fear, according to a 1987 study.[37] "We were picked on. We were called 'queer' and 'faggot' and a host of other homophobic slurs," recalled one young homosexual. "We were also used as punching bags by our classmates, just for being different"[38]

> I was harassed a great deal before I came out. When I was a freshman, like all freshman, I had to take gym. And a group of girls in my class decided that I was a lesbian because I was taller and stronger than the other girls in my class. The first time they bashed me was in the locker room. And I had finished getting dressed and they pulled me to the ground and started kicking me and screaming, "queer, faggot, dyke—stop looking at us." And I got up and just bolted from the room, and I stopped dressing for gym after that. The second time they bashed me I was playing field hockey and one of them had her hockey stick in her hands and just clubbed me to the side of the forehead with it. I fell to the ground and the rest of them circled me and started beating me with their hockey sticks, screaming the same epithets…my gym teacher said if you're going to behave that way you deserve it.[39]

Conclusion

Attitudes in the general public toward homosexuality are changing, and it is only a matter of time before gay and lesbian individuals are afforded the same rights and privileges as heterosexuals. It has been thirty-three years since organized psychiatry and psychology viewed homosexuality as an illness. Same-sex civil marriage is now supported by the American Psychiatric Association, which recognizes that homosexual couples have the same psychological, social, and economic reasons for getting married as heterosexual couples.

Although it is heartening to see these changes, it remains unacceptable to see the continuing hatred and violence directed toward LGBT individuals, especially toward our most vulnerable youth. Instead of looking at empirical evidence, society continues to hold attitudes based on religious and cultural beliefs. It is now past time to stop antihomosexual bias and violence and to question the underlying beliefs and attitudes that cause such hatred and discrimination.

To effect change we must all confront our individual and institutional antihomosexual biases. Like organized psychiatry of over thirty years ago, we must face these biases and recognize their detrimental effects on homosexuals.

Once we become fully aware of our biases, we need to provide accurate information about homosexuality to all health care providers, educators, clergy, youth, family members, and our communities. For example, the current seventh- and eighth-grade science textbook for North American Seventh-day Adventist schools refers to homosexual orientation as "part of Satan's effort to sabotage God's plan for men and women."[40] This text, and others, needs to be revised or replaced with more accurate information.

If we do not do all that we can to stop antihomosexual bias, we will continue to be responsible, in part, for the pain and deaths of LGBT individuals.

The author would like to acknowledge the invaluable ideas and support for this paper from Janice Wang, Kia Wang Nevarez, and Jose Mateo.

Questions for Discussion

1. Why was the psychologist Evelyn Hooker's 1957 paper on the psychological functioning of gay men so important?
2. What were the key factors that led the American Psychiatric Association to change its views of homosexuality in 1973?
3. Why does the author state that lesbians of color who are part of a religious community belong to a "quadruple minority"?
4. Why do gay and lesbian youth attempt suicide at a rate two to three times higher than do heterosexual youth?

5. What can be done to make our schools safer for lesbian and gay youth?

Notes and References

1. K. Hausman, "Assembly Backs Gay Marriage, Asks Board to Share Power," *Psychiatric News* 40 (2005):1–5. Position statement can be found at <http://www.psych.org/edu/other_res/lib_archives/archives/200502.pdf>, accessed Mar. 26, 2006.
2. R. Bayer, *Homosexuality and American Psychiatry* (Princeton, N.J.: Princeton University Press, 1987), 19.
3. Ibid.; J. Money, "History, Causality, and Sexology," *Journal of Sex Research* 40 (2003):237–39.
4. In *Letters of Sigmund Freud*, E. Freud, ed. (New York: Basic Books, 1960), 423–24; and Bayer, *Homosexuality and American Psychiatry*, 27.
5. Bayer, *Homosexuality and American Psychiatry*, 28–30.
6. I. Bieber et al., *Homosexuality: A Psychoanalytic Study of Male Homosexuals* (New York: Basic Books, 1962).
7. A. Kinsey, W. Pomeroy, and C. Martin, *Sexual Behavior in the Human Male* (Philadelphia: Saunders, 1948).
8. C. Ford and F. Beach, *Patterns of Sexual Behavior* (New York: Harper, 1951), 125–43.
9. E. Hooker, "The Adjustment of the Male Overt Homosexual," *Journal of Projective Techniques* 21 (1957):18–31.
10. M. Freedman, *Homosexuality and Psychological Functioning* (Belmont, Calif.: Brooks/Cole, 1971); R. Friedman and J. Downey, "Homosexuality," *New England Journal of Medicine* 331, no. 14 (1994):923–30; J. Gonsiorek, "The Empirical Basis for the Demise of the Illness Model of Homosexuality," in *Homosexuality Research Implications for Public Policy*, eds. J. Gonsiorek and J. Weinrich (Newberry Park, Calif.: Sage, 1991), 115–36; and idem, "Results of Psychological Testing on Homosexual Populations," in *Homosexuality: Social, Psychological, and Biological Issues*, eds. W. Paul, J. Weinrich, J. Gonsiorek, and M. Hotvedt (Beverly Hills, Calif.: Sage, 1982), 71–88.
11. J. Krajeski, "Homosexuality and the Mental Health Professions," in *Textbook of Homosexuality and Mental Health*, eds. R. Cabaj and T. Stein (Washington, D.C.: American Psychiatric Press), 21.
12. Bayer, *Homosexuality and American Psychiatry*, 102–5.

13. M. Kirby, "The 1973 Deletion of Homosexuality as a Psychiatric Disorder: 30 Years On," *Australian and New Zealand Journal of Psychiatry* 37, no. 6 (2003):674–77; J. Lenzer, "John Fryer Obituary," *British Medical Journal*, Mar. 22, 2003, 662; and "81 Words" (episode 204), *This American Life*, Jan. 18, 2002, accessed online Mar. 26, 2006, at <http://www.thislife.org/pages/archives/archive02.html>.
14. L. Lamberg, "Gay is Okay with APA—Forum Honors Landmark 1973 Events," *Journal of the American Medication Association* 280 (1998):497–99; and Bayer, *Homosexuality and American Psychiatry*, 118.
15. Bayer, *Homosexuality and American Psychiatry*, 118.
16. Ibid., 119.
17. R. Stoller et al., "Should Homosexuality Be in the APA Nomenclature?" *American Journal of Psychiatry* 130, no. 11 (1973):1211–12.
18. Bayer, *Homosexuality and American Psychiatry*, 126; and "81 Words."
19. B. Fisher and J. Akman, "Normal Development in Sexual Minority Youth," in *Mental Health Issues in Lesbian, Gay, Bisexual, and Transgender Communities*, eds. B. Jones and M. Hill (Washington, D.C.: American Psychiatric Press, 2002), 4.
20. B. Moyer, "A Cry from the Valley of Death," *Ministry*, Nov. 1996, 23–25, 29.
21. R. Troiden, "The Formation of Homosexual Identities," *Journal of Homosexuality* 17 (1989):43–73; and C. Ryan and D. Futterman, *Lesbian and Gay Youth* (New York: Columbia University Press, 1998), 10.
22. A. D'Augelli and C. Patterson, eds., *Lesbian, Gay, and Bisexual Identities and Youth* (New York: Oxford University Press, 2001); V. Cass, "Homosexual Identity Formation: A Theoretical Model," *Journal of Homosexuality* 4 (1979):219–35; idem, "Sexual Orientation Identity Formation," in *Textbook of Homosexuality and Mental Health* (Washington, D.C. American Psychiatric Press, 1996), 227–51; E. Coleman, "Developmental Stages of the Coming Out Process: Homosexuality and Psychotherapy," *Journal of Homosexuality* 7 (1981–82):31–43; J. Sophie, "A Critical Examination of Stage Theories of Lesbian Identity Development," *Journal of Homosexuality* 12 (1985–86): 39–51; R. Troiden, "Homosexuality Identity Development," *Journal of Adolescent*

Psychiatry, Antihomosexual Bias, and Challenges

Health Care 9 (1988):105–13; idem, "Formation of Homosexual Identities," 17 (1989):43–73; and M. Rotheram-Borus and M. Fernandez, "Sexual Orientation and Developmental Challenges Experienced by Gay and Lesbian Youth," *Journal of Suicide and Life Threatening Behavior* 25 (1995):1–10.

23. R. Garafalo et al., "The Association between Health Risk Behaviors and Sexual Orientation among a School-Based Sample of Adolescents," *Pediatrics* 101, no. 5 (1998):895–902.
24. B. Fergusson, L. Horwood, and A. Beautrais, "Is Sexual Orientation Related to Mental Health Problems and Suicidality in Young People?" *Archives of General Psychiatry* 56 (1999):876–80.
25. "Suicide and Attempted Suicide," *MMWR Weekly*, June 11, 2004, accessed online Feb. 20, 2007, at <http://www.cdc.gov/mmwr/preview/mmwrhtml/mm5322a1.htm>; P. Gibson, "Gay and Lesbian Youth Suicide," in *Death by Denial* (Boston: Alyson, 1994), 16; and H. Kulkin, E. Chauvin, and G. Percie, "Suicide among Gay and Lesbian Adolescents and Young Adults," *Journal of Homosexuality* 40, no. 1 (2000):1–15.
26. A. Faulkner and K. Cranston, "Correlates of Same-Sex Sexual Behavior in a Random Sample of Massachusetts High School Students," *American Journal of Public Health* 88, no. 2 (1998):262–66; Fergusson, Horwood, and Beautrais, "Sexual Orientation"; and Garafalo et al., "Health Risk Behaviors."
27. E-mail from former Pacific Union College student to Harry C. Wang, July 28, 1999, in possession of the author.
28. Interview of Kelli Peterson by Terry Gross, *Fresh Air*, June 8, 1999.
29. "HIV Prevalence, Unrecognized Infection, and HIV Testing among Men Who Have Sex with Men—Five U.S. Cities, June 2004–April 2005," *MMWR Weekly*, June 24, 2005, accessed online Feb. 20, 2007, at <http://www.cdc.gov/mmwr/preview/mmwrhtml/mm5424a2.htm>.
30. Office of National AIDS Policy, *Youth and HIV/AIDS 2000: A New American Agenda* (Washington, D.C.: White House, 2000).
31. Centers for Disease Control, "Deaths, Percent of Total Deaths, and Death Rates for the 15 Leading Causes of Death in 10-year Age Groups: United States, 2002," accessed online Feb. 20, 2007, at <http://www.cdc.gov/nchs/data/dvs/LCWK2_2002.pdf>.

32. S. Hershberger and A. D'Augelli, "The Consequences of Victimization on the Mental Health and Suicidality of Lesbian, Gay, and Bisexual Youth," *Developmental Psychology* 31 (1995):65–74; and R. Savin-Williams, "Coming Out to Parents and Self-Esteem among Gay and Lesbian Youths," *Journal of Homosexuality* 18 (1989):1–35.
33. N. Pilkington and A. D'Augelli, "Victimization of Lesbian, Gay, and Bisexual Youth in Community Settings," *Journal of Community Psychology* 23 (1995):33–56.
34. Gibson, "Gay and Lesbian Youth Suicide," 5; and G. Kruks, "Gay and Lesbian Homeless/Street Youth: Special Issues and Concerns," *Journal of Adolescent Health* 12 (1991):515–18.
35. Testimony of Troix Bettencourt in The Governor's Commission on Gay and Lesbian Youth, *Prevention of Health Problems among Gay and Lesbian Youth* (Boston, Mass.: n.p., 1994), 28.
36. Harris Interactive and GLSEN, *From Teasing to Torment: School Climate in America, A Survey of Students and Teachers* (New York: GLSEN, 2005), accessed online Feb. 20, 2007, at <http://www.glsen.org/binary-data/GLSEN_ATTACHMENTS/file/499-1.pdf>.
37. G. Remafedi, "Adolescent Homosexuality: Psychosocial and Medical Implications," *Pediatrics* 79 (1987):331.
38. The Governor's Commission on Gay and Lesbian Youth, *Making Schools Safe for Gay and Lesbian Youth* (Boston, Mass.: n.p., 1993), 8.
39. Interview of Kelli Peterson, June 8, 1999.
40. R. Ritterskamp and D. Wyrick, *Exploring God's World* (Nampa, Idaho: Pacific Press, 1996), Chapter 9–4, "Sexual Issues."

Response: Science and Sexual Orientation

By Aubyn Fulton

Is homosexuality a choice? Is it a mental disorder? Over the years, I have participated in a lot of conversations about sexual orientation with fellow Seventh-day Adventists, and these two questions are almost always asked. This is more surprising than it might seem, for the answer to neither question is determinative of a theological or moral response to homosexuality. Still, there are good reasons why biological and psychiatric considerations play an important role in any discussion of sexual orientation and religion. First, we are all vulnerable to the tendency to mistake our prejudices for evidence. The more clearly and accurately we understand the biological and mental health issues, the better our religious and moral judgments will be. Second, both biology and psychiatry can help us recognize and serve those in our community who are suffering. Ben Kemena and Harry Wang provide the church with the kind of biological, psychiatric, and historical information that must be wrestled with if Adventists are to engage in just and loving conversation about sexual orientation. They both also pose startling, even painful challenges to the church. A prayerful and careful consideration of both the evidence and the challenges are long overdue.

Ben Kemena's subtitle for his chapter on "Biological Determinants of Homosexual Orientation" is particularly revealing: "Is It a Choice or Innate—Biology or Sin?" It is imperative that we correct rampant misinformation about the causes of sexual orientation in the church—and many Christians have either been kept ignorant about the explosion of scientific evidence that has established strong biological factors, or been (mis)taught to be irrationally suspicious of its validity or conclusions. Kemena's article should help enormously on this front. But it may be that his tracing of the modern history of the social construction of homosexuality is even more important—and ironically this history explodes the narrow dichotomy of "Biology or Sin" reflected in his subtitle.

The "Biology or Sin" dichotomy is problematic at several levels. It implies that the only "causes" of human behavior are biological ones, ignoring the clear lesson from social science that many of the most powerful forces that shape or "cause" human behavior are in the environment. Conditioning, modeling, and internalization of social roles are just some examples of powerful nonbiological forces that shape our behavior, most often outside any conscious awareness or "choice." The dichotomy also implies that biologically caused behaviors cannot be considered sinful, even though we can all think of behaviors that would still be considered sinful even if strong biological contributions were identified (for example, murder or stealing). Most fundamentally, the "Biology or Sin" dichotomy conflates two different categories. Biological factors contribute to sexual orientation either a little or a lot, and the only credible way of answering that question is scientifically. Whether or not homosexuality is a sin is an entirely different sort of question, and science can perhaps inform, but certainly not decide, the answer. Accepting the "Biology or Sin" dichotomy encourages avoiding responsibility for making ethical and moral judgments that in the end cannot really be avoided.

Another problem with trying to answer the "Biology or Sin" question is that it risks overemphasizing the biological role, since that is the only role it asks about. Kemena notes "genetics are likely combined with environmental factors to create a spectrum of human sexual desire" (P2-15) and acknowledges there is a lot we still do not know about human sexuality (P2-18), but by attempting to address the issue of whether homosexuality is biological or sinful, he does naturally place a lot of emphasis on biology. I do not dispute the validity of his summary of this evidence. There is no real argument any longer about the existence of a strong biological contribution to sexual orientation, and to deny this is to stand outside reasonable discourse on the subject. But the evidence points to something more that can be

Response: Science and Sexual Orientation

easily overlooked: Just as clearly there are nonbiological factors that contribute to sexual orientation.

Here's one example to make the point: The evidence about concordance rates for homosexuality in identical twins, discussed by Kemena (P2-14), are significantly higher than the general population, but nowhere near 100 percent (the concordance rates have been reported to be between 20 and 50 percent). This almost certainly means that, although as many as half of the determiners of sexual orientation are genetic, at least half are nongenetic. We should note, however, that much of the nongenetic part of the explanation might be factors that have their effect on the in utero environment, thus mediated by biological processes in the developing fetus.

It is important to understand that this is not the same as saying that sexual orientation is partly determined and partly chosen; rather, it says that some of the causes of sexual orientation are biological and others are nonbiological (for example, psychological or social). As Kemena shows so well, even if we are not completely sure of what all the specific causes of sexual orientation might be, it is now clear that the majority of us do not "choose" our sexual orientations. For most of us, our sexual orientations are part of our identity, part of who we are, which develops subtly and imperceptibly but is often in place by the end of the fifth year, as the data from Green and his colleagues (discussed by Kemena on pages P2-13-14) shows.

The role of choice in sexual orientation has been confused in the public's mind in recent years. Psychiatrist Robert L. Spitzer published an article in 2003 on his study of 143 men, referred by so-called "ex-gay" ministries, who reported that at one time they were homosexual and had become heterosexual as a result of some kind of "conversion therapy."[1] This study was widely misrepresented in the conservative Christian community as "proving" that homosexuality was a choice. In fact, Spitzer never made such a claim. He limited his conclusions simply to the observation that some men, a very small minority, report having changed their sexual orientation. In his paper, he concludes that 11 percent of his highly selected, highly motivated sample had changed their orientation, and in personal communications I have had with him he has stated that, for most homosexuals, orientation is highly stable and extremely resistant to change. We do not have enough good evidence to know how many homosexuals could change their orientation, mostly because the groups that engage in such practices do not permit independent investigators to review their data—as Kemena points out. However, Spitzer reported that he would be surprised if the number were higher than 3 percent. This must be put in the context of the existing data on the potential for harm in such change practices. Kemena notes that Arial Shidlo and Michael Schroeder found that less than 4 percent of gay men who have undergone "conversion therapy" have been able to refrain from homosexual behavior. As important, the investigators found that 77 percent of this sample reported significant negative side effects of the change attempts, including significant increase in depression, anxiety, serious self-harmful behavior, and heavy substance abuse.[2]

Kemena uses Alfred Kinsey's 10 percent estimate of the prevalence of male homosexuality, whereas most contemporary social scientists would put the figure at between 3 and 6 percent.[3] Whatever the exact percentage, and whatever the relative balance of biological and nonbiological causes of sexual orientation, it now seems clear that, for most of us, orientation is well-established early in life and stable and highly resistant to change, and that change efforts are very likely to result in significant risk of serious harm.. The likelihood of change is so low, and the likelihood of harm is so high, that it is difficult to see any ethical basis for encouraging someone to try to change their orientation. Certainly, the Adventist church must at the very least consider a moratorium on any formal or informal program of referring gay and lesbian church members or workers for "conversion therapy."

Although the article is framed by the "Biology or Sin" dichotomy, Kemena repeatedly breaks through it, most clearly in his location of Western, Christian attitudes toward homosexuality in the "degeneracy pyramid," based on the belief that "different types of human beings [have] different value and worth" (P2-15). The argument here is not that homosexuality is not a sin because it is biological and beyond personal control. The argument is far more radical—and more Christian. The "degeneracy pyramid" that Kemena discusses is the very power hierarchy that was the primary target of the ministry of Jesus. It is hard to imagine an idea more violently opposed to the central teachings of the gospel and the principles of the kingdom of God. If the homo-negative attitudes of the Adventist church are influenced even a little by internalization of this anti-Christian power hierarchy, then Kemena has turned the discussion of homosexuality and the church on its head. The question is no longer (as it is often framed) "will Christians water down their commitment to the gospel to accommodate modern science and social norms?" but "will Christians have the

Response: Science and Sexual Orientation

courage to live out the true meaning of the gospel, even when it challenges their own personal biases and prerogatives?"

Of course, no member of the Adventist church would consciously endorse the idea of the degeneracy pyramid—that some humans (conveniently, usually white, male, wealthy, and powerful) have more inherent value than others. But our experience with other aspects of this pyramid suggests that it is all too easy for us to internalize this hierarchy unconsciously and, most shockingly, actually confuse it with Christian morality. It was not that long ago, after all, that it was taken for granted in many Christian communities—even Adventist ones—that the Bible required us to accept the conclusion that blacks were inferior to whites, or women inferior to men. The role of biology in such a discussion is not to let the church off the hook of making hard moral judgments because of sympathy for homosexuals who somehow "can't help themselves." The role of biology is simply to help us gain a more accurate understanding of the full range of the human family, helping us to see more clearly who our neighbors are. Thus equipped, we are better able to see what our neighbors need to be healthy and safe, and how our own too-human tendencies to create boundaries and elevate our self-interest can get in the way. At that point, our obligation is clear.

Harry Wang begins his chapter by correcting a common misconception among many Christians that a few radical homosexuals forced the American Psychiatric Association to remove homosexuality from the official list of mental disorders, perhaps out of some godless antipathy for the family or the Bible. The real story, told well by Wang, is quite different. It was not politics that took homosexuality off of the list of mental disorders; it was politics that put homosexuality on the list in the first place. It certainly was not scientific evidence that put it there, since there was not then, and never has been, scientific evidence that homosexuality is a mental disorder.

Of course, the concept of "disorder" itself can never be purely scientific. It rests on certain assumptions of what normal "order" is in the first place, and there will always be cultural and political dimensions to that judgment. The current definition of disorder used by the American Psychiatric Association requires evidence of a syndrome in the person that is associated with either distress or disability (DSM-IV TR, xxi). There were no scientific studies of representative samples showing that there was something in a homosexual orientation associated with increased distress or dysfunction when psychiatry pathologized homosexuality; that decision was made because the ones with the power to make them were prejudiced against homosexuals. As Wang has shown, the scientific evidence is now clear—homosexuality is not associated with distress or dysfunction, and by the established criteria is not a mental disorder. This is not to say that politics played no role in the removal of homosexuality from the DSM—all disorders in the volume have been listed there as a result of some degree of political process. But in this case, politics functioned to remove barriers to objective consideration of evidence.

By the mid-1970s, the mental health profession was becoming more aware of the need to base psychiatric diagnosis on objective evidence. As Wang shows, this coincided with a growing awareness by the leadership of the American Psychiatric Association that some of its leading colleagues, known to be psychologically healthy, were in fact homosexuals. Up to that time, most psychiatrists had based their conclusions that homosexuals were mentally disordered on their familiarity with gay patients, who, of course, by definition had psychological problems. When the first courageous gay psychiatrists came out to their leadership, their decision provided precious information—that homosexuals were just like heterosexuals, no more or no less healthy. It is neither coincidental nor surprising that as a result of these honest relationships psychiatry took its first steps toward a more accurate understanding and civil treatment of homosexuals. The evidence has consistently shown that the best predictor of positive attitudes toward homosexuals is the number of homosexual friends and relatives a person has.[4] The hostile climate common in most Seventh-day Adventist churches toward homosexuals is not only destructive for homosexuals, but also makes the kind of open and honest relationships with homosexuals necessary for accurate and full understanding almost impossible. As psychiatry did forty years ago, the church today continues to assume and perpetuate the lie that homosexuals are sick, then acts in such a way as to make it difficult to correct the lie.

Although homosexuality is not a source of distress, the pervasive negative climate many homosexuals are forced to grow up in is. Wang closes his chapter by carefully explaining the devastating consequences of this oppressive, hostile, and often violent environment, especially for children. Parents, pastors, teachers, and church members who somehow have convinced themselves they are acting in the name of Jesus treat gay children with such hatred and contempt that they are anxious, depressed, and far too often suicidal. Wang presents the

Response: Science and Sexual Orientation

findings from the Gay, Lesbian, and Straight Education Network nationwide study on bullying showing that LGBT students were three times more likely to feel unsafe, 50 percent more likely to be attacked at school, and a quarter more likely to drop out of school. Adventist schools should be safe places for our children, but they may well be even more dangerous than public schools. We desperately need good studies of this issue.

Several years ago I accompanied a gay student at one of our Adventist colleges to a meeting with his residence hall dean. The student had been the victim of verbal and physical violence throughout the school year and had finally worked up the courage, after months of prayer and counseling, to ask the dean for help. I was deeply saddened and ashamed to find that the dean—a sincere member of the church in good standing—at first suggested that the student had brought the assaults on himself by his nonconformity to what the dean considered acceptable styles of masculine dress and personal style. It was only after I basically resorted to legal threats that the dean agreed that this kind of hostile and violent environment was inappropriate on an Adventist campus.

This is where Wang's analysis poses a difficult challenge for the church—even more difficult, perhaps, than he has let on. If homosexuality is not a mental disorder (and, clearly it is not) and if gay young people are vulnerable to assault and oppression (as clearly they are) what is our responsibility as a Christian community? Wang closes with an argument: "If we do not do all that we can to stop anti-homosexual bias, we will continue to be responsible, in part, for the pain and deaths of LGBT individuals" (P2-40). True enough. But this means more than simply intervening when we observe a gay or lesbian young person being attacked—though of course we must do at least that. It also requires that we proactively identify and seek to modify those attitudes and values that lead to such abuse. We do not all need to agree that homosexuality is not a sin; all of us need to agree that not treating homosexuals as our neighbor *is* a sin. How many Adventist K–12 schools and colleges have systematic and intentional programs in place to address these issues in a developmentally appropriate way with their students? I suspect the answer would be embarrassing.

But it is even more challenging than this. It is not enough to stop current acts of assault, and it is not enough to develop proactive programs to reduce them from ever occurring. Wang's outline of the developmental needs of young people raises the issue of what we are doing to help LGBT adolescents come to terms with their own identity. Though it may be disturbing to some, perhaps it is time to consider how we can support young gay and lesbian Adventists, rather than creating an environment so toxic that we force them to find out about themselves outside the safety of the church. I am not sure how to create supportive spaces for gay and lesbian youth to meet and talk and socialize in the church without moving too fast for members who define all homosexuality as sinful. I do know that the material reviewed by Wang demonstrates it is imperative that we start looking for ways now.

Kemena and Wang both provide important answers to some of the most common questions that Adventists ask when they start talking about homosexuality. What are the biological factors? Is it a mental illness? Can it be changed? But the questions they raise and the challenges they pose are even more important. If we take these chapters seriously, we can no longer ignore or dismiss homosexuals as degenerates, willfully choosing a harmful or sick lifestyle, deserving of whatever harm comes their way. We will need to recognize that a significant fraction of our human family suffers from social and often physical oppression simply for being who they are. We will need to wrestle with gospel imperatives to open wide our definition of neighbor, treat all with justice and love, and be willing to think again about pet biblical interpretations and theories we have inherited but perhaps not examined closely enough. This might mean finding ways to make sure we treat all the members of our family with respect and compassion, even before we have resolved every theological and moral conundrum. The challenge for the Adventist church is not just to find a way to reconcile our biblical understanding with less hostility toward homosexuals; the challenge is that, as followers of Christ, Adventists have an affirmative moral and spiritual duty to create a loving and just community in which homosexuals can participate.

Questions for Discussion

1. How and why does the moral or theological status of homosexuality change if we assume that sexual orientation is biologically determined? If it is partly a result of non-biological factors, does that necessarily make it a choice?
2. Are there ways in which sexual orientation is similar to other core, personal identities like gender or ethnic identity?

Response: Science and Sexual Orientation

3. Christians often assume that the Bible requires the condemnation of homosexuals. Given Kemena's discussion of the degeneracy pyramid, is it possible that the Bible actually requires Christians to embrace homosexuals?
4. What definition of "normal" would support labeling homosexuality "abnormal" without opening all other minority groups that do not conform to some aspect of majority values as abnormal as well?
5. Why is it that the more homosexual friends and relatives a heterosexual knows themselves to have, the more supportive their attitudes are towards homosexuality? What are the implications of this fact for the church?
6. What obligations does the Seventh-day Adventist Church have for correcting negative and hostile treatment of LGBT children and adolescents in its schools, colleges and universities? Is the standard "hate the sin, but love the sinner" approach sufficient to provide for the well-being of these students?

Notes and References

1. Robert L. Spitzer, "Can Some Gay Men and Lesbians Change Their Sexual Orientation?" *Archives of Sexual Behavior* 32, no. 5 (Oct. 2003):403–17.
2. Arial Shidlo and Michael Schroeder, "Changing Sexual Orientation: A Consumers' Report," *Professional Psychology: Research and Practice* 33, no. 3 (June 2002):249–59.
3. See Gregory M. Herick's Web site, *Facts about Homosexuality and Mental Health*, at <http://psychology.ucdavis.edu/rainbow.html/facts_mental_health.html>.
4. Annie L. Cotton-Huston and Bradley M. Waite, "Anti-Homosexual Attitudes in College Students: Predictors and Classroom Interventions," *Journal of Homosexuality* 38, no. 3 (2000):117–33.

Part Three
Behavioral Science Perspectives

Part 3-2

Interaction and Angst: The Social Experiences of Gay and Lesbian Seventh-day Adventists

By René D. Drumm

What is it like to grow up in the Seventh-day Adventist (SDA) Church and in that growing up process discover you are gay or lesbian? Given that homosexual behavior is sinful according to traditional interpretations of SDA doctrine, how does a person make such a discovery? How does that discovery then impinge on gay and lesbian Adventists' daily lives? This chapter addresses what social science does and does not support in terms of how sexual orientation develops and how stable it is. Spanning more than ten years of research into the social aspects of gay and lesbian Adventist life, it offers information about the social reality of growing up in a setting poised for rejection. This chapter discusses the influences of the family, school, church, and other social institutions on the lives of gay and lesbian people brought up in Adventist homes. The chapter concludes by offering suggestions to enhance our responses to these members of the Adventist family. All of the names used are pseudonyms to protect the identities of the people who contributed information for this chapter.

Sexual Orientation 101: The Components of Sexual Orientation

Sexual orientation refers to a configuration of dynamics that work together categorizing people as heterosexual, bisexual, or homosexual.

René D. Drumm

Sexual orientation forms along several continuums that contribute to the overall sexual orientation label with which a person identifies. Four of these components include the biological or physical aspects of personhood that are granted at birth, the gender identity people develop over time, their emotional attractions, and their sexual preferences.

Biological Factors

Biological components of a person that contribute to determination of sexual orientation include the anatomical features that society has labeled as "male" or "female." For example, "males" are distinguished by possessing testicles and penises, whereas people with vaginas and breasts are labeled "females." A common myth exists that people are biologically "either or," either biologically male or biologically female. In reality, people are much more complex. Some individuals are positioned along the continuum between male and female. For example, people who possess indistinct genitalia are known as hermaphrodites, or currently more often as intersexed people. In addition, type of genital is a factor that determines a particular gender label and hormones play a powerful role in the biological determinants of our emotions and behavior. Hormones such as testosterone and estrogen occur along the biological continuum and differ in levels from individual to individual.

Biology Continuum

Male	Hermaphrodite	Female
XY Chromosomes		XX Chromosomes
Penis, Testicles, Prostate	Mix of Genitalia	Vagina, Ovaries, Clitoris
Testosterone	Mix of Hormones	Estrogen

These two facets of biology provide important inputs toward sexual orientation formation. Researchers have noted very specific differences between homosexually and heterosexually oriented individuals.[1]

Gender Identity and Gender Role

The gender identity of a person is determined by a combination of societal expectations and individual preferences. Society decides what

Interaction and Angst

specific behaviors or characteristics are appropriate for each gender. For example, in the United States, girl babies are identified by pink blankets, whereas boy babies are given blue blankets. Boys are "supposed to" play with trucks, and girls with dolls. Just as in biology, gender identity plays out across the entire continuum. The interplay of biology and gender identity begins the unfolding of sexual orientation and societal labeling. For example, people with penises and testicles (biologically male) who like shopping and cooking are often labeled effeminate. Biological young females who like to climb trees are called "tomboys."

Gender Continuum

Male/Masculine   **Androgynous**   **Female/Feminine**

Culturally defined mannerisms, personality traits, clothing, grooming

Researchers who study gender identity as a component of sexual orientation formation have provided insights about how gender identity contributes to sexual orientation formation. Bailey and Zucker found that childhood sex-typed behavior was significantly predictive of adult homosexual orientation in men in their review of forty-eight studies that examined the relationship between childhood sex-typed behavior and sexual orientation. Childhood sex-typed behavior refers to behaviors identified as indicators of gender identity and gender role, such as preference for same- or opposite-sex peers, toy interests, and fantasy play. Bailey and Zucker maintain that a significantly large number of homosexual men and a smaller but still significant number of lesbians recall childhood cross-sex-typed behavior.[2] Building on these and other studies, Bem has developed a theory that explains how gender identity plays a role in both homosexual and heterosexual development.[3]

Emotional and Cognitive Functioning

The emotional and cognitive functioning of a person are key elements in determining sexual orientation. Emotional functioning addresses the issue of who a person is drawn to emotionally and who that person can truly "love." The key issue in emotional identity focuses on which gender the person is attracted to most on an emotional level. Cognitive functioning centers on erotic fantasies and who people picture themselves with as life mates. Research indicates that the emotional and cognitive components of sexual orientation are fairly stable. In one research report that attempted to highlight change in sexual orientation, eight out of eleven individuals (73 percent) who claimed to have changed their orientation from homosexual to heterosexual retained their same-sex dreams, fantasies, or impulses.[4] Friedman and Downey, who have published in the *New England Journal of Medicine*, conclude "there is little evidence that permanent replacement of homosexual fantasies by heterosexual ones is possible."[5]

Emotional and Cognitive Continuum

Male only　　　　**Both Men and Women**　　　　**Women only**

"Who is this person attracted to emotionally?"
"Who does this person fantasize about?"

Sexual Preference

A fourth component in understanding sexual orientation is sexual preference. Sexual preference refers to the gender of a person whom another finds appealing as a sexual partner. Whereas the biological, gender identity, and emotional aspects of sexual preference are known fairly early in life, as a general rule, the sexual preference aspect of sexual orientation appears sometime after puberty. This helps explain why some people seemingly "become" homosexual later in life. Sexual preference can be suppressed by external factors such as societal and religious expectations. Only after concerted effort to understand their sexual orientation do some people come to recognize their sexual preference. Research indicates that sexual preference is rather fluid and malleable, particularly among women.[6]

Sexual Preference

Male only　　　　**Both Men and Women**　　　　**Women only**

"Who is this person sexually attracted to?"

Interaction and Angst

Using these continua, social scientists have created labels to describe people who intersect along the continua in various configurations. For example, a biological female who sees herself as a male (gender identity) is known as a transgendered person, regardless of her emotional identity or sexual preference. A biological male who likes shopping and cooking, feels that he can be a soul mate to women, and prefers sexual intimacy with women is considered an effeminate heterosexual. A biological male who likes fast cars (gender identity), experiences emotional intimacy with men, and prefers men as sexual partners is known as a homosexual. A person who can be emotionally intimate with and sexually satisfied by either sex is labeled bisexual. Labels for some configurations still do not exist. For example, society does not have a label for a biological female who sees herself as a male and is attracted emotionally and sexually to females. Although some people may label this orientation as lesbian, the psychology speaks more of a heterosexual person than a homosexual one.

From this information, is it clear that sexual orientation is an extremely complex issue. Sexual orientation is not determined easily or clearly at times. It is important to recognize the multifaceted nature of sexual orientation in order to have an appropriate context for understanding information about the experiences of gay and lesbian Adventists.

What Sexual Orientation Is Not: Issues That Do Not Explain Sexual Orientation

Just as it is important to understand the complexity of sexual orientation, it is also imperative to understand factors that are unrelated to sexual orientation. This section explores some myths about sexual orientation formation through social research studies that address each common issue.

Sexual Orientation Is Not Simply about Sexual Behavior

Sexual orientation cannot be understood by concentrating exclusively on sexual behavior; it is much more complex. Research that looks solely at same-sex sexual behavior indicates that among men who engage in anonymous sexual encounters with men, the majority identify themselves as heterosexual and more than half (54–58 percent) are married.[7] In another study that examines sexual labeling of men who have had sex with men and have requested an HIV blood test, 25 percent reported a heterosexual orientation.[8] If sexual behavior *determines* homosexuality, these studies suggest a 25–30 percent homosexuality rate. This possibility is highly unlikely. Instead, a more plausible explanation for this type of same-sex behavior is a person's desire to seek sexual variation, not their sexual orientation. This is an important point to consider when discussing change in sexual orientation. Although people can change *behavior*—such as unhealthy anonymous sexual encounters—change in sexual orientation from exclusive homosexuality to healthy functioning heterosexuality is extremely complex and remains undocumented in controlled studies.

Sexual Orientation Is Not a Choice

A common myth exists that sexual orientation is a choice. Sexual behavior is a choice; however, the configuration of sexual *orientation* depends on many factors, as stated above, and some of those factors are ascribed. In addition to the biological and gender differences that research demonstrates (see citations above), original research into the lives of gay and lesbian Adventists attest to the lack of choice in orientation. One of the clearest findings from my research into the lives of gay and lesbian Adventists is that from all accounts, their sexual orientation was, for them, never a choice. All of the people I interviewed told of many ways they tried *not* to be gay or lesbian.[9] Had a choice been available at the time they discovered their sexual orientation, their choice would have been for heterosexuality. For some people, many years were spent searching for a technique, a connection with God, some revelation that would change their orientation—all to no avail. The following quotes from people I interviewed offer insights into their experiences of self-discovery and desire to be heterosexual.

> At a very early age, I started praying earnestly that God would not allow me to be gay. I did not want to be gay. Who in their right mind would choose to totally ignore what is considered normal attractions, the norms of society? Who would want to face the consequences of such a decision to be ridiculed, to be discriminated against, to be called a child molester, a sick-o, a freak? To be made fun of, to have to live in fear of your personal safety, your life. Who chooses to put themselves into such horrible circumstances? Well, not I. I

Interaction and Angst

wished I could have a girlfriend, be good at sports, and be one of the guys. (Todd)

One thing that I knew from an early age—I was gay. I fought it with all of my strength. I prayed to God daily and many, many, many, times begged God to take this cup away from me. I didn't want to be gay and I wanted to have a wife and family just like most people that I knew. I experienced a fair amount of frustration when God did not take away my same sex attraction. (Gregory)

If I could just take a pill to change this, I would in a second. (Mitch)

Sexual Orientation Cannot Be Explained by Poor Parent Relationships

Early research literature on families in which children grow up to be gay indicated that homosexuality was a result of unsatisfactory relationships with parents.[10] For example, psychology has "blamed" homosexuality on a mother- or father-dominant configuration, insecure relationships with a mother or father, or child sexual abuse.

In contrast, the gay and lesbian Adventists I interviewed recalled generally typical childhood experiences and close relationships with their parents. It is clear through discussions about family life with gay and lesbian Adventists that their homosexuality was not caused by poor parental relationships or any particular configuration of parent interaction. By far, the majority of gay and lesbian Adventists I interviewed described relationships with their parents as loving and warm.

A quotation that I have published elsewhere illustrates this closeness.[11]

"I come from a very loving and caring family. We are very close to this day. I call them all the time and assure them that I love them. They do the same." (Donald).

Not all of the people I interviewed remembered a perfect family life. Elwin recalled, "My dad was an alcoholic and my mom was codependent. As a result, I attend Al-Anon meetings. I never had really positive role models."

René D. Drumm

Growing Up Gay and Adventist

For gay and lesbian Adventists, growing up in an Adventist family appears to be no different than growing up Adventist as a heterosexual person. Adventist families where gay and lesbians are reared hold values and traditions similar to those in families with only heterosexual children. Gay and lesbian Adventists go to Sabbath School and church; attend church schools, academies and Adventist colleges; adhere to vegetarian diets; avoid tobacco and alcohol; and felt guilty when they attend movie theaters. One illustration of just how "Adventist" many of these people are has been quoted in other published works.[12]

> To answer the question of how I became an Adventist, I'd have to say that I don't know what else I could have been. I was born in an Adventist hospital (on the Sabbath, no less), to SDA parents who had graduated from SDA schools, sent there by their SDA parents. I went only to SDA churches and my parents socialized almost exclusively with SDAs. My aunts and uncles were SDAs. One set were missionary doctors, another uncle was an academy Bible teacher. My mother's father had been a missionary to Japan. (Marvin)

The gay and lesbian Adventists who shared the stories of their life journeys with me came from homes just like any other Adventist who grew up in the United States at that time. Their stories reflect similar journeys through common experiences of cultural Adventism. But their stories vary a great deal beginning with the onset of puberty and the struggle to understand their lives as a sexual minority in a context that does not allow such an option.

Coming Out in an Adventist World

What happens in the Adventist world when one of its own declares himself or herself to be homosexual? Coming out involves the private and public understanding of and declaration of being a homosexual person. One of the first obstacles lesbian and gay Adventists reach is "coming out." Coming out is shorthand for coming out of the closet, or no longer concealing a homosexual orientation. When someone tells friends and family members that he or she is gay or lesbian, this is referred to as coming out. This section offers information about the coming out experiences of gay and lesbian Adventists. It examines

Interaction and Angst

coming out to self, parental reactions, and coming out to friends and spouses. Because many of the people to whom I talked worked for Adventist institutions, coming out at work is discussed here as well.

Coming Out to Self

The first step in coming out to others is to come out to self, to acknowledge one's own homosexuality. Coming out, even to oneself, is often a difficult and sometimes lengthy process for gay and lesbian Adventists. The following quotes from interviews reveal the emotional turmoil of coming out to self.

> While I began to acknowledge my homosexual tendencies, I was only able to deal with bits and pieces at a time. Months, even years went by when I would ignore these issues again. (Joanne)

> I came out to myself in the summer of 1980. I was twenty years old and a summer student in the university living in San Francisco. I knew I was gay and I was scared…scared of myself and frightened of my passions. (George)

> Coming to accept myself has been a long, arduous journey. (Leon)

After coming out to self, lesbian and gay Adventists come out to others either voluntarily or by being discovered. The information that follows highlights gay and lesbian experiences in coming out to parents, spouses, and friends.

Parental Reactions

Parental reactions varied greatly as parents heard from their children that they were gay or lesbian. Some parents received the news through stunned silence, others with fearful questioning or angry outbursts, and some with confusion mixed with love. One of the most heartbreaking stories of coming out I have heard was that of an Adventist pastor's son that has been printed in a book chapter on gay religion.[13] Nathan recalled the night he came out to his parents: "My dad took it hard. At one point he came into my bedroom and said, 'if your mother and I would have known about this [your homosexuality], she would have had an abortion.'" The words of his father were still etched in Nathan's mind at the time of the interview.

René D. Drumm

Beyond cruel words, some lesbian and gay Adventists were forced out of their homes when they came out to their parents.

> One night I was out late and returned home. My parents started questioning me. They said, "We both think you are homosexual, tell us the truth, are you?" "Yes," I told them. My mother immediately burst into tears, "What did we do wrong? What made you do this?" My dad, on the other hand, stormed out of the room and slammed the door. He came back about thirty minutes later and said, "I won't tolerate you in my house any more. Pack up and leave." And so I did. I left home at age eighteen." (Joel)

Not all of the gay and lesbian Adventists were treated harshly by their parents at their coming out. The following quote illustrates a more moderate parental reaction.

> I wanted to tell my mother, so I took her shopping at the mall and then went to a very nice restaurant. I figured that it was the best time to tell her. I was twenty-two or twenty-three at the time. As the main course was arriving, I said, "I think I'm bi-sexual if not gay." She froze. The first words out of her mouth were, "Doesn't it hurt?" I replied, "I don't know, maybe I'll find out and tell you." Later she asked, "Do you have anything to tell me about diseases or anything? Do you have any bad news to tell me?" She also said, "I love you." (Elwin)

Some of the parents of lesbian and gay Adventists supported their children as they disclosed their homosexuality. The quotes that follow are from individuals who had a positive experience coming out to their parents.

> One of the first people I had "the conversation" with was my stepmother. She is very important to me, my best friend in a motherly way. It was a wonderful experience. She had it figured out before I ever brought it up. She was only concerned that I was okay and acting responsibly and safely. She is also perfectly okay with the eventuality of me visiting with my life partner—when I finally snare him. It was very comforting and encouraging to have someone who I respect and love this much to be this supportive. (Robert)

Interaction and Angst

At first, after I came out, my parents didn't say anything, they got up and hugged me and then told me that they loved me. My mom said, "We don't understand, but there isn't anything that you can be or do that would make us stop loving you!" My dad said basically the same thing and that he was glad I had the courage to tell them. They both said they didn't understand, but I told them that it took me a while to understand it and that maybe we could as a family reach an understanding! We sat on the couch for a long time with our arms around each other. (Charlie)

Spouses

Gay and lesbian Adventists who where heterosexually married generally avoided coming out to spouses until some direct confrontation required them to come out.

Finally, as AIDS was in the news more and more, my wife asked me point blank if I had been having any sex with men. Although I had been living a lie for years, I was certainly not able to lie bold-facedly, so I told her that I had. It was one of the most painful experiences of my life. We continued in the marriage until she decided to ask me to move out. (Adam)

I came out to my wife after she found some pictures I had downloaded from the Internet. When she confronted me about my sexuality, I decided to tell her the truth. (Brandon)

In some cases, denial would have been useless even if a person would have liked to continue concealing their homosexuality from their spouse. The following quote is from a former Adventist pastor who was arrested for soliciting an undercover police officer who posed as a male prostitute.

My wife could tell that something was the matter. After kids went to bed, I said, "I was arrested." She cried and said, "We'll work it out." My wife knew I was gay because of a previous incident where I had a reaction from a blood test and we needed treatment. I told her what had happened and we both thought it was a phase. Then, another time, she said, "Something's the matter." I said, "Yes, I'm gay." (Leon)

René D. Drumm

Friends

Sometimes close friends of gay and lesbian Adventists were the ones entrusted with the secret of their homosexuality. Meg explained, "The only person I ever discussed my same-gender attractions to was my best girlfriend. I was so afraid to be discovered and feared so much the ramifications of others finding out that I stayed deeply closeted." Risking the loss of friendship, gay and lesbian Adventists shared their homosexual orientation with their friends often with fear. One person I interviewed came out to his best friend soon after that friend had asked him to be best man in his wedding. Mitch told his friend he was gay and then asked, "Do you still want a fag to be your best man in the wedding?"

His friend replied, "Mitch, you're not that; I want my best friend to be my best man. I want you in my wedding."

In addition to telling their friends directly about their homosexual orientation, people might write coming out letters to friends and family.

> "Despite the difficulties involved in coming out, I proceeded with strengthening my new found self-acceptance by refusing to pretend anymore. I sent a coming-out letter to all of my close family and friends." (Joanne).

The reactions from friends varied greatly. One person summed up his experience, "Most of the people I've come out to have been supportive, but the truth is some have been brutal. Makes you wish you could rush back into the wardrobe and even hope there would be a door into Narnia....alas, once you're out to someone, there's no going back." (Robert).

Coming Out at Work

Many lesbian and gay Adventists have been fired from church-related employment because of their homosexuality. The following excerpts from interviews illustrate the heartbreak and difficulties associated with denominational employment among Adventist homosexuals.

> That morning when I got to work I got a call from the financial vice president's office wanting me to go there for a meeting. When I arrived my director was there also. It seems that "anonymous people" had reported two things to them: first, that I had been seen in the local airport kissing a man on

Interaction and Angst

the lips; second, that someone had found nude pictures of me on the web. I was suspended with pay for two weeks. I needed to turn in my keys and passwords. Two weeks later, after the investigation was finished, I had the option of resigning with benefits to be negotiated or be fired with all of this put on my record. (Harold)

The fateful night came in 1990 when the dean of the school where I was teaching called me in her office. She had heard about my "gay sympathies," and she wanted to hear nothing more. I would either publicly declare my heterosexuality and take a wife or I could leave quietly at the end of the academic year. I was to disclose this to no one, and if I was discreet, the dean promised to endorse my departure with a letter of recommendation. On July 1, 1991, I quietly left. (George)

For their employment status to be secure, lesbian and gay Adventists choose self-employment or work for nonchurch-related organizations. I did speak with one person who worked for an organization that uses the Adventist name, although he was not a denominational employee, and he recalled a positive experience.

I came out to my boss and she said, "I don't see it [your sexuality] as an issue." Then she told the president of the company, and the president said the same thing. (Brandon)

Although this reaction represented the exception rather than the rule, it is notable that not all Adventist organizations fire gay or lesbian employees solely on the basis of sexual orientation. However, many gay or lesbian workers remain closeted until they find other work, as illustrated by the following quote.

I couldn't come out. I knew I would risk losing my job and church membership. I finally decided to quit and seek employment in the private sector. I just walked away from everything. It was one of the most difficult yet one of the best life-changing decisions I have ever made. (Cindy)

Experiences in Adventist Schools

Gay and lesbian students in Adventist schools experienced a wide variety of interactions and reactions with teachers, administrators, and fellow students in terms of gay acceptance. Some of the most difficult circumstances existed when students exposed another student's sexual orientation.

> I was a sophomore at [a Seventh-day Adventist] university. I was confused about the feelings I was experiencing. I knew something was different but was so afraid because I thought I was the only one experiencing these feelings. I was attracted to someone in the dorm. One evening, we were talking on the phone and he said he wanted to take our relationship to the next step with me that night. His roommates were going to be gone for a few hours that evening and wanted me to come down to his room. I was so excited. In my mind I was going on my first date. I was nervous. I walked down to his room at eight o'clock that evening. I entered into his room. He had the room all romanced out with black lights and everything. We talked for a moment then I placed my hand on his upper leg. At that point he stood up and said, "What the [explicative]?" He turned on the main lights and the few friends I had and his roommates jumped out of the closet or from under the bed. My world came to crashing halt. I was so distraught and at that point I was ready to kill myself. (Tom)

Administrators were also known to discover and expel gay students.

> When I was a resident advisor in the dorm, I was pulled into the witch hunts and the administration wanted me to tell on friends and confirm that they were gay. The purpose was to dismiss them because they were a bad influence. With about thirty to forty people that I knew on campus at various stages of coming out/self-acceptance, telling on one or two was not going to change the scene. I did not comply with any of their requests and somehow survived them myself. (Hector)

In contrast, some faculty members at Adventist institutions helped gay and lesbian students deal with their struggles. The first quote below notes the help of an Adventist professor, the second from an Adventist university administrator.

> It was an Adventist professor who helped me accept who I was. This professor came and spent an afternoon with me going over the Scriptures and helped me to understand what those Scriptures were really saying and what they were not

Interaction and Angst

saying. The turning point for me was when this person asked me, "Did you ask God to change you?" I told her yes, many times. She replied, "Do you think God is big and powerful enough to answer those prayers?" I, again, answered in the affirmative. She then said to me some profound words, "Did it ever occur to you that God doesn't want you to change or he would have answered your prayer? Maybe you are asking for the wrong thing. Maybe, God wants you to be the best gay man that you can be under the direction of an almighty God." Those words stuck with me and for the first time in my life the war inside of me was over, that war that I carried for years, decades now were over!!! What peace I enjoyed. (Gregory)

I went to see him [the administrator] and I told him, "This is who I am [lesbian]," and I asked him "What does this mean spiritually?" He pulled out books that explained Bible texts with the real Hebrew meaning. I took it from there. It was like the whirlwind inside me stopped and I was able to meld my spiritual and sexual identities. (Irene)

Experiences in Other Adventist-Supported Institutions

One notorious experiment of the Seventh-day Adventist Church in addressing homosexuality was the development and support of a residential treatment facility called Quest Learning Center. Quest's founder and director was Colin Cook, an Adventist minister who claimed to be a reformed homosexual. Colin was married and developed a program that he said would free individuals from homosexuality. The following paragraphs offer insights from two individuals as they encountered Quest Learning Center.

My first experience at getting help [to change my sexual orientation] was at a Seventh-day Adventist-supported ministry in Reading, Pennsylvania, run by Colin Cook. I went there for help and I trusted the church and its belief system that the idea of "change" was good religion and good psychology. Instead, I found mostly unproven claims being pushed by untrained persons who had perpetrated an intellectual dishonesty on the church and the public. While at Quest, Cook approached me and asked me to take off my clothes and grabbed me in my private parts to offer prayers for it and its ability to have an erection, etc. During my sojourn in the "change ministry" world, I saw no one who was changed. I did see a lot of people making great claims like snake oil salesmen but no one went from homosexuality to heterosexuality. In the long run, making people go through this seemed to make the problems worse rather than better, and this just to make a parent feel better or the church feel better. (Gregory)

    My experience with a change ministry began when I was a student missionary. One of my fellow student missionary friends received *Ministry* magazine and left it in the common area of the mission. I found it and was fascinated to read an autobiographical account about an Adventist minister who was a reformed homosexual and now ran a treatment center in Reading, Pennsylvania. The article gave this strong sense that the church was very supportive, very open to the subject of change and very affirming of these efforts. I gained a great sense of peace and courage. The article seemed almost revolutionary to me. I wrote [the director] and he wrote back encouraging me that I, too, could experience freedom from homosexuality and opened the possibility of having a family and a wife. The director suggested that I consider taking some time out, preferably a year, and relocate to the treatment center to deal with this issue and then move on with the rest of my life. I ordered the tapes he had for sale, *Homosexuality and the Power to Change*, a ten-tape series. The director was extremely open and frank on the tapes. I was diligent in wanting to begin doing what he suggested. I transcribed the tapes and I would write about it in my journal. I did that for the next six months as he indicated. I started to believe that I was seeing the world through faith and through heterosexual eyes.

    I went back to North America, rented a car, drove to Pennsylvania, and had my first introduction to Colin Cook. It was liberating. I felt for the first time more connected to another human being than I had ever felt before because I was telling and sharing my history, struggles, and fears, and he was also open and frank about his. His wife was not at the center the weekend I arrived, so we had one or two days alone. We talked and talked, which was an extremely positive experience

Interaction and Angst

for me. I left feeling exhilarated and hopeful. That's how I felt despite an experience in that first weekend at which others would be appalled.

The only way now that I can explain why I allowed it, why I didn't question it, or tell anyone else about it was because of my naïveté, my vulnerability and neediness. In that weekend, as he became a sort of a surrogate, a caretaker of me, I became a victim of sexual abuse. Without anything being said explicitly, I entered into Colin's secret world completely. I knew that weekend that Colin was not true to his word, to his wife or the public; I knew he was homosexually active and that was demonstrated with me. Colin was able to maneuver me into a position where I was naked, teaching me to affirm myself physically. The treatment incorporated positive, exciting, new, elements of secretiveness that Colin explained as necessary. "We know what we're doing, but others might not understand." I took it all—hook, line, and sinker.

I was the type of person who would not have gone to a non-Adventist counselor. When I grew up, the phrase *peculiar people* grabbed hold. Everything that happened I allowed because I trusted that it was beneficial to me because it was Adventist.

I moved down to Pennsylvania intending to spend about a year there, but I only stayed five months. I felt an ongoing struggle with who I was and who I was not becoming. I also learned about what Colin did with other counselees—the boundary violations between counselor and counselee was incredible. I did experience him as sort of forcing himself on me on all different levels and degrees, from him wanting a hug from me and me not really wanting to hug him, to sexual encounters. I became confused and left. (John)

These individuals suffered fraud at the hands of this Seventh-day Adventist-supported institution. There was and is no "cure" for homosexuality—although church leaders wanted to believe there might be. The only "cure" is a life of sexual abstinence, which for most people is a setup for sporadic promiscuity. The recovery from the disappointment and abuse suffered at the center proved a long and difficult journey for the participants. The experience left significant emotional scars on the victim-survivors that they later had to address.

René D. Drumm

Surviving as a Gay Adventist

What happens after the dust settles from the whirlwind of coming out and people realize that their sexual orientation will not change? How do individuals deal with the gay/lesbian *and* Adventist parts of themselves? I have published specific multiple strategies of identity integration elsewhere.[15] This section offers highlights that address the intricacies of weaving together these two seemingly opposite identities. The three primary processes that occur when a person desires to retain both identities are to come to a new understanding of Scripture in reference to same-sex activity, to find supportive people who have integrated their identities, and to be connected with an accepting church congregation.

New Scriptural Understanding

To remain a gay or lesbian Adventist, a person needs to reconcile traditional church doctrines about homosexuality with their knowledge about sexual orientation. This usually involves discovering alternate understandings of Bible texts that discuss same-sex activity. Three examples that typify these alternate explanations are offered below.

> I began a real sincere prayer and study campaign, desiring to know only the truth in regards to homosexuality and the Scripture. I was willing to accept whatever direction God would lead. Having spent my entire life on the side of believing homosexual behavior was a sin, I was still most comfortable with that belief. I spent weeks, and months, in prayer and study. And over that time, my picture of those few scriptural texts that are used to condemn homosexuals began to change. I had a friend who took me to an MCC [Metropolitan Community Church] and I went to hear a study. The title was "Homosexuality in the Bible," and it made me look at Bible texts differently, especially those particular texts [that refer to same-sex behavior]. I realized that I could be gay and Christian. (Joanne)

> Did the spider spin a deceptive web before sin or was the lion capable of digesting meat? Probably not, but we can only admire the ingenuity, adaptability and, yes, "beauty" in some of these changes. If we allow that homosexuality may have

Interaction and Angst

followed as a result of sin, does that mean we cannot find beauty in it, or even allow it to exist within the framework of God's plan? If other changes occurred after the fall which we readily accept, should homosexuality be different? (Peter)

Leviticus 18:22 talks about man not lying with mankind as with womankind because it is unnatural and an abomination. I don't lie with mankind as I would lie with womankind. I am gay. I have never had sex with a woman—*that* would be unnatural for me. This verse must be taken contextually with what is natural for the individual. Also stated, the same terminology used here is that which is used in reference for the pagan rituals of prostitution [heterosexual men having gay sex] and the pagan idolatry practices. This verse is in the same set of ceremonial laws that includes forbidding of the wearing of two different types of fabric together, and many other forgotten laws. It is always interesting how people forget the ones they want to but remember the ones they think they can use. (Todd)

Organizational Support

Besides coming to understand Bible texts differently from the traditional Adventist interpretation, many gay and lesbian Adventists rely on support groups such as SDA Kinship International, KinNet, or IMRU? to help integrate their identities. SDA Kinship International is an organization that began in the 1970s and offers networking and support for lesbian, gay, bisexual, and transgendered Adventists. KinNet is an Internet group initiated by members of Kinship that facilitates dialog among gay, lesbian, transgendered, and bisexual people who have or have had ties to Adventism. IMRU? is a listserve for current or former Adventist gays and lesbians who are under the age of thirty and in need of support, connection, and friendship. The following quotes illustrate the importance of Kinship and KinNet in the lives of lesbian and gay Adventists.

Now Kinship has become my Adventist family. Since the time that I joined I've been comfortable as a gay person. (Stan)

> Soon after we got our computer and were connected to the Internet, I started surfing and found KinNet. I couldn't believe it! I screamed out to my partner, "Oh, my God! There are gay Adventists." I contacted them right away and they have been like family to me. (Tammy)

Local Church Response

A third area important for identity integration is local church acceptance of gay and lesbian members after they come out. There is much variation among gay and lesbian Adventists in how their churches and pastors dealt with homosexuality. Some church members show love and support, whereas others become hostile and rejecting. Some churches withdraw church membership, whereas others welcome their gays and lesbians. The following quotation illustrates one individual's experience with trying to transfer her membership after she came out as a lesbian.

> When I requested my church membership transferred here, the church board in the other state voted not to transfer it. Instead, they decided I was no longer a "member in good and regular standing," and my name was removed from the church books. (Nan)

In contrast, when a married pastor acknowledged his sexual orientation as a gay man, the members of his church were supportive. His memory is related below.

> Most members made it clear that it made absolutely no difference to them who/what I was, and that they realized this was an extremely difficult issue for our family. I got several dinner invitations to church members' homes—I had to schedule Thanksgiving meal appointments, and ended up with three of them! Quite a few told me that if I ever needed a place to stay, I was always welcome at their home, and that I must make sure to keep them posted as to how I was doing. (Peter)

Besides receiving support from church members, some gay and lesbian Adventists find their pastors encouraging and welcoming. When gay and lesbian Adventists are accepted by pastors, they often feel gratitude and respond through attendance and participation. The quotation below

Interaction and Angst

reveals Carol's resolve to remain attached to the Seventh-day Adventist Church.

> My involvement with the church has been less than average in the last six years. It's not that I don't believe—I do—but I was limited because of how I thought the church may perceive me. But lately I've found a refuge in my church. When I go to prayer meeting, my partner comes with me. The pastor said that if the gay fellowship in his church increases, he would be more than happy. People in this church are warm and accepting, or at least not mean. So, I've started to go back to church more and try to teach my partner, who is not an Adventist, more. (Carol)

The experience of many gay and lesbian Adventists lies between the polar opposites of outright rejection and loving support. Although I risk stereotypical imagery, my observation is that the gay and lesbian Adventists I know are extremely gifted and use their gifts freely within the church, when allowed. One way that congregations have responded to gay or lesbian church members is to exclude them from active service. Ignorance abounds, and some Adventist church members still fear that gay members could lead someone "astray" or make children vulnerable. I address these myths in recommendations at the end of this chapter. The quotation below illustrates the experience of gay and lesbian Adventists excluded from active service in the church.

> The church I attend is small, about forty members. It is the church of my childhood. Many members know I am gay. The church members were surprised, to say the least, when I came out to them. I have been rather silent on the subject since realizing that my orientation would not change. A few members know I am in a relationship—most who do are understanding, if not supportive, but last Friday my pastor came by for a visit. We have talked several times about being gay and all the related issues for me. This visit, I assumed, was not going to be out of the ordinary. Someone at church approached him last week and asked him if he knew I was a "practicing" homosexual. To this point he had never asked and I choose not to volunteer the information [that I had a life partner]. So he asked me. I did not deny it. The result is that I am not allowed to continue teaching the children's Sabbath

School or to speak during church. The next few months are going to be awkward, distressing, embarrassing, painful and unpredictable. I feel betrayed and my experience negated. (John)

Conclusions and Recommendations

Sexual orientation is a multifaceted phenomenon that is complex and cannot be explained simplistically. Science seems to offer more questions than concrete answers as to the etiology of sexual orientation or its stability. It is important for Adventist scholars in the social and biological sciences to become educated and informed about the scientific aspects of sexual orientation. Continued research among gay and lesbian Adventists is especially needed.

Gay and lesbian Adventists are faced with an almost-impossible situation as they endeavor to understand themselves as homosexuals and Adventists. From birth, Adventists are taught that the Bible contains the answers to right and wrong behavior, and they are taught that same-sex behavior is sinful. The enigma is that lesbian and gay Adventists have same-sex desires and fantasies and no amount of prayer or force of will seems to change that fact.

The pain of growing up in a system that sets up gays and lesbians for rejection is clear and heart-wrenching. It is the duty of parents, friends, teachers, and every Adventist who comes in contact with gay and lesbian Adventists to support their efforts to understand themselves and live their lives as best they can. I offer the following recommendations for dealing with gay and lesbian Adventists and grappling with the issue of homosexuality in the Adventist Church.

1. Get to know gay and lesbian people—both Adventists and non-Adventists. The scriptural mandate, "Love your neighbor as yourself," is reason enough to do so. If you do not know your neighbor, how can you love him or her? It is important to get acquainted with and include homosexuals in your circle of friends. Determine to come to the point in your life that you would go out of your way to minister (show friendship and fellowship) to someone who is gay or lesbian.
2. Be aware of resources for gay and lesbian Adventists and their families. SDA Kinship International is an excellent resource for gay and lesbian Adventists to find support and understanding. Its Web site is: <www.sdakinship.org>. Another important resource

Interaction and Angst

for families and friends of gay and lesbian Adventists is *Someone to Talk To*. *Someone to Talk To* is a Web site hosted by Carrol Grady that specifically seeks to help friends and families of Adventist gay and lesbian persons. The Web address is: <www.someone-to-talk-to.net>.

3. Get educated about sexual orientation. Be able to distinguish between fact and myth concerning the formation of sexual orientation. For example, there is no research-based information indicating that sexual orientation is a choice.
4. *Never* suggest that a gay or lesbian person engage in a sexual orientation change endeavor such as Exodus or change therapy. There is no science-based evidence that such programs work and much evidence that they do great emotional harm to participants. Change ministries hold out hope that is ill-conceived and highly inappropriate for most Seventh-day Adventist gay, lesbian, and bisexual individuals. In addition, change ministries can expose participants to possible sexual abuse by the leaders and/or other participants. Given the likely outcomes, referring to these types of programs is unethical and immoral.
5. *Never* suggest that heterosexual marriage might "heal" homosexuality. It doesn't. The following quote addresses the misconception that marriage "cures" homosexuality.

    Even if I found out that I have to be celibate, then that would be better for me than living like this [married]. The church's position is that even if you're gay, you can find release with a straight woman and that is terribly wrong. That hasn't helped me and she deserves more than that. She deserves someone to appreciate her in every way. I can't appreciate her for the sexual creature she is. (Mitch)

6. Recognize and block any communication within your hearing that represents slurs to gay or lesbian individuals. It is never appropriate to tolerate negative characterizations of children of the King.
7. Don't be afraid to expose your children to gay and lesbian persons. One common myth is that gay men, in particular, are sexual predators. The truth is that 90 percent of all sexual offenses occur at the hands of heterosexual males. A second, related myth is that homosexuality is somehow contagious, that gay and lesbians have the power to "recruit" heterosexual young people to the "other

Part 3-25

side." Because of the biological roots of sexual orientation, there is no danger for children to be exposed to homosexuality. It cannot be "caught"; neither can it be "taught."

Questions for Discussion

1. What are the primary components that form sexual orientation?
2. What specific issues do not explain sexual orientation?
3. What do you think about programs that propose to cure homosexuality?
4. How have gay and lesbian Adventists been able to survive?
5. What are some recommendations for Adventists in dealing with gay and lesbian issues?

Notes and References

1. S. LeVay, "A Difference in Hypothalamic Structure between Heterosexual and Homosexual Men," *Science* 253 (5023):1034–37; L. S. Allen and R. A. Gorski, "Sexual Orientation and the Size of the Anterior Commussure in the Human Brain," *Neurobiology* 89 (1992):190–202; D. F. Swaab et al., "Sexual Differentiation of the Human Hypothalamus: Differences According to Sex, Sexual Orientation, and Transsexuality," in *Sexual Orientation: Toward Biological Understanding*, eds., L Ellis and L. Ebertz (Westport, Conn.: Praeger, 1997), 129–50; and D. F. Swaab et al, "Sex Differences in the Hypothalamus in the Different Stages of Human Life," *Neurobiology of Aging* 24, supplement 1, (2003):S1–16.
2. J. M. Bailey and K. J. Zucker, "Childhood Sex-typed Behavior and Sexual Orientation: A Conceptual Analysis and Quantitative Review," *Developmental Psychology* 31, no. 1 (1995):43–55.
3. D. J. Bem, "Exotic Becomes Erotic: A Developmental Theory of Sexual Orientation," *Psychological Review* 103, no. 2 (1996):320–35.
4. E. M. Pattison and M. L. Pattison, "Ex-gays: Religiously Mediated Change in Homosexuals," *American Journal of Psychiatry* 137, no. 12 (1980):1553–62.
5. R. Friedman and J. Downey, "Homosexuality," *New England Journal of Medicine* 331, no. 14 (1994):923–29.
6. L. M. Diamond and R. C. Savin-Williams, "Explaining Diversity in the Development of Same-Sex Sexuality among Young

Interaction and Angst

Women," *Journal of Social Issues* 56, no. 2 (2000):297–313; C. Kitzinger and S. Wilkinson, "Transitions from Heterosexuality to Lesbianism: The Discursive Production of Lesbian Identities," *Developmental Psychology* 31, no. 1 (1995):95–104; D. P. Keys, "Instrumental Sexual Scripting: An Examination of Gender-Role Fluidity in the Correctional Institution," *Journal of Contemporary Criminal Justice* 18, no. 3 (August 2002):258–78; and R. F. Baumeister, "Gender Differences in Erotic Plasticity: The Female Sex Drive as Socially Flexible and Responsible," *Psychological Bulletin* 126, no. 3 (2000):347–74.
7. Laud Humphreys, *Tearoom Trade: Impersonal Sex in Public Places* (New York: Aldine, 1970); and Frederick J. Desroches, "Tearoom Trade: A Research Update," *Qualitative Sociology* 13 (1990):39–61.
8. L. S. Doll et al., "Homosexually and Non-homosexually Identified Men Who Have Sex with Men: A Behavioral Comparison," *Journal of Sex Research* 29, no. 1 (1992):1–14.
9. René Drumm, "Gay and Lesbian Seventh-day Adventists: Strategies and Outcomes of Resisting Homosexuality," *Social Work and Christianity* 28, no. 2 (2001):124–30.
10. Pattison and Pattison, "Ex-gays"; and I. Bieber, H. J. Dain, and P. R. Dince, *A Psychoanalytic Study* (New York: Basic Books, 1962).
11. Drumm, "Gay and Lesbian Seventh-day Adventists"; and René Drumm, "No Longer an Oxymoron: Integrating Gay and Lesbian Seventh-day Adventist Identities," in *Gay Religion*, eds. S. Thumma and E. Gray. (Walnut Creek, Calif.: AltaMira Press, 2005).
12. Drumm, "Gay and Lesbian Seventh-day Adventists"; and idem, "No Longer an Oxymoron."
13. Drumm, "No Longer an Oxymoron."
14. Ibid.
15. L. A. Greenfield, *Sex Offenses and Offenders: An Analysis of Data on Rape and Sexual Assault* (Washington, D.C.: U.S. Department of Justice, Office of Justice Programs, Bureau of Justice Statistics, 1997).

The Caring, Welcoming Church? The Seventh-day Adventist Church and Its Homosexual Members

By Ronald Lawson

In 1983, Charles Bradford, the president of the Seventh-day Adventist Church in North America, invented a new slogan, which was disseminated widely: Adventism styled itself "The caring church."[1] Some twenty years later, the newly reelected president of the world church, Jan Paulsen, preaching on the final Sabbath of the General Conference Session in 2005, laid out his vision of a "welcoming church." Throughout his sermon, Paulsen frequently referred to the need to open the Church's doors. He "encouraged the widely diverse church to welcome everyone into the church, not keep them out because of their differences." "God has set before us an open door," he said, "which is not our privilege to close and keep others out.…I have a word of caution to anyone who is looking for bad grapes in the church: only God can safely grade people. God loves all people globally.…I want the Adventist family around the world to be known as a compassionate family."[2]

This paper tests the truth of both slogan and vision by exploring the evolution of the relations between the Adventist Church and its homosexual members. It asks to what extent the church welcomes and cares for a group of members who are stigmatized by society.

The findings reported here draw on part of my research for a massive study of international Adventism, which will appear in a book titled *Apocalypse Postponed*. The research used four research methods: historical research, in-depth interviewing, surveys, and participant observation.[3] The latter included eighteen years when, as church liaison for Seventh-day Adventist Kinship International, Inc., I had the role of trying to communicate with church leaders, institutions, and members on behalf of gay and lesbian Adventists.

Religious and Civil Context

Condemnation of homosexuality by Christian churches long fostered discrimination against homosexuals in many countries. This was reflected both in law, where criminal penalties were often harsh, extending to capital punishment in some parts, and in public opinion, where it was invoked to justify ridicule, physical violence, eviction from housing, and loss of employment. However, growing concern for justice and civil rights in the United States during the 1960s, beginning with discrimination against blacks and women, was extended at length to homosexuals. The new current fostered the emergence of the gay liberation movement in 1969. This quickly garnered support from key organizations such as the American Bar Association, the American Psychiatric Association, and the American Psychological Association. The American Bar Association issued a call for the decriminalization of homosexual behavior between consenting adults in 1973, and the American Psychiatric Association voted to remove homosexuality from its official list of mental disorders the same year. The more liberal Protestant churches also responded: the United Church of Christ and the Unitarian Universalist Churches voted to ordain openly gay and lesbian pastors, and other mainline churches began to debate such issues; some congregations declared that they welcomed gay members.

Conservative religious groups, however, quickly mounted a sustained counterattack: in their continuing zeal to roll back progress toward liberalized laws and attitudes, they have mounted several political crusades that tapped deep reservoirs of hatred and prejudice within society. For example, when, in 1977, Anita Bryant successfully took the lead in the campaign to reverse a civil rights ordinance that had helped protect homosexuals in Dade County, Florida, against discrimination in employment and housing, her campaign spawned bumper stickers that urged people to "Kill a gay for Christ."

In the succeeding decades the U.S. Supreme Court has ruled state sodomy statutes unconstitutional, several cities and states have chosen to recognize and protect same-sex relationships, and the Supreme Court of Massachusetts has recognized same-sex marriage. The Episcopal

The Caring, Welcoming Church?

Church has ordained openly gay and lesbian priests and consecrated its first openly gay bishop. Meanwhile, the conservative Religious Right, made up of fundamentalists, Mormons, and many Catholics and Evangelicals, has cast aspersions at people with AIDS, has gained political influence, and is pursuing state votes and a constitutional amendment that defines marriage as being limited to heterosexual couples.

Where does the Adventist Church fit into this evolving picture?

Emergence of Gay Issues

The Seventh-day Adventist Church largely ignored the topic of homosexuality until the early 1970s. The Adventists' prophet, Ellen White, never referred to it directly in her vast published works or correspondence.[4] The church never saw reason to commission a study of the topic. The *Seventh-day Adventist Bible Commentary,* published during the mid-1950s, merely repeated the traditional interpretations of the passages that have been used by conservative Christians to condemn homosexuality; other church publications rarely mentioned the topic.

Church leaders generally assumed that there were no homosexuals among their members: the categories *Adventist* and *homosexual* were regarded as mutually exclusive. This assumption was wrong. However, most homosexual members were deeply closeted, living lonely lives. Their discomfort caused many to exit the church, and those who were discovered often faced rejection by their families and church, expulsion from church schools if they were students, loss of their jobs if they were church employed, and exposure to guilt, shame, and humiliation. For example, Vernon Hendershot, who was president of the Adventist seminary when it was located at the General Conference complex in Washington, D.C., disappeared suddenly after being arrested during a police raid on a gay meeting place in 1952.[5] Such experiences were repeated throughout the global Adventist church. A student at Avondale College in Australia in the 1970s, who confessed to being homosexual between his final examinations and graduation, was not allowed to graduate and was never awarded his degree.[6] Church entities were concerned primarily with protecting their purity and their reputations rather than supporting such members.

Although most "sins" committed by church employees could be forgiven, this was not true of sexual sin. Of these sins, homosexuality was considered the worst. In 1983, when Grady Smoot, the president of Andrews University, the present location of the Adventist Seminary, was arrested on charges that he had propositioned an undercover vice officer, it was reported to me that several dispirited church leaders had exclaimed, "If only it had been with a woman!"[7] Although the number of church members whose homosexuality was discovered so dramatically was relatively few, the proportion of gay and lesbian members who grew up in the church was no doubt about average, and many others also joined as adults.[8]

Many Adventist pastors, evangelists, and publications seized on the emergence of the gay liberation movement in 1969 as a sign of the end of the world and of the imminent return of Christ.[9] The flow of similar comments—in articles, pamphlets, public pronouncements, and two books that dealt with sex—continued throughout the 1970s, strengthening especially after mid-decade. Some condemned gay activists who demanded acceptance rather than wanting to change their behavior, and the Annual Council of the General Conference altered the rules for divorce, voting that homosexual behavior by a spouse was a biblical cause for divorce.[10] In an anthology of Ellen White's writings bearing on mental health, published in 1977, the editors inserted a caption that identified homosexuality as "Sodom's Particular Sin."[11]

Although the majority of the articles and pronouncements urged that those with aberrant drives should seek deliverance through God, both books on sex recognized that change in orientation was unlikely and urged that divine strength be enlisted to resist temptations.[12] Most of these publications assumed that the issue they addressed was exterior to the church; however, they elicited several letters to editors that suggested the presence of many homosexuals among its members.

In 1977 a number of gay Adventists in Southern California, emboldened by the gay movement to seek out their own mutual support, formed an organization they ambitiously named Seventh-day Adventist Kinship International. By following networks and placing advertisements in gay and lesbian publications, Kinship began to expand around North America and to reach out overseas.

As time passed, pressure on church leadership to respond somehow to the needs of gay Adventists began to build. A series of articles published in *Insight*, the church youth periodical, in 1976 proclaimed that victory over homosexuality through faith was possible.[13] These were authored by Colin Cook, a former pastor who, after being dismissed from the ministry in New York following discovery of his

The Caring, Welcoming Church?

homosexual behavior, had sought spiritual healing for his unwelcome drives and eventually married.

When these articles drew a spate of letters from persons who desired help, Cook began counseling those who were willing to go to Reading, Pennsylvania. In 1978, he prepared ten hours of tapes, which were widely distributed under the title *Homosexuality and the Power to Change*. In another contribution to *Insight* in 1980, he estimated that there were between ten and twenty thousand homosexuals within the Adventist Church in the United States alone, and chastised the church for failing to foster ministries to help these members.[14]

In 1979, James Londis, pastor of Sligo Church in suburban Washington, D.C., spoke to groups of clergy in Southern California and around Washington, D.C., about the plight of gay Adventists. His sensitivity to the issue had been raised by the trauma experienced by a gay sibling. Estimating that there must be tens of thousands of gay Adventists in North America, he questioned the two solutions usually offered homosexuals within the church when he suggested that it was not possible for most to live lives of sexual abstinence and stated that he doubted whether cure was possible for all. Reviewing modern biblical scholarship, which disputed traditional interpretations of key biblical passages, he urged that scholars study the issues thoroughly and that the Church prepare itself to minister to its gay children.[15]

First Kinship Kampmeeting

Church leaders were forced to address the issue of gay Adventists early in 1980, when Kinship invited three seminary professors and two pastors to participate in its first national Kampmeeting. Searching for spiritual nurture and help in answering their most agonizing questions, Kinship leaders had turned to prominent figures. However, when three of those who responded positively realized that they were all from the Seventh-day Adventist Theological Seminary at Andrews University, they concluded that they could not attend without first asking permission. Neal Wilson, president of the church's General Conference (GC), responded sympathetically, perhaps because he is reputed to have two gay members within his family. When he found opposition to the request on the President's Executive Advisory Council (PREXAD), he avoided taking a vote there and took responsibility for the decision himself.[16]

During the final negotiations, Duncan Eva, who represented Wilson, said, "You have approached us; it is the responsibility of the church to reach out to you." However, he insisted on two conditions: Kinship could not use the participation of clergy as an opportunity to claim in the press that the General Conference had accepted homosexuality; and Colin Cook, whose claim to be able to help homosexuals change their sexual orientations was attracting favorable attention among church leaders, should be added to the five invited.[17]

The most emotional experience at the Kampmeeting was telling and listening to personal narratives, which were dubbed "the horror stories." One person after another told of the isolation each had felt because almost all had been convinced he or she was the only gay Adventist in the world; of years of unavailing struggle and unanswered prayer for a miracle that would make them heterosexual; of overwhelming guilt and self-rejection; of consequent difficulty in establishing relationships; of promiscuous patterns and more guilt; of rejection by their families and estrangement from their congregations. Since they had been taught that it was impossible to be both Christian and gay, but had found themselves gay, they had despaired because they assumed that they were eternally lost. Some told how deep depression had led to suicide attempts. Almost everyone had found no one within the church to whom they could turn for help; those who had sought counseling there had met platitudes such as, "It's only a phase. Get married and everything will turn out all right." But the stories of those who had married were especially poignant, with guilt and defeat within their marriage relationships and sorrow over ultimate estrangement from their children.

The biblical scholars had been asked to help address the issue of whether or not it was possible for gays and lesbians to be Christians, and thus they researched what the Bible had to say about the topic for the first time from an Adventist viewpoint. They concluded, as a result of their study in advance of the Kampmeeting, that the Bible was silent about persons with a homosexual orientation and that the little it said there was directed to heterosexuals. They argued that homosexuals, like heterosexuals, were called to faithfulness within a committed relationship and to chastity outside of such a relationship. The biblical proscriptions were also the same for homosexuals as for heterosexuals: sexual exploitation, promiscuity, rape, and temple prostitution. Wilson probably did not anticipate such an accepting response. The clergy were deeply moved by the stories they heard at the Kampmeeting of the trauma of growing up as gay Adventists.[18]

These scholars also drew up recommendations to take to the church

The Caring, Welcoming Church?

leadership, most of which PREXAD initially accepted. However, these were soon submerged behind a series of raging but unrelated theological and fiscal controversies, which increased leader sensitivity to the criticisms of conservative members.[19] Consequently, church leaders quailed before a letter campaign, orchestrated by an independent right-wing publication, querying whether the participation of GC-sponsored clergy in a homosexual "kampmeeting" indicated that the denomination had "accepted homosexuality." The North American Division (NAD) Committee then voted that the church could not condone practicing homosexuals, that it could not negotiate with organized groups who called themselves SDA gays and lesbians, or even engage in "diplomatic relations" with them, since church members would interpret this as "recognition and endorsement of a deviant philosophy and lifestyle." Indeed, it voted to seek legal counsel "as to what appropriate action can be taken to prevent such groups from using the name of the church."[20]

The General Conference acted on only one recommendation from the Kampmeeting clergy: that a list of sympathetic counselors be prepared. A letter seeking suggestions for such a list revealed the conflicting pressures that church leaders felt and the direction in which they were tilting. It mentioned a wish to reorient homosexuals, complained about gays who held that reorientation was impossible, and asked that word that church leaders were working on "redemptive plans" be treated discreetly because members with a "critical bent" would not favor such a concern and church leaders wished to avoid giving the impression to members that they faced "some big new threat" or that "corruption" existed "to an alarming extent in the church."[21]

Estrangement

A series of mailings that Kinship sent to college administrators, teachers, students, and pastors caused heartburn among many Adventists. The *Adventist Review* explained that Kinship was not associated with the church in an editorial titled "The Church and the Homosexual." Although the editorial reiterated the usual statements that homosexual practice is immoral and that celibacy is the only morally acceptable alternative to marriage, and that erring members "must reach out for divine power to conquer the problem," it also recognized that the testimonies "about the ostracism homosexuals have faced in the Adventist church and the almost total absence of people—ministry and laity alike—who seem capable of treating homosexuals with compassion...[indicate] that the church has failed its mission."[22]

Church leaders, feeling the need to take a stand on the issue of homosexuality, had the Biblical Research Institute (BRI) solicit papers from scholars. David Larson, a Loma Linda University ethicist whose consciousness had been raised by the grim experiences of his gay brother, wrote the first. In it he urged the Church to nurture gay relationships as the best option available; however, this suggestion generated considerable hostility and the paper sank into oblivion.[23] The BRI then commissioned a second paper, this time from Ronald Springett, a New Testament scholar from Southern Adventist College. On learning about this, I phoned him to invite him to participate in Kinship's 1984 Kampmeeting so that he could have an opportunity to find out about the issues homosexual Adventists face first-hand. He was initially eager to accept the offer, but on reflection concluded that to do so would endanger his job since two of his colleagues had recently been fired on theological grounds. He explained further that the position a biblical scholar would arrive at vis-à-vis homosexuality was likely to depend on his overall view of the Scriptures, and that if he showed his hand in that respect he would really court dismissal. Consequently, he would be forced to adopt a conservative view of the Scriptures for this paper and thus toward homosexuality. When he presented a draft of his paper to the BRI in 1985, it was greeted as a major contribution and later published as a book.[24]

The church administrators also set out to add a statement on homosexuality to the *Church Manual*. The new statement, which was voted at the 1985 General Conference Session, for the first time labeled these "practices" as unacceptable and a basis for discipline.

In a further effort to distance the church from Kinship, the church leadership demanded later that year that all traces of the name of the church be deleted from Kinship's official name: "The problem is the use of 'Seventh-day Adventist' and 'SDA' in conjunction with 'Kinship International.' Church leaders feel strongly that the combination implies official endorsement of Kinship International, and those leaders object strongly to that implication," wrote church counsel Robert Nixon in a letter to the author in 1985. The letter explained that Kinship had dragged the name of the church into the mud by participating in Gay Pride parades with banners that bore its full name. But it was that name that pulled watching Adventist homosexuals from

The Caring, Welcoming Church?

the sidewalk into the street to ask with excitement for information about how to get in contact with Kinship. Its Adventist roots and identity were central to the reasons for its existence and ministry. Kinship's response to the demand was that such a decision could be made only at a Kampmeeting, the next of which was scheduled for August 1986.

In May 1986 Kinship mailed material to all dormitory students at Andrews University. This included an invitation to call Kinship's new 800 number for information. Dismayed, the General Conference discussed preparing counter-materials for distribution and took further steps toward suing Kinship over use of the Seventh-day Adventist name. In June it requested copies of Kinship's incorporation papers from the office of the secretary of state in California. In August Eva sent a letter to personnel at Adventist schools: "Perhaps there is no greater challenge to our faith and our preaching of the gospel of the grace of God than the challenge which homosexuality and those who teach it as an acceptable alternative Christian lifestyle presents to our church today. Does the gospel we proclaim have power to change or does it not?"[25]

Quest Learning Center

Church leaders were much more comfortable with the approach of Colin Cook, a self-described "recovered homosexual," who had founded the Quest Learning Center in late 1980. His program, which proclaimed "deliverance from homosexuality," advertised that it brought homosexuals together in Reading, Pennsylvania, for a year or more of counseling and involvement in a support group called Homosexuals Anonymous (HA). Within a few months, the General Conference opted to fund Quest and provided more than half of its budget. The Adventist Church thus became the first denomination to fund a "healing ministry" for homosexuals.

Church periodicals provided the Quest-HA program with extensive publicity within Adventism, presenting it as the answer to homosexuality. Adventist pastors and school counselors began to recommend that anyone who came to them with a homosexual issue contact Quest. *Ministry*, the church's publication for ministers, broadened the network of people aware of Cook's program by recommending Quest when it featured a long interview with Cook in an issue distributed free to 300,000 clergy of other denominations.[26] As

Quest grew, it attracted a great deal of attention from both the press and TV and radio talk shows and drew endorsements from conservative clergy of other denominations, who were relieved to be able to recommend a solution when condemning homosexuality. Adventist leaders basked in the favorable publicity: for example, they made a church 800 number available to handle inquires that resulted from Cook's appearance on the *Phil Donohue Show* in 1986.[27] Homosexuals Anonymous spread rapidly, peaking at sixty chapters around North America in that year.

    The Adventist Church never conducted a study of the impact of the program on counselees, nor did it even require a written report before extending funding. It ignored Kinship's informed questions and listened only to the glowing reports of Director Cook and to orchestrated testimonies from counselees who were still in the midst of their time at Quest. It failed to understand that the reported healings were claimed by faith rather than achieved in experience. Church leaders eagerly extended funding when Cook and his wife appeared hand-in-hand before the Annual Council of the church leaders: Cook became their representative "ex-gay."[28]

    The denominational role in financing and publicizing the Quest program helped make church members more conscious of homosexual Adventists. Three articles published by *Spectrum,* an independent Adventist journal, in the spring of 1982 had a similar effect. These reported in detail on the 1980 Kampmeeting, recounted ten of the personal stories shared there, and in order to provide "balanced" coverage, provided Cook an opportunity to describe the Quest program.[29] The arrest of the president of Andrews University during the Annual Council in 1983 and of an associate pastor of the congregation who served many General Conference officials the following year, both on vice charges, brought further awareness. The leaders' sense that they were under scrutiny made them more eager to proclaim the success of their program in changing sexual orientations and more careful to avoid appearing as if they were accepting of homosexuals.

    As part of my sociological study of international Adventism, I conducted a series of interviews with fourteen Quest participants, completing them in the fall of 1986. These revealed that the Adventists who uprooted themselves to move to Reading to participate in the Quest program were usually fragile, very conservative church members with high levels of guilt and self-rejection because of their homosexual inclinations. Even if they had heard about Kinship, they were so frozen

The Caring, Welcoming Church?

in their guilt that they could not bring themselves to make contact with it: Quest, the church-endorsed program for "recovery," was their only hope.

But Quest turned out to be a nightmare experience for them—one that they did not describe in their testimonies before church leaders. Suddenly, they found that they were no longer the only homosexual Adventists in the world: isolation was replaced by community, a community under stress because its members were trying to change their orientation, and yet were often sexually attracted to one another. The immediate result was confusion, turmoil, and considerable sexual contact. Their confusion was greatly heightened when Cook, the director of the program, made repeated sexual advances to them.[30] None of the interviewees reported that his sexual orientation had changed, nor did any of them know anyone who had changed. Indeed, eleven of the fourteen had come to accept their homosexuality.[31]

I had thought Quest's claims and testimonies of "healing from homosexuality" hard to believe, so I was not surprised to discover that those claims were made "in faith" that transformation had occurred, when in fact no one in my interview sample had actually been "changed." However, I was taken aback by the evidence that Cook had sexually used and abused almost every counselee. Realizing that I had a moral obligation to report such abuse, I wrote to the General Conference president, Neal Wilson, in October 1986, telling him what I had unexpectedly found at Quest.[32] To try to ensure that Wilson would not ignore my letter, I sent copies to twenty-nine other church leaders and academics. Cook admitted that my findings were correct and was removed within a week. Church leaders decided shortly afterward to close the Quest counseling program, but to continue support for Homosexuals Anonymous chapters.

The Adventist press initially ignored the closing of Quest and the removal of its director, so that the widespread image of the program as *the* solution to the problem of homosexuality remained uncorrected. Eventually, I asked the editor of the *Adventist Review* about this omission, and he responded with a "newsbreak" announcing merely that Quest had been closed because of the resignation of Colin Cook as its director.[33] In September 1987, eleven months after the situation was disclosed, *Ministry* published another long interview with Cook which, although indicating that there had been improprieties, strongly endorsed Cook's methods as the answer to homosexuality and announced (in a photo caption apparently left in by mistake) that he

Part 3-39

would "soon resume leading seminars for recovering homosexuals."[34] By December, Cook had recovered enough confidence to announce, in a report addressed to Wilson and copied to forty others, that he had launched Quest II and was working with his first two counselees.[35]

In 1989 an article by Cook appeared in the Evangelical publication *Christianity Today* trumpeting how he had "found freedom" from homosexuality. Cook was beginning to find new sources of support among evangelicals and ultimately the Religious Right, which because of its frequent attacks on homosexuals sorely needed a "solution" to showcase.[36] In 1993 Cook moved to Denver, where he founded a new ministry, FaithQuest. This grew and became prominent thanks to close alliances with organizations such as James Dobson's Focus on the Family, which referred potential counselees to him, and Colorado for Family Values, which gave him publicity by advertising him as a speaker in its antigay Time to Stand seminars, whose goal was to use a referendum to roll back the gay civil rights legislation that had been enacted in some of the state's cities. Cook also reappeared once again on national television on the *Phil Donohue Show.* He spoke frequently at Adventist churches in Denver and began to get invitations to speak at Adventist colleges, such as a chapel service at Pacific Union College in California in December 1993.[37] These opportunities in Adventist circles emerged because of the failure of the church press, which had earlier publicized Cook's program, to inform Adventists of his fall. Consequently, young Adventists troubled by their homosexual desires continued to contact him for help.

My interest in Cook and his ministries was rekindled when two of his new counselees brought their new painful stories to my attention. They had discovered that the would-be healer was still a sexual predator, and had learned about my earlier role in unmasking him via the Adventist grapevine. Consequently, I set out to research Cook's activities in Denver. Since one of the counselees was willing to share with me tapes he had made of many of his counseling sessions and a detailed diary of several days of intense "counseling" while living in Cook's house in Denver, the data were full and compelling. In an endeavor to prevent further abuse, I provided the results of my research to the religion reporter at the *Denver Post,* who then carried out a full investigation of her own. Her report, published as a front-page story, was the beginning of a wave of publicity that caused the Religious Right to back off.[38] FaithQuest and Cook largely disappeared from view while the furor subsided. The Adventist Church announced that it

The Caring, Welcoming Church?

was not connected to Cook's seminars and counseling activities.[39] Meanwhile, Cook was greatly hampered because his wife, who had separated from him earlier, then divorced him.[40] Shortly afterward, he happened to ask a female researcher, whom he did not realize was a friend of mine, for help in finding a replacement since he needed a wife to give his program legitimacy.

General Conference vs. Kinship

In December 1987 the General Conference filed suit against Seventh-day Adventist Kinship International, Inc., in the U.S. District Court for the Central District of California for "breach of trademark."[41] Because the suit had to be shaped to address commercial law, it did not even mention that Kinship members are homosexual and Adventist: its case had to be shaped in terms of unfair commercial competition. Its brief consequently made the absurd claims that by using the name *Seventh-day Adventist* or its acronym as part of its name, competition from Kinship's newsletter was undermining the church's publishing empire and that Adventists were likely to contribute heavily to Kinship, mistaking it for the church's official tithe/offering conduit. However, the accompanying press release, titled "Church Moves Against Homosexual Support Group," made it clear that the General Conference was rejecting Adventist homosexuals and the ministry of Kinship.[42] In addition to seeking to compel Kinship to change its name, the suit also demanded "exemplary, punitive, and treble" monetary damages.

This Goliath-versus-David suit was poorly timed from the church's point of view, for it coincided with the media's belated discovery of the Quest scandal and the filing of a suit against the church by abused counselees. Although the latter suit was independent of Kinship, the press drew all these issues together, which resulted in considerable negative publicity for the Church.[43]

In filing this suit against an organization with fewer than one thousand members, church leaders expected an easy pushover. The General Conference hired two major law firms to present its case, at an admitted cost of more than two hundred thousand dollars.[44] However, it failed to take the strength of the gay movement into account: the case was accepted by National Gay Rights Advocates, which arranged for Fullbright and Jaworski, a major legal firm, to defend Kinship on a pro bono basis. Depositions were taken in the fall of 1990, and the case was argued in the federal court in Los Angeles in February 1991. The legal proceedings were traumatic for Kinship members. However, in its verdict, which was announced in October, the court rejected the suit, thus allowing Seventh-day Adventist Kinship International Inc., to keep its full name.

In her opinion Judge Mariana Pfaelzer pointed out that the term *Seventh-day Adventist* has a dual meaning, applying to the church but also to adherents of the religion. She found that the SDA religion pre-existed the SDA Church, that the uncontested use of the name by schismatic groups such as the Seventh-day Adventist Reform Movement indicated that it does more than suggest membership in the mother church, and that, as used by Kinship, the name merely describes that organization in terms of what it is, an international organization of Seventh-day Adventists. Consequently, she found that "as used by SDA Kinship, the terms 'Seventh-day Adventist,' and its acronym 'SDA' are generic, and are not entitled to trademark protection."[45] Left with no good grounds on which to appeal the decision, and fearing a more devastating loss in the court of appeals, the General Conference chose not to appeal this result.

The fact that a group of gays and lesbians could continue to identify themselves as Seventh-day Adventists, and that nothing could be done about this, continued to irritate church leaders. The church spurned Kinship's overtures after the verdict, which suggested that enmities be forgotten and communication begin concerning such common problems as AIDS.[46] The church press also persisted in referring to "Kinship International" rather than "Seventh-day Adventist Kinship International."

Church Statements and Political Involvement.

The General Conference followed up on the change to the 1985 *Church Manual* by issuing increasingly frequent statements that focused on gay-related issues starting in 1994. In that year a member of its legal department felt ethically obliged, for reasons related to the earlier suit against Kinship, to inform General Conference president Robert Folkenberg that he had been invited to speak at a Kampmeeting. Subsequently, the president announced that the General Conference Administrative Committee had passed the following resolution:

> HOMOSEXUAL GATHERINGS—SPEAKING

The Caring, Welcoming Church?

> INVITATIONS. In view of the fact that homosexual behavior is clearly contrary to biblical teachings, Church beliefs,...and in order to avoid the appearance of giving the sanction of the Church to such behavior, it was
>
> > VOTED, to request all General Conference personnel to decline invitations to speak to gatherings of homosexuals.[47]

Nevertheless, Folkenberg did not intervene to stop the person who had raised the issue from participating in the Kampmeeting.

In 1996, the General Conference Administrative Committee voted "An Affirmation of Marriage." This reminded homosexual Adventists that their only acceptable option was celibacy: "However, the estate of marriage is not God's only plan for the meeting of human relational needs or for knowing the experience of family. Singleness and the friendship of singles are within the divine design as well....Scripture, however, places a solid demarcation socially and sexually between such friendship relations and marriage."[48]

In 1999, as gay issues came increasingly to the fore in political debate and court cases, the Annual Council voted a new "Seventh-day Adventist Position Statement on Homosexuality":

> The Seventh-day Adventist Church...believe[s] that by God's grace and through the encouragement of the community of the faith, an individual may live in harmony with the principles of God's Word....[S]exual intimacy belongs only within the marital relationship of a man and a woman....The Bible makes no accommodation for homosexual activity or relationships. Sexual acts outside the circle of heterosexual marriage are forbidden....For these reasons Adventists are opposed to homosexual practices and relationships.[49]

This statement was more sweeping and negative than the one added to the *Church Manual* in 1985.

As the new millennium dawned, Adventism became directly involved in the raging political debates. In February 2000, when the state of Hawaii seemed to be on the verge of recognizing same-sex marriage, Thomas Mostert, president of the Pacific Union Conference, and Alan Reinach, head of its Department of Public Affairs and Religious Liberty (PARL), published articles in the *Pacific Union Recorder* calling on Adventists in California to support the Knight Amendment, also known as Proposition 22, which aimed at adding the clause "Only marriage between a man and a woman is valid or recognized in California" to that state's constitution. Reinach explained that "The California Protection of Marriage Initiative, Proposition 22, is designed to insure that California need not recognize gay marriages when and if they become legal in other states." He added, "We need not sit on the sidelines on this issue, assuring ourselves that Adventists avoid political issues.... We can assist in efforts to educate our neighbors, and to get the word out, as well as urging our own church members to vote."[50]

In May 2000, as Vermont was in the process of adopting legislation that recognized civil unions between same-sex couples, officials of the Atlantic Union and the North New England Conference raised their voices in opposition to it. In contrast, the administration of the Netherlands Union remained aloof from the debate when that country embraced same-sex marriage in 2001. However, when the courts of British Columbia and Ontario launched the process that resulted in the recognition of such marriages in Canada, the director of PARL there described it "an assault on marriage," and declared that "Adventists have a responsibility to make their voices heard on this issue."[51]

In April 2003 Reinach opposed legislation in California that would have required any organization that contracted to supply goods and services to the state to provide the same benefits to domestic partners as to married couples, because it did not include a conscience clause exempting Christian organizations. He launched a petition against the bill and urged church members to sign it, arguing that the legislation would force hundreds of church-related educational, health care, and day care institutions to observe the law or close, ultimately resulting in a tax increase. As the bill progressed through the legislative process, Reinach requested that churches make announcements urging that members sign his petition, and later, after the legislature passed the measure, he launched a petition drive demanding that Governor Gray Davis veto it.[52] Adventists were allied with Mormons, Protestant Fundamentalists, many Pentecostals, conservative Catholics, and other elements of the Religious Right in their stance. Their opposition failed. After rereading Reinach's news releases early in 2006, I wrote him to ask how many of the institutions he had predicted would close with passage of the law had actually closed. He replied that he did not know, an answer that suggests he had "cried wolf."[53]

Meanwhile the U.S. Supreme Court had shocked such Adventist officials when, in *Lawrence vs. Texas*, it overturned a Texas sodomy statute on the grounds that it did not treat homosexual and heterosexual persons equally. When the British government announced plans to

The Caring, Welcoming Church?

introduce civil unions in order to eliminate one source of discrimination against homosexuals, the British Union Conference announced its opposition to the measure.[54] When Canada expanded its hate crimes law to add disparagement of "sexual orientation" to the list of crimes for which perpetrators could be charged with the equivalent of a felony in the United States, the Adventist News Network reported that pastors there were afraid that their preaching against homosexuality could result in them falling afoul of the law.[55]

After a decision of the Massachusetts Supreme Judicial Court legalized same-sex marriage there, Reinach attacked the ruling in an e-mail newsletter and suggested that Adventists support President George W. Bush's Defense of Marriage Act (DOMA), which was designed to override that decision. Adventists committed to the long-held position of separation between church and state then held their breath, wondering if the General Conference would embrace DOMA, and thus set a new precedent where the Adventist Church gave official support to legislation that the Religious Right designed and supported.

By then a number of cities had begun to perform same-sex marriages, attracting a great deal of attention from the media. These developments, together with the growing number of nations considering the legalization of same-sex unions, led the General Conference Administrative Committee in March 2004 to issue a "Seventh-day Adventist Response to Same-Sex Unions—A Reaffirmation of Christian Marriage." This proved to be fairly mild: although it restated the church's narrow position on homosexuality, it said nothing about the wisdom of legalizing civil unions or domestic partnerships or aligning the church with attempts to amend the U.S. Constitution.[56]

The official positions announced by church leaders have become narrower and more polarizing over time. Although the statements often declare that all people, including homosexuals, are children of God and that abuse, scorn, and derision aimed at them are unacceptable, the dominant tone of these statements is an insistence that gay and lesbian Adventists lead celibate lives. When questions that focus on homosexuality have been raised in the televised chat sessions that the current president of the General Conference, Jan Paulsen, has had with Adventist youth, his answers have been conservative to the point of being retrogressive. For example, when asked advice by a gay youth who felt called by God to become a pastor, he replied, "the biblical expectation is for those who believe they have a homosexual orientation to live a celibate life or to limit sexual activity to within a husband-and-wife marriage situation."[57] In suggesting that a gay person enter a heterosexual marriage, Paulsen was repeating bad advice that Adventist counselors had frequently given in yesteryear.

The attempts of some church officials to involve Adventism in political debates on the side of traditional heterosexual values raised the possibility of moving the Adventist Church away from its traditional position in opposition to the enactment of morality-based law. If Adventists had taken that path in the past, it might have led them to support those who had given them the greatest trouble on such issues as freedom to observe the Saturday Sabbath. In the 1880s well-meaning Protestants, with references to saving the family, attempted to legislate morality through laws by declaring Sunday a holy day—legislation that would have harmed Adventists severely through compromising their religious freedom. However, 120 years later some Adventist spokespersons now attempt to legislate morality by making gay marriage impossible. Although Adventists officially continue to realize the importance of taking a stand against simple majoritarian rule in matters of religious liberty and race, attempts to press for majoritarian legislation that would outlaw same-sex marriage seem to undermine their traditional commitment to church-state separation.

Adventist Ministries to Homosexuals

In 1995 Pacific Press published *My Son, Beloved Stranger*, which recounted the story of a mother's distress on realizing that her son was gay and the events that followed.[58] The mother, Carrol Grady, was well-known in the church, for she was married to a pastor and both had worked at the General Conference for years. Although she had published under a pseudonym, the book resulted in invitations for her to speak at Adventist meetings and to publish articles in church-related magazines. Her experience with her son had led her to realize that Adventist parents of gay or lesbian children had nowhere to turn for support. She started a newsletter, *Someone to Talk To...*, in 1996 and a support group by the same name for families and friends of Adventist gays and lesbians in 1999, and she launched a Web site in 2000.

A variety of ministries aimed at gay Adventists emerged near the end of the millennium. Redeemed!, located in San Jose, California, sought to be an "ex-gay ministry" offering Christian support for those who wanted "freedom from homosexuality." It was founded by a

The Caring, Welcoming Church?

mother of a gay son whose rejection of his orientation had totally alienated him from her. In her attempts to find a way to "save" her son, she formed a connection to the National Association for the Research and Therapy of Homosexuality (NARTH). The lifespan of this ministry, however, was short.

God's Love—Our Witness (GLOW) was founded in 1997 by Inge Anderson, a board member of SDANet, an Internet discussion list, where some conservative members had engaged in a series of heated attacks on others who had admitted that they were gay or lesbian. It became a Web discussion list/support group that tried to steer a "middle course": on the one hand, it accepted the reality of homosexual orientations and therefore rejected the likelihood that change of orientation is possible for most; on the other hand it was "designed to support those who wish to order their lives in line with a fairly literal interpretation of Scripture, which reserves sex for those covenanted to each other for life in the holy covenant of (heterosexual) marriage." Given the close match between GLOW's position and the statements that the General Conference has issued since Quest proved to be an embarrassing failure, GLOW's leaders hoped to gain the official blessing of the church and to grow fairly rapidly. However, GLOW has experienced a considerable flow-through of members, and in spite of some growth, remains fairly small, about one-tenth the size of SDA Kinship. Its leaders have subdivided it into two overlapping groups: Gay and Lesbian Adventists (GLADVENTISTS) is restricted to Adventists, whereas GLOW has a broader membership, of which about one-third are Adventists.[59]

Meanwhile a ministry was launched in the San Francisco Central Adventist Church by an aging gay couple who, after many years' absence from Adventism (during which time they had owned and operated a gay bar), had returned to the church and committed themselves to celibacy within their relationship. This program took an exhibit booth during the gay-sponsored Castro Street Fair as part of an attempt to reach out to the gay community. On its Web site, the congregation declared that "homosexual orientation is not a choice," but that nevertheless "homosexual acts" are forbidden by God, who had designed that human sexuality should be expressed within heterosexual marriage. However, "we recognize that it is not our right nor responsibility to pry into the private lives of persons, whether they are homosexual or heterosexual." Duke Holtz, the main mover behind this ministry, later added a second related ministry, God's Rainbow, which was intended to be the umbrella for all officially recognized church programs for gays and lesbians. He gained some recognition from the Central California Conference for this initiative. Duke was aggressive in pressing for acceptance of celibate homosexuals within the church, presenting them as moral, whereas practicing gays were immoral. Both of Holtz's programs collapsed in 2004, when he moved out of the area following the death of his partner.

A similar small ministry, Rainbow of Promise, took the form of a newsletter. It was operated by a former pastor, Ben Anderson, who had lost his job, home, family, and church about twenty-five years earlier, when he was discovered to be gay. After living in the gay community for most of the interim, he turned his back on it, returned to the Adventist Church, and established this ministry, which advocated celibacy as a means of developing a close relationship with God.

Surprisingly, it was during this period, when ministries with differing philosophies emerged to compete with it, that SDA Kinship grew most rapidly in the United States and Canada and internationally. Kinship supports committed relationships among its members, and its meetings and activities provide opportunities for gay and lesbian Adventists to meet one another and pursue such relationships. It also nurtures, without judging, all gay, lesbian, bisexual, transgendered, and intersexed persons who approach it. Most members are Adventist or of Adventist background, with most of its non-Adventist members being partners of Adventists. Kinship's spiritual message, which has often brought encouragement and healing to homosexuals who felt estranged from God and rejected by their church, is that God loves and accepts them the way they are.

The Adventist Press

The church press was largely silent about homosexuality until the 1990s, apart from the earlier articles by Colin Cook and those publicizing and then attempting to rehabilitate him, and the knee-jerk criticisms. However, it then became much more willing to publish articles that addressed homosexuality and related issues. In 1992, the youth magazine *Insight* published a major article, "Redeeming Our Sad Gay Situation: A Christian Response to the Question of Homosexuality," authored by the editor, Christopher Blake.[60] Blake admitted that the church should have issued a public apology following the collapse of the Quest Learning Center and that it had not moved

The Caring, Welcoming Church?

ahead with any other approach to help gay and lesbian church members. In many respects, the article represented a real advance in understanding, especially in its sections titled "Nobody Chooses to Be Homosexual," "'Gay Bashing' Is Never Acceptable, Especially for Christians," "Many Fears about Homosexuality Are Irrational," "Homosexuals Are Not by Nature Necessarily Promiscuous or Child Molesters," "Changing One's Homosexual Orientation Is Difficult and Rare," and "Homosexuals Can Be Genuine, Model Christians." However, the article defined such model Christians as those who "battle against their orientation all their lives" because "homosexual activity is sinful" and cannot be condoned.[61]

In November 1996 *Ministry*, whose designated audience is pastors, published an issue that addressed the question "What do homosexuals need from a pastor?" All articles stayed within the officially recommended behavioral guidelines for homosexuals. The lead article, by John Cress, campus chaplain at Walla Walla College, stated that the beginning point in dealing with homosexuals was to recognize the difference between orientation and behavior; he urged that pastors and churches "be both prophetically clear and genuinely compassionate," and approvingly quoted an alumnus who had returned to the church when he had advanced AIDS and who told a student audience shortly before he died that the "gospel imperative" for his life was "no sex with other people and no sex with myself."[62]

Insight has published ten articles dealing with homosexuality since 1992. In general, these have not contravened the official church position. One, authored by a student at a non-Adventist college whose ex-high school boyfriend had later told her he was gay, told of the trauma for both of them caused by the sharing of this news.[63] A sidebar by an Adventist recommended change and support ministries, for homosexuals, their families, and friends. The author had included SDA Kinship in his original list of recommended organizations, but the editor omitted it.

Another article by a mother of a gay son, writing under a pseudonym, appeared in *Women of Spirit* in 2000.[64] She told of traveling to meet her son's partner for the first time and of finding herself eating with three gay guys and a lesbian, who unexpectedly asked her about her faith and church. Warming to her responses, one commented that he knew little about Christianity, but would like to learn more. He then asked, "Could I go to your church? Would they be like you?" She replied: "No, Jed, my church isn't ready for you yet."

Ministry published an article by Carrol Grady in 2003, now written under her own name and bolder and more independent in tone, asking pastors how they treat gay people.[65]

As the issue of same-sex marriage became politically prominent in the United States, the tone of some articles in church publications became much more strident. In October 2003, for example, Roy Adams, associate editor of the *Adventist Review*, published an editorial, "Marriage under Siege," which featured a photo of Bishop Gene Robinson, the first openly gay bishop elected by the Episcopal church. Adams referred to "the concerted push for full acceptance by a well-heeled, well-financed homosexual lobby, the media falling all over itself to push the agenda." He listed the overturning of the Texas anti-sodomy law and the acceptance of same-sex marriage by the Netherlands and Belgium and its advance through the courts in Canada and Massachusetts, and posed the question, "What is to be our stance as a church?" Declaring that "the spiritual crisis of the last days" is here, that we are seeing "a brazen, deliberate, concerted attack on the three foundational pillars of the book of Genesis: Creation, Sabbath, and…marriage," he asserted that in spite of the historic embrace of the separation of church and state by Adventists, "Silence is not an option. The stakes are too high. And normal considerations of tolerance and political correctness cannot apply—in fact, would be irresponsible. This is the time for faith communities to speak out."[66]

Editor William Johnsson wrote a supporting editorial statement, asserting that observance of the Sabbath had long set Adventists apart, but now the other two fundamental beliefs rooted in the first two chapters of Genesis, creation and marriage "also seem destined to mark us out as distinctive."[67]

In 2004 an issue of *Liberty* set a similar tone. This was surprising, given the publication's historic purpose to promote religious freedom and, in the United States, the separation of church and state. In an editorial, Lincoln Steed proclaimed that "those who see no threat to religion in recent moves to legalize same-sex marriage don't understand the movement's long-ago articulated intention to dismantle religious values." "We give away too much," he insisted, "by allowing the homosexual agenda to be framed as a civil rights argument."[68] Elaborating on this fear in "Why Silence Is Not an Option," Barry Bussey stated, "Religious communities that view sexual relations outside the traditional marriage of one man and one woman as immoral and a 'sin' ought to prepare for the greatest assault on religious

The Caring, Welcoming Church?

freedom in recent memory"—both externally from the state and internally from dissident church members.[69] The lead article, "Civil Rights and Homosexual Rights: A Flawed Analogy," tried to argue that there is no parallel between African-American civil rights and gay and lesbian civil rights.[70]

The ultraconservative independent press within Adventism, often considerably to the right of the official press, has had little to say about homosexuality, and what has appeared there differs little in tone and content from most of the articles published by the official publications. The main ultraconservative to write, Samuel Koranteng-Pipim, a Ghanaian who lives in the United States, suggested that attitudes toward gays and lesbians within Adventism are changing. He challenged interpretations of biblical scholars who have concluded that the proof texts used to condemn homosexual relationships are misused.[71]

In contrast the publications of the liberal independent press concerning homosexuality are often very different from the official publications, reflecting increased polarization over this issue. In 1995 *Adventist Today* published "Kampmeeting Supports Gay Adventists," which described the program, participants, and interaction at Kinship's annual week-long retreat the previous summer and summarized Kinship's history and goals.[72] The gathering was portrayed as a regular, successful event of interest to all Adventists. In 1999, *Adventist Today* published a cluster of six articles, including three personal accounts of finding one's self or one's son to be gay and its impact on self, marriage, and family, and two contrasting interpretations of the biblical passages often used to condemn homosexuality. In an editorial introduction, John McLarty warned of the dangers and unfairness of heterosexual church leaders demanding that homosexuals live celibate lives.[73]

In the winter 2000 issue of *Spectrum*, Aubyn Fulton compared two "official statements" approved by the Annual Council in 1999. He concluded that the statement on birth control "largely succeeds in creating a moral context within which couples can make responsible reproductive decisions."[74] In contrast, the "Seventh-day Adventist Position Statement on Homosexuality" was concerned more with public relations than with pastoral functions:

> Absent…is a tone of respect for a full range of Christian perspectives, or recognition of related complexities and subtleties. The document lacks evidence of underlying redemptive and pastoral

concern....It is hard to see how a simple "we're against it" can be of much help if it ignores complex biblical evidence as well as growing scientific data regarding the biological basis for a great deal of sexual orientation and resistance to change that orientation.[75]

Spectrum's summer 2002 issue contained a cluster of five articles on sexuality, including research on the lives of gay and lesbian Adventists, an autobiographical narrative, and a book review that surveyed a diversity of Christian views of homosexuality. In the winter 2004 issue, Gary Chartier argued that even those who condemn homosexual activity should support the legalization of same-sex marriage in order to foster social stability.[76]

Several articles in the March-April 2004 issue of *Adventist Today* explored Adventist positions on gay marriage. Two were reprints: a letter from Thomas Mostert, president of the Pacific Union Conference, to legislative leaders in California, announcing the church's opposition to a bill that could recognize gay marriage; and an article by Alan Reinach urging Adventists to "speak up" on the "marriage debate."[77] As an opposing view, I argued that "Supporting the 'Marriage Amendment' would place the Adventist Church in opposition to what is a civil rights—not a religious—issue....The recent decisions of the U.S. Supreme Court, the Canadian courts, and the Massachusetts Supreme Judicial Court have nothing to do with religious freedom or religious rites."[78]

Adventist Schools and Colleges

By the mid-1990s, Adventist colleges had moved away from witch hunts focused on suspected gay students to policies of "don't ask, don't tell." In part, this is because they have gotten more accustomed to the presence of some openly gay students, but another ingredient is that they can no longer afford to lose tuition income. However, students found in compromising situations are still likely to face expulsion or perhaps some lesser form of discipline. Attitudes vary from one college to another. For example, in 1997 La Sierra University, in Southern California, asked a lesbian couple, who had been kissing and caressing one another around the campus, to be more discreet. This was a dramatic change from the automatic removal of yesteryear. The following year it accepted a former Adventist and self-identified lesbian who planned to seek ordination in the gay-oriented Metropolitan Community Church into its M.A. program in religion.[79]

The Caring, Welcoming Church?

Some colleges have gay support groups among students. These depend on the presence of support among the faculty and a secure administration, but especially on the presence of students with the courage to act. The visibility of each group rises and falls as active students graduate and newcomers become involved. The first such group was formed by two Hispanic students at Pacific Union College in the late 1980s; it faded after the two founding leaders graduated. By 1996, there were more substantial and active groups at Walla Walla College in Washington state and at Columbia Union College in Maryland, near the District of Columbia. Others formed at La Sierra in 1998 and at Southern Adventist University more recently.[80]

Although public surveys suggest that younger people are generally more accepting of gays and lesbians than the older generations, students on Adventist campuses are more conservative than average, so gay students there face mixed reactions if they "come out." In 2000, the *Student Movement* at Andrews University reported the results of a survey of 111 students who were asked how the Adventist Church should treat homosexuals: 55, almost exactly 50 percent, chose the option "excommunicate them."[81] A previously closeted gay student wrote a letter to the editor in which he "came out" and commented that he had concluded "there is no possible channel for talking about homosexuality on campus."[82]

Loma Linda University, the site of the Adventist Medical School and other related programs, has long had a reputation of being especially inhospitable to gay and lesbian students. In September 2000, its president, Lyn Behrens, declared in an interview with a local newspaper that faculty were fired and students expelled if caught or suspected of breaking the university rules banning homosexual conduct. Student records were marked that the dismissal was because of immorality, and they were not given supporting letters or help in finding other schools. When this came to the attention of the American Civil Liberties Union, it warned the LLU administration that such policies could violate a new state antidiscrimination law that went into effect in January 2001.[83] When its letter of warning was ignored, the ACLU decided to focus attention on the university. It placed a follow-up article in the newspaper in February 2001.[84] This caused a furor on campus because it coincided with LLU's reaccreditation process. The administration felt vulnerable at this time because the university had earlier experienced problems with accreditation. When Ben Kemena, a former faculty member fired earlier because of his sexual orientation, showed members of the university administration a notice on the ACLU Web site that invited persons who had experienced discrimination and harassment at LLU to approach them, and informed them that more than twenty had already come forward and were willing to bring charges and testify, the university's leadership agreed to protect homosexual faculty and students who did not practice homosexuality, and to help others, when found, to relocate to other schools.[85]

Nevertheless, in an August 2002 article in the *Adventist Review*, the LLU vice president for diversity reported being asked about the university's position on sexual orientation after making a presentation on health care and diversity at a national conference. His answer had been "Loma Linda has one standard applicable to both hetero- and homosexual persons: celibacy before marriage; monogamy within marriage." In response to another question, he had added that Loma Linda does not knowingly hire practicing homosexuals or extend benefits to their partners, but that there are no witch-hunts.[86] Loma Linda University has not yet become a welcoming environment for gay and lesbian Adventists.

In spite of indications of change at Adventist educational institutions reviewed here, faculty, and especially biblical scholars, have remained afraid that their careers could be damaged if they published their positive conclusions about homosexuality. Kinship has invited many such scholars to discuss what the Bible says about sexuality at its Kampmeetings since 1980. This was a new topic for almost all of them, but their presentations showed a remarkable degree of agreement that the Scriptures do not address sexual orientation and that homosexual Adventists are called to the same standards as heterosexuals—to faithfulness within their relationships. It would have been very helpful to the debate within the church if these scholars had published their conclusions. However, until recently, the only one to do so published under a pseudonym in the *Kinship Connection*, which meant that his article had no opportunity to make a broader impact within Adventist circles.[87] The current volume is therefore a major breakthrough.

Congregations and Pastors

Given the negativity of the Adventist Church's official statements, the diversity of voices within it, and the bitter debates within society about civil rights for homosexuals, to what extent have Adventist congregations and pastors in the United States and Canada become caring and welcoming toward homosexuals? In 1992, an article published in *Insight* concluded that "Homosexuals, as long as they are not practicing homosexuals, can be members in good and regular standing of any Seventh-day Adventist church. They can hold church offices." According to the article, "If an alcoholic who never drinks alcohol can hold any church office, a homosexual who never practices homosexuality can hold any church office."[88]

But, in fact, there is considerable difference from one congregation to another. This was well illustrated by two interviews I completed back-to-back in Los Angeles. One of the questions on the interview schedule for pastors asked, "How many gay members do you have?" When I asked this of the pastor of a large Hispanic church, his first response was "none," which he quickly changed to "maybe one." He then told me of a member who had been disfellowshipped because of his homosexuality, and who had later been rebaptized because he claimed to have been "cured." But because the members did not believe this claim, they shunned him when he attended church. The pastor did not speak to him either because, he said, this would have offended the lay leaders in the congregation. Following this interview, I made my way to a predominantly white church only a few miles away. When I asked the pastor there the same question, he told me that his youth leader, who was highly admired, was widely known to be gay and that he and his partner often sang duets in services.[89]

Most Adventist churches follow an unwritten, unstable version of "don't ask, don't tell." This means that it is acceptable if a gay member is single and discreet, and especially if he or she has professional stature, for a commitment to celibacy is often assumed. It is frequently acceptable for a couple to attend together as "friends," and lesbian couples have often been able to live together, and even follow one another from one city to another as they change jobs, without raising overt suspicion. However, if a gay member is open about a same-sex relationship, severe problems are likely to emerge. At this point, only a handful of congregations are known to be accepting of members known to be gay or lesbian. Because they are so few, and the church hierarchy has adopted a rigid, antagonistic position, the pastors of these churches have to be careful. Sadly, such accepting situations are also fragile and uncertain, for a loving pastor can be replaced by a crusader, new antagonistic members may set out to "cleanse" the church, or the conference can suddenly intervene, and in each case the previously loving community may then become poisonous.

One example of such a dramatic change occurred at San Francisco Central Church, where several gay members had found a spiritual home and also support in a ministry to reach out to members of the broader gay community. It was mentioned above that the ministry folded in 2004 when its leader moved away after his partner died. This allowed two ultraconservative newcomers to the church to change the accepting dynamic, kill the outreach program, and intimidate the remaining gays and lesbians in the congregation. Another example occurred at the North Oshawa Church in Ontario, Canada, which had supported and integrated a gay couple. Later, however, the conference intervened, and a new pastor was appointed and new, compliant lay leaders were elected. Both the gay couple and the former leaders were made to feel so unwelcome that they started a new, independent congregation. The final irony was that these events so offended the United Church congregation from which the Adventist congregation rented its facilities that it refused to continue the rental arrangement, thus leaving the restructured Adventist congregation homeless.[90]

A gay or lesbian Adventist can also be left without a spiritual home if he or she needs to move to another area. In the late 1980s, a Kinship member was nominated to be head elder of his church in suburban Philadelphia. Surprised by this development, he felt it necessary to inform his pastor that he was gay. He was assured that his sexual orientation would not disqualify him, and when he added that his roommate was his partner, the pastor remained steadfast. Later, the gay elder bought a house on the opposite side of the metropolitan area, and began to attend a church nearby. However, when he gave the pastor there the same information, he was disfellowshipped. He was so hurt by the experience that he exited from Adventism.[91]

Many Adventist pastors do not know how to minister to gay members. I have heard many complaints about derisive statements about homosexuals from the pulpit, and even jokes at their expense, from pastors who are apparently oblivious to the fact that there may be closeted lesbians and gays sitting in the pews. Some pastors have also betrayed those who have confided in them.[92]

The evidence suggests that Adventist congregations and pastors usually offer their members conditional, rather than unconditional love. Because of this, the best way for a gay or lesbian member to survive there is to remain closeted—but this prevents strong bonds from developing because these members must try to hide who they really

The Caring, Welcoming Church?

are. This forces them to turn instead to the gay community for genuine, caring friendships. The closet is an uncomfortable space in which to be confined. Given the negative situations that they must often endure, it is amazing how many gay Adventists remain committed to their congregations.

Homosexual Adventists around the World

Adventism has grown rapidly in recent years, especially in the developing world, resulting in a relative decline of the membership located in the United States and Canada, which now stands at only 7 percent of the total. The membership in most other parts of the developed world—Europe, Australia and New Zealand, and Japan—is quite small. Nevertheless, the Adventist Church has now become a global church, with members in almost every country, and it is especially strong in Africa, Latin America, the Caribbean, and parts of Asia and the South Pacific Islands.

SDA Kinship has grown rapidly since 2001. In July of that year, it noted that, although it had accumulated 3,000 names in its database, it had lost contact with all but 288. However, in the four years since then, it has added 1,400 new members, and it has recruited widely because Adventists in many countries have found it after searching the Web. In 2005, its members could be found in 51 countries and 16 percent of its total lived outside the United States. Countries with active clusters of members include Australia, New Zealand, Canada, Germany, England, the Netherlands, Brazil, Mexico, Columbia, the Philippines, South Africa, and Uganda. Europe has had its own Kampmeeting for several years, and Australia and New Zealand are planning their first. But many members are still isolated: twenty-six countries have only one each. The Internet, however, has greatly increased communication among members.[93]

The situation of gay and lesbian Adventists in much of the developing world is grim. There are undoubtedly thousands who live in total isolation because they have never heard of Kinship or have no means of making contact with it. Many of those who have contacted Kinship have yet to meet another gay Adventist face-to-face. Moreover, they typically confront a church even more rejecting of homosexuals than in North America, and they often live in cultures that are hostile.[94]

While traveling the world doing research on international Adventism, I not only asked pastors and administrators wherever I went how many homosexual members they had, I also tried to find opportunities to meet and interview gay members personally. One in Lima, Peru, explained that he had left the church as a youth because he had realized that it had no room for homosexuals. Indeed, he was aware of many homosexuals who had been Adventists—all had exited the church, either because it had disfellowshipped them or because they realized it had no place for them. One gay couple in Buenos Aires, Argentina, had grown up in one of the largest congregations there, but it had disfellowshipped the two after discovering their homosexuality. Still being Adventists at heart and wishing to worship God in an Adventist setting, they began to attend the headquarters church as visitors, not members. However, they were soon told explicitly that they were not welcome at services.[95]

When I conducted interviews in Africa, I was almost always told that there were no homosexuals there. However, Kinship today has one hundred members in Uganda alone. About twenty of these were Adventists and the rest have come from other communions, including about ten who were Muslims: they share the experience of being cast out by their religious groups. Several, who are of school age, were expelled from their schools and homes when their sexual orientation was discovered. When I asked a gay former pastor about the impact of growing up as Adventists on gay and lesbian Ugandans, he replied, "It is the most difficult thing you could ever think of—they tell you that you are already condemned, going to hell. No one tells you that God loves you."[96] All of them also face a situation where homosexuality is illegal and can result in long prison sentences. That is, they face harassment and ostracism from both church and state. Another former Adventist pastor, whom I shall call Pastor Joseph, has gathered Kinship members together into a nonsectarian worshiping community. Joseph, who was also disfellowshipped after discovery of his homosexuality five years ago, spoke with excitement about finding Kinship on the Internet. A young woman assists him, leading the lesbians in separate activities. Pastor Joseph believes that God has called him to minister to homosexuals, especially Adventist homosexuals, in Uganda. He says that many gay Adventists remain hidden in the church, living miserable, closeted lives. However, all discovered, or even suspected, homosexuals have been disfellowshipped—often secretly. He mentioned that some gay Adventists have committed suicide after being discovered.[97]

The Caring, Welcoming Church?

AIDS

Acquired Immune Deficiency Syndrome (AIDS) was first diagnosed in 1981, and it was initially known as Gay-Related Immuno-deficiency Disorder (GRID) because it was first found among gay men in America. At the first Adventist conference that focused on the disease, sponsored in 1990 by the *Adventist Review* and Sligo Church in suburban Washington D.C., Fritz Guy challenged Adventists: "It would seem that responding to AIDS would be a natural for Adventism, because we claim that healing and caring are part of our mission, and because a sexually transmitted disease is immediately relevant to our understanding of the wholeness of man."[98]

In fact, however, church leaders were slow to recognize that AIDS impinged on Adventism. Since it was a gay disease, they saw it as God's judgment on willful sinners and a sign that the end of the world was imminent. That is, they were repelled, and frozen in inaction, because of their own homophobia. While the disease raged and gay Adventists died, the General Conference broadened the Adventist definition of adultery to include homosexual behavior as a legitimate ground for divorce, and it sued SDA Kinship in an attempt to force it to remove the part of its name that identified it with Adventism. When *Message,* the missionary magazine addressed to African-Americans, published a cluster of articles that dealt with AIDS, it omitted any reference to homosexuality and drug abuse, fearing that this could be interpreted as approval of such lifestyles.[99]

Neither did the hospitals in Adventism's large hospital system in the United States go out of their way to treat people with AIDS (PWAs). Indeed, its flagship hospital, Loma Linda University Medical Center, became the object of special criticism following reports of neglect and demeaning behavior toward PWAs. The reasons given to explain this pattern included fear of infection, moral disgust with the patients, and the risk of financial problems attendant on providing care for patients who often lacked medical insurance, yet often required long stays in hospitals.[100]

This pattern created a striking contrast with the role that Adventist hospitals played during the polio epidemic of the 1950s, when they had stood at the forefront. Indeed, their work among children who had contracted the disease so impressed the members of a prominent Ohio family that they donated a four-hundred-bed hospital, the Charles F. Kettering Memorial Hospital in suburban Dayton, to the church.

Although the church regarded the children as innocents, it saw those infected with AIDS differently.

Adventism's major response to the AIDS epidemic was to affirm its stance against "sexual immorality." The epidemic never became a focus during all the hype about "The Caring Church." There was no systematic education of clergy or church members in North America, and little coverage of it in Adventist schools, in spite of studies showing that students there were engaging in at-risk behavior.[101] Neither did the church raise its voice in advocacy on behalf of PWAs. Most Adventist PWAs slipped away from their congregations without putting them to the test, and their families were shamed into silence. I interviewed several mothers of PWAs during the 1980s, and not one of them had told her pastor, her Sabbath School class members, or her church friends about the cloud that hung over her family.[102]

A few church members became prominent AIDS activists. One was Eunice Diaz, who became active in 1981, almost as soon as the disease was identified, while working with the Los Angeles County Health Department. Later, while employed by the Adventist White Memorial Medical Center, which is located in the major barrio in Los Angeles, she tried to bring people together around AIDS. However, the hospital administration demanded that she drop the issue because the visibility she brought the hospital created a "negative image." As a result, she resigned her position in 1988 and became a health care consultant for government and private agencies. Within months after she left the Adventist hospital, President George H. W. Bush appointed her to the National Commission on AIDS, which was commissioned to advise the president and Congress on all matters pertaining to HIV and AIDS.[103] When church periodicals trumpeted this news, Diaz responded sadly: "With the minimal response of our church, I don't go around waving a flag saying I'm a Seventh-day Adventist." She explained, "The church has turned its back on the AIDS issue because it cannot come to grips with the issue of Homosexuality. The leadership of the church is afraid of becoming identified with something it finds embarrassing."[104]

Another prominent Adventist activist is Harvey Elder, a physician and specialist in infectious diseases at the Veterans Hospital in Loma Linda, California. When he saw his first AIDS patient in January 1983, he realized he was strongly prejudiced against homosexuals and drug users. However, as he interacted with his patients and learned their stories, he realized that if Jesus were in his place he would reach out to such patients; Elder accepted this as his calling. By the mid-1980s, he

The Caring, Welcoming Church?

could see that a frightful epidemic was spreading, and, after meeting with Eunice Diaz, the two set out to prod the Adventist Church to become involved. Both received appointments to the General Conference AIDS Committee when it was created in 1987, and they served on it for a decade. However, they became frustrated when its meetings did not result in actions. Elder responded by launching a lonely crusade aimed at persuading Adventism to embrace the disease and PWAs.[105]

The AIDS Committee failed in its attempt to persuade church leaders to put AIDS on the program of the General Conference Session in 1995. However, its members were given twenty minutes to address the Annual Council of church leaders in 1996. Since many pastors interested in the disease found that speaking about it led people to suspect that either they or their children were gay, a result that created a caution that silenced others, the committee's speakers urged the General Conference to acknowledge that AIDS was a major crisis. They also asked that the church advise couples in areas with high rates of infection to be tested before marriage and to use condoms if one of them were found to be HIV-positive. They also urged that the Adventist seminaries teach about AIDS, if only because the students needed to be prepared to preach suitable sermons at the funerals of PWAs. In spite of considerable opposition to the use of condoms under any circumstance, the leaders voted in favor of all of the items. However, there was little attempt to implement the measures, which deeply disappointed the committee members.[106]

It is still true that the church in North America has never really made AIDS its concern. According to the committee, "We don't have any idea of the prevalence of HIV/AIDS in the North American church. There is still so much shame and stigma that family members do not speak and those at risk do not attend church."[107] Although Adventist hospitals now treat PWAs—as those with any other disease—Elder is "not aware of any SDA hospital that has made AIDS a priority."[108] When the Health Department of the General Conference sponsored a conference on AIDS at Andrews University just before the General Conference Session in June 2005, only two of the one hundred attendees were from North America. A survey of the churches here, in an attempt to discover levels of interest in the topic, found that AIDS was not seen as a major problem when compared to other medical problems. Only about 20 percent of respondents expressed some interest, the majority from black congregations.[109]

An AIDS epidemic broke out in Africa shortly after the disease was identified in the United States. Sexual contact also transmitted it, but this time transmission was primarily heterosexual. In 1990, I interviewed Bekele Heye, president of the Eastern African Division of the church, where AIDS was rampant, and at that time he declared that "AIDS is not an Adventist issue!"[110] This was because he associated it with sexual promiscuity, and since the church forbad that, he was not interested in the disease. The lack of interest no doubt contributed to the fact that I had found Adventist hospitals in his division cavalier about the risk of spreading the contagion through the use of untested blood supplies and through reusing needles when I visited in 1988–89. Heye also ignored the fact that thousands of new members were pouring into the church there, and he could not speak to their sexual habits before their baptism. Indeed, I also stumbled onto considerable evidence of sexual promiscuity among church members and pastors during my three research-related visits to Africa. Heye's attitude was therefore totally unrealistic.

As late as 1996, in an article titled "AIDS and the Church in Africa," Saleem Farag, former long-term head of the Health Department in the East African Division, and Joel Musvosvi, ministerial secretary of the division, made no mention that Adventists had AIDS or that the disease had affected the church. Neither was there acknowledgment that African Adventists were often highly promiscuous. Instead, the authors referred to U.S. data and recommended emphasis on morality and evangelism opportunities among PWAs.[111]

The General Conference AIDS Committee had chosen to focus its efforts on education to prevent the spread of the disease in the developing world, and thus on promoting "moral behavior" there. This focus allowed church leaders once again to avoid dealing with homosexuals, for AIDS in these regions was found primarily among heterosexuals. However, with the evidence that an epidemic was galloping through Africa, it started to dawn on church leaders that AIDS was just another disease rather than God's judgment on homosexuality. Nevertheless, the church took a long time to realize that the infection rate among Adventists in Africa was high. In fact, General Conference president Robert Folkenberg did not realize that the church was infected until Elder warned him that a significant number of pastors there were infected and Folkenberg himself saw firsthand during a subsequent visit to Africa that pastors and midlevel church

The Caring, Welcoming Church?

administrators were dying.[112] Alan Handysides, current head of the Department of Health at the General Conference, gained the attention of administrators when he pointed out that the cost of medical care for one church employee with AIDS equals the salaries of four or five pastors.[113] Only recently have church leaders in Africa acknowledged that multiple sex partners, incest, and rape are major problems within the church there.[114] Independent studies show that the average number of sex partners that African Adventists have is only slightly lower than for people in the general population. Discouragement of the use of condoms, primarily because of Farag's views while health director in the East African Division and support he received from the General Conference, made the situation even more dangerous. Africans tend to see things in black-and-white terms, and ultraconservatives among them coined slogans such as "conduct not condoms." Only now is this view starting to change. The Adventist Development and Relief Agency (ADRA) has helped, partly by introducing a new slogan, "Protection for People with an Unregenerate Heart."[115] General Conference president Jan Paulsen recently endorsed the use of condoms at an AIDS Conference in Africa.[116]

When I visited South Africa and Zimbabwe in 1999, I found churches in Swaziland that had only women and children members because their husbands were away working in the mines. Pastors there told me that the men returned once a year to see their wives and "give them AIDS," which many had contracted as a result of active sexual lives while away.[117] In Zimbabwe, I saw the results of a confidential survey among unmarried members of the largest Adventist congregation in Bulawayo, where more than 80 percent of the males and 75 percent of the females admitted to being sexually active. I was dismayed to learn that the promise of confidentiality had been broken for respondents who had admitted to having had a homosexual experience.[118]

Handysides became head of the Health Department at the General Conference in 1998. By the following year, he realized that AIDS was an enormous problem for the church because of the large number of members in Africa, where the epidemic was worst. He pushed to have an AIDS office established in Africa and headquartered in Johannesburg. Since then, the office has worked to persuade Adventist universities in Africa to teach a course on AIDS in their ministerial training programs as both a warning and a call to minister to PWAs, to make every Adventist church an AIDS support center where PWAs can sew and bake goods for sale, and to help reduce transmission of AIDS from mother to child through testing and treating. However, the director's shoestring budget severely hampers his efforts.[119]

Elder's crusade has taken him to Africa many times since 1989, and he has endeavored to raise the consciousness of the church there about the epidemic. In 1991, he designed an AIDS course currently being taught in four of the African Adventist universities, because he felt that too little was being said to the church youth. "I fervently hope that [the course] changes the attitude about the infected, and helps the students realize what are dangerous behaviors," he told me. "When it comes to protection, being an Adventist does not work nearly as well as a condom!"[120] Handysides concurs: he explained that HIV/AIDS challenges some beliefs that Adventists have about their purity, such as the assumption that they will not be infected by such an epidemic.[121]

An Adventist AIDS conference in Harare in 2003 represented a turning point, at least in acknowledging that Adventism had been slow to respond to the epidemic, that many Adventists were infected, and that those who had contracted the disease frequently faced stigmatization in their churches.[122] Pardon Mwansa, president of the division, bravely acknowledged that a member of his family was infected with AIDS. He insisted that Adventists acknowledge the disease as their problem. Elder had demanded that the conference schedule a separate meeting for union presidents and health educators, and that these meet with Adventist PWAs. As a result of Elder's urging, presidents who attended the meeting confessed to the PWAs that they had sinned against them by lying to them about God and about them to their members.[123]

The Adventist Church is learning to respond to heterosexual Africans who transmit AIDS through multiple partnering as it has come to realize the extent to which Adventists are infected. However, it continues to do next to nothing about the disease in the United States because it started as a gay disease there—and it continues to reject both gay Adventists who put themselves at risk of contracting AIDS, as well as those who live in committed relationships as equally promiscuous.

Conclusion

This chapter set out to test both the fit of the slogan, "The Caring Church," for Adventism and the extent to which the hope of General Conference president Jan Paulsen that it be a "welcoming church" has

The Caring, Welcoming Church?

been realized in treatment of homosexual members. As measured here, the Adventist Church fails the test because it has proven itself more concerned with rules and image than with the needs of its people.

Despite the failure of the "change" program it supported and the sexual exploitation of young, fragile counselees by its director, church leaders helped restore him to a place where he could resume his activities, and it continued to insist that only homosexuals who struggle to change their orientation will be accepted. The prejudice of these leaders led them to sue SDA Kinship in order to distance themselves from gay Adventists, and it prevented them from seeing the relevance of the AIDS epidemic for Adventism, especially in places that initially considered it a "gay disease." There is currently growing awareness in the church of homosexuality as well as gay and lesbian Adventists, but a profound distaste for and fear of them also exists, and this has fostered growing polarization over the issue.

It is no surprise that context strongly influences and shapes churches, like any other human collectivity. It is disappointing, however, that the Adventist Church has so largely succumbed to the example of the American Religious Right. Adventists have taken a strong position against majoritarian rule in religious matters ever since their founding mother prophesied that they would face persecution, especially in the United States, and attempts at legislation during the 1880s that would have made Sunday sacred by law seemed to indicate that the fulfillment of that prediction was at hand. The logic of the long-held position should surely be that government may not refuse equal status and protection to any group. However, although Adventists have come to support equal civil rights in the areas of race and gender, they generally continue to withhold support for such rights in relation to sexual orientation. Indeed, they have followed the Religious Right's attempts to take away recent gains.

There have been some positive shifts, however, at the local level, where individual cases are most often addressed. These shifts seem isolated and incremental because of diverse situations. Nevertheless, in the years since the first Kinship Kampmeeting, a remarkable change has occurred in the tone of stories that newcomers tell about growing up gay in the Adventist Church. For the first few years of Kinship, these were known as "horror stories." Such a designation is rarely apt today in North America or much of the rest of the developed world, even though the stories often still reflect pain, confusion, isolation, and rejection. A number of factors have made a remarkable impact: the very existence of SDA Kinship; the fact that gay Adventists currently find it more easily and at a younger age; the ready availability of information on the Web; and changing attitudes in society and church, especially among Adventist parents. This is not yet the case in the developing world, where both church and society still typically reject gays and lesbians and where "horror stories" still abound.

Kinship continues to make an extraordinary contribution in the name of the church, sometimes to the latter's chagrin. Kinship is reaching out with increasing effectiveness to young Adventists who have questions about their sexuality; no longer does it need to send mailings to Adventist campuses because most young homosexuals find it easily on the Web. It nurtures gay Adventists spiritually, encourages them to think through the ethics of being a gay Christian, and fosters stable relationships among them. Its members have proved, even through the long ordeal of the suit that the General Conference brought against Kinship, astonishingly tenacious with their Adventist heritage.

Yet the main message of Adventism to its gay and lesbian members—a slogan that appears in some form in almost all official statements that bear on homosexuality, and is repeated again and again in publications and sermons—is that Adventists "love the sinner, but hate the sin." This attitude, in fact, judges the faith and lives of the people whose sin is "hated," and may best be translated as "we will truly love you only when and if you meet our standards." It thus offers conditional rather than unconditional love. This is neither welcoming nor caring.

Questions for Discussion

1. What do you feel it would be like to be a committed Adventist who finally comes to the conclusion that his/her orientations are gay/lesbian? How would you react if your son/daughter told you that he/she was gay/lesbian?
2. Looking back at the history of the Adventist church and its gay members, what were the best things done by the church? What were the worst things?
3. What actions should the church take now to make its churches and institutions accepting and nurturing environments for its gay members? What should our local church do?
4. If you were a gay or lesbian in a same-sex committed relationship and the church told you must separate from your partner to

The Caring, Welcoming Church?

become or continue as a church member, what decision would you make? Why would a gay or lesbian member be deeply distressed over a suggestion to he/she should exit the church?
5. Where did the Adventist involvement with "change ministries" go wrong? Where did the "change ministries" go wrong?
6. In the past, young Adventists who have approached their pastors or school counselors for help when distressed over their gay attractions have often been advised to pray about it, date a woman and marry her. Is this the most loving advice in this situation?

Notes and References

1. Owen A. Troy, "Caring-Church Seminar Held," *Adventist Review*, Feb. 24, 1983, 17; and "First Union-Wide Caring Church Seminar Conducted," *Adventist Review*, Nov. 17, 1983, 24.
2. Jan Paulsen, report of sermon at General Conference Session, *Adventist News Network*, July 9, 2005.
3. I completed thirty-five hundred interviews in fifty-six countries. Since I promised most interviewees confidentiality, I have identified such sources simply as "interviews."
4. For example, her extended discussion of Sodom and Gomorrah linked their destruction to a variety of sins, but did not mention homosexuality. See Ellen G. White, *Patriarchs and Prophets* (Battle Creek, Mich.: Review and Herald, 1890); and Michael Pearson, *Millennial Dreams and Moral Dilemmas: Seventh-day Adventism and Contemporary Ethics* (Cambridge, Eng.: Cambridge University Press, 1990).
5. Interviews; and General Conference Committee Minutes, 1951–52, available online at <www.adventistarchives.org>.
6. Interviews.
7. Ibid.
8. This statement is based on personal stories told at SDA Kinship Kampmeetings.
9. Kenneth Wood, "Power to Counter All Deviation," *Adventist Review*, July 15, 1971, 2; and Dan Day, "What about Homosexuality?" *Insight*, Dec. 14, 1971.
10. Miriam Wood, "Anita Bryant and Homosexuality," *Adventist Review*, Oct. 6, 1977; Robert Pierson, press statement, June 24, 1977, quoted in Pearson, *Millennial Dreams*, 248; and "Annual

Council Passes Action on Conciliation, Divorce, and Remarriage," *Adventist Review*, Feb. 17, 1977, 18.
11. Ellen G. White, *Mind, Character, and Personality* (Nashville, Tenn.: Southern Publishing Association, 1977), 232. When he found this, Larry Hallock, a Kinship member, conducted a long correspondence with the Ellen G. White Estate, which eventually agreed that the quotations used under this caption had been taken out of context. It promised to change the caption if there were ever another edition (Hallock to White Estate). However, when the estate published *Testimonies on Sexual Behavior, Adultery, and Divorce* in 1989, it included a heading "Homosexuality" with out-of-context passages where White had referred to Sodom.
12. C. E. Wittschiebe, *God Invented Sex* (Nashville, Tenn.: Southern Publishing Association, 1974), 187; and S. Kubo, *Theology and Ethics of Sex* (Nashville, Tenn.: Southern Publishing Association, 1980), 83.
13. Colin Cook, "God's Grace to the Homosexual," parts 1, 2, and 3, *Insight*, Dec. 7, 14, 21, 1976.
14. Colin Cook, "The Church's Responsibility to Homosexuals," *Insight*, Dec. 16, 1980, 9–11.
15. Interviews.
16. Neal Wilson, interview, *Walla Walla College Alumni Review*, winter 1981; and idem, personal conversation with the author, May 1981.
17. Ronald Lawson, notes from participant at LaGuardia Airport meeting, May 1980, in author's possession. Those present at the meeting, which took place at LaGuardia Airport, in New York City, were Eva, Professor James Cox, and the author (representing Kinship).
18. Anonymous, "Growing Up Gay Adventist," *Spectrum* (May 1982):38–48. One of the five clergy invited by Kinship (Londis) knew at that time that his brother was gay. Two others later discovered they had a gay sibling and gay son, and then thanked Kinship for the preparation that the Kampmeeting experience had provided in helping them relate to that family member. I was the one who compiled the selection of personal stories that appeared in *Spectrum*: the editor insisted that it appear without attribution.
19. The firing of theologian Desmond Ford, whose trial occurred immediately following the Kampmeeting; what became known as the Davenport Affair, where church leaders had invested the

The Caring, Welcoming Church?

funds of church entities in a pyramid scheme operated by Doctor Davenport that went bust; and the research of Walter Rae, an Adventist pastor, which suggested that Ellen White had plagiarized other sources when preparing her "inspired" writings.

20. North American Division Committee, minutes, Apr. 4, 1981; and "Spring Council Report," *Adventist Review*, May 21, 1981, 14–15.
21. Duncan Eva to Josephine Benton, Jan. 13, 1981, in author's possession.
22. "The Church and the Homosexual," *Adventist Review*, Apr. 26, 1984.
23. Interviews.
24. Ronald M. Springett, *Homosexuality in History and the Scriptures* (Washington, D.C.: Biblical Research Institute, 1988).
25. Duncan Eva to Adventist educators, Aug. 16, 1986, in author's possession.
26. Robert Spangler, "Homosexual Healing," *Ministry*, Sept. 4–13, 1981.
27. *Atlantic Union Gleaner,* Mar. 25, 1986.
28. Interviews.
29. Elvin Benton, "Adventists Face Homosexuality," *Spectrum* (April 1982):32–38; Anonymous, "Growing Up Gay Adventist"; and Colin Cook, "Church Funds Program for Homosexuals," *Spectrum* 12.3 (May 1982):46–48.
30. This had been the experience of thirteen of the fourteen interviewees, and, according to them, of many of their fellow counselees throughout the history of Quest. The only exception was an older man in his fifties.
31. Ronald Lawson, "The Quest Learning Center/Homosexuals Anonymous: Trouble in an Ex-Gay Ministry," Paper Presented at the meeting of the American Sociological Association, Chicago, Aug. 1987.
32. Ronald Lawson to Neal Wilson, Oct. 23, 1986, in author's possession.
33. "Newsbreak," *Adventist Review*, May 21, 1987. Ironically, the same issue included a full-page advertisement urging Adventists to subscribe to the *Review* with the heading, "It's my church. I want an honest picture of what's going on."
34. Robert Spangler, "Homosexual Recovery—Six Years Later," *Ministry*, Sept. 4–9, 1987.

35. Colin Cook to Neal Wilson, Dec. 14, 1987, in author's possession.
36. Colin Cook, "'I Found Freedom': One Christian's Struggle with Homosexuality and How He Found Healing through God's Grace," *Christianity Today*, Aug. 18, 1989, 22–24.
37. Interviews.
38. Virginia Culver, "Sessions with Gays Criticized," *Denver Post*, Oct. 27, 1995, 1, 8A, and 9A.
39. "NAD Leaders Comment on Colorado News Stories," *Adventist Review*, Dec. 14, 1995, 6.
40. Interviews.
41. The General Conference had taken steps to register the denominational name in the spring of 1980 and had done so by November 1981. The case was filed in this jurisdiction because Kinship was incorporated in California.
42. "SDA Church Moves Against Homosexual Support Group," *Adventist Review*, Feb. 4, 1988.
43. A. Japenga, "It's Called Change Counseling: Troubled Pioneer Maintains His Faith in Program," *Los Angeles Times*, Dec. 6, 1987; and "Desperate Quest: Cook's 'Cure' Much Worse than 'Disease,'" *Reading Eagle*, Feb. 16, 1988, 4.
44. Kenneth Edward Piner, "'Seventh-day Adventist' not Always a Trademark," *Spectrum* 22.1 (Mar. 1992):63–64.
45. *General Conference of Seventh-day Adventists vs. Seventh-day Adventist Kinship International*, USDC, CD CA, 1991, Case No. CV 87–8113 MRP, unentered.
46. Michael McLoughlin to Robert Folkenberg, Oct. 1991, and Bob Earl Jacobs to Michael McLoughlin, Jan. 15, 1992, both in author's possession and SDA Kinship files.
47. General Conference Administrative Committee, May 17, 1994, available in the General Conference Archives.
48. General Conference Administrative Committee, "Seventh-day Adventist Affirmation of Marriage," *Messenger*, June 21, 1996, 5, also available online on the Web site of the Seventh-day Adventist Church <www.adventist.org/beliefs/statements/main_stat53.html>.
49. Available online on the Web site of the Seventh-day Adventist Church <www.adventist.org/beliefs/statements/main_stat46.html>.

The Caring, Welcoming Church?

50. "Adventists Reaffirm Traditional Marriage; Call for Support of Legislation," *ANN Bulletin*, Jan. 19, 2000.
51. "Adventists Respond to Court Decisions on Same-Sex Marriage in Canada," *ANN Bulletin*, Oct. 20, 2002.
52. Bulletins distributed by Seventh-day Adventist Church-State Council, Apr.-Oct. 2003.
53. Ronald Lawson to Alan Reinach, Jan. 3, 2006; and Reinach to Lawson, Jan. 20, 2006, both in author's possession.
54. "British Opposition to Government Plan to Introduce Civil Unions," *ANN Bulletin*, July 8, 2003.
55. "SDA Fears about Canada's Expansion of Its Hates Crimes Law," *ANN Bulletin*, July 2004.
56. "Seventh-day Adventist Response to Same-Sex Unions—A Reaffirmation of Christian Marriage," *ANN Bulletin*, June 6, 2004. "Homosexuality is a manifestation of the disorder and brokenness in human inclinations and relations....It is very clear that God's Word does not countenance a homosexual lifestyle....Seventh-day Adventists believe that the biblical teaching is still valid today."
57. Paulsen's remarks, from a televised program where he answered questions from Adventist youth, can be found on the Web at <letstalk.adventist.org> under Q&A—Pop Culture and Society.
58. Kate McLoughlin, *My Son, Beloved Stranger* (Nampa, Idaho: Pacific Press, 1995).
59. Inge Anderson to Ronald Lawson, Dec. 26, 2005, in author's possession.
60. Christopher Blake, "Redeeming Our Sad Gay Situation: A Christian Response to the Question of Homosexuality," *Insight*, Dec. 5, 1992, 4–16.
61. Ibid., 10–11.
62. John C. Cress, "Compassion—An Alternative Lifestyle," *Ministry*, Nov. 6–9, 1996. Carrol Grady, the mother of a gay son, wrote one of the articles in this issue. Kate McLoughlin, "A Homosexual in My Congregation?" *Ministry*, Nov. 1996, 10–11, 29. Writing first under a pseudonym and more recently under her own name, Grady has published a stream of articles in the church press that she discusses in her chapter elsewhere in this volume.
63. Sheyanne Williams, "A Match Made in Heaven," *Insight*, Dec. 12, 1998, 8–13.
64. Tessa Willow, "Still Our Son," *Women of Spirit,* May/June 2000.

65. Carrol Grady, "Listen and Love: How Do You Treat Gay People?" *Ministry* (Aug. 2003):25–26, 29.
66. Roy Adams, "Marriage under Siege," *Adventist Review*, Oct. [2], 2003, 34–36.
67. William Johnsson, "Biblical Marriage," *Adventist Review*, Oct. [2], 2003, 6.
68. Lincoln Steed, "Behind Closed Doors," *Liberty* (Sept./Oct. 2004):30.
69. Barry Bussey, "Why Silence Is Not an Option," *Liberty* (Sept./Oct. 2004):16–19.
70. Jonathan Sorum, "Civil Rights and Homosexual Rights: A Flawed Analogy," *Liberty* (Sept./Oct. 2004):8–13.
71. Samuel Koranteng-Pipim, "Born a Gay or Born Again? Adventism Changes Attitudes towards Homosexuality," *Journal of the Adventist Theological Society* 10 (spring-autumn 1999):141–83; and "Homosexuality in the Church: Should this "Born-a-Bay" Lifestyle Be Baptized?" *Adventists Affirm* 14 (Spring 2000):11–19, 47–58.
72. Robert Bouchard and Harvey Elder, "Kampmeeting Supports Gay Adventists," *Adventist Today* (Nov./Dec. 1995):16.
73. John McLarty, "Let's Talk about Homosexuality," *Adventist Today* (July/Aug. 1999):2.
74. Aubyn Fulton, "Making a Stand: Official Statements Bring out the Best and Worst in the Church," *Spectrum* (winter 2000):69–72.
75. Ibid., 71–72.
76. Gary Chartier, "Marriage in 2004," *Spectrum* 32 (winter 2004):4–6.
77. Thomas Mostert to California Assembly members Mark Leno and Ellen Corbett, quoted in Robert M. Johnston, "Pacific Union Conference Oppose Gay Marriage Bill," *Adventist Today* (Mar./Apr. 2004): 13; and Alan Reinach, "Should Adventists Speak Up on Marriage?" *Adventist Today* (Mar./Apr. 2004):12.
78. Ronald Lawson, "Adventists and the Proposed 'Marriage Amendment': The Constitution and Same-Sex Relationships," *Adventist Today* (Mar./Apr. 2004):14–17.
79. Interviews.
80. Ibid.
81. Chris Holland, "Unacceptable," *Student Movement*, Jan. 16, 2000, 15.

The Caring, Welcoming Church?

82. Daniel Scarone, "The Real Issue," *Student Movement*, Feb. 2, 2000, 13.
83. Interviews.
84. Sharyn Obsatz, "Gays Urge Policy Shift: Loma Linda University Calls Its Sexual Standards a Way to Promote Chastity, Homosexuals Call It Bias," *Riverside Press-Enterprise*, Feb. 11, 2001, A1.
85. Interviews.
86. Leslie N. Pollard, "Upstream," *Adventist Review*, Aug. 1, 2002, 45.
87. Derek Easton, "The Old Testament and Homosexuality," *SDA Kinship Newsletter*, Jan., Mar., May 1982.
88. Blake, "Redeeming Our Sad Gay Situation," 16.
89. Interviews.
90. Ibid.
91. Ibid.
92. Ibid.
93. Fred Casey to Ronald Lawson, 2005, in author's possession.
94. Ibid.; and interviews.
95. Interviews.
96. Ibid.
97. Ibid.
98. The AIDS Conference took place at Sligo Church over three days, April 5–7, 1990. Guy was one of two people who shared the preaching at the Sabbath morning worship service on April 7. The *Adventist Review* reported on the conference in a "Newsbreak" and sidebar titled "AIDS Conference Challenges Adventists" and "Adventists with AIDS," respectively. *Adventist Review,* Apr. 26, 1990, 6–7.
99. Delbert W. Baker, address to AIDS Conference, Sligo Seventh-day Adventist Church, Apr. 5–7, 1990.
100. Douglas R. Hegstad: "AIDS—A Call for the Wisdom of Solomon, the Grace of Christ," *Spectrum,* 18.1 (Oct. 1987): 15–18; and interviews.
101. Joyce Hopp, "A Study of Adventist Academy Students in California Concerning AIDS At-Risk Behaviors," unpublished paper; and Gary L. Hopkins and Joyce Hopp, "AIDS and Adventist Youth," *Ministry*, July 22–23, 1996, 25–27.
102. Interviews.
103. Ibid.

104. Kevin G. Richards, "AIDS, Adventists, and America (An Interview with Eunice Diaz)," *Kinship Connection*, June 1992, 6–12.
105. Interviews of Harvey Elder by the author, 2005 and 2006, in author's possession.
106. Interviews.
107. Interview of Harvey Elder by the author, 2005, in author's possession.
108. Ibid.
109. Interview of Alan Handysides by the author, Sept. 2006, in author's possession.
110. Interview of Bekele Heye by the author, Aug. 1990, in author's possession.
111. Saleem Farag and Joel Musvosvi, "AIDS and the Church in Africa," *Ministry*, July 1996, 10–13.
112. Interview of Harvey Elder by the author, 2006, in author's possession.
113. Interview of Alan Handysides by the author, Sept. 2006, in author's possession.
114. Interview of Harvey Elder by the author, 2005, in author's possession.
115. Interview of Alan Handysides by the author, Sept. 2006, in author's possession.
116. Interview of Lester Wright by the author, Oct. 2006, in author's possession.
117. Interviews.
118. Ibid.
119. Interviews.
120. Interview of Harvey Elder by the author, 2005, in author's possession.
121. Interview of Alan Handysides by the author, Sept. 2006, in author's possession.
122. "Zimbabwe: Church Leaders Stress Urgent, Practical Involvement in AIDS Crisis," *ANN Bulletin*, Mar. 11, 2003.
123. Interview of Harvey Elder by the author, 2006, in author's possession. According to Elder, "When a person demeans any Christian because of behavior or illness, they take the name of God in vain. They are saying that God hates that person—a blatant lie."

Response: Social Experiences in the "Caring Church"

By Catherine Taylor

Seventh-day Adventists are a people of context. Since our beginnings we have pointed to our connection with the lessons taught in Eden. We have named ourselves after the hope of the Second Advent of Christ on Earth to take us home to Heaven. We have made endless time charts to clarify our position in the line of history. We have developed programs to place ourselves in the same arena as the Good Samaritan. Ellen White called our midweek prayer groups "social meetings" to focus on the importance of both horizontal and vertical connectedness. Given this heritage, it is particularly valuable that René Drumm and Ronald Lawson focus on context: the environments in which gay and lesbian Seventh-day Adventists begin to integrate their orientation and their spirituality (self, parents, spouses, friends, work, schools, and congregations) and the structured religious organization in which Seventh-day Adventists attempt to live their spiritual lives. As we read their chapters, we should keep in mind the components that make environments viable for human existence and growth. In this Christian context, we need to compare the contexts described in the writings of Drumm and Lawson with Heaven's behaviors and value systems.

    Lawson introduces his chapter by sharing the ideals of a "welcoming church" and a "caring church" that Charles Bradford and Jan Paulsen set forth as goals for Seventh-day Adventists. Those attributes fit the heavenly lessons mentioned in the very first pages of the Bible. Genesis describes beginnings filled with both gifts and mandates.

Two are particularly germane to the discussions shared by Lawson and Drumm. The first is the gift of relationship: face-to-face communion with God as well as the opportunity to build emotional intimacy with family, community, and other citizens of the earthly/galactic/universal/heavenly realms. Although the relationships in Eden had original intents, the changes that time has brought are not always condemned.

The second gift and responsibility was God's delegation to us of dominion over the Earth. Like the relational bequest, dominion was an object lesson of Heaven's way of responding to creation. Dominion was an opportunity to use power to benefit others; to be a servant of creation; to utilize strength to protect, maintain, and nurture those who lived in humanity's domain. This mandate has never been changed, mutated, or abrogated. The Sabbath Commandment in Exodus 20 reminds us that the ideal reflected in that weekly heavenly time capsule of an object lesson is that vulnerable members of the community (women, children, foreigners, animals) are all to be cared for. Isaiah 58, a text that Ellen White has instructed Seventh-day Adventists to memorize and follow, states that our work is to "loose the chains of injustice." The shepherds mentioned in Ezekiel 34 are cursed because "my shepherds did not search for My flock," but often devour it. In John 10, Jesus describes a true shepherd as one "the sheep will follow [into the safety of the sheep pen] because they know his voice." In no biblical illustration does the shepherd push a sheep out of the safety of the sheep pen. Those in church leadership today are shepherds entrusted with the hungry, the vulnerable, and the scattered of the flock. I believe that how modern-day spiritual shepherds utilize their dominion is of intense interest to God and to Heaven. It is those shepherds that Lawson addresses in his chapter.

Drumm describes some of the changes that have occurred in human beings over the last several millennia. Instead of "male" and "female," we now have a continuum of biology affected by shifted chromosomes, physiology, and hormones. Instead of one orientation, she describes a continuum that includes homosexual relationships, as well as heterosexual ones. Biblical stories also describe changes, uncondemned ones. In the first chapters of Genesis, there seem to be no alternatives other than procreating with siblings or very near cousins. The custom was still in practice when Abraham married his half-sister. By the time

Response: Social Experiences in the "Caring Church?"

of Leviticus, sibling marriage was forbidden. By the time of the letter to the church in Corinth, marriage to near relatives was shocking. The original ideal is pictured as two-person monogamy. Abraham was reprimanded for his relationship with Hagar because it showed his lack of faith in God's promise of a child to him and Sarah. However, there is no reprimand at the time of his death (in Genesis 25) for his relationships with his concubines and their children, as well as to his second wife, Keturah. The main focus seems to be an insistence that the lineage of the Messiah be clearly filled with miraculous covenant-based births, as opposed to being an insistence on monogamy. Esther's membership in a Persian harem is pivotal to her ability to access the king of that empire and save thousands upon thousands of Jews. Instead of being condemned for being part of a polygamous arrangement, she is lauded and memorialized for her courage and her gift of life to her people. Liaisons with Moabites are condemned after the debacle with Balaam and Balak lead to idolatry on the shores of Canaan's Jordan River. Despite this, Ruth becomes one of the progenitors of the beloved King David and, through him, the Messiah. Perhaps more powerfully, she is an object lesson of someone who leaves a safe home, where she is loved, to go to a foreign land, where she is subject to the death penalty. She has an understanding of and willingness to live covenant-based love. Ruth, a cursed woman, is a type of the Savior.

    These people have several things in common. They are committed to having a relationship with God. They exhibit a willingness to follow God wherever he leads them. The welfare of God's people is important to them; it is something for which they may even risk their own lives. They are willing to use their gifts, talents, and resources in the cause of God. God did not refuse to use Abraham, Esther, and Ruth because they were different or did not fit easily into the prevailing belief system of their times. In fact, God used their difference to his glory. These people were willing to learn the lesson of being authentic, honest individuals in the cause of God and in the relationships in which God placed them. It is when they were most authentic and honest about their lives that these people were most powerful, most able to use their God-given gifts, most able to help his people, most able to be examples of his love. Proper, upstanding religious conservatives would have condemned these people on the basis of "biblical" teachings. Being religiously conservative is not necessarily the same as being biblically observant.

Catherine Taylor

René Drumm's chapter gives a clear and cogent description of the details and causes of gender and orientation diversity. I am struck by the difficulty we Seventh-day Adventists have with the variety among people who are modern-day believers. Many of the gay and lesbian people she describes have the same commitment to following God's leading as did biblical heroes. I am puzzled that we insist in condemning those who are God's creation, redemption, and heartfelt love because of what we perceive as God's decision to condemn anything that has not stayed the same as we were in Eden. If that perception were accurate, no one would eat salads. Greens were designed to be eaten by "the beasts of the earth and all the birds of the air and all creatures that move on the ground" (Gen. 1:30). Humans were supposed to eat only "seed bearing plants and every tree that has fruit with the seed in it" (Gen. 1:30). It should follow that we would be even more gentle with human beings than we are with diet.

God did not design that we should be alone. Authenticity, honesty, and safety are essential components of powerful intimate relationships. God created a safe environment for the first humans, where the other qualities could develop and flourish. In Eden, God gave us spousal relationships so we could understand a microamount of the intimacy among members of the Trinity. That emotional intimacy was so powerful that conversing with his father though the night hours rejuvenated Jesus when most of us would need sleep. That emotional intimacy was so powerful that when Jesus felt sin separate him from his Father, his heart shattered. That emotional intimacy was so powerful that when God called Jesus from the tomb, the power of intimate love shook the earth and destroyed the web of death. No human being could have given Jesus that particular intimate bond because we are not like him. God designed us to be with beings who could match our relational needs. We were designed to be with people like ourselves.

Drumm's stories point out the lengths to which lesbian and gay people will go in their attempt to have honest, intimate spousal/partnership relationships. She and Lawson have pointed out the pain inflicted on vulnerable people as they made those attempts. They pointedly describe a Seventh-day Adventist culture that discourages authenticity, safety, and honest communication. People who were trusted with information about gay or lesbian Seventh-day Adventists were described as "brutal" (P3-14). Hardworking employees were fired as they became more honest and authentic about their orientation (P3-

Response: Social Experiences in the "Caring Church?"

14–P3-16). Students were humiliated and denigrated (P3-16). The destruction of honesty and emotional intimacy is the purview of the evil ones. Revelation 21:6 states, "all liars will have their place in the fiery lake of burning sulfur, the second death." I do not believe that a church focused on the Second Coming of Christ should create an environment where lying is encouraged in order to maintain church membership, school safety, employment, or friendships.

Lawson quotes Jan Paulsen, in his role as General Conference president, saying "the Biblical expectation is for those who believe they have a homosexual orientation to live a celibate life or to limit sexual activity to within a husband and wife marriage situation" (P3-46). When church leadership insists on a requirement of celibacy for lesbian and gay believers, that leadership is directly opposing God's plan that "Adamah" should not be alone. Human beings, like the members of the Deity, need to be coupled with someone who is "like" them, who can understand them. Gay and lesbian believers are not able to be intimate with partners of the opposite sex. In my work as a family therapist, I have read much research that indicates human beings live longer when they are able to be in a committed long-term relationship. Following this research to its logical conclusion would indicate that people living celibate lives die earlier. What does it say about the "caring church" that it would encourage or force a life on its members that would lead to early death?

In a religion whose focus is spiritual development, René Drumm and Ronald Lawson describe a church that attempts to deny the power experienced by Abraham, Esther, and Ruth to its lesbian and gay members. The church does this by creating a culture where a substantial percentage of its members understand they need to live closeted or facade-based lives in order to participate in Seventh-day Adventist projects or outreach. We will not be able to "press together," as Ellen White said, or to "bear one another's burdens" if we are facades of our true selves. Modern believers, like biblical ones, have unique gifts to match their unique experience, relationships, and mission. When we, as a body of believers, amputate some of our unique members and their influence, we are going against Genesis mandates, prophetic warnings, and Paul's counsels to the early church.

When there is a blaming environment of secrecy, open communication is impossible. How will we learn to pray honestly to our God if we spend the rest of our lives needing to keep secrets from fellow mortals? I have heard stories of many couples that included one gay member who married because the gay person believed they had a mandate either to remain celibate or enter into a heterosexual marriage. The stories of loneliness for both partners that come out of those marriages is heart wrenching. The anger at God, as well as the church, is often tangible and permeates a community. The remarkable part of René Drumm's presentation is the lengths to which gay, lesbian, bisexual, transgendered, and intersex members of the body of believers will go to be able to live honest, authentic lives. These are people genuinely attempting to live with qualities that encourage intimacy that can reflect the love and bond of the Trinity. Seventh-day Adventist Christians need to be looking for a variety of members whose bond is their commitment to building their relationship with God, a willingness to follow wherever he leads, to be concerned about and work toward building the community of God and using their gifts and talents for that work. These are biblical priorities, and the church would be richer if we followed them with our gay and lesbian members.

First Corinthians 12, Romans 12, and Ephesians 4 discuss the gifts of God's Spirit. Galatians 5:22 discusses the fruits of that Spirit. These texts are all clear that both the gifts and the fruits given to the sheep in Heaven's fold come from God. If someone exhibits these qualities or talents, God has blessed them. These gifts were not given only to those who were Jewish or male or slave or Pharisee. They were given to individuals as God chose and chooses to give them. They were and are given for the building of the body and the community of God. God did not instruct the church leadership to assess the worthiness of members to receive these gifts. The church membership did not have input on whether these gifts were to be used. The gifts were and are given by God to build up God's work. When the shepherds, the church leadership, begin to decide that they will control whether the gifts of Spirit of the Holy God will be used, they put themselves in the place of God—even if the people who exhibit any of the gifts and fruits are lesbian or gay. According to Isaiah 14:12, putting oneself in the place of God is very dangerous.

Ronald Lawson describes the history of the Seventh-day Adventist Church in relation to our gay and lesbian members. It includes lawsuits and decisions to send vulnerable, frightened human beings to a "treatment center," where they were exposed to unwanted and unexpected sexual assaults by someone in the powerful roles of counselor and pastor. The history includes assaults on spiritual integrity by the Adventist press and the decision of a health-oriented

Response: Social Experiences in the "Caring Church?"

denomination to ignore one of the health pandemics of our generation. Shepherds are to use their dominion to protect the sheep, to provide the poor wanderers with shelter. Lesbian and gay men growing up in the homophobic culture of the Seventh-day Adventist Church can experience poor self-esteem, have bad images of their bodies, and confront difficulties being able to protect their own boundaries. These qualities can lead to anxiety, depression, and vulnerability to abuse.

As a therapist who has worked with sexual abuse in the Seventh-day Adventist Church for more than fifteen years, I have been appalled by clinical stories I have heard that describe the sexual abuse and predatory behavior demonstrated by Colin Cook and other leaders of "change ministries." Many gay and lesbian youth have left these programs feeling more hopeless, less spiritual, and more self-hating than when they arrived. Additionally, they have needed to address the sequelae of sexual abuse that may not have even existed before they attended Quest or similar programs. I have heard many stories about young men subjected to bullying and hazing when fellow students in Seventh-day Adventist schools came to believe that no protection would be given to vulnerable members of the body perceived as "faggots." I have heard about a school administrators who said, "Well, boys will be boys," and did nothing to protect a member of God's creation from being tormented or physically harmed by members in good standing of "God's remnant people." When we pressure vulnerable human beings to go to venues or situations with a history of abuse, we become party to that abuse.

Shepherds have charge of congregational communities. They have a large influence on the way varieties of people are accepted. They are often, as John 10 describes, the gatekeepers, as well as those who search for the wandering. Pastors are the equippers who nurture and encourage the gifts the Holy Spirit has bestowed on each member. They facilitate church board and business meetings. They encourage or discourage church discipline. They are the gatekeepers of priorities. Ellen White has written that the two worse sins in the church are backbiting and self-sufficiency. In a chapter titled "Judge Not that Ye Be Not Judged," in her book, *Thoughts from the Mount of Blessing,* she writes that we are not to confront or correct anyone unless, at that point, we are willing to give our life for them. Unless church leaders make these two belief priorities their own, we abrogate our role as shepherds of the flock. We no longer follow the mandates of Genesis dominion or of Isaiah's description of true believers.

Catherine Taylor

These stories and Lawson's chapter paint quite the picture of how the shepherds called by God have utilized their power and the dominion God has entrusted to them. In looking at this history, it is important to understand that modern-day Seventh-day Adventist shepherds were given the commission to invite the sheep into the sheepfold and search for the scattered ones (Ezek. 34). It is essential to understand that these shepherds were given the Isaiah 58 mandate to "life up the heavy yoke…loose the chains of injustice…set the oppressed free…avoid the pointing finger and the malicious talk." Comparing the actions of the Seventh-day Adventist hierarchy described by Drumm and its history chronicled by Lawson with biblical counsel, I am concerned that our "shepherds" are exposing themselves to the judgment of God.

Ronald Lawson, with the clarity of a modern prophet, has pointed out how the leadership of the Seventh-day Adventist Church has abdicated its God-given responsibility. He has given clear and specific indicators of the ways the church hierarchy has negated the very goals set forth by Bradford and Paulsen to be a welcoming and caring church. In the list of recommendations found at the end of her chapter, René Drumm points back to an Edenic model that focuses on honesty, compassion, community, intimacy, and the spirituality modeled in Heaven. We would do well to listen.

Questions for Discussion

1. As Seventh-day Adventist Christians deal with the issue of gay and lesbian members, what do you believe are the Biblical principles we should be following? By what method or with what process do you think we should assess the policies of the church on this issue?
2. How has the Seventh-day Adventist Church chosen which Biblical edicts to follow and which to set aside? How do we respond to these edicts as individuals?
3. What might be some ways that people who are homosexual and Adventist could benefit our denomination and our congregations?
4. How do you differentiate between individual sins and the shifts in our world that sin has caused which are not condemned?
5. Since Jesus acted contrary to accepted teachings of his day, what was the basis on which he made his priorities? How would his value system apply to this discussion?

Part Four
Scriptural and Theological Perspectives

Part 4-2

"In Christ There Is Neither…": Toward the Unity of the Body of Christ

By John R. Jones

For Seventh-day Adventists, human considerations matter.[1] But such considerations do not suffice. As "people of the Book," we instinctively turn to Scripture for guidance. We want help, and we want it on authority that transcends anecdotal or "common sense" appeals. So it is with questions of our sexual relationships. Early in any discussion of how we should sexually express our love for one another, the question of "what the Bible says" urges itself upon us. We experience it as foundational, a priori.

I write from the perspective of a heterosexual Caucasian male who through schooling and practice has arrived at certain insights into scriptural interpretation. My sociocultural location inevitably affects my perspective, even as I seek to listen sincerely to the voices (scriptural and contemporary) engaged in this conversation. As a student of Scripture, I come to the text with the scholarly tools of both traditional historical analysis and more recent literary approaches. These two locations—sociocultural and academic—I take as grounds for humility and continuing open-mindedness in proffering what follows.

We will cut through much underbrush if we keep our questions framed correctly. In asking, *What biblical implications can we find for the ethics and boundaries of sexual expression in the context of loving same-sex relationships?* we can immediately set aside the horrific stories of Genesis 19 and Judges 19 as irrelevant. These accounts may have much to say about patriarchal hospitality codes, male control over women's sexuality, and ethnic/tribal identity in ancient Israel; but we can only regard the same-sex aspect as serving at most to underscore the sense of contravention of boundaries.[2] Sodom and Gomorrah subsequently function in Hebrew Scripture as bywords for a variety of evils from pride to oppression, but without reference to homosexuality.[3]

The Holiness Code

Leviticus 17–26 encodes the legal framework of Israelite society as attributed back to Moses.[4] This framework structures an ethic of ritual purity, a code of sacral taboos through which Israel is to maintain a state of holiness before God. Always fragile and subject to threat, this state is constantly to be reinforced not only through ritual ceremonies, but also through meticulous observances in the sphere of everyday life. Included among its injunctions are the two instances of outright prohibition of same-sex intercourse to be found in the Bible: "You shall not lie with a male as with a woman; it is an abomination" (18:22); and "If a man lies with a male as with a woman, both of them have committed an abomination; they shall be put to death, their blood is upon them" (20:13).[5]

Throughout the Holiness Code, it is only the adult males of the community, the "sons of Israel," who are addressed; what women do sexually with women is not on the horizon. In the prohibition in Chapter 18, together with its sanction in Chapter 20, the wrongness resides in the feminizing treatment of one male by another: "as with a woman." This pattern of concern over the blurring of distinctions in the conventional order is evident in many of the ceremonial law's stipulations.[6]

Such stipulations forbid the mixing of two kinds of crops in one field, the wearing of garments composed of more than one type of fabric, or the crossbreeding of animals (Lev. 19:19).[7] Some of them have to do with dietary practices (17:10–16), some with degrees of consanguinity for sexual relations (18:6–18), some with the trimming of hair and beard (19:27), and much else. In all, the expressed intent is to avoid contamination by association with any practices that characterize other peoples. "You shall be holy to me; for I the Lord am holy, and have separated you from the peoples, that you should be mine" (20:26). This holiness, then, is marked not only by separation of themselves from surrounding nations, but also by observance of other separations that the Israelites understood to express the canonic order of the universe.

Further, the proscription against sex between males is understood to apply only to penetrative sex, for only so is the ancient taboo against the mixing of kinds violated. With regard to the distinction between sexes, such a practice caused a man to be used as a woman—as a passive recipient of male "seed." With regard to the cultic identity of Israel, it contaminated their ceremonial purity by bringing in activities identified with the Canaanites. On both counts, the concern was not over an individual's sexual orientation or expression per se; homosexuality as we understand it today from the standpoint of the individual was simply absent from the thinking behind these injunctions.[8] Rather, the concern was wholly corporate: it was to protect the symbolic markers between Israel and her neighbors. In this perspective, one's sexual conduct was no mere personal matter; it was loaded with overtones of cultural and national identity. And it was these overtones that determined the attitudes and sanctions regarding sexual behavior.

All of this, of course, comes to us as background. It participates in that larger conversation between Judaism and Christianity that began in New Testament times. And it poses again for us, as for the earliest Christian thinkers, the question, *How does scriptural fidelity relate to a religious heritage that vests its sexual norms in precisely those distinctions that are overcome in Christ?*

This chapter turns on that question. In the New Testament, the question brings into conversation three religio-cultural worlds—the ancient Israelite, the Hellenistic Roman, and the emerging Christian. Although early Christians interact with both their Hebraic heritage and the thought world of Gentile society, they are nonetheless shaping a new moral order. And in that order, they see themselves pushing beyond their two roots. It started with Jesus: he was understood to have both demonstrated and authorized the process. In him, questions of gender roles and relations, of the Holiness Code, of Jew/Gentile interactions and much else are laid open to new perspectives.

With explicit regard to same-sex relations, however, we must wait for Paul to open the discussion; here the canonical Gospels provide no input from Jesus.[9]

John R. Jones

The Gospel According to Paul

For Paul, the fact that the core of the gospel is the divine initiative toward humankind, centering in Jesus' death and resurrection, provides the lodestone from which he constantly takes his theological and ethical bearings. His construction of Christian theology around the cross of Christ provides the decisive standard for Christian life; nothing must be allowed to impinge on the believer's freedom, purchased at highest cost.[10] It is for the sake of freedom that Christ has liberated us. This is no trivial matter; we are summoned to stand firm in that freedom, refusing to compromise the efficacy of Christ's cross by reintroducing superstitions of either pagan or Judaic origin into our walk by faith.

At the same time, this is no license for irresponsible or profligate behavior. "For you were called to freedom, brothers and sisters; only do not use your freedom as an opportunity for self-indulgence" (Gal. 5:13; compare v. 16). For Paul, flesh and spirit represent two opposite principles at work in human life. Even with all of his instinctive holism, he juxtaposes the works of one and the fruits of the other as setting the terms of our reach toward wholeness and freedom in Christ.[11]

The implications are many and far reaching. But when it comes to how we shall live as Christians in this world, Paul is nowhere more pointed than in his famous summation at the close of Galatians 3: "As many of you as were baptized into Christ have clothed yourselves with Christ. There is no longer Jew or Greek, there is no longer slave or free, there is no longer male and female; for all of you are one in Christ Jesus. And if you belong to Christ, then you are Abraham's offspring, heirs according to the promise." This single visionary statement demonstrates what the cross of Jesus means for Paul. It provides a focal lens through which to view all of his pronouncements on human relations, and points the trajectory for our own ongoing hermeneutic as we take up the task of appropriating his principles for our own time.

In light of Paul's first pairing above, our first question, "What biblical implications can we find for the ethics and boundaries of sexual expression in the context of loving same-sex relationships?" gets pulled directly into the second, "How does scriptural fidelity relate to a religious heritage that vests its sexual norms in precisely those distinctions that are overcome in Christ?"

We have observed the Levitical conviction that sex between

"In Christ There Is Neither..."

Israelite males breaches the ethnic identity of the Hebrew people, who defined their chosenness and ceremonial purity in terms of their descent from Abraham. Now when these cultural and national bounds are transcended in Christ, the ground is cut out from under the proscriptions in Leviticus 18 and 20. When Paul affirms the equality of Jew and Gentile before God, he is dismantling the framework on which these proscriptions stand.

To be sure, the distinction remains between God's holy people ("saints," as Paul regularly addresses them) and an unholy world. But if the distinction is now to be marked along nontribal lines, then any of the traditional markers must now be shown to carry other water, or go the way of that central symbol of tribal identity, circumcision. Paul's principle becomes more interesting as he pushes further: Just how far does this erasure of difference, in Christ, extend?

Clearly it goes far enough that when Paul wants to differentiate between life in the Spirit and the life of fleshly indulgence, he can readily reach beyond the Judaic pale to Gentile norms for support. His frequent use of catalogs of vices (as well as of virtues) appears to be shaped not so much by one-to-one correspondences with specific behaviors in a given situation as by conventional listings in popular Greco-Roman literature of the day.[12] Whether appropriated directly from commonplace moralizing in the larger world or mediated through Hellenistic Jewish tradition, these concatenations provide Paul with ready-made markers for the bounds of conduct for those who belong to the Kingdom.[13]

Sexual references make limited appearances in these lists. Unsurprisingly, the general term *pornos*, designating a fornicator, adulterer, or otherwise sexually immoral person, is the most common sexual term in such New Testament catalogs, occurring at 1 Corinthians 5:9, 10 and 11; 6:9; 1 Timothy 1:10; and Revelation 21:8 and 22:15.[14]

Same-sex considerations do, however, arise at two points, in 1 Corinthians 6:9 and 1 Timothy 1:10, with the terms *arsenokoites* and *malakos*.

The Pauline Vice Lists

In 1 Corinthians 6, Paul is working against the readiness of some Christians to go to court against their fellow believers over perceived wrongs. In reproving them, he lists the kind of people in the world to whom they are turning for justice: "Do you not know that wrongdoers will not inherit the kingdom of God? Do not be deceived! Fornicators, idolaters, adulterers, male prostitutes, sodomites, thieves, the greedy, drunkards, revilers, robbers—none of these will inherit the kingdom of God" (6:9–10). Where the 1952 Revised Standard Version has "homosexuals," the 1972 edition has "sexual perverts." In either case (as with the New International Version's "homosexual offenders"), these expressions combine a pair of terms in the Greek text, *malakoí* and *arsenokoitaí*. These two terms stand behind the expressions *male prostitutes* and *sodomites* in the NRSV.

Paul is progressively building up a conventional catalog of kinds of people who carried some stigma in the larger society, to make his point of Christian distinctiveness. To the four examples in 5:10, he adds two more in verse 11 and an additional four in 6:9–10:[15]

1 Corinthians 5:10	1 Corinthians 5:11	1 Corinthians 6:9–10
immoral	immoral	immoral
greedy	greedy	idolators
robbers	idolators	adulterers
idolators	revilers	*malakoì*
	drunkards	*arsenokoitaí*
	robbers	thieves
		greedy
		drunkards
		revilers
		robbers

This may be evidence that Paul is here depending on pre-established catalogs, without focusing on any particular item. The lists lengthen for rhetorical effect.[16] As for *malakoì* and *arsenokoitaí*, the two terms are not grammatically paired—as are the "greedy" and the "robbers" of the first list. Rather, they are separated by the same "or" as are the other terms. Accordingly, we will consider them separately.

Malakos. Used adjectivally, this term carries the basic quality of "softness." In the New Testament, it appears three times in this usage (twice in Matt. 11:8; and in the parallel, Luke 7:25), modifying the noun *clothing.* Jesus contrasts the ruggedness of anyone who lives in the desert with those who live luxuriously in palaces, and his peasant hearers would have appreciated the jibe. But the fact that this saying is preserved in the Gospels implies that it also resonated later with Christians in the larger Roman world who found themselves under duress from the rulers of their day. If soft living was a marker of the

"In Christ There Is Neither..."

oppressor, then by contrast the oppressed were bound to see themselves at its opposite, more stringent pole. Such a stance could stiffen their resistance to persecution, strengthening spines by means of a certain hard-edged style.

So natural was this tendency that it could descend into outright bravado. Again it is Matthew and Luke who give us the picture of a macho Peter at the Last Supper, avowing his steadfastness and prompting his fellow disciples to join in (Matt. 26:33–35 = Luke 22:33–34). The incident, surely, is recorded as a cautionary word to later believers, as to how the threat of persecution is to be met: not with swagger but with the steadfast firmness of faith.[17] Evidently the caution was needed.

This connotation provides an important interpretive frame for the one time the term *malakos* appears as a noun in the New Testament. In its plural form, *malakoí* is included in the listing of unworthy types in 1 Corinthians 6. Polycarp (d. 155 C.E.), himself a voluntary martyr, similarly uses it in his listing of those who will not inherit the Kingdom.[18] By contrast, when Polycarp enters the arena of his death, he hears a voice from heaven: "Be strong, Polycarp, and play the man [*andrizou*]."[19]

For a community under such pressure, it is hardly surprising that a certain semantic polarity would evolve between the strength of character that endures and the kind of weakness that folds. And given the dualistic assumptions of the Greco-Roman world, it was equally predictable that the former would be invested with overtones of manly virtue, whereas the latter would be projected as effeminate.[20]

Such a construct, under life-and-death conditions, goes well beyond mere dismissals of wimpiness as a personal affect. This was serious business. The gospel's summons, even in its call to freedom, was also a summons to a certain stern and austere ethos. Paul's military metaphors draw upon what was doubtless the standard view, in early Christian circles, of their situation. They saw themselves as engaged in a vital "struggle" (Eph. 6:12) against forces both spiritual and physical (Rom. 8:38–39). They were called to become "more than conquerors" (8:37) over the hardship, distress, persecution, famine, nakedness, peril, and sword they confronted in an alien world. Such conditions inevitably shape the social codes of any group so positioned. Clearly, early Christians found themselves threading their way between the two extremes of overassertiveness and capitulation.

Even short of voluntary martyrdom, then, there could be little room for "softness." That *malakoí* would come to appear among conventional listings of undesirables in such circles is hardly surprising. In such a world, whether in a Palestinian Jewish setting or a Gentile Christian context, Jesus' dig at voluptuaries who wear soft clothing would have served to caricature who the oppressors were—and who his followers were not. With or without intimations of any particular sexual conduct, the term would certainly have addressed a larger issue, having to do with the integrity of the community: Would they all prove faithful under duress? Were they made of the right stuff?

Viewed through sociological glasses, a certain rough-hewn ethos would seem to have already been natural to the underclass who made up much of the Christian community in Corinth (1 Cor. 1:26–28). Prior to their conversion, it would have served as a class marker, and now as Christians they could readily carry forward that same code to mark their even greater distance from the alien world of privileged social elites who were additionally becoming their oppressors. Within the faith, Paul could play to such attitudes by contrasting the "super-apostles" (2 Cor. 11:5; 12:11), who always escaped hardship, with his own sufferings for Christ (11:23–29). All the more, then, could he appeal to that code as a way of distancing the believers from the outsiders to whom they were turning for redress of disagreements among themselves. How could they take individual recourse to such *malakoí*, the silken magistrates of a legal system that was the instrument of their oppression as a group?

None of this, of course, negates the possibility that the term *malakos* included male homosexual behavior. It simply locates the opprobrium where it belongs: as part of a larger pattern of self-indulgent, lustful living that was precisely the opposite of the values the threatened underclass of Christians espoused.[21] Under the duress of worldly challenges and the shortness of the hour, even heterosexual marriage could be but grudgingly accommodated as an alternative to "burning" (1 Cor. 7:6–9). Given the universal assumption of the day that homosexual relations were motivated simply by fleshly passion, neither the conduct nor the self-indulgent style of which it was perceived to be a part had any place in the beleaguered community's life.

Arsenokoites. This noun, composed as it is of two Greek words *arsen* (male) and *koite* (a bed, euphemistically used for sexual intercourse), invites a straightforward interpretation as a male who

"In Christ There Is Neither..."

engages sexually with other males. But if we take seriously the appropriate cautions against mechanically turning to etymologies—actual or supposed—to define the semantic domain of a term, we must dig deeper.[22] Given the fact that meaning is contextually determined, a term's signification is best traced by observing its function in as many contexts as possible—especially those closest in time and subject matter.

When it comes to the noun *arsenokoites* or the verb *arsenokoitein*, however, we have few such resources. The term appears to be a coinage of the Jewish community of Paul's day; the first instances of any form are its two appearances in the New Testament letters (*arsenokoitai*, 1 Cor. 6:9; *arsenokoitais*, 1 Tim. 1:10). The two halves of the word appear as separate words in the Septuagint, the Greek translation of the Hebrew Scriptures, at the two Levitical prohibitions considered above.[23] The composite term, then, may well have been a common usage in Hellenistic Jewish circles, derived from these Levitical texts.

Essentially, we are dependent on the appearances of this term in the vice lists of the Greek Christian writings. Still, certain clear pointers reside there, providing important guidance. First, the vices in the conventional catalogs of undesirable behaviors can be seen to cluster themselves in overarching categories, such as sexual misconduct, violence, injustice, and others. Second, in the two New Testament occurrences of the term, it appears precisely in between sexual and other sins—especially greed, selfishness, and exploitation. Third, the same ordering appears in a comparable list in a second-century Christian treatise by Theophilus of Antioch, *To Autolychus*. This pattern suggests that the sequence may have been conventional and the term may well have incorporated both elements—exploitive and selfish behavior of a sexual sort. This implication of the ordering receives some reinforcement from the term's occurrence in another second century source, Aristides' *Apologia*, where it is connected with the idea of being "an obsessive corrupter of boys."[24]

Indeed, if we ask which of the two aspects is the leading one, the emphasis may well be on that of economic or even violent coercion. At an earlier point in Theophilus's work there is a similar listing, in which *arsenokoites* is separated from sins of sexual immorality, to appear among those of economic injustice.[25] The case is bolstered by other extracanonical examples, drawn from the *Sibyllene Oracle* (2:70–77) and from the second-century *Acts of John* (2:279–82), showing that *arsenokoites* occurs in these vice lists, "not where we would expect to find reference to homosexual intercourse—that is, along with adultery (*moicheia*) and prostitution or illicit sex (*porneia*)—but among vices related to economic injustice or exploitation."[26] The plural form *koitai* (as in Rom. 13:13) evidently points to repetitive conduct, excessive sexual behavior, whether as obsession or prostitution. It is quite possible "that the author attached to the compound a meaning like 'male prostitution.'"[27]

So we almost certainly have to do with homoerotic activity of an exploitative sort. This is about as far as the rather cryptic references in vice lists can get us.

The Significance of Romans 1

Romans 1:24–27 contains the Bible's only substantive consideration of homosexual conduct. The two sentences in verses 26b and 27 are the interpretive crux of debates concerning scriptural teachings on same-sex relations. Yet even here this matter is subsidiary to Paul's larger and more central purpose in writing to the Christian community in Rome: winning acceptance both for himself personally and for his understanding of the gospel. And he is trying to do this among people whom he has not met and who number both Jewish and Gentile believers—among whom there were bound to be tensions. So he has thought out his approach with care.

Building on his conviction that in Christ there is neither Jew nor Gentile, he wants to unite both groups of believers at the foot of the cross. He is headed for the point (in Chapter 3) where he can speak of the central revelation from God: all are equally sinful, and all, whether or not they have the Judaic law in their background, are equally justified on the basis of faith (3:21–26). So in Romans 1:16–17, Paul boldly sets out the good news of God's righteousness: "The one who is righteous will live by faith."

To bring out the implications for Jews and non-Jews alike, Paul then makes the standard move of Christian evangelism. He steps back to a prior revelation that is not news—certainly not to his Jewish-Christian audience, whom he is especially addressing here: God's wrath has already been revealed against all who suppress the truth (1:18). This case is developed through four paragraphs in Chapter 1, beginning with verses 18, 24, 26, and 28, respectively.[28] The first paragraph (1:18–23) makes clear that this entire section (1:18–32) is an

"In Christ There Is Neither..."

indictment of non-Jewish inhabitants of the Greco-Roman world. Their idolatry is the source of the problems in the following verses, for they have turned away from the divine revelation that they have received via the observable world, exchanging the Creator's glory for images of the creatures—human and subhuman:[18]

> For the wrath of God is revealed from heaven against all ungodliness and wickedness of those who by their wickedness suppress the truth.[19] For what can be known about God is plain to them, because God has shown it to them.[20] Ever since the creation of the world his eternal power and divine nature, invisible though they are, have been understood and seen through the things he has made. So they are without excuse;[21] for though they knew God, they did not honor him as God or give thanks to him, but they became futile in their thinking and their senseless minds were darkened.[22] Claiming to be wise, they became fools;[23] and they exchanged the glory of the immortal God for images resembling a mortal human being or birds or four-footed animals or reptiles.

The next three paragraphs unfold God's continuing withdrawal in consequence of this idolatry. This progressive divine resignation can be traced through two levels of depravity, one having to do with impurity (*akatharsia*, uncleanness), and the other with moral evil (*adikia, poneria*, wickedness, evil). The distinction is marked: on the second level, in the two paragraphs dealing with the dishonoring of their bodies in impurity (1:24), Paul disparages their conduct along lines of Hellenistic Jewish propaganda against Gentiles, which in turn draws upon attitudes of certain Greco-Roman thinkers themselves.[29] The fourth paragraph (1:28–32) returns to the "ungodliness and wickedness" (*asebeia, adikia*, v. 18) of the first level and the first paragraph:

Level 1 moral evil	Paragraph 1 18–23	Paragraph 4 28–32
Level 2 ceremonial impurity	Paragraph 2 24–25	Paragraph 3 26–27

There is a certain crescendo in all this, discernable even within Level 2. In true rhetorical style, Paul rounds off his second paragraph with a ritual invocation of God's name:[24]

> Therefore God gave them up in the lusts of their hearts to impurity, to the degrading of their bodies among themselves,[25] because they

exchanged the truth about God for a lie and worshiped and served the creature rather than the Creator, who is blessed forever! Amen.

It goes without saying that the "Amen" signals a chorus of assent from his Jewish hearers.

That interruption, however, requires him to repeat his refrain with the beginning of his third paragraph:[26]

For this reason God gave them up to degrading passions. Their women exchanged natural intercourse for unnatural,[27] and in the same way also the men, giving up natural intercourse with women, were consumed with passion with one another. Men committed shameless acts with men and received in their own persons the due penalty for their error.

Then Paul's technique of the ascending effect becomes more marked as he shifts levels. Again the refrain, "God gave them up," at the beginning of his fourth paragraph:[28]

And since they did not see fit to acknowledge God, God gave them up to a debased mind and to things that should not be done.[29] They were filled with every kind of wickedness, evil, covetousness, malice. Full of envy, murder, strife, deceit, craftiness, they are gossips,[30] slanderers, God-haters, insolent, haughty, boastful, inventors of evil, rebellious toward parents,[31] foolish, faithless, heartless, ruthless.[32] They know God's decree, that those who practice such things deserve to die—yet they not only do them but even applaud others who practice them.

This extensive vice list deepens the wrongness from what is shameful (literally, "shameless," "disgraceful") and unnatural to outright evil. Such moral language is anticipated in the first paragraph but is absent in the middle two paragraphs, which deal with same-sex relations. At the same time, the matter of same-sex relations is lacking in the catalog of evils in the final paragraph.[30] Even as his cadence quickens, Paul's declamation deepens his charge.

In all of this, we see the dynamic of a new religious movement in conversation with its religious and philosophical precedents. This process is just getting under way in the first Christian century.

Vis-à-vis Greco-Roman thought, three main issues emerge: attitudes toward pleasure, attitudes toward procreation, and understandings of natural order. The first two considerations interact to some extent. Already with Plato, any sexual act pursued for the sake of pleasure over the citizen's duty to produce offspring for the state is a personal defeat in one's struggle against self-indulgence.[31] The Stoics would largely have concurred, primarily on grounds of natural law.[32]

Paul's admonition to make no provision for gratifying fleshly desires (Gal. 5:16) would at first seem to be of a piece with the stern voice of self-governance (*autarcheia*) as a Greco-Roman ideal. Yet even though his attitude toward marriage is concessive, his reminder to couples to attend to each other's sexual desires (1 Cor. 7:1–7) grants the legitimacy of pleasure in the Christian life.[33] And with time in this world running out (7:29), Paul would hardly have subordinated sexual fulfillment to an imperative for procreation. In these two regards, then, he stands over against an important current of his time. In Romans 1, however, his opposition lies elsewhere.

With the expression "unnatural" (*para phusin*, "contrary to nature") Paul moves into conversation with both the Gentile and Judaic perspectives. On the Greek side, Plato had already used the expression to characterize male homogenital sex.[34] Additional instances from around the ancient Mediterranean world, using the same expression as a regular reference, can readily be cited.[35]

In what senses is homogenital sex thought of as contrary to nature in the Gentile world? Its nonprocreative character is part of the picture, together with the popular notion that animals, as exemplifying the "natural" order, engage only in opposite-sex mating.[36] Greco-Roman writers do not seem to be personalizing the matter, as if same-sex intercourse were a contravention of the particular individual's heterosexual nature.[37] It is possible, but less likely, that *para phusin* is to be translated in these references as "beyond natural passion," given popular notions of the day that associated pederasty with excessive lustfulness.[38] Essentially, it means that which is nonstandard, outside the norm. While the expression in Gentile usage could refer to a number of sexual practices, it certainly included same-sex intercourse, as here in Romans 1.[39]

The issue, of course, is to what extent this commonplace way of referring to homogenital sex involved a moral judgment in Hellenistic Roman society. It is true that "the concept of 'natural law' was not fully developed until more than a millennium after Paul's death, and it is anachronistic to read it into his words."[40] Even so, four popular notions seem to have entered into conventional ideas about homogenital sex in relation to what was understood to be natural.[41] First, while heterosexuality and homosexuality as constructions of the self, together with any underlying considerations of biology, psychology, or sociology, were far from the conceptual horizon of that day, the standard assumption was that same-sex intercourse was a deliberate overriding of a universal "natural" desire for the opposite sex. It was, in short, regarded as a choice. Second, that choice was assumed to be motivated by inordinate and overly indulged sexual appetites. Third, the practices of the time, whether involving pederasty, male prostitution, or male/male intercourse between master and slave, were uniformly understood to involve established relations of dominance and submission—thus demeaning a male into assuming what was "naturally" the female role. The ostensible natural order was thereby being confused. Fourth, it was feared that homoerotic practice could lead to infertility—with potential for the extinction of the human race. This was predicated on an assumption that, just as heterosexual attraction was the natural and universal norm, so same-sex attraction was a temptation for everyone.

Two key observations immediately follow. First, what passed for "natural" in the Greco-Roman world was in fact "what was culturally prevalent and socially accepted."[42] Second, homogenital sex, at least between males, was starting to be disparaged as indecent conduct. Although there were several reservations about the practice, they converged in the appeal to what nature, however construed, seemed to imply. It was not condemned on moral grounds; but by Paul's time, even the Gentile world was beginning to voice disapproval.[43]

Paul builds on this. In so doing, he has ample precedent from Jewish sources, which in turn found ready ammunition in the reservations emerging in the larger Roman world. So the Jewish philosopher Philo writes from Alexandria at about the same time, disparaging same-sex practices as a Gentile vice. For him, the epitome of the problem was its shameless alteration of nature. "In fact, the transformation of the male nature to the female is practiced by them as an art and does not raise a blush."[44]

Just as Paul shares the common assumption among Greeks and Jews about same-sex relations as flying in nature's face, so he also shares the common conception as to what nature is. First, he consistently uses the term *phusis* to refer not to an overarching principle, but to specific instances of the "nature of" some particular person or thing.[45] Second, of the eleven occurrences of "nature" (*phusis*) or "natural" (*phusikôs*) in the Pauline writings, this passage in Romans 1 is the only one into which one could read a moral principle.[46] Third, Paul is as indebted to his contemporary cultural norms for his allusions to "nature" as are his Gentile counterparts.[47] It is this cultural

"In Christ There Is Neither…"

element that accounts for the shading of "unnatural" (*para phusin*) over into "shameless" (*aschemosune*) in Romans 1:27, a common judgment on pederasty in Paul's time. These considerations, taken together, locate Paul's reference to nature within the conventional grounds on which Hellenistic Roman criticisms were being expressed.

The Jewish perspective, however, does impose a further judgment on homoerotic acts, beyond the Gentile reservations. Standard Jewish associations of homoerotic sex with pagan idolatry do add an overlay of moral judgment, which comes through in the first paragraph (that is, Level 1) of this passage. The most obvious connection is with temple prostitution, though Paul, like his fellow Jews, views the whole matter more broadly. Here in Romans 1, homogenital sexual practices symbolize the whole problem of the estrangement from God that follows from false religion.

This, of course, is a rhetorical choice on Paul's part. From a Christian standpoint all false divinities are nothing.[48] But here in Romans 1, Paul chooses another stance, involving a twofold shift of perspective. First, the practitioners are envisioned here apart from any reference to Christianity; it is their pagan devotion to the creature rather than to the Creator that, ironically, leads them to act against the nature they claim to venerate. Second, Paul is speaking here in the voice of pre-Christian Jews in echoing their denunciations of what they especially regarded as a Gentile vice.

While Paul is indeed driving toward a united community of Gentile and Jewish Christians at the foot of the Cross, the only way to get there, he understands, is to bring home to each group their absolute dependence on God's forgiveness. There is to be no distinction: all have sinned and fallen short of God's glory; all are now justified only by God's grace (Rom. 3:22–24). Any vestige of their pre-Christian superiorities toward each other will prevent their acceptance of what Christ has done for all. Hence the double shift: In order to get at the problem of any such vestiges, Paul has clearly backed up to the pre-Christian conditions and attitudes of both groups.

Paul's primary target in this is his fellow Jews. The point, ultimately, is less what Gentiles have done than what the Jews' attitude toward them has been.[49] His strategy, accordingly, is to bring to the surface those old judgments so as to deal with them from a Christian standpoint. By aligning himself with the pre-Christian Jewish perspective in Romans 1, Paul positions himself to hold up a mirror before their eyes in Chapter 2.

To be sure, when he gets there he will undercut Jewish judgmentalism, not by defending the Gentiles' behavior but by extending the guilt to their Jewish critics. "Therefore you have no excuse, whoever you are, when you judge others, for in passing judgment on another you condemn yourself, because you, the judge, are doing the very same things" (Rom. 2:1). Even so, his point of departure in Romans 1 is a judgment that has its native roots in ancient Hebraic convictions—and so owes nothing to the reservations that were beginning to arise in the surrounding Gentile world.[50] Paul must engage his compatriots on their own terms. In so doing, he falls back upon the locutions of his years of proclaiming the gospel in Jewish synagogues.[51]

This helps us understand why Paul as a Christian relies on pre-Christian Jewish sources for his language. There is hardly a word in Romans 1:24–27 that does not echo Hellenistic Jewish propaganda against Gentiles.[52] Paul's indebtedness brings with it the language of impurity (*akatharsia*), dishonor (*atimazesthai, atimias*), and shame (*aschemosunen*).[53]

None of this implies that Paul does not disparage the conduct in these verses; he clearly does. But in aligning himself with traditional Jewish judgments he reverts into that earlier world of condemnation. Here the ancient cultic taboos still operate. Here the wrongness once again expresses the tribal markers. Level 2 (paragraphs 2 and 3) of this passage reprieves precisely those elements of Judaic separatism that Paul wants to evoke.

If his Jewish compatriots regard homogenital relations as the epitome of pagan difference from themselves, Paul moves to shift the ground of the discussion. He can indeed speak of godlessness (*asebeia*), wickedness (*adikia*), outright evil, and malice (*poneria, kakia*). This deeply moralizing language of Level 1 (paragraphs 1 and 4) makes clear that, for Paul, the first and deepest result of idolatry is outright sinfulness, as catalogued in the longest and most explicit vice list in his writings.[54] On this Level 1, devoid of all reference to sexual misconduct, Paul will eventually turn the table on his compatriots, accusing them too of openly flouting the divine will. Then, having already been filled up with such evil, the Gentiles further experience the impurity to which God resigns them.[55] This is the second, and secondary, negative outcome of idolatry, which Paul carefully restricts to Level 2 of the passage, and for which he uses quite different language.

Here in Romans 1 the real conversation between Christianity and

"In Christ There Is Neither…"

Judaism has not yet begun. It will begin with the Jews' culpability in Chapter 2 and will emerge more fully with the divine remedy in 3:21f. But in our present passage, Paul has so positioned himself that no daylight yet opens up between the Judaism of his day and his rhetorical stance. It is mistaken, then, to look here for the definitive word on same-sex relations or anything else from a developed Christian standpoint.

What the Texts Mean for Us Today

Our overarching question, "What biblical implications can we find for the ethics and boundaries of sexual expression in the context of loving same-sex relationships?" turns in part on the subsidiary question, "How does scriptural fidelity relate to a religious heritage that vests its sexual norms in precisely those distinctions that are overcome in Christ?" So let us consider them in reverse order, with particular reference to Romans 1.

Today's discussion of Romans 1 centers primarily on the issue of the moral status of the same-sex conduct that Paul adduces there. There is no question of his strongly negative perception; the question is, "What are the grounds for that negativity?" Several issues feed into the various attempts to answer this question. One's answer can largely be predicted from which of these issues rises to the top in the eyes of a given interpreter.

Sin or uncleanness? For some who take their cue from Paul's expression "unnatural" (*para phusin*), the determinative considerations remain those of natural law.[56] For such, this principle moves to the fore as a divinely ordained creation order, despite the culturally conditioned character of the gender assumptions reflected in the New Testament and the Greco-Roman world. This approach regularly accompanies a reading of the Levitical taboos as absolute, definitive scriptural injunctions for all times and circumstances. By privileging this issue of natural law, these interpreters seek to present the Holiness Code as still morally binding in Christ. Paul's language in Romans 1:26f, though admittedly couched in terms of impurity, is then regarded as a reaffirmation of unexceptionable regulations reflecting a universal order.

But the difficulties remain: the ancient Holiness Code did indeed proceed from a perceived creation order, but it is at most an open question whether such an order as a theological principle can be traced through Romans 1. If so, it has to be taken as a singular use of an argument from nature as a cosmic principle of morality on Paul's part. If so, one must explain the marked difference between Levels 1 and 2 in this passage, where Paul so consistently references homogenital sex in cultic rather than moral terms.

Above all, we are left with the reduction of morality to casuistry. The focus on homosexual acts can become a device for working around contemporary insights into sexual orientation: one can treat same-sex orientation as a morally neutral phenomenon, while proscribing its expression as a moral evil.[57] But so behavioral an approach, while mirroring that of the Levitical codes, falls short of an adequately Christian perspective.[58] "If homosexual practice is to be discussed in a Christian context as culpable in all cases, it should be articulated as sin and not as uncleanness—because the New Testament has delegitimized the latter category."[59] In regarding uncleanness as sin, we risk collapsing together categories that, even prior to Christ, are distinguished in Scripture.

Alternatively, interpreters who recognize the strongly cultic nature of the Level 2 language in the Romans 1 passage do not attempt to stretch it beyond the symbolic world of ritual purity. From this standpoint, it is enough to state,

> While Paul wrote of such acts as being unclean, dishonorable, improper, and "over against nature," he did not apply the language of sin to them at all. Instead, he treated homosexual behavior as an integral if unpleasingly dirty aspect of Gentile culture. It was not in itself sinful, but had been visited upon the Gentiles as recompense for sins, chiefly the sin of idolatry but also those of social disruption.[60]

Such a reading has the advantage of allowing the texts to function in the mode in which they actually speak. By respecting the distinction Paul himself observed, it avoids the fallacy of arguing that somehow in Christ the two levels are collapsed into one.

Seventh-day Adventists have been particularly sensitive to the distinction between the ceremonial and the moral law, taking the seventh-day Sabbath's inclusion in the Decalogue precisely as the criterion of its endurance into the Christian era.[61] The ceremonial law, by contrast, fades out in the face of the new reality that Christ brings.[62] The question now becomes one of our readiness to indeed accept that new reality in Christ.

"In Christ There Is Neither..."

Christian or pre-Christian? All of these interpretations take some passing notice of Paul's rhetorical strategy in the opening chapters of Romans. His intent, it is universally understood, is comparable to that of a parable in which the hearer is drawn in to a particular perspective, then is caught by surprise as that perspective is applied to the hearer in unanticipated ways. So the Jews here, having had their judgments against Gentiles brought to the surface, are to be shown their own need of divine grace. But as correct as this observation is, Paul's strategy of speaking requires to be met on our part with a more considered strategy of reading. Most interpretations proceed from an apparently unexamined assumption that Paul's voice in Romans 1:18–32 is that of a Christian theologian making definitive pronouncements about homoeroticism. This flattening of the text simply fails to catch the voice in which Paul speaks.

For here in Romans 1:18–32 it is not fully Paul's own Christian voice. Indeed, even in Romans 2, where he turns the table on his compatriots, he is still addressing them simply as Jews, not yet as converts to Christ. This is not to make of his presentation a pretense; he is utterly serious about what he is saying. But he is saying it in a way that reaches back behind the Jewish Christians' experience of Christ. In so doing, both his terms and his tone deepen the Jews' revulsion toward Gentiles by starting with the way they have traditionally regarded them. Shortly this will play out into some explicit lessons as to how they shall regard themselves, and then into their regard for their Gentile fellow believers from the Kingdom's fresh perspective. But all of that comes later. Here in his opening chapter, it is enough for Paul to locate himself, the Jews, and even his Jewish Christian hearers in their conventional Judaic ways of thinking about these things.

It becomes important, then, to cut the question of our passage in Romans 1 in two ways: The traditional standard inquiry as to "sin or uncleanness?" needs to be complemented with the further question, "Christian or pre-Christian?" Helpful as it is for setting up his topic of the universal need for deliverance, Paul's approach is not aimed at sketching the Christian life. The only way questions of same-sex relations could be pressed into such an agenda, beyond simply flagging the very boundaries Paul means to break down, is to show when and how homogenital intercourse in and of itself came to be deepened into sin. And here Paul does not oblige us. His two sentences in Romans 1, for all their vehemence, have served his rhetorical purposes; he doesn't pursue the matter for its own sake.

Our reading, then, will respect Paul's purposes and allow him to speak to them in his own way. We do Paul no justice when we seize upon a subsidiary point and make it function beyond his intent. What we owe him is serious attention to what he is about: the tragic consequences of human sinfulness, especially stemming from various forms of idolatry, and the rifts that can result in the Body of Christ when arrogance on either side, indecent conduct, moral evil, and religio-cultural elitism take hold. These are the problems that occupy the body of his letter; the cultic issues re-surface only afterward, in Chapter 14. The contours of our reading, then, are to match those of Paul's writing.

Paul's world and ours. We have noted in his letter something of the interactions between Paul's own conceptual horizon and those of his various audiences. This is important for how we are to read him. But if we are to read him without wresting his thought, we must further consider the relationship between Paul's frame of reference and our own.

Part of the disconnection between Paul's interests and ours derives from the difference between our thought categories and his. The difference first arises with the English term *homosexual* itself. Given that both the label and the concept behind it are of comparatively modern origin, we can too glibly assimilate his frame of reference into our own.[63] But "what we mean by the term 'homosexuality' in the late twentieth century is for the most part rather different from what the biblical texts are discussing." This is not a trivial problem. Indeed, in order to preclude reading our modern understandings of homosexuality anachronistically back into the biblical texts, "we should stop talking about what the Bible has to say regarding 'homosexuality.'"[64]

And yet Scripture matters. It matters to the extent that we can establish legitimate overlaps in fields of meaning between scriptural conceptions and ours. In holding together certain people and certain biblical passages—all individuals who engage in homogenital sexual activity of any kind and context together with all texts that mention such activity of any kind and context—we can legitimately get a partial overlap. The scriptural condemnations of various exploitative and lustful sexual behaviors (same-sex or opposite-sex) in Paul's time are rightly applied to such behaviors (same-sex or opposite-sex) today. But let us note that the two horizons—textual and contemporary—are now converging around the relational and character issues rather than around the question of sexual orientation as such.

"In Christ There Is Neither..."

Clearly in Romans 1 we have to do with at least a partial incongruence between conceptual horizons, between the box within which Paul was writing, and our box into which we want to fit him. In our quest for answers concerning "homosexuality" as a condition (even if we regard it as a mutable condition) we are asking Paul to address a category of being that was essentially uncomprehended in his world. If the Greeks assumed everyone was at least potentially, bisexual, the Jews assumed everyone was naturally heterosexual.[65] The standard models of the day for same-sex eroticism were all exploitative to one degree or another, and understood to be more or less transitory—whether involving pederasty, temple prostitution, or master/slave relations. Thus for Paul and all other ancient writers, Christian or not, the horizon of possibilities hardly provided for a developed notion of inherent homosexuality or, concomitantly, of loving, enduring bonds between same-sex partners in committed, consensual, and exclusive relationships.[66]

Here we must recognize that our essentializing of homosexuality can lead us into inappropriately limiting our selection of texts when we look for scriptural guidance today. We illegitimately try to force an overlap when we attempt to stretch the ancient models to cover the entire contemporary spectrum. For this leads us into category errors. If we want to hear the Scriptures fully, we must allow them to point us toward additional legitimate lines of thought that can broaden our selection of texts—thus enabling the Bible to build its own bridges between its world and ours. On doing so, we find that there are indeed pertinent axes of connection that provide some real guidance without forcing the text.

What are the criteria of this legitimacy? For present purposes, two. First, a Christian interpretation must be carried out within a Christian framework. This does not exclude pre-Christian scriptural passages from Christian reflection, but the early Christian communities, through many challenges, pointed the way: they understood that their interpretations of the Scriptures, like interpretations of the meaning of Jesus himself, must be carried out from within the new perspectives that Jesus brought to the human situation. The implications and outcomes of this process were not always self-evident to those pioneers of faith; this was no simple matter. When we trace the dynamics of their struggles we see how surprised they were at God's gradually emerging intentions for them. And we are astonished at their gutsiness, ultimately, as they tried to follow where the Spirit was leading.

Even so, their advances were partial—which brings our second criterion: It is not required that everything must be fully realized in Scripture. It is required that the Scriptures genuinely point the way to any values and truths we espouse. This is because Scripture remains authoritative for us. In modeling for us the faithful discipleship of the first followers of Christ, the Bible sets our feet on the path of our own onward pilgrimage. A legitimate trajectory between scriptural understandings and our own is necessary; but it is just that: a trajectory. Our task is to extend that potential into our own lives, and to do this along lines consistent with the Christian perspectives that Scripture itself provides for us.

These principles of reading bring us to the pay-off, in principles for our living. How shall we then live?

Sexual Expression in Loving Same-Sex Relationships

We return to the first question with which we opened this chapter: "What biblical implications can we find for the ethics and boundaries of sexual expression in the context of loving same-sex relationships?" How might this look, as we seek scriptural fidelity today? Three broad brushstrokes follow, as illustrations of characteristic features.

The first brushstroke has to do with the ethics of our interpretations.[67] Discussions of issues of homosexuality (as of much else) too often take place on only one of two planes, without allowing either to intersect the other. For some, the strong inner sense of self-evident right and wrong leads them to turn away from Scripture as simply not helpful. Others, unwilling to abandon the Bible as authoritative for faith and practice, refuse to set its witness aside. The latter may, however, take exegesis to be a process of drawing out a single particular message as the text's only potential meaning. This way of thinking can fail to see that all readings, including those of scholars who mean to be as objective as possible, reflect the perspectives one brings to the text. Meaning, it turns out, arises in the encounter between text and reader.[68]

In this light, our very act of reading assumes an ethical dimension. We must own responsibility for the impact that our interpretations exert in the lives of others. Far from presenting our findings with a take-it-or-leave-it shrug that absolves us of accountability toward those impacted by our ostensibly objective analyses, we must recognize the potential for additional insights when the Bible is read by other believers. Seen through other eyes, the Bible provides other connections through other texts that too often escape our own limited vision.[69]

The ethics of reading and interpretation require that those who have most at stake in the outcomes actively participate as equals in the interpretive conversation. We must complement our reading with our listening, so that the planes of our responsibility to the text and of our accountability toward others can be brought into interaction. Only so can we continue something of the dynamic give-and-take that characterized the process of evolving revelation among the earliest communities of Christian believers. By definition, this process will not be unidirectional, and will not always move in a "liberalizing" direction. Nonetheless, it comprises a vital aspect of our accountability to one another, in the Christian unity toward which Paul summons us.

In certain denominations today, the debates have turned deeply rancorous. This may be, in part, because they have not truly been conversations—exchanges in which all voices have equal expression and are equally heard. One of the most telling undertones of Paul's approach to Jew/Gentile relations in the opening two chapters of Romans is the recognition of some arrogance on the part of both groups, against which he has to warn both in the body of his letter. The problem is not that there were some tensions. A creative theological dynamism will always entail tensions. The point is to harness the energy of those tensions, under the reign of Christ, as part of a process of mutual speaking and hearing, in which we truly hear one another, render account to one another, and trust one another. This has happened in the most formative periods of Christian history, and under the guidance of the Spirit can certainly happen again.[70]

This dynamism in the theological life and thought of the first Christians comprised only the beginnings of the conversation to which the church is called for all time. Even as theological benchmarks continue to be established along the way, these are not grounds for stasis.

Interpretation through conversation. Sexual expression in the context of loving same-sex relationships in Christ will answer to and build upon interpretive parameters established through shared perspectives, voiced in conversations, rather than through any dominant structure of authority—ecclesiastical, academic, or other.

The second brushstroke is a double one, addressing the wellsprings of our moral life. With regard to sexual morality, the first and most important truth is the one most visible in Paul's guidance to the

Corinthians. Their lives are now to be different, simply because they are now in Christ. The famous profligacy of their city, in which some of them had previously shared (1 Cor. 6:11), has no more place in their lives.[71] Christ has lifted them above the pagan temples to a new respect for others and for their own bodies as temples of the Spirit (6:19). This is precisely the result of their newfound freedom in Christ; they are delivered from the old enslavements. The fundamental principle of *agapaic* love, as Paul sets it forth (1 Cor. 13), means that there is no place for any kind of sexual immorality (*porneia*), exploitation, or idolatry in the Christian life.

Moral quality. Sexual expression in the context of loving same-sex relationships in Christ does not stand beyond the pale of divine sovereignty. Rather, as with all of holistic Christian life, it comes under the governing framework of Christian morality—with all that this implies for commitment, faithfulness, bodily discipleship, and spiritual growth.

The second aspect of this brushstroke has to do with our deliverance not only from the grip of sin and idolatry but also from ritual strictures. Paul explicitly parallels both kinds of bondage in Galatians 4:1–11, warning against replacing one with the other. In Christ, faithfulness in our sexuality, as in all things, reaches beyond codes of ceremonial purity to deeper levels of responsibility. When Paul in Romans 14 returns to these cultic issues from within his own explicitly Christian stance, he shows the way. There we see that he is less interested in the details of dietary practices or calendrical observances than in the solidarity and mutuality of the congregation. In other words, his concern on the cultic level, as on the moral level, is the same: that all of Christ's followers live in ways that express the unity of the Body. The only difference is that he gets at this via moral principles of salvation theology when dealing with our moral sinfulness, whereas on the level of cultic observances he is quite indifferent as to how his hearers negotiate their harmony.

For most of us under the banner of the new order in Christ, the ancient ritual taboos have largely been emptied; yet we still feel something of the shock Paul's readers must have felt on hearing his pronouncement, "I know and am persuaded in the Lord Jesus that nothing is unclean in itself" (Rom. 14:14). He is talking about matters that in the eyes of some of his fellow believers were as sensitive as homosexual practice. Yet in Christ Paul can go on to relativize the whole scheme of ceremonial purity acknowledging that ritual

"In Christ There Is Neither…"

contamination exists in the eye of the beholder. "But it is unclean for anyone who thinks it unclean."

Like some of the Corinthian believers (1 Cor. 8:7), not all in Rome know that. So Paul seeks to carry his hearers along with him as he moves them toward fuller knowledge—from a pre-Christian to a Christian stance. He obviously understands the lingering distaste on the part of some of his fellow Jewish believers; he may well share it. As far as same-sex relations are concerned, there can be little doubt that he thought of such as unworthy behavior, even this side of the Cross. But given popular understandings of the day, this may have differed only in degree from his reservations toward heterosexual marriage, which he saw primarily as an outlet for sexual passions.

So if Paul retains something of the Judaic aversion toward same-sex relations, he also retains the Judaic assignment of the matter to the level of ceremonial observance. That assignment points the direction. His open-eyed understanding of Calvary's implications, and his principled devotion to those implications as the core of his gospel, lead Paul to treat the ceremonial matters as nothing more than occasions for mutual forbearance in Christ. The questions of dietary and other observances emerge in Romans 14 as clear parallels to the sexual issues in Romans 1. We may wish that Paul had returned to an explicit showing of how this works out in the Christian's sex life, but he is content to allow the matter to stand. In his analogies of food and festival he has provided sufficient guideposts for the day when the church would be ready to follow through.[72]

That day will be marked by an erasure not only of difference between Jew and Greek, but also of difference between "weak" and "strong." Whatever Paul's personal predilections may be, when it comes to matters of ritual observance he consistently positions himself with the "strong" while urging those like himself to respect the sensibilities of the "weak." Until the happy day of collective spiritual maturity, as far as the ritual observances in Romans 14 are concerned, each believer is to make up his/her own mind (14:5) and, by implication, to give every other believer room to do the same.[73] This conclusion is obviously a major leap for many, and Paul has pressed it quite far enough for his time. It remains for us in our time to consider anew whether the Spirit is leading us further in continuation of this process.

Beyond ritual observance. Sexual expression in the context of loving same-sex relationships in Christ will be validated on the grounds of a deeper morality that goes beyond ritual observance, in the context of a faith community that sees itself as growing in Christian understanding toward a unity that transcends "weak" and "strong."

The third brushstroke has to do with our selection of scriptural themes and passages that emerge as relevant. Our discipleship in Christ means being faithful to the Christian principles that Scripture provides to govern our sexual relations. At the same time, this very faithfulness broadens the definition and thus multiplies the lines of our accountability in Christ to scriptural mandates. Now that the issues define themselves as issues of relational responsibility and integrity, genuine morality, and *agapaic* love, new potentials emerge for bridges between the ancient text and our lives today.

Limiting our quest for guidance to those texts that deal explicitly with same-sex relations, especially given their focus on particular acts as viewed from perspectives of ceremonial uncleanness, proves inadequate precisely because such a limitation derives from a category error on our part. From a Christian standpoint, it is fair to ask whether our questions today about homosexuality are more naturally addressed in just those passages that point to the new levels of responsibility Christ brings into all our relationships, especially our domestic ones. Once the revolutionary message of mutuality between life partners is received, if this message is predicated on the core value of Christ's modeling and salvation, its leverage must extend across all relations. If under Christ's lordship, husband and wife are led beyond conventional cultural norms to new levels of mutuality and consideration toward one another (1 Cor. 7), ought not the same principles govern the relationships of all couples in Christ?

New perspectives; other Scriptures. Sexual expression in the context of loving, same-sex relationships in Christ manifests the qualities of mutuality, equality, respect, and consideration that derive from scriptural passages that address heterosexual couples in Christ.

While not exhaustive, these three brushstrokes suggest some characteristic features of scriptural fidelity in regard to these issues today. Taken together, they illustrate the same spirit of accountability to fellow believers, agapaic love, profound and genuine morality, and deliverance from ceremonial law that guides all of Christian life.

Conclusion

"There is no longer Jew or Greek." The struggles among early

"In Christ There Is Neither…"

Christians over ethnicity in all its implications were no less riveting than those we are encountering today over homosexuality. Indeed, given that issues of homoeroticism were perceived from the outset as having to do with the distinction between Jews and Gentiles, the erasure of the barriers between them, in Christ, carries implications for how we should regard same-sex relations today.

As we follow Paul's thought we see that this is not merely a matter of juxtaposing a "modern" concept of sexual orientation against an ancient one, as if we simply "know better" now. Rather, it involves coming to terms with theological developments already emerging in early Christian reflection. Precisely because in Christ there is neither Jew nor Greek the symbols of ethnically defined sanctity lose their substance.

"There is no longer slave or free." In part, the Christian rejection of slavery's accompanying sexual abuses (whether across gender lines or not) may have contributed to the evolving Christian instinct that this polarity, as well, must erode in Christ.

"There is no longer male and female." With this pronouncement, Paul's vision continues to challenge the church. Given that much of the ancient and contemporary objection to same-sex relations is predicated on the alleged confusion of this distinction, the implications of Christ's reign in this regard still summon us beyond our conventional assumptions. The biblical associations of sexism with patriarchalism should alert us to our unfinished work here.

There is no question that the Spirit's onward call, from comfortable stasis to destabilizing rethinking in line with Christ's rule, will continue to affront many. And I realize how readily the perspective represented in this chapter can be cheapened with a dismissive label of "situational ethics." But this perspective does not mean that "anything goes." For all of us, true discipleship can only mean that all aspects of our lives are gladly placed under the criteria that we have identified above: full acceptance of what Christ has done on Calvary, genuine morality, honest engagement with the Scriptures, accountability to one another, openness to new light, sincere regard for the conscience of others and for the unity of Christ's Body. If we citizens of the Kingdom are to continue our journey toward ever-fuller living out of that Kingdom's values in this world, we can only seek to grow beyond the level of mechanical obedience to ordinances that Paul calls "bondage," and into the joyous discipleship that he calls "freedom" (Gal. 5:1).

John R. Jones

How else shall we move beyond Hellenism's (admittedly increasingly reserved) acceptance of even exploitative same-sex activities, and Judaism's unqualified condemnation of every homoerotic expression (no matter what the relational context) on grounds of ethnic and ceremonial separateness? We must follow Paul's pointing; we must do what he did not fully spell out, but which he pointed us toward. If Paul doesn't get us there, he nonetheless opens up the way for us to go there in accord with his principles.

John's Gospel, the latest of the canonical lives of Jesus, still points his readers forward to the Spirit's continuing revelations in the life of the church. Among his final words to his followers, Jesus says "I still have many things to say to you, but you cannot bear them now. When the Spirit of Truth comes, he will guide you into all the truth; for he will not speak on his own, but will speak whatever he hears, and he will declare to you the things that are to come" (John 16:12-13). If John's Gospel, in which the new wine is better (2:10), still speaks to us today in new ways, can we now bear to hear? For Jesus, who is the same yesterday, today, and forever (Heb. 13:8), still reserves the right to surprise us.

Questions for Discussion

1. What are the implications for this discussion, of the fact that Seventh-day Adventists have consistently defended the seventh-day Sabbath as a Christian observance on the grounds of its presence in the Moral Law rather than the ceremonial?
2. What are the threats to the Galatians' new-found freedom in Christ, against which Paul has to warn them in his letter?
3. What does it mean, to speak of extending the trajectories of early Christian thought (as we can trace these in the New Testament) into our lives today? How do the quite different understandings of our sexuality, between their time and ours, figure into this process?
4. In the first chapter of his letter to the Romans, Paul speaks of two divine revelations: of God's grace (1:16, 17) and of God's wrath (1:18). Which of these comes before the other, in Paul's thought? Which of these two revelations is he dealing with, in the rest of his first chapter? From which perspective or standpoint does he write the second half of this chapter?
5. Who owns the process of scriptural interpretation? Who should participate in it, and in the conversations that flow from that

"In Christ There Is Neither…"

process? What if these conversations bring underlying tensions and disagreements to the surface?

Notes and References

1. We may be a little nervous about Jesus' dictum concerning the relation between humankind and the Sabbath in Mark 2:27, but we do accept it.
2. Among those who deny that these stories have anything to do with same-sex intentions is D. Sherwin Bailey, *Homosexuality and the Western Christian Tradition* (New York: Longmans, 1955), 1–28, as discussed at length in John J. McNeill, *The Church and the Homosexual*, 4th ed. (Boston: Beacon, 1976, 1993), 42–50. I do not concur. It is, however, a mark of the common tendency to essentialize "homosexuality" that these stories have been drawn into considerations of homoerotic behavior. It is rather the gang-rape aspect that both epitomizes the evil and negates the accounts' applicability to our purposes here.
3. Amos 4:11; Isa. 1:9–10; 13:19; Jer. 49:18; Lam. 4:6; Ezek. 16:46, 48–49, 53, 55–56; Zeph. 2:9; Deut. 29:22; 32:32. The expression "abominable things" in Ezek. 16:50 is too broad to depend on connections with Lev. 18:22 and 20:13. So also in the New Testament: Matt. 10:15, 11:23–24; Luke 10:12, 17:29; 2 Pet. 2:6; Rev. 11:8.

Jude 6–7, drawing on the apocryphal first book of Enoch, cites ancient contraventions of the barriers between humans and angels as a warning against false teachers in the early church who may have been claiming that their mystical experiences brought them into sexual contact with the "glorious ones" (v. 8), an order of angelic beings. Whether initiated from the side of angels (Gen. 6) or of humans (Gen. 19), such mixing of kinds is labeled as profoundly blasphemous (v. 8). The explicit parallel between the two Genesis examples makes clear that the wrong in both cases is "going off after other flesh" (*sarkos heteras*), as the Greek of v. 7 explicitly puts it—an expression whose import is missed by such renderings as the NRSV's "pursued unnatural lust." The underlying assumption seems comparable to Paul's in 1 Cor. 15:39–41, where he argues on the basis of just such distinctions between our present bodily existence and that of our glorified physical state in the resurrection: God makes various kinds of flesh. See L. William Countryman, *Dirt, Greed and Sex: Sexual Ethics in the New Testament and Their Implications for Today* (Philadelphia: Fortress, 1988), 133–34.

4. Although Karl Heinrich Graf in 1866 first identified the literary integrity of these chapters as forming a separate body of material within Leviticus having its own style and theology, it was August Klostermann who in 1877 first named it the "Holiness Code" (*Heiligkeitsgesetze*) in light of its regular invocation of holiness formulas. These insights have since been borne out by continuing scholarly investigation of a particular circle or "school" of Israelite thinkers, distinguished from the "priestly" tradition.

5. The term *abomination* (Heb *to'evah*) denotes anything that is culturally or ritually forbidden in Jewish law. The Septuagint translates it with "uncleanness" (*akatharsia*) in several places, for instance Prov. 3:22, 6:16, 16:5. In Lev. 18:22, 20:13, the Septuagint uses *bdelugma*, a ritual offense.

6. This insight has enabled Mary Douglas to unlock the structures underlying the Levitical code of distinction between clean and unclean animals. For example, those that are seen to deviate in some way from a perceived order in which characteristic modes of locomotion pertain to particular realms (land, air, water) are unclean—thus polluting and dangerous. See Mary Douglas, "The Abominations of Leviticus," in *Purity and Danger* (New York: Routledge and Kegan Paul, 1966, 2002), 51–71. This is a telling illustration of the way in which the cultural "grid" of an ordered universe, in which holiness is defined as conformity to divinely ordained categories, extends to the classifications of humankind as well. Thus a contravention of gender distinctions among the people who are summoned to holiness implies a contravention of the ethnic and ritual distinctions between them and the Egyptians or Canaanites—as the opening verses of Lev. 18 make clear. Compare Lev. 11:44f.

7. The term *kil'ayim*, used in all three of these prohibitions, means a separate or distinct kind. Similar injunctions in Deut. 22:9–11 also forbid yoking an ox and ass together for plowing.

8. As a construction of the self, the concepts of "homosexuality" and "heterosexuality" appear to arise only in the late nineteenth century. See Seward Hiltner, "Homosexuality: Psychological and Theological Perspectives," *Bulletin of the Christian Association for Psychological Studies* 3, no. 4 (1977):4: "At least in its

"In Christ There Is Neither..."

reference to homosexuality, therefore, the Bible does not speak at all to the principal way in which homosexuality must be understood today." The term *sodomite* is unknown to either the Hebrew or the Greek Scriptures, even simply denoting citizens of Sodom. It is an English coinage imposed on certain English translations.

9. Jesus' saying about eunuchs in Matt. 19:12 envisions three categories. It is possible that the first class, "eunuchs who have been so from birth," could be understood as males who had a physical deformity and/or whose sexual orientation was toward males. Accordingly, it is further possible that the Ethiopian officer whom Philip baptized (Acts 8:26–40) may have been an individual whom we today would call homosexual. It is also possible that the centurion's servant, who was precious to him and whom Jesus healed (Matt. 8:5–13 = Luke 7:1–10), may have been understood as serving his master in sexual as well as in other ways. Plato, *Republic* IX, 574b-c, speaks of a man's erotic love toward a young boy (*pais*, the term used in John 4:51) who has become "dear" (*entimos*) to him—the same term as used in the Lucan account.

10. Regarding the importance of the cross: "For I decided to know nothing among you, except Jesus Christ, and him crucified" (1 Cor. 2:2). In regard to freedom: "For freedom Christ has set us free. Stand firm therefore, and do not submit again to a yoke of slavery" (Gal. 5:1). All scriptural quotations in this chapter are from the New Revised Standard Version (1989), except for the allusion to Gal. 3:28 in the title, which uses the familiar wording of the King James Version (1611).

11. See the juxtaposed vice and virtue lists in Gal. 5:16–24.

12. For vices: Gal. 5:19–21; 1 Cor. 5:10, 11, 6:9, 10; 2 Cor. 12:20; Rom. 1:19–31, 13:13; compare 1 Tim. 1:9, 10; 2 Tim. 3:2–5. Regarding virtues: Gal. 5:22, 23; 2 Cor. 6:6; Phil. 4:8; compare 1 Tim. 6:11. For examples of popular listings, see Robin Scroggs, *The New Testament and Homosexuality* (Philadelphia: Fortress, 1983), 102, n. 6, cites Maximus of Tyre XVIII.84b; XIX.90a; *Sibyllene Oracles* III.36–39; and Epictetus II.16.45, with the observation, "One finds such catalogs everywhere."

13. Philo Judaeus, *Sacrifices of Abel and Cain* 32, comes up with a list of 147 vices.

14. William F. Arndt and F. Wilbur Gingrich, *A Greek-English Lexicon of the New Testament and Other Early Christian Literature*

(Chicago: University of Chicago Press, 1957), q.v. *pornos*. Apart from vice lists, the term *pornos* is also used in Eph. 5:5, and Heb. 12:16, 13:14, as well as twice in the Septuagint (Sirach 23:17). The abstract noun *porneia* appears twenty-five times in the New Testament, including three references to the decision of the Jerusalem Council (Acts 15:20, 29; 21:25).

15. In this arrangement, I am following Scroggs, *New Testament and Homosexuality*, 103.
16. Ibid., 104–5.
17. The phenomenon of voluntary martyrdom, which soon became an issue in some congregations, was an extreme but not uncommon expression of the assertive tendency. The ecclesiastical disavowal of such spontaneous initiatives (*Martyrdom of Polycarp* IV.1) attests the practice among some who may have been motivated by desire for approval among their fellows. Christians' endurance of torture and death could appear steadfast to some, but Marcus Aurelius's passing reference to their stubbornness as distinguished from principled death (*Meditations* II.5) appears to reflect an equally popular impression that they were simply obstinate people. The attitude and conduct of some Christians may have fed the impression.
18. Polycarp, *To the Philippians* 5.3: "Likewise also let the younger men be blameless in all things; caring above all for purity, and curbing themselves from all evil; for it is good to be cut off from the lust of the things in the world, because 'every lust warreth against the Spirit, and neither fornicators (*pornoi*) nor the effeminate (*malakoi*) nor sodomites (*arsenokoitai*) shall inherit the Kingdom of God,' nor they who do iniquitous things." *The Apostolic Fathers*, trans. Kirsopp Lake (Cambridge, Mass.: Harvard University Press, 1912, 1959), 1:289, 291.
19. *The Martyrdom of Polycarp* IX.1; *Apostolic Fathers*, 2:323.
20. The feminine cognate *malakia* is regularly used to express illness, weakness, or faint-heartedness. See Arndt and Gingrich, *Greek-English Lexicon*, viz. *malakia*.
21. Dale B. Martin, "Arsenokoites and Malakos: Meanings and Consequences," in *Biblical Ethics and Homosexuality: Listening to Scripture*, ed. Robert L. Brawley (Louisville, Ky.: Westminster John Knox, 1996), 125–26, finds that in Greco-Roman culture, "In fact, *malakos* more often referred to men who prettied themselves up to further their *heterosexual* exploits" (emphasis original).

"In Christ There Is Neither..."

Compare 127: "The word *malakos* refers to the entire ancient complex of the devaluation of the feminine. Thus people could use *malakos* as an insult directed against men who love women too much."

22. See, for example, James Barr, *The Semantics of Biblical Language* (London: Oxford University Press, 1961), 107: "Etymology is not, and does not profess to be, a guide to the semantic value of words in their current usage, and such value has to be determined from the current usage and not from the derivation."
23. "You shall not lie (*koimethesei*) with a male (*arsenos*) [as with] the lying (*koiten*) of a woman" (Lev. 18:22; similarly in 20:13).
24. For this observation I am dependent upon McNeill, *The Church and the Homosexual*, 52–53.
25. See Robert M. Grant, *Ad Autolycum* (Oxford: Clarendon, 1970), cited in Martin, "Arsenokoites and Malakos," 122: "*Arsenokoites* is separated from the sexual sins by three terms that refer to economic injustice. Would this be the case if it was understood as a condemnation of simple male homosexual intercourse? Furthermore, as Grant notes, Theophilus takes these terms, with the exceptions of *phtheoneros* and *hyperoptes*, from vice lists in the Pauline corpus. Therefore, it is notable that Theophilus places *arsenokoites* in a different position. Grouping it with economic sins, I suggest, reflects his understanding of the social role to which it referred and his rhetorical goal of grouping the vices by category."
26. Martin, "Arsenokoites and Malakos," 120.
27. McNeill, *The Church and the Homosexual*, 53.
28. In NRSV; the Greek text originally had no chapter or verse divisions, much less modern paragraphs.
29. As pointed out by Scroggs, *New Testament and Homosexuality*, 109–10; and Jeffrey S. Siker, "Gentile Wheat and Homosexual Christians: New Testament Directions for the Heterosexual Church," in *Biblical Ethics and Homosexuality*, 142–43.
30. There are in fact no sexual references at this level in either paragraph. The term *poneria* ("evil") is better attested in the ancient manuscripts at v. 30 than is the alternative reading *porneia*, which would be a general reference to sexual immorality.
31. Plato, *Laws* 772d-e, 773b, 840c.
32. This despite the known same-sex preferences of Seneca and certain other Stoic figures.

33. The chapter "Same-Sex Love" in this book explores the theological significance of giving and receiving pleasure in the Christian life.
34. Plato, *Phaedrus*, 250e.
35. Plutarch, *Erôtikos* 751c, for example, has Daphnaeus refer to pederasty as a "union contrary to nature," in contrast to heterogenital sex. Athenaeus, *Deipnosophists* XIII, 565c (Egypt, c. 200 C.E.), quotes a dinner guest as warning philosophers against indulging in passion that is contrary to nature.
36. This opinion is expressed as a common assumption in several Greek and Roman sources, including Plato, *Laws* 836c. 840d-e; and Plutarch, *Whether Beasts are Rational* 990d-f.
37. John Boswell, *Christianity, Social Tolerance and Homosexuality: Gay People in Western Europe from the Beginning of the Christian Era to the Fourteenth Century* (Chicago: University of Chicago Press, 1980), 58: "Terms for these categories [homosexual and heterosexual] appear extremely rare in ancient literature, which nonetheless contain abundant descriptions and accounts of homosexual and heterosexual activity. It is apparent that the majority of residents of the ancient world were unconscious of any such categories."
38. Used with the accusative case (as here) the preposition *para* has the basic spatial meaning of "alongside." Used metaphorically, it typically means "against," "contrary to," or, more mildly, "in contradistinction to." So used, it does sometimes carry the comparative idea of "more than." F. Blass and A. Debrunner, *A Greek Grammar of the New Testament and Other Christian Literature*, 9th ed., trans. Robert W. Funk (Chicago: University of Chicago Press, 1961) §236.
39. At least with reference to males, in Rom. 1:27. As for females (v. 26), despite the contrary view by interpreters from St. Augustine to Daniel Helminiak, *What the Bible Really Says about Homosexuality* (Tajique, N.M.: Alamo Square, 1994, 2000), 87–89, the *homoiôs* between vv. 26 and 27 sets up a parallel between the two genders, which surely must include engagement in same-sex activities since that is what is in view here.
40. Boswell, *Christianity, Social Tolerance and Homosexuality,* 110.
41. Victor Paul Furnish adduces these four points in "The Bible and Homosexuality: Reading the Texts in Context," in *Homosexuality in the Church: Both Sides of the Debate*, ed. Jeffrey S. Siker

(Louisville, Ky.: Westminster John Knox, 1994), 26–27. Siker recapitulates them in "New Testament Directions for the Heterosexual Church," in *Biblical Ethics and Homosexuality*, 142–43.

42. Helminiak, *What the Bible Really Says*, 85.
43. At least with regard to adult Roman citizens, especially in passive roles. See Boswell, *Christianity, Social Tolerance and Homosexuality*, 74–75.
44. Philo Judaeus, *Special Laws* III.37, quoted in Scroggs, *New Testament and Homosexuality*, 74–75. Compare Plato, *Laws* I.636c, in Scroggs, *New Testament and Homosexuality*, 59–60: "When male unites with female for procreation, the pleasure experienced is held to be due to nature (*kata phusin*), but contrary to nature (*para phusin*) when male mates with male or female with female."
45. For example, "Formerly, when you did not know God, you were enslaved to beings that by nature [that is, by their nature] are not gods" (Gal. 4:8).
46. The occurrences are in Rom. 1:26; 2:14, 27; 11:21, 24; 1 Cor. 11:14; Gal. 2:15; 4:8: Eph. 2:3. God, indeed, works "contrary to nature" (*para phusin*) in grafting the Gentiles into the trunk of the Hebrew heritage (Rom. 11:24). According to Furnish, *Bible and Homosexuality*, 30, the scholarly consensus is that "no such 'creation theology' as that alleged for Rom. 1:26–27 is evident in any of Paul's other references to what is 'natural' or 'unnatural'." To the contrary, Robert A. J. Gagnon, *The Bible and Homosexual Practice: Texts and Hermeneutics* (Nashville, Tenn.: Abingdon, 2001), 246–70 passim, sees in Paul's conception of nature the principle of the divinely created order established in Genesis 1, with theological implications for moral conduct.
47. For example, "Does not nature itself teach you that if a man wears long hair, it is degrading to him, but if a woman has long hair, it is her glory?" (1 Cor. 11:14, 15).
48. So Paul can quote with agreement the slogan of some in Corinth that "no idol in the world really exists" (1 Cor. 8:4).
49. In this, Paul's approach is comparable to the one he adopts in Rom. 14, where he is less interested in the rightness or wrongness of one or another position regarding diet or observance of holy days than in allaying the spirit of mutual judgment that is destroying the unity of the body of Christ. The issues here, in fact,

appear to line up with the Jew/Gentile polarities Paul is addressing in the first chapters of his letter.

50. Paul's treatment, in common with the Jewish thought of his day, is utterly uninterested in distinguishing among any of the various forms of same-sex interactions that shape discussions from the Hellenistic standpoint. For the Greco-Roman world, there were male-male relations between teachers and students, between temple prostitutes and their clients, between masters and slaves. The character of these interactions certainly varied from one context to another. The Greek vocabulary itself tells the story: One could speak, for example, of a *paiderastes* ("boy-lover"), a *kinaidos* or *erômenos* (a beloved one), or even a *paidophthoros* (a seducer or kidnapper of boys). Thus any particular Gentile discussion tends to be about one or another of these defined interactions, rather than about an overarching topic of same-sex relations as such.

When Paul, by contrast, baldly treats the matter in terms of the act itself, his thought runs along lines of classic rabbinic casuistry—ethical judgments of specific deeds in and of themselves. Such a model essentializes all same-sex activity in ways that reflect the Jewish perspectives of Paul's time more than those of his larger world.

51. This is not the last place in Romans where Paul will provisionally ally himself with the prejudices of his Jewish Christian hearers, in order to keep them with him. He employs similar strategies in dealing with their impatient demands. The erasure of difference between Jewish and Gentile worlds is not attained by the assimilation of one to the other, as if the Gentiles, even in Christ, had to become Jews. The earliest Christian believers wrestled with that notion before awakening to the full reach of their new reality: that both previous categories are now transcended, and so rendered moot, in Christ.

Yet even Paul, the most clear-eyed proclaimer of this new vision, knows in his letter to the congregants in Rome that his fellow Jewish Christians will object. "Then what becomes of our advantage?" "What, after all, did our human father Abraham gain?" "Has God rejected his people?" In his letter he anticipates their questions—questions long shouted at him from non-Christian Jewish audiences and that continued to bedevil Jew/Gentile relations in Christ. In dealing with these, he mollifies his fellow

"In Christ There Is Neither…"

Christian Jews in much the way he has come to do with his non-Christian Jewish hearers: They are entrusted with the oracles of God (3:2). To them belong the adoption, the glory, the covenants, the giving of the law, the worship and the promises. The patriarchs, even the messiah, arise from them (9:4f). Yet these turn out to be trophies of a fading past. "Are we Jews any better off?" Ultimately, Paul must say "No, not really" (3:9). With this, the mask comes off and the gospel can stand forth in its full truth. All of this represents rhetorical strategies developed during his years of verbal give-and-take in the synagogues. The doxology at the end of 1:25, like the one at the end of 9:5, is an obvious vestige of that verbal experience.

52. Furnish, *Bible and Homosexuality*, 28, notes, "It is apparent from both the wording and the content of Paul's remark in Romans that he shared the common Hellenistic-Jewish view of 'homosexuality.' There is nothing distinctively Pauline, or even Christian, about that remark. Philo himself could have written it—and so could any number of pagan moralists, given just a few changes."

53. Countryman, *Dirt, Greed and Sex*, 115–16, points out that the "error" (*plane*) at the end of Rom. 1:27 is best understood as the Gentiles' idolatry. The result, then, in accord with the rest of the passage, is the Gentiles' impure passions and practices.

54. In accord with the grammatical principle that the demonstrative pronoun "such things" (*toiauta*) in v. 32 should take as its antecedent the nearest possible referent, it is the vices of 1:28–31 that deserve death, not the homogenital acts back in vv. 26–27.

55. Helminiak, *What the Bible Really Says*, 96; and Countryman, *Dirt, Greed and Sex*, 116, both correctly catch the implication of the perfect participle *peplerômenous* in v. 29. In parallel with v. 28, God surrendered the Gentiles to their homoerotic practices in the wake of their profound sinfulness.

56. For example, Gagnon, *Bible and Homosexual Practice*, 255–56, where natural law is an expression not so much of culturally defined gender roles as of the sheer physical complementarity of the sexes: "For Paul it was a simple matter of commonsense observation of human anatomy and procreative function that even pagans, otherwise oblivious to God's direct revelations in the Bible, had no excuse for not knowing."

57. So Stanton L. Jones and Mark A. Yarhouse, *Homosexuality: The Use of Scientific Research in the Church's Moral Debate*

(Downer's Grove, Il: InterVarsity, 2000), 179: "(1) homosexual behavior violates God's revealed will, (2) homosexual behavior is contrary to God's creational purposes for sexual intimacy, (3) the state of having homosexual desires is of uncertain moral status but certainly must be viewed as a deviation from the Creator's intent for those individuals and must be seen as representing an occasion for sin (just as does heterosexual lust)...." Similarly, Gagnon, *Bible and Homosexual Practice*; also, Hays, *Moral Vision of the New Testament*.

58. Part of the problem is our tendency to single out individual verses and absolutize them by reading them in isolation from their religio-cultural matrix. In the case of the Levitical materials this masks from us the larger issues of the overall attitude expressed throughout the individual prohibitions. As Gary David Comstock, *Gay Theology without Apology* (Cleveland, Ohio: Pilgrim, 1993), 63–64, says, "One looks in vain for an example of inclusive community, egalitarian principles, or a theology of loving outreach and pluralistic justice in Leviticus."

59. Dan O. Via, "The Bible, the Church, and Homosexuality," in Dan O. Via and Robert A. J. Gagnon, *Homosexuality and the Bible: Two Views* (Minneapolis: Fortress, 2003), 28. Ibid., 27, captures the larger hermeneutic issue: "It is precisely the concept of the unclean that regards certain objects, processes and actions as manifesting a certain contagion that automatically contaminates without regard for motives or intentions. Gagnon's assimilation of homosexual practice to the unclean brings him into conflict with those important strands in both testaments that maintain the reciprocal interaction between actions and dispositions of the heart. To ignore the latter is to have a reduced view of the structure of human existence." Jones and Yarhouse, *Homosexuality*, 168–70, illustrate the way such a reading-stance pulls one back toward a reappropriation of theocratic civil and ceremonial regulations into our life in Christ today.

60. Countryman, *Dirt, Greed and Sex*, 117. Compare Helminiak, *What the Bible Really Says,* 101: "Paul's terminology in Romans 1 presents male homogenital acts as socially unacceptable or impure—but not as ethically wrong."

61. M. L. Andreasen, *The Sabbath* (Washington, D.C.: Review and Herald, 1942), 145, is typical of the classic line of argument among Seventh-day Adventists: "These ceremonial and temple

"In Christ There Is Neither..."

laws terminated when the temple service ceased to be of value at the death of Christ. All Christians believe that they were abolished and annulled in the great sacrifice on Calvary. Col. 2:14. It is not of these laws that we speak, but of the law of God contained in the ten precepts. This law we believe to be of as much force as ever, and binding upon Christians and upon all men in all ages."

62. "These are only a shadow of what is to come; but the substance belongs to Christ" (Col. 2:17).
63. For example, Michel Foucault, *History of Sexuality I: An Introduction*, trans. Robert Hurley (New York: Random House, 1978), 43, traces out the notion of sexual orientation, analyzing how the construction of same-sex orientation as a clinical or psychological "disorder" first arose in the nineteenth century.
64. Siker, "Gentile Wheat and Homosexual Christians," 140.
65. The myth of human origins in Plato, *Symposium* 189c–193d, hinting at a primordial third sex oriented toward its own gender does not refute this.
66. The point is not how relatively common or uncommon such examples are. It is enough that they do exist, and that as will be indicated below, the Scriptures do have pertinent words to apply to such.
67. This point is prompted by the challenge presented to the Society of Biblical Literature by Elizabeth Schüssler Fiorenza, in a presidential address, "The Ethics of Interpretation: Decentering Biblical Scholarship," *Journal of Biblical Literature* 107 (1988):3–17. The issues she raises of responsibility to the scholarly disciplines of textual interpretation and accountability to others deserve much more consideration in connection with this present topic.
68. This does not reduce the text to a mirror, merely reflecting the reader's own preconceptions. The text does exert controls, by means of its underlying structures of meaning-potential. Such potential is variously actualized, however, through varied acts of reading. Even so, the resultant meanings do have the potential to cut across a given reader's preconceptions, awakening new insights.
69. For example, Comstock, *Gay Theology*, Chap. 3, finds insightful parallels between the situation and response of Queen Vashti in the book of Esther and his experience as a homosexual male in today's society.

John R. Jones

70. Carl S. Dudley and Earle E. Hilgert, *New Testament Tensions and the Contemporary Church* (Philadelphia: Fortress, 1987) trace out the way in which deep disagreements were not papered over in the early church but were used as occasions for fuller understanding and theological advancement when the tensions were worked through with mutual respect.
71. There is some evidence that already by Paul's time a verb "to Corinthianize" (*korinthiazesthai*) had been coined to denote living in a luxurious and profligate manner. A century later, Pausanius, *Description of Greece* II.3.2, quotes a common saying among sailors of the time: "Not for every man is the voyage to Corinth."
72. That Paul and his converts saw direct parallels between issues of dietary and sexual purity is clear in 1 Cor. 6:12–20, where he argues by analogy from the former to the latter.
73. Compare Jesus: "And why do you not judge for yourselves what is right?" (Luke 12:57). Evidently, the priesthood of every believer is to be exercised under the high priesthood of Christ who sympathizes with our limitations (Heb. 4:15) in ways that give us courage to grow as new insights become available (5:11–14).

Same-sex Love: Theological Considerations

By Fritz Guy

The best approach to thinking theologically about same-sex love and its accompanying physical intimacy is to consider this kind of relationship in the broader context of romantic love and sexuality in general. Only in this way can a sound theological understanding of same-sex love be developed.

The theological considerations outlined here consist of a series of affirmations:

1. Physical pleasure and sexual intimacy belong to the created goodness of humanness.
2. Sexual intimacy symbolizes a profound personal and moral relationship.
3. The moral quality of physical intimacy does not depend on the sex of the partners.
4. Scripture does not condemn all same-sex love.
5. Same-sex love is not "unnatural."
6. Antagonism toward same-sex love has deep psychosocial roots.
7. Christians should affirm caring, committed same-sex love.

Fritz Guy

1. Physical pleasure and sexual intimacy belong to the created goodness of humanness.

Physicality—along with mentality, sociality, and spirituality—is a defining characteristic of humanness. Although physicality is not a distinguishing characteristic (since all forms of life on planet Earth are physical), to be human is necessarily to be physical. Not to be physical is not to be human.

The essential goodness of human physicality is confirmed by three theological considerations. First, the biblical narrative of the creation of humanity affirms its essential embodiment: humanity was not a creation out of nothing *(creatio ex nihilo)*; it was creation out of the most mundane form of matter available—soil from the ground (Gen. 2:7). Even the name given to this new kind of reality, "Adam" (Heb. *'adam*), reflects its formation from the ground (*'adamah*), and might be translated "groundling." A human being is not essentially a spiritual reality housed in a material body, but a physical reality enlivened and maintained by the divine power that underlies and sustains all natural and spiritual processes. Second, in the person of Jesus of Nazareth, God "became flesh"—that is, existed physically (John 1:14). It was "in the body" that Jesus suffered and died" (2 John 7), and anyone who says otherwise should be regarded as a deceiver (1 Pet. 4:4; 3:18). And third, the ultimate future of humanness is a thoroughly physical, resurrected existence in the presence of God. Jesus, whose own resurrection was a prototype of eschatological resurrection, called explicit attention to the physicality of his resurrection existence (Luke 26:39).

Physical pleasure, the enjoyment of one's body beyond the maintenance of physical health and the absence of pain, is one of the blessings of physical existence and part of the created goodness of humanness.[1] Physical pleasure is intrinsically good, to be valued in and for itself. It becomes morally problematic only when it is sought or experienced at the expense of other values essential to one's overall well-being or the well-being of others.

Adventist thinking has long emphasized the multidimensional unity of human personhood. The idea of the wholeness of persons has proceeded from theology to health care, and to the inclusion of spiritual nurture as part of "whole person" health care. All this attention to human physicality leads logically to a recognition of physical pleasure as a proper function of bodies and in itself an entirely appropriate

Same-sex Love: Theological Considerations

reason to be as healthy as possible.[2] It is right to take good care of bodies—one's own and others'—and it is right also to enjoy them. Physical pleasure as such is a created good, not an evil seduction.

Sexuality, the desire for and act of sharing physical intimacy and pleasure with a partner, involves all of the senses to one extent or another, and a prominent characteristic of physical intimacy is the pleasure of orgasm. Regrettably, however, much of the Christian tradition has taken a negative view of the body and especially of physical pleasure, often regarding it as the cause of sin. In the earliest centuries, the sexual ideal was certainly not celebration, or even procreation, but renunciation.

Augustine (354–430), the most influential figure in Christian theology after the apostle Paul, believed that physical intimacy was an evil to be avoided as far as possible, even in marriage. He recognized that physical intimacy yields "the greatest of all bodily pleasures"—and that was the problem. "So possessing indeed is this pleasure, that at the moment of time in which it is consummated, all mental activity is suspended."[3] Augustine believed also that the reason human beings are born with a tendency to sin is that they are conceived through an act of sexual passion.[4] Jesus, of course, was the one miraculous exception to this universal depravity, and the fact that he was conceived without a sexual act explains why he, and only he, was "without sin" Heb. 4:15. Later theologians followed Augustine's lead down this wrong road, and some went even farther, warning married couples that the Holy Spirit left their bedrooms whenever they engaged in sexual intercourse.[5]

But sexuality, like the physicality of which it is an aspect and including the physical pleasure it generates, is intrinsically good—although, like everything else that is human, in practice it is often distorted and morally flawed. Sexual intimacy and pleasure do not need to be legitimated by an intention or possibility of procreation, which is only one of its functions. Otherwise, sexual intercourse between persons unable (or no longer able) to bear children would be morally wrong. And the intrinsic goodness of sexual intimacy is not a recent discovery; at least by the seventeenth century, some Protestants realized that "loving companionship, not procreation, is the central meaning of sexuality."[6]

There are both biblical and theological reasons to regard sexuality as a reflection of God's relationship to creation, especially to humanity, in both creativity and vulnerability. God's attitude toward humanity is often expressed in Scripture by means of marital and sexual metaphors.

"As the bridegroom rejoices over the bride, so shall your God rejoice over you" (Isa. 62:5).[7] There is, of course, no reason to suppose that deity is, like humanity, intrinsically physical, and good reasons to suppose that it is not.

2. Sexual intimacy symbolizes a profound personal and moral relationship.

Human sexual intimacy is a symbol that both points to a reality beyond itself and participates in that reality, thus opening up levels of reality that human beings would not otherwise be able to experience.[8] The reality to which sexual intimacy points and in which it participates is a relationship of permanent, preeminent concern for and commitment to the total well-being of one's sexual partner. Sexual intimacy expresses this reality and also enriches it. Conversely, the experience of sexual intimacy is enhanced by an awareness of this symbolic meaning in the same way that the enjoyment of a meal is enhanced by the presence and participation of a cherished friend. The food itself does not actually taste better, but the total experience is certainly better. As humans, we are not only *homo sapiens* but also *homo symbolicus.*

Because humanness is by its very nature multidimensional, physical intimacy is intrinsically relational. This is why there is no such thing as "casual" intimacy, although many people want to be casual *about* it. Even if it is not a celebration of an intimate *relationship,* every occasion of sexual intimacy "does constitute some kind of bond with the partner."[9] Besides its expressive dimension as a "natural symbol," it has also a biopsychological dimension, and both contribute to personal bonding.[10]

Thus sexual intimacy carries inevitable and often profound consequences for whatever relationship exists, whether or not the partners intend them.[11] What both partners need—and at some level really want—is the intimacy of two persons blended into one emotionally and spiritually. When this occurs, the result can be an ecstatic, self-transcending experience of love in which two persons let go of themselves and concentrate their attention on enhancing the physical pleasure and emotional fulfillment of the other. Although for many men sexual intercourse "does not mean *in the first instance* loving intimacy, sensuous playfulness, babies, or the *eros* that draws us into communion with all else" but may be merely "a happening, a sexual event involving our genitals," there is no good reason to

Same-sex Love: Theological Considerations

suppose that profoundly meaningful sexual experience is unavailable to men, including men in relationships of same-sex love.[12]

Since human fulfillment and flourishing entails morality, the moral dimension is essential to sexuality's distinctively human quality. The depth and power of sexual desire and the exquisite pleasure of sexual intimacy make the moral considerations especially significant—even though, as in other human activities, much sexual intimacy is morally ambiguous.

In the light of biblical materials such as the Seventh Commandment (Exod. 20:14) and the Golden Rule (Matt. 7:12), specific moral criteria for optimal sexual intimacy are immediately evident.

- It does not compete with any other relationship or violate any prior commitment.
- It is not coercive, exploitive, or manipulative. It is not instrumental or strategic, an exchange for some other desired good—financial consideration, professional advancement, or other favorable treatment.
- It is truly mutual and egalitarian. The desire to experience pleasure does not in the long run exceed the desire to give pleasure, or in the short run overwhelm it.
- It respects the vulnerabilities it engenders. It includes concern for each other's safety, security, and comfort in the broadest and deepest sense.
- It presupposes and expresses trust, and it evokes and sustains trust.

Taken seriously, these moral criteria carry important practical implications. They call for a rigorous self-discipline and an "ethic of tenderness"[13] They exclude sexual seduction. They also explain why a genuinely loving relationship intended to be permanent provides a uniquely valuable context in which mutually vulnerable, intimate knowing is facilitated and the intrinsic goal of love can be given fuller expression.

These criteria, furthermore, are theologically significant insofar as sexual intimacy at its best symbolizes the desire of Divine Reality to give pleasure to, and (in some sense beyond our comprehension) receive pleasure from, human reality. Thus, in spite of its motivation by a negative view of human physicality, the traditional allegorization of the Song of Songs as a metaphor for the relation between God and humanity is not entirely misguided. The mistake is denying the obvious meaning of the Song's sexual content instead of seeing in just that content a symbol of God's own desire to give to and receive pleasure from human reality.

3. The moral quality of physical intimacy does not depend on the sex of the partners.

Although the theologically based moral criteria of optimal sexual intimacy specify the *quality of the personal interaction* of the partners, both in the interpersonal context and in the actual experience of sexual intimacy, these criteria do not involve the *sex* of the partners. Obviously the vast majority of people choose to experience sexual intimacy with partners of the other sex, and the majority of persons who choose to experience sexual intimacy with a partner of the same sex have a deep-rooted, persistent inclination to do so. But "what describes most couples need not prescribe for every couple."[14] Most people are right-handed, although a minority are left-handed and a very few are truly ambidextrous; but we do not make the characteristics of the majority a requirement for every individual.

Nor is the moral quality of same-sex physical intimacy dependent on sexual orientation. Although a combination of genetic, biological, and experiential factors may significantly influence one's choice of sexual partners, the moral quality of physical intimacy is determined neither by the sex of the partner nor by the factors involved in the choice, but only by the moral quality of the intimacy itself, as defined by the kind of criteria identified above. In fact, some same-sex couples clearly meet the moral criteria for optimal sexual intimacy better than many opposite-sex couples. An Adventist psychotherapist at a community mental health clinic reports his experience:

> For about six months, I had two interesting couples scheduled for the same day, one at 2:00 p.m. and the other at 3:00 p.m. They provided me with two different visions of a biblical marriage.
>
> The 2:00 p.m. couple, both members in good standing at a local Seventh-day Adventist Church (where one of them was the head elder), was miserable. He had never physically assaulted his wife, nor had he been sexually involved with other women. He took seriously his interpretation of the curse of Genesis 3:16 (echoed, he thought, in Eph. 5:22–24), where

Same-sex Love: Theological Considerations

God condemns Eve (and, all of her daughters) to be "ruled over" by her husband. He ruled with a firm, though (in his mind) fair hand. His wife had almost no autonomy or control in her life, and was expected to comply with her husband's directives. He insisted that he was in faithful compliance with Paul's commission to husbands to love their wives as Christ did the Church (Eph. 5:25). His directives to his wife were always in what he saw as her best interest and designed to keep her clean, radiant, and blameless (5:26–27). If they sometimes disagreed about where her best interests lay, well, as he saw it, Scripture was pretty clear about whose view must prevail. Fifteen years into their marriage—after giving birth to three children and regularly performing all of her wifely duties—the head elder's wife decided to stop having sexual relations with her husband. As I say, they were miserable.

The 3:00 p.m. couple attended a Christian church of a different denomination, where one was also an elder. They had been together for about fifteen years, as well. They were miserable, too, but for a different reason—one of them had breast cancer and was probably going to die soon. They had spent a decade and a half sharing real intimacy and companionship with each other, providing for each other what they saw as the biblical imperative of a "suitable helper" (Gen. 2:18 NIV). They made their decisions together and resolved conflict by searching for common ground, values, and goals. They had each made sacrifices for—and accepted them from—the other. They had raised two children together, and had looked forward to watching them grow up together. They had been sexually faithful to each other throughout their relationship, and continued to fulfill each other in that way, as well. They were in therapy to get support and to help them deal with anger and grief over the likely too-early death of one and the loss of their shared future. Both of them, of course, were women.[15]

Diversity in the choice of physical intimacy with persons of the same or the opposite sex goes beyond the usual categories of "heterosexual," "homosexual," and "bisexual." The complex interaction of diverse genetic, cultural, and experiential factors yields a wide variability of dynamics in the choice of partners. Some persons are not attracted to, and are even repelled by, the possibility of sexual intimacy with a person of one sex or the other. Others, however, are basically capable of physical intimacy with either sex but may, by experiences with male or female persons, be disinclined toward intimacy with one sex or the other. Still others are guided not by the sex of a potential partner but by individual attractive factors such as intellectual interests, emotional compatibility, and personal values and concerns. Thus, besides the continuum of sexual preferences and choices reflected by the Kinsey scale, a complex web of specific personal factors may also be involved.

In modern Western culture, in contrast to other cultures (including those that were the context of biblical revelation), sexual intimacy with a person of the other sex is much less closely connected with procreation. The ready availability of contraceptive measures means that such intimacy is far from a *sufficient* condition for procreation, and the possibility of artificial insemination means that it is no longer a *necessary* condition. Perhaps coincidentally, these scientific and technological developments have been accompanied both by a growing awareness of the positive role of sexual intimacy in marital relationships and mental health, and by an increasing openness to same-sex love. For more and more people, religious as well as secular, same-sex love is "hardly a moral question."[16]

There are no evident theological or psychological reasons for condemning same-sex love. It is neither a sin nor a sickness. It is not a psychological, moral, or spiritual aberration, much less a "perversion." It is a "problem" only because of the widespread and profound prejudice against it. But "if we define sickness as the inability or unwillingness to conform to society's regulations, then many others besides those with the homosexual way of life—including many religious groups such as the Christians of the first centuries of our era [and the Adventists of the mid-nineteenth century]—would come under this designation."[17]

Nevertheless, two kinds of objections to same-sex love call for serious consideration—namely, the claim that Scripture condemns such love, and the argument that it is "contrary to nature," not only because it cannot result in procreation but also because it disregards the natural complementarity of male and female. An objection that does not merit detailed consideration here is that an affirmation of same-sex love is a radical departure from historic Christian and Adventist thinking and is a capitulation to modern culture. From its beginning, Adventist Christianity has understood itself as called not only to theological

Same-sex Love: Theological Considerations

criticism of traditional religious thinking, but also to theological self-criticism. The theological question is never whether a belief or attitude is orthodox, but always whether it is true.[18]

4. Scripture does not condemn all same-sex love.

The widespread belief that the Bible condemns all same-sex love is the result of a serious misunderstanding and misuse of Scripture. Underlying this misunderstanding and misuse may well be a psychological need to rationalize, absolutize, and universalize one's own sexual attractions and aversions. If so, what feminist understandings of Scripture have done to supplement, enrich, and sometimes correct traditional ("masculist") interpretations may eventually be paralleled by the enrichment and correction of traditional ("straight") interpretations of Scripture as a result of gay and lesbian understandings.[19] In any case, it is a logical mistake to trivialize such new understandings as "biased." Traditional understandings carry an even greater risk of bias, because along with the inevitable bias of cultural context and individual experience, the religious and theological tradition itself engenders an inevitable (although usually unrecognized) bias.[20]

Eight scriptural passages are frequently cited as condemning same-sex erotic relationships, beginning with two narratives—the attempted rape of Abraham's guests in Sodom (Gen. 19:4–11) and the actual rape of the Levite's concubine (Judg. 19:22–25).[21] The legal texts of Leviticus include a prohibition of lying "with a man as with a woman" (18:22) and a mandated death penalty (20:13). In the New Testament, there are three Pauline references—the designation of the "shameful lusts" of female and male homosexual intimacy as consequences of idolatry (Rom. 1:26–27), the inclusion of male homosexual intimacy among the activities that keep a person from participating in God's program in the world (1 Cor. 6:9–10), and as contrary to "sound teaching" (1 Tim. 1:10).[22] Finally, the brief letter of Jude associates the cities of Sodom and Gomorrah with "sexual immorality" and "immoral lust" (vs. 7).

But the theological and moral implications of these passages are not as clear as many readers suppose. While it is evident that none of the references approves physical intimacy between persons of the same sex, it is equally evident that none of them explicitly refers to the kind of loving sexuality that meets the moral criteria for all sexual relationships and is the focus of these theological considerations. The narratives explicitly involve violence and humiliation that are in no circumstances morally tolerable. Other references may well involve pagan worship, temple prostitution, or the extramarital sexual intimacy that was common in Greco-Roman society.

Nevertheless the scriptural fact remains that, as the popular quip goes, "God made Adam and Eve, not Adam and Steve." In the cultural environment in which the Genesis accounts originated, with its familial and societal need for procreation, the majority practice of physical intimacy with a person of the other sex had the practical value of fulfilling the mandate to "be fruitful and multiply" and "fill the earth" (Gen. 1:28). But this functional fact hardly translates directly into a theological conclusion that physical intimacy between persons of the same sex is morally wrong. The early chapters of Genesis provide no reason to suppose that the first humans represented all of the subsequent variations of human ability and personality. We simply do not know when humans first experienced same-sex love, any more than we know when they first became introverts and extraverts.

Moreover, there is significant precedent for taking as morally normative broad scriptural *principles* rather than specific *prescriptions*. It is Scripture *as a whole* that is properly the "rule of faith and practice." Slavery is explicitly approved in the Hebrew Bible (Exod. 21:5–6; Num. 31:26–47) and accepted in the New Testament (Eph. 6:5–9; Phil. 16), and 150 years ago these scriptural facts were cited as justification of Christian ownerships of slaves. The Hebrew Bible also contains numerous other explicit instructions that are not now regarded as normative, and in some instances, such as the sayings in the Sermon on the Mount (Matt. 6:17–48; see also Heb. 1:1–4), the teachings of Jesus represent a conscious moral and religious development beyond the Hebrew Bible.[23]

Some same-sex friendships described in Scripture may actually have included physical intimacy. One possible instance is the profound and intense affection between David and Jonathan. From the beginning of their relationship "the soul of Jonathan was bound to the soul of David, and Jonathan loved him as his own soul….Jonathan made a covenant with David….Jonathan took off the robe he was wearing and gave it to David, along with his armor, and even his sword, his bow, and his belt" (1 Sam. 18:3). Jonathan's father (Saul) was outraged by the relationship: "You son of a perverse, rebellious woman! Don't I know that you've chosen the son of Jesse to your own shame and the shame of your mother's nakedness? As long as that son of Jesse lives on the earth, neither you nor your kingship will be secure" (1 Sam. 20:30). Saul's language implies a suspicion that the relationship between Jonathan and David went beyond that of "best friends." After Jonathan's death in battle, David expressed his bereavement in romantic terms: "To me you were greatly beloved. Your love to me was wonderful, greater than the love of women" (2 Sam. 1:27).

Another possible instance involves the Roman military officer who asked Jesus to heal his *pais* ("boy"). On the basis of this report (Matt. 8:5–13), the *pais* could have been the officer's son, slave, or (in a culture where teenagers were often sold into marriage or homosexual relationships) sexual partner. But a parallel Gospel account (Luke 7:1–10) refers to a *doulos* ("slave" or "servant") who was *entimos* ("valuable," "precious"); and since in ancient Greek *doulos* never referred to a child, the *pais* was evidently an especially valuable slave who might well have been the officer's sexual partner.

A third possible instance is the Ethiopian government official who was encountered by the Christian evangelist Philip on the road to Gaza (Acts 8:26–40). This official is consistently described in English translations as a "eunuch," a straightforward transliteration of the Greek *eunouchos*, regularly used to refer to a castrated male. But etymologically *eunouchos* meant "one having charge of the bed"—that is, a male serving at the royal court as supervisor of the harem. Having been castrated, and thus regarded as having been "deprived of his manhood, the eunuch was also deprived of his identity with his fellow men. This, in turn, made him even more suitable as a guard to the harem, and because of the social ostracism, increased his loyalty towards this master."[24] But *eunouchos* was also used metaphorically, as reflected in a saying of Jesus that employs the word five times (three times in the plural, and twice in a verb form): "Some *eunouchoi* are from the mother's womb, and some *eunouchoi* are 'eunuchized' by humans, and some *eunouchoi* have 'eunuchized' themselves for the sake of heaven's program" (Matt. 19:12). Of these three kinds of *eunouchoi*, the second almost certainly involved some form of castration and the third probably involved self-chosen celibacy.[25] The first more plausibly involved an intrinsic aversion to heterosexual intimacy (which might have been the result of a preference for same-sex intimacy) than a physical deformity, which was arguably as rare then as now. This might also have been the Ethiopian official's situation. Ancient Jewish and secular literature indicates that "eunuchs" were sometimes described in terms remarkably similar to modern stereotypes of homosexual men.[26]

These possible instances are, of course, highly conjectural, and many heterosexual readers may regard them as implausible if not utterly unthinkable. None of the stories contains an explicit recognition, much less an endorsement, of same-sex love. What is not at all conjectural, however, is the fact that "Jesus scandalized his pious contemporaries by his willingness to accept highly dubious people."[27] And since Christians believe that Jesus was the incarnation of God, this means that Jesus' acceptance of people was in fact God's acceptance. Given what we know about human nature and same-sex love, statistically it is highly probable that *some* of the figures in the scriptural narratives were participants in same-sex erotic relationships.

The selectivity with which Christians cite Scripture as the ground of their moral convictions is clear evidence that historical, cultural, and social factors are also at work. It is always useful to remember the theological principle cited earlier—that "there is no excuse for anyone in taking the position that there is no more truth to be revealed, and that all our expositions of Scripture are without an error," that "age will not make error into truth," and that "truth can afford to be fair."

5. Same-sex love is not "unnatural."

It is true that Scripture usually links sexual intimacy with procreation, beginning early in the human story: "Adam lay with his woman Eve, and she became pregnant and gave birth to Cain" (Gen. 4:1). But there are two especially significant instances in which Scripture does not make this connection. The narrative presentation of the origin (and hence fundamental meaning) of male-female duality does not mention procreation. Instead, the whole point of the story is the necessity and goodness of companionship, and the preeminence of this egalitarian relationship over attachment to one's birth family (Gen. 2:23–24).[28] Equally important is the fact that the biblical poetry devoted to the celebration of (hetero)sexuality in the Song of Songs does not mention procreation either. It is wholly devoted to the mutual desire for sexual intimacy, ecstasy, and fulfillment.

The nonprocreative aspect of human sexuality distinguishes it most decisively from the sexual activity of other biological species and is an important ingredient in human flourishing. Therefore, to insist on a necessary connection between sexual intimacy and procreation as its

Same-sex Love: Theological Considerations

"natural" function is to deny its role in human companionship and to ignore that which gives human sexuality its unique morality. Such an insistence presupposes an essentially biological understanding—what has been called a "barnyard view"—of sexuality, and thus undermines the symbolic and theological function of sexual intimacy and the moral requirement of sexual mutuality.[29]

Philosophical considerations of same-sex love raise the issue of sexual complementarity—that is, "the strangeness of the other gender" and the fact that "heterosexual arousal is arousal by something through and through other than oneself, and other as *flesh.*" But the argument, based partly on the complementarity of male and female genitalia, that "gender distinctions play a constitutive role in the sexual act" and that same-sex love is therefore different from, and in some sense inferior to, opposite-sex love, is highly speculative and experientially dubious, and is properly acknowledged as "certainly far from a proof."[30] Although the differences between women and men involve far more than anatomy and physiology, the most significant personal differences vary much more widely among men and among women than between men and women in general. And, in fact, partners in caring, committed same-sex relationships exhibit a sense of personal complementarity; for every profoundly human interaction with another person entails a recognition, affirmation, and celebration of otherness.

The most plausible conclusion is that the dominant factor in the evaluation of same-sex love as immoral is the profound aversion to what is "other" and "different," and a consequent disinclination to admit even morally qualified diversity in the sensitive area of sexual behavior. "Unnatural" properly describes such practices as bestiality and necrophilia; "immoral" properly describes pedophilia and sadomasochism. Neither term properly describes same-sex love as such.

6. Antagonism toward same-sex love has deep psychosocial roots.

People tend to make the usual the norm—it seems so "natural"—rejecting and denigrating the unusual as "unnatural," "against nature," "perverse," and therefore "contrary to God's will." What is not "normal" is judged as "abnormal." Sometimes the "abnormality" is relatively innocuous (as in the case of left-handedness) and generally ignored. Sometimes the "abnormality" evokes mildly negative or merely curious comment (as in the case of unusual height or hair color). But to many people in contemporary Western culture, the sex of one's partner in sexual intimacy seems anything but innocuous, and an "abnormality" in this area often evokes deep-seated fear—the literal meaning of "homophobia"—that leads to social contempt and moral condemnation.[31] Whatever choices one cannot imagine oneself making, and whatever intimacies one cannot imagine oneself experiencing, are passionately denounced.

One reason for this passionate denunciation is the fact that same-sex love is often felt (sometimes subconsciously) as profoundly threatening to the social order. The question then is, What aspect of the social order is thus threatened? An easy response is that such relationships jeopardize "family values" in general and "traditional marriage" in particular. Although it has never been explained precisely *how* this is so, the claim seems to give a moral legitimacy and righteous motivation to the hostility. In fact, however, a far more likely connection between traditional marriage and same-sex erotic relationships is the convenient availability of the latter as a scapegoat for the widely documented defects in the former.

The primary, though unacknowledged, locus of vulnerability is the almost universal tradition of hegemonic masculinity—the notion that men are innately superior to women and therefore rightly dominate society and the church. This domination, sometimes labeled "headship" or "leadership," is regarded not only as a male right but also as a male responsibility. So for a man to relate to another man in the ways in which men normally relate to women is nothing less than subversive of the social order—a kind of sexually perpetrated treason. A similar dynamic occurs when a woman relates to another woman in the ways in which women normally relate to men, suggesting that men may not be as essential to the fulfillment of womanhood as many (mostly male) people think.

So it is hardly surprising that the increasing equality of women and men in contemporary society (and in the church), in itself a disturbing indication of the decline of male dominance, has been followed by increasingly vocal hostility to same-sex love. "The times they are a-changin'," and to many that feels like bad news indeed. The good news for all, however, is that "God is clearly more comfortable with diversity than we are."[32] This is one of the most obvious results of the incarnation and self-revelation of God in and as Jesus of Nazareth, who was also condemned for allegedly subverting the social order.

Same-sex Love: Theological Considerations

7. Christians should affirm mutually caring, committed same-sex love.

If the reasoning outlined here is sound, it is theologically and morally imperative for serious Christians—Adventist and otherwise—to welcome, affirm, celebrate, nurture, and support individual choices for caring, committed same-sex relationships. This conclusion entails several practical implications.

- Christians should address their moral attention and educational efforts to the monumental task of improving the moral and spiritual quality of the sexual intimacy of all Christians. Common street language reflects an element of violence and hostility (as in "screw you"), and that is all too common in the sexual intimacies of the most conservative Christians as well as other people. For many women, heterosexual intimacy is a symbol of power and submission "governing the nature of the relationship" between the partners, and "from such an angle, sex is always rape."[33] Although this claim is surely exaggerated, it appropriately calls attention to the fact that any element of physical or psychological coercion is at the very least disrespectful and calls for explicit moral criticism and educational effort.
- Christians should discontinue their moral condemnation of same-sex intimacy in caring, committed relationships. Jesus emphatically opposed misguided moral judgments: "Take the plank out of your own eye," he said, "before you try to get the speck out of someone else's eye" (Matt. 7:5). "You strain out gnats and swallow camels" (23:24). "The person who is without sin should throw the first stone" (John 8:7). Nowhere in the Gospel accounts of the teachings of Jesus is there any reference to opposite-sex vs. same-sex love.[34]
- Christians should encourage their spiritual brothers and sisters living in caring same-sex relationships to communicate not only their experiences of rejection and oppression (especially within the community of faith), but also their hearing and understanding of Scripture, especially when that hearing and understanding differs from that of the larger community.
- Christians should encourage their congregations to welcome, affirm, and support persons engaged in morally appropriate same-

sex relationships.[35] Like their teacher, these Christians should speak clearly and act courageously in behalf of those who are oppressed and marginalized by the larger society—even if, again like their teacher, they evoke social hostility from persons inside and outside their communities of faith.

In these and other ways serious Christians can contribute to the realization of God's intention for all humanity and the actualization of God's loving will "on earth as it is in heaven" (Matt. 6:10).[36]

Questions for Discussion

1. If you have friends who are same-sex lovers, how does their relationship compare with that of other-sex couples?
2. Can you think of any objections to same-sex love besides those mentioned in this chapter?
3. What might other-sex couples learn from same-sex couples?
4. Based on your understanding of the values and attitudes of Jesus, what advice do you think he would give to same-sex Christian couples today?
5. How do you react to the suggestion that some biblical characters may have been in same-sex love relationships?
6. Does it seem plausible to you that Scripture does not directly address the kind of loving, committed same-sex relationships described in this chapter?

Notes and References

1. The physical senses—sight, hearing, taste, smell, touch—are of course involved in other, more intellectual kinds of enjoyment, such as that which comes from experiencing art, discovering truth, and encountering God. "Physical pleasure" here indicates the most immediate and intense bodily pleasure. Physical existence includes the colors of a sunrise, the fragrance of a carnation, the sound of a symphony, the taste and feel of an ice cream cone, the relaxation of a massage or a warm bath.
2. For more than 140 years Adventist thinking has been interested in diet (and recently the rest of the world has begun to catch up). So far, however, this interest in diet has been focused on nutrition; good food is important because it facilitates good health. It is right

also to be interested in the actual *enjoyment* of food, to want to have food that *tastes* good.
3. Augustine, *City of God* 14.14. The passage continues: "What friend of wisdom and holy joys, who being married, but knowing, as the apostle says, 'how to possess his vessel in sanctification and honor, not in the disease of desire, as the Gentiles who know not God' [1 Thess. 4:4–5], would not prefer, if this were possible, to beget children without this lust, so that in this function of begetting offspring the members created for this purpose should not be stimulated by the heat of lust, but should be actuated by his volition, in the same way as his other members serve him for their respective ends?"
4. Augustine, *On Marriage and Concupiscence* 1.24 (27).
5. Yves of Chartres, cited by Letha Dawson Scanzoni, *Sexuality* (Philadelphia: Westminster, 1984), 46, advised Christians to abstain from sexual relations on Thursdays in remembrance of Christ's arrest in the Garden of Gethsemane, on Fridays in remembrance of the Crucifixion, on Saturdays in honor of the Virgin Mary, on Sundays in celebration of Christ's resurrection, and on Mondays in respect for their departed loved ones. Besides the long Christian theological tradition, philosophy, all the way to the Enlightenment and beyond, also felt Augustine's impact. Immanuel Kant, for example, considered sexual love as belonging to the "degradation" of the human condition. See his *Lectures on Ethics*, trans. L. Infield, new ed. (New York, 1963), 164. Kant never married.
6. James B. Nelson, *The Intimate Connection: Male Sexuality, Masculine Spirituality* (Philadelphia: Westminster, 1988), 132.
7. Consider also the pathos of the story of Hosea and the explicit sexual imagery of Ezekiel.
8. On the function of symbols, see Paul Tillich, *Systematic Theology* (Chicago: University of Chicago Press, 1951–63), 1:240–41; *Dynamics of Faith* (New York: Harper, 1957), 41–42.
9. L. William Countryman, *Dirt, Greed and Sex: Sexual Ethics in the New Testament and Their Implications for Today* (Philadelphia: Fortress, 1988), 263.
10. See Mary Douglas, *Natural Symbols: Explorations in Cosmology*, 2d ed. (New York: Routledge, 2003).
11. This inescapable dynamic is central to the plot of the film *Fatal Attraction* (Paramount, 1987). The film's primary moral deficiency

is not its gratuitous violence but its implication that an insistence on the relational meaning of sexual intimacy is the result of a disordered (female) personality, whereas a healthy (male) person, duly forgiven his marital infidelity by a loving spouse, can expect to live happily ever after. It is true that sexual intimacy tends to be more personally relational for women than for men, but this is a sign of intelligent realism, not mental illness.

12. Nelson, *Intimate Connection*, 34; italics his.
13. See Paul Ricoeur, "Wonder, Eroticism, and Enigma," *Cross Currents* 14.1 (spring 1964): 137.
14. Aubyn Fulton, "Genesis Marriage," *Spectrum Online,* <http://www.spectrummagazine.org/onlinecommunity/sabbathschool/060116fulton.html>, accessed Jan. 22, 2006.
15. Ibid.
16. Morton Kelsey and Barbara Kelsey, *Sacrament of Sexuality: The Spirituality and Psychology of Sex* (Rockport, Mass.: Element, 1986), 200–201.
17. Ibid., 194.
18. See, for example, Ellen G. White, "Christ Our Hope," *Advent Review and Sabbath Herald,* Dec. 20, 1892, 785; reprinted in *Counsels to Writers and Editors* (Nashville, Tenn.: Southern Publishing Association, 1945), 35: "There is no excuse for anyone in taking the position that there is no more truth to be revealed, and that all our expositions of Scripture are without an error. The fact that certain doctrines have been held as truth for many years by our people is not a proof that our ideas are infallible. Age will not make error into truth, and truth can afford to be fair. No true doctrine will lose anything by close investigation." See also, idem, "The Mysteries of the Bible a Proof of Its Inspiration," *Testimonies for the Church* (Mountain View, Calif.: Pacific Press, 1948), 5:706–9 (1889); "Open the Heart to Light," *Advent Review and Sabbath Herald*, Mar. 25, 1890, 177; "Search the Scriptures," *Advent Review and Sabbath Herald,* July 26, 1892, 465, reprinted in *Counsels to Writers and Editors,* 37; *Selected Messages from the Writings of Ellen G. White* (Washington, D.C.: Review and Herald, 1958–80), 1:37; *The Great Controversy Between Christ and Satan* (Mountain View, Calif.: Pacific Press, 1911), 677–78; *Education* (Mountain View, Calif.: Pacific Press, 1903), 305. As for the alleged "capitulation to modern culture," the same charge was made in regard to the movements toward racial and gender

Same-sex Love: Theological Considerations

equality in the past century. "Cultural capitulation," furthermore, more accurately describes an endorsement of the traditional condemnation of same-sex love.

19. See, for example, Gary David Comstock, *Gay Theology Without Apology* (Cleveland, Ohio: Pilgrim Press, 1993), 61–90; Jeff Miner and John Tyler Connoley, *The Children Are Free: Reexamining the Biblical Evidence and Same-sex Relationships* (Indianapolis: Jesus Metropolitan Community Church, 2002). Compare Part 2, "Biblical Witness," in Walter Wink, ed., *Homosexuality and Christian Faith: Questions of Conscience for the Churches* (Minneapolis: Fortress, 1999), 31–60; and Jack Rogers, *Jesus, the Bible, and Homosexuality: Explode the Myths, Heal the Church* (Philadelphia: Westminster John Knox, 2006).

20. Whether or not this tradition-engendered bias is a hindrance to sound theology is debated. Its inclusion in the "Wesleyan quadrilateral" of Scripture, tradition, reason, and experience reflects a positive valuation. Being more critical of tradition, I do not regard it as a theological resource alongside Scripture, reason, and experience, but take account of it as part of corporate Christian experience.

21. See also the detailed examination of the relevant biblical materials in the chapter by John R. Jones in this volume. One suggested additional narrative involves Noah's son Ham (Gen. 9:20–27), who, some scholars argue, may have committed an incestuous homosexual rape of his father. See, for example, Robert A. J. Gagnon, *The Bible and Homosexual Practice: Texts and Hermeneutics* (Nashville, Tenn.: Abingdon, 2001), 63–71. This incident may, however, have been a much less dramatic case of filial disrespect.

22. My translation of *basileia tou theou* as "God's program" rather than "kingdom of God" is unusual, but hardly idiosyncratic. The standard translation unfortunately encourages the (mis)understanding of the "kingdom" as an eschatological realm rather than a present-and-future functional project.

23. Other examples of instructions not currently considered normative include the status of women as the household property of men (Exod.20:17), the imposition of capital punishment for desecrating the Sabbath (Exod. 31:15; Num. 15:32–36) or cursing one's parents (Exod. 21:17; Lev. 20:9), and divinely ordered genocide in

the slaughter of Amalekites (Exod. 17:14–16; Deut. 25:19) and the residents of Jericho (Josh. 6:17, 21).
24. Charles Humana, *The Keeper of the Bed: The Story of the Eunuch* (London: Arlington Books, 1973), 12.
25. The Christian theologian Origen (ca. 185–ca. 254), as reported by the historian Eusebius (ca. 260–ca. 340), took Jesus' words literally and castrated himself.
26. Miner and Connoley, *Children Are Free*, 40–42.
27. John Polkinghorne, *Exploring Reality: The Intertwining of Science and Religion* (New Haven: Yale University Press, 2005), 76.
28. "This is now bone of my bones and flesh of my flesh. She will be called 'woman,' for she was taken out of a man. Therefore a man leaves his father and mother and unites with his woman, and they become one flesh."
29. This view may have been encouraged by Plato, who was highly influential in early Christian thought. His proposal for regulating human reproduction appears in his *Republic,* Book 5, 457b–461e.
30. Roger Scruton, *Sexual Desire: A Philosophical Investigation* (London: Weidenfeld and Nicolson, 1986), 310–11.
31. John B. Cobb, Jr., "Being Christian about Homosexuality," in Wink, *Homosexuality and Christian Faith*, 90–91.
32. Richard Rohr, "Where the Gospel Leads Us," in Wink, *Homosexuality and Christian Faith*, 86.
33. Nancy Mairs, *Plaintext* (Tucson: University of Arizona Press, 1986), 84.
34. Ironically, vigorous condemnation of same-sex love seems to be generally ineffective or even counterproductive. See Kelsey and Kelsey, *Sacrament of Sexuality*, 197: "In societies where there is little attempt to discourage homosexual activity, cultural studies show that most young males and females pass through a homosexual phase to a heterosexual adjustment and that only about one percent remain in a homosexual lifestyle. In societies with violent antagonism to homosexuality somewhere between six and ten percent remain in a homosexual adaptation."
35. This view consciously differs from that of Stanley J. Grenz, *Welcoming, but not Affirming: An Evangelical Response to Homosexuality* (Philadelphia: Westminster John Knox, 1998), 153–57.
36. See suggestions and recommendations elsewhere in this volume.

Same-sex Love in the "Body of Christ"?

By Roy E. Gane

The question of how Christians should relate to same-sex love is not an easy one. So it is wise to harness the energy of our tensions "under the reign of Christ, as part of a process of mutual speaking and hearing," as John Jones counsels. I agree that while our primary accountability is to God, we are also accountable to each other. Aside from questions of exegesis and theology, the issue of homosexuality is highly charged on an emotional level because many of us, including myself, have homosexual friends and/or relatives who crave acceptance within our community of faith and desire eternal salvation through Jesus Christ. Whatever our theological and biblical conclusions may be, compassion for people in a devastatingly difficult situation must be an important part of the way we relate to them.

The present discussion is limited in scope. It is not about promiscuous lifestyles of gays with multiple sexual partners, which are clearly out of harmony with biblical principles. Nor are we addressing the civil rights issue of respect and fair treatment of homosexuals within the context of secular society and our (nontheocratic) civil governments, which Christians who accept the freedom of separation between church and state should affirm. Neither do we question whether persons with homosexual tendencies who refrain from sexual activity with persons of the same gender can be saved if they have a saving relationship with Christ, and whether they can enjoy full membership in the Seventh-day Adventist Church if they accept Adventist teachings. Close friendships between persons of the same gender are no problem, as long as these are not sexual relationships.

Fritz Guy and Jones argue that sexual intimacy between persons of the same sex is morally acceptable to God and the Church, provided that it is only enjoyed within the context of a loving, mutual, committed, exclusive relationship analogous to a monogamous marriage between heterosexual partners. Any Adventist can wholeheartedly endorse the values of unselfish, caring, and loyal (heterosexual) marriages that include enjoyment of pleasurable physical relations, as described by Guy and Jones. But does the presence of these values in a same-sex union legitimate such a relationship in God's sight so that it is not sinful?

Response to Fritz Guy

Guy's concern for accepting diversity and caring for homosexuals is commendable, and many will welcome his conclusion, which resonates with the current ethos. Unfortunately, however, Guy's present instance of "thinking theologically" is fraught with such major logical and exegetical flaws that his conclusion actually receives little more than emotional support:

1. He compiles a list of moral criteria for sexual intimacy and applies them as if these were the only relevant biblical criteria.
2. He finds no biblical passage that explicitly condemns the kind of loving same-sex union that he condones. But by hastily making an argument from silence, he overlooks the reason for the lack: The Bible explicitly condemns all homosexual activity in crystal clear, nontechnical language (Lev. 18:22, 20:13; Rom. 1:26–27). Why should Scripture explicitly condemn one kind of active homosexual relationship when all such practices are already forbidden? If God permitted at least one kind of homosexual union, we would expect to find it mentioned (and likely regulated) in the Bible. Guy's "moral criteria" are simply irrelevant to the question of whether the Bible allows homosexual unions because there is a deeper biblical criterion/principle that he has dismissed: only male-female human sexuality, which God set up in the beginning (Gen. 1–2), is morally legitimate.
3. Although Guy correctly points out that not all laws in the Hebrew Bible have modern applications, he does not consider criteria for

knowing which ones apply today and which do not. Space is lacking here for analysis of this crucial question, on which I have written elsewhere.[1] Suffice it to say that (1) while the Ten Commandments present examples of paramount moral principles, there are timeless moral laws elsewhere in the so-called Mosaic laws (for instance, Lev. 19:11), and (2) the laws prohibiting homosexual relations are timeless moral laws, along with laws that prohibit other immoral behaviors, such as adultery, incest, and bestiality (Lev. 18, 20; see further below).

4. Guy fails to see the relevance of 1 Corinthians 5, where Paul commands that a man living in an incestuous relationship with his stepmother should be disfellowshipped, in hope of saving his soul by showing him his need for repentance. All of the reasons Guy uses to condone same-sex unions would also support continuation of the Corinthian incest, that is, if he and his stepmom interacted in a loyal, loving way according to Guy's moral criteria. But Paul doesn't even ask about these factors. The union is wrong because these two individuals should be sexually inaccessible to each other. It is true that incestuous unions produce genetically weakened offspring. But this alone does not account for the biblical prohibition, which does not permit an incestuous union when reproduction is not a factor, such as after a woman reaches menopause. Neither did Paul permit the Corinthian couple to maintain their cohabitation if they simply refrained from having children (for example, by practicing coitus interruptus). Thus we can conclude that the advent of modern birth control methods do not legitimate incest. It is wrong because God said so—in Leviticus 18, 20, precisely where he said homosexual activity is wrong.

5. Guy does not adequately explain why the "natural" argument regarding genitalia carries no validity. How is it true that there is more variety within than between the sexes? Is it not biologically self-evident that the penis was made for the vagina rather than an orifice of elimination? What about Paul's language condemning "unnatural" relations among both homosexual males and lesbians (Rom. 1:24–27)?

Response to John R. Jones

John Jones presents much more careful scholarship, with detailed exegesis that involves instructive anthropological and linguistic background material illuminating the cultural contexts addressed by relevant biblical passages. Unlike Guy, who wanders into peripheral speculations (regarding David and Jonathan, and so forth), Jones concentrates his attention on the passages that matter most—Leviticus 18, 20 and certain Pauline texts—although he too has overlooked 1 Corinthians 5.

Like Guy, Jones immediately sets aside the narratives of Genesis 19 and Judges 19 as irrelevant. It is true that these horrific stories involve complex cultural and moral dynamics, such as lack of hospitality, gang rape, and violation of boundaries. But perhaps the most disturbing element of these stories (aside from the Levite quartering and parcel posting his dead concubine; Judg. 19:29), is the fact that females were offered to rapists in place of males. In Judges 19, at least, this cannot simply be attributed to the imperative of hospitality that involved protection of guests at any cost. Although the Levite's concubine was a guest, the elderly host offered her along with his virgin daughter in order to prevent (homosexual) rape of the Levite (vv. 22–24). It is true that the concubine was of lower social status than the Levite, but so was the Levite's male servant (vv. 11–13). Why not also offer him? Was homosexuality regarded as such a great evil that it had to be avoided at all cost?[2] This question and its implications should at least be addressed.

In his section on the so-called Holiness Code, Jones examines the two prohibitions against consensual male-male sexual intercourse, which is labeled "an abomination" and carries the death penalty (Lev. 18:22; 20:13). Jones argues that limitations to male homosexuality and penetrative sex here are due to the wrongness residing in "feminizing treatment of one male by another," which involves violation of "distinctions in the conventional order" through causing a male to be used as a woman to receive male "seed."[3]

Jones is right that orderly distinctions were an important element of the portion of Leviticus that emphasizes holiness and that Israel's holiness included separation from contamination with defiling practices of other peoples. But he is apparently unaware of a major difference, well recognized by Leviticus scholars, between the remediable ritual/ceremonial impurities regulated earlier in Leviticus (in the so-called "P" = "priestly" portion; especially in chapters 12–15) and the irremediable moral "impurities" of serious, defiling sins (including homosexual activity) covered in chapters 17–27 (in the so-called "H" =

"Holiness" portion). Jacob Milgrom explains:

> H's metaphoric use of P's cultic terms is highlighted by *âme*. In P, it is ritual impurity; in H, moral impurity. Ritual impurity (P) is remediable by ritual purification, but moral impurity is irremediable. It is a capital crime, punishable for the individual by *kâret* and for the community by exile....[4]

So Jones is incorrect when he says that homosexual activity "contaminated their ceremonial purity by bringing in activities identified with the Canaanites." Yes, there was a corporate concern, including protection of "symbolic markers between Israel and her neighbors." But the impurity of homosexual practice was not ceremonial, but moral.

Jones concentrates the bulk of his efforts on references to homosexuality in the writings of Paul. Having already decided that "the Levitical conviction that sex between Israelite males breaches the ethnic identity of the Hebrew people, who defined their chosenness and ceremonial purity in terms of their descent from Abraham," Jones deduces from Galatians 3:28 that "when these cultural and national bounds are transcended in Christ, the ground is cut out from under the proscriptions in Leviticus 18 and 20. When Paul affirms the equality of Jew and Gentile before God, he is dismantling the framework on which these proscriptions stand." Applying this Christological hermeneutic to the question of homosexuality leads Jones to the conclusion that the categoric, comprehensive prohibitions of Leviticus 18:22; 20:13 do not apply within the context of the Christian church because their applicability was based on an obsolete ethnic distinction.

Jones's argumentation is fatally flawed on two major counts:

1. Although the legislation in Leviticus 18 and 20 was certainly intended to keep the holy Israelites from becoming like their unholy neighbors, a temporary kind of distinguishing function by no means exhausted the rationale of this timeless moral instruction any more than temporary honoring of the Sabbath in the Israelite cult (Lev. 24:8; Num. 28:9) and enforcement of Sabbath rest under the theocracy (Num. 15:32–36) nullifies the ongoing validity of Sabbath observance.[5] The laws of Leviticus 18 and 20 are not like circumcision, the temporary ethnic covenant marker. This is confirmed by the fact that in Acts 15, which releases Gentile Christians from circumcision, the "Holiness Code" prohibitions

against meat offered to idols, sexual immorality in general (*porneia*; not only adultery), and meat from which the blood is not drained at the time of slaughter (vv. 20, 29; compare Lev. 17–20) remain in force for Gentiles.[6]

2. Jones misapplies Galatians 3:28 by greatly overextending its scope. Paul's point is that all who belong to Christ, no matter what their ethnicity, gender, and social status may be, are justified the same way through faith in Christ's remedy for sin. In this sense, all true Christians are spiritual heirs of Abraham and recipients of God's promise to him. This passage does not neutralize the relevance of gender distinctions in Christian social contexts, including those regulated by God's moral law. Sexual immorality as defined by Leviticus 18 and 20 is still sexual immorality in the Christian church (for instance, 1 Cor. 5).

Regarding condemnation of homosexuals in the Pauline vice lists (1 Cor. 6:9; 1 Tim. 1:10), Jones draws on biblical and Greco-Roman sources to effectively show associations of the relevant Greek words with "self-indulgent, lustful living" and "homoerotic activity of an exploitive sort." Such associations tend to draw attention away from homosexuality per se. But Jones admits that the compound word *arsenokoites* "male homosexual" (from "male" + "lie") appears to be derived from the Septuagint terminology of Leviticus 18:22 and 20:13, where, I would add, the other associations are not in view. Whether *arsenokoites* was coined on the basis of Leviticus 18 and 20 or not, this term used by Paul provides an intertextual link to the "Holiness Code" passages, supporting their ongoing applicability (against Jones's overall conclusion).

In his fascinating, extensive discussion of Romans 1:24–27, which condemns lesbianism along with male homosexuality, Jones demonstrates that Paul echoes pre-Christian Jewish condemnation of Gentiles and their vices in order to bring old Jewish judgments concerning Gentiles to the surface and address them from the new Christian perspective. Here Jones continues to reference the Greco-Roman background, which shows that homogenital sex was to some extent becoming regarded as contrary to "nature" even among Gentiles, although this negative assessment was not based on morality as we think of it.

There is no question that Romans 1:24–27 is embedded in a rhetorical context that draws upon already existing Jewish and Gentile

Same-sex Love in the "Body of Christ"?

attitudes toward homosexual behavior in order to show that Gentiles are tragic sinners who desperately need the mercy of God that is available only through Christ. But Jones makes a logical leap when he concludes that because Paul's rhetorical stance here identifies with the Judaism of his day, it is mistaken "to look here for the definitive word on same-sex relations or anything else from a developed Christian standpoint." Deficiencies of this trajectory of thought include at least the following factors:

1. The fact that Paul's demonstration of Gentile sin draws upon pre-Christian condemnation of homosexual behavior in order to persuade his audience regarding a larger point does not nullify the fact that his overall discussion is Christian. Paul's Christianity clearly shares the pre-Christian norms, or his logic would fail. If homosexuals are no longer guilty before God, why would they now need the grace of Christ?

2. Paul's allusion to Gentile condemnation of sexual vice as unnatural implies an *a fortiori* argument: If even Gentiles know there is something wrong with this behavior, shouldn't those who have received God's law know it even more? Compare the way in which Paul shames the Corinthian Christians for continuing to grant Christian fellowship to a man who continues to commit sexual immorality "of a kind that is not found even among pagans" (1 Cor. 5:1 NRSV here and in subsequent biblical quotations).

3. Elsewhere, Paul does not hesitate to address and stress discontinuity between pre-Christian norms and attitudes and new Christian freedom in Christ (for example, Rom. 4, 14; 1 Cor. 8; and the entire epistle to the Galatians). So if homosexual unions were now allowed in the Christian church, why would Paul not even mention that?

4. In Romans 1, Paul's enumeration of Gentile sins includes not only homosexual behavior, but also idolatry (vv. 23, 25), covetousness, malice, envy, murder, strife, deceit, and so forth (vv. 29–31). Does the fact that these Gentile moral faults would also be condemned by pre-Christian Jews (and Gentiles) mean that they (or some limited forms of them) would be acceptable within Christian life? Hardly!

In his section, "What the Texts Mean Today," Jones interprets the language of "impurity" in Romans 1:24–27 (see v. 24) as cultic rather than moral. He commits a "category error" by missing the fact that

Paul is referring to the "impurity" of the "Holiness Code," which is moral impurity = sin (see above).

Jones goes on to point out differences between Paul's conceptual horizon and ours. Granted there are differences, and modern science has analyzed and nuanced various forms and aspects of human sexual life in many ways. But none of this changes the unequivocal biblical teaching that sexual activity between same-sex partners is morally wrong, and there is no exception for same-sex partners in loving, committed, consensual, and exclusive relationships.

Conclusion

Guy and Jones have illustrated the futility of trying to harmonize Scripture with acceptance of some active homosexual practice within a religious community that accepts the Bible as its authoritative guide to faith and practice. Not even Jacob Milgrom succeeded in that through elegant casuistry (regarding Lev. 18:22; and 20:13).[7]

True compassion for homosexuals pleads that we stop wasting time on this dead-end road of attempted harmonization, which prolongs the agony, builds false hopes and security that can result in eternal loss, and diverts our focus and energy from the only truly redemptive approach: Helping homosexuals in their brutal battle to overcome their overwhelming desire to gain sexual fulfillment with a same-sex partner. This victory can be won only through faith in the mighty, transforming power of Christ and the Holy Spirit, against the tide of political correctness and postmodernism that regard sexual fulfillment of choice between consenting adults as an inalienable right. Homosexuals, who are often highly sensitive individuals, desperately need our support through friendship, prayers, tears, and unfailing love. Sometimes this needs to be "tough love" to remove the danger of false security, so that the person can have the redemptive opportunity to realize the need to submit to God in order to be saved (compare 1 Cor. 5).[8]

There is no doubt that homosexual behavior is one of the most challenging lifestyle issues to overcome, and comparing it with other problems invariably diminishes the reality of its difficulty. In fact, for many or most it may be impossible in human terms (as psychologists affirm). But this is an opportunity for highlighting the magnitude of the authentic gospel miracle, for nothing is impossible with God (Luke 1:37), and "I can do all things through him who strengthens me" (Phil. 4:13). Even the "vice list" of 1 Corinthians 6, where Paul says that wrongdoers, including (active) homosexuals, "will not inherit the kingdom of God" (vv. 9–10), is followed by resounding hope: "And this is what some of you used to be. But you were washed, you were sanctified, you were justified in the name of the Lord Jesus Christ and in the Spirit of our God" (v. 11). Homosexuals, too, can hear Christ say, "Neither do I condemn you. Go your way, and from now on do not sin again" (John 8:11). They, too, can be redeemed, transformed, and experience full peace with God. They, too, can contribute their talents and testimonies to the church.

While the church has no biblical license to sanction the practice of homosexuality in any form, Christ's approach demands that it be a haven of support to help precious people—including gays, lesbians, and bisexuals—in their often painful and traumatic journeys of recovery from all kinds of lifestyles. To restore the church as the trusted friend rather than the enemy of sinners requires a major shift of attitude on our part.[9]

Questions for Discussion

1. What is the relationship between biblical teachings on sexuality and current "political correctness"?
2. How do attitudes of our modern culture influence interpretations of biblical passages dealing with homosexuality?
3. What does the Bible teach regarding divine forgiveness and/or empowerment available to persons who choose to follow God's lifestyle principles in spite of extreme difficulty?
4. How can Seventh-day Adventist Christians provide better spiritual, social, and emotional support for persons with homosexual tendencies?
5. How can biblically based boundaries for church membership be maintained in a consistent, constructive, and redemptive way?

Notes and References

1. Roy Gane, *Leviticus, Numbers*, NIV Application Commentary (Grand Rapids, Mich.: Zondervan, 2004), 305–10.
2. Compare the analyses of these passages by Richard Davidson in *Flame of Yahweh: Sexuality in the Old Testament* (Peabody, Mass.; Hendrickson, 2007), 145–49, 161–62 (in his comprehensive treatment of "Human Heterosexuality versus Homosexuality,

Transvestism, and Bestiality" in the Old Testament, against its ancient Near Eastern background, 133–76).
3. But in regard to male homosexuality and penetrative sex, see ibid., 149–50.
4. Jacob Milgrom, *Leviticus 17–22*, Anchor Bible 3A (New York: Doubleday, 2000), 1,326; see also, for example, Jonathan Klawans, *Impurity and Sin in Ancient Judaism* (Oxford: Oxford University Press, 2000), especially 21–31; Jay Sklar, *Sin, Impurity, Sacrifice, Atonement: The Priestly Conceptions* (Sheffield: Sheffield PhoenixPress, 2005), 139–53.
5. Compare Roy Gane, "The Role of God's Moral Law, Including Sabbath, in the 'New Covenant,'" 10–11; online at <http://www.adventistbiblicalresearch.org/documents/> (select "Gane Gods moral law.pdf").
6. "In Acts 15 the four categories of prohibitions imposed upon Gentile Christians are precisely the same four, in the same order, as those listed in Lev. 17–18 that are applicable to the stranger, with the final prohibition, *porneia,* summarizing the illicit sexual activities described in Lev 18. Clearly the NT covenant community saw this reference to the "alien" as an indication of the transtemporal and transcultural nature of these laws, including the law prohibiting homosexual activity." Davidson, *Flame of Yahweh*, 155.
7. Milgrom, *Leviticus 17–22*, 1,786–90. My answer to the question, "Do the biblical prohibitions against homosexuality and incest apply to Christians today?" in Gane, *Leviticus, Numbers,* 325–30, includes a critique of Milgrom's interpretation (326–28).
8. On grace, redemption, welcoming homosexuals, and humbly recognizing our own sexual fallenness, compare Davidson, *Flame of Yahweh*, 175–76.
9. Gane, *Leviticus, Numbers*, 330.

Is the Church Ready for Same-sex Sex?

By Richard Rice

The question that same-sex love presents to the Seventh-day Adventist Church arises from an experience that is common to many of us.[1] We know men and women who occupy responsible positions in society, who contribute to the lives of others in important ways, who are spiritually sensitive and dedicated to their faith, and who find personal fulfillment in same-sex relationships. There seems to be no significant difference between them and anyone else in the Church except for problems created for them by those who look askance at their choice of sexual partners.

As Christians, we also take the Bible as our rule of faith and practice, and there are biblical passages that condemn same-sex relations in very strong terms. So the question is how to bring together the evidence of experience and the statements of Scripture. How should Christians today respond to those in committed same-sex relationships in light of the biblical perspective on human sexuality?

In their contributions to this volume, Fritz Guy and John R. Jones present carefully developed answers to this question. Although they argue along different lines, they begin and end in much the same way. They share the conviction that same-sex relationships are natural and fulfilling, they argue that the Bible does not support a blanket condemnation of them, and they conclude that the Church should accept and affirm same-sex couples as valued members of the community.

Guy begins his theology of sexual experience by affirming the value of physical pleasure in general and sexual pleasure in particular. He notes that there are varieties of sexual preferences, and insists that their moral quality depends on characteristics such as mutuality, trust, and care—not on the sex of the partners. Indeed, a number of biblical figures, such as David and Jonathan, may have been involved in same-sex relationships. Despite its condemnation of certain same-sex practices, he argues, the Bible as a whole does not lead to the "conclusion that physical intimacy between persons of the same sex is morally wrong." Broad biblical principles, as distinct from certain specific prescriptions, support a different conclusion, just as they do in the case of slavery. Though same-sex love does not lead to procreation, this does not make it inferior to heterosexual love, nor mean that it is "unnatural." Same-sex partners can "complement" each other in significant ways just as well as heterosexual partners. Finally, the long-standing opposition to same-sex love is attributable to deep-seated prejudices and fears, of the sort that lie behind sex discrimination, for example. In light of these considerations, Guy concludes, "Christians should encourage their congregations to welcome, affirm, and support persons engaged in morally appropriate same-sex relationships."

Though he reaches more or less the same conclusion Guy does, Jones's path takes him through a detailed analysis of the Bible's strongest statements against same-sex activities: the proscription of male-male sexual relations in the Holiness Code of Leviticus 17–26, and the condemnation of same-sex relations in Romans 1.

The Holiness Code contains two references to male-male sexual relations. "You shall not lie with a male as with a woman; it is an abomination" (18:22). "If a man lies with a male as with a woman, both of them have committed an abomination; they shall be put to death; their blood is upon them" (20:13).

The passage in Romans refers to both male and female same-sex relations. "For this reason God gave them up to degrading passions. Their women exchanged natural intercourse for unnatural, and in the same way also the men, giving up natural intercourse with women, were consumed with passion for one another. Men committed shameless acts with men and received in their own persons the due penalty for their error" (1:26–27).

For Jones, the Holiness Code refers to the special identity and

Is the Church Ready for Same-sex Sex?

responsibility of the Jewish people. Consequently, it does not apply to members of the church. The Christian community is much more inclusive and its identifying marks are quite different.

Jones's treatment of the statements in Romans is more intricate and extensive. He develops three considerations that lead to the conclusion that we should not construe this passage as a condemnation of all same-sex relations.

The first is the cultural background that lies behind the passage. What we have here is not "fully Paul's own Christian voice," but a summary of widely held attitudes toward same-sex activities in the ancient Mediterranean world. To the Greco-Romans, who regarded everyone as essentially bisexual, it was a form of willful self-indulgence. To the Jews, who regarded everyone as essentially heterosexual, it was a perversion, closely connected to idolatrous practices. Paul thus appeals to, rather than arguing for, the widely accepted view of his day that those who indulged themselves with members of the same sex were violating natural law. Same-sex activity was characteristic of a generally self-indulgent lifestyle that was acceptable neither to Jews nor to thoughtful pagans.

A second consideration arises from a careful analysis of Romans 1:18–32. According to Jones, this passage refers to two levels of depravity, one involving cultic impurity, the other, moral evil. Sexual sins, significantly, are located only on the first level, indicating that Paul viewed same-sex relations in cultic rather than moral terms. This is extremely important, because later in Romans Paul relativizes the whole scheme of ceremonial purity when he declares concerning food, "Nothing is unclean in itself" (14:14). With this, the apostle acknowledges "that ritual contamination exists in the eye of the beholder," and indicates that ceremonial matters, including same-sex relations, represent "nothing more than occasions for mutual forbearance in Christ." Since the apostle's readers would have been just as sensitive about dietary matters as we are about homosexual intercourse, Jones maintains that Paul's treatment of them provides a "guidepost" for the church in the future.

A third consideration is Paul's overall theological concern. The Romans 1 passage serves a specific rhetorical function within Paul's argument in the book as a whole. His overarching concern is to show that the cross of Christ creates a new reality in the world, a reality available to both Jews and Gentiles. It is available to all because all are saved on the same basis, that of grace received by faith, and because all have the same need of salvation: all have sinned. The first step in the initial phase of this argument—to establish that all have sinned—is to show the well-deserved wrath of God against the pagan world. This is a point that his intended audience, Hellenistic Jewish Christians living in Rome, would no doubt agree with. Once he brings this group on board he can move to the second step in this initial phase, and show that they, too, are the object of divine wrath. With the whole world thus standing under divine condemnation, no one has an advantage over any other; all are dependent on God's grace for salvation; and all therefore stand on equal footing within the new social reality that the cross of Christ creates, namely, the Christian church.

These three considerations lead to three conclusions. First, Paul's frame of reference did not include the notion of a fundamental same-sex orientation, let alone the possibility of loving, committed same-sex relationships. Indeed, it was not until much later in history, until the nineteenth century actually, that people began to understand the subtle way in which sexuality and personality are connected. We have a different understanding of same-sex relations today—unknown and unavailable in the ancient Mediterranean world.

Second, the cultic context of Paul's condemnation of same-sex relations in Romans 1 puts the issue in an entirely different light. Paul relegated homogenital sex to the level of ceremonial observance, and elsewhere he treats ceremonial matters as occasions for mutual forbearance in Christ. Accordingly, the preference for heterosexual or same-sex relationships is the sort of thing that should be settled on the level of individual conscience, and each church member should respect the decisions of others.

Third, viewed in both its literary and historical contexts, the condemnation of same sex relations in Romans 1 turns out to be a specific illustration of a preliminary point in Paul's extended argument, not necessarily the enunciation of a principle binding on human beings for all time. Furthermore, the burden of the larger argument in Romans, as well as in Paul's letters generally, is to break down the divisions in the ancient world that threatened unity among Christians, such as the differences between Jews and Gentiles, slaves and free, and so forth.

So, even though Paul himself no doubt shared the view of same-sex relations as his contemporaries, the trajectory of the principles he articulated leads us to a different perspective in our time and place. The disjunction between clean and unclean is not one that matters to us, and when we realize that this is the background of the biblical comments on same-sex relations, and that a new understanding of same-sex relations is available today, that is to say, loving, committed relationships, we should be willing to follow the logic of Paul's argument and accept people in such relationships as fellow members in the body of Christ. Following the trajectory of Paul's theology to our own day, we should view the division between heterosexual and same-sex orientations as something to be overcome in Christ.

The essays by Guy and Jones contain exemplary theological reflection. Both scholars are conversant with a wide range of relevant literature, thoughtful in their interpretation of the Bible, sensitive to the complexities of human experience, and committed to the welfare of the Church.

The purpose of this volume, as I understand it, is to stimulate a discussion of the topic by considering various perspectives. My particular task is to respond to the contributions of Guy and Jones with that objective in mind. A number of other Christian scholars have approached the issue with the same concerns and commitments evident in Guy and Jones's discussions. They, too, have a strong sense of biblical responsibility and deep sensitivity to the personal and emotional aspects of the issue. Yet they come to quite different conclusions. The points raised in the following paragraphs are drawn in large measure from the work of two of these scholars, Stanley Grenz and Richard B. Hays.[2] I offer them, not because I fully endorse them, but in the hope that they will extend our conversation on this important issue.

An initial question concerns the appropriate course of theological reflection. There is always an interchange in theology between the Bible and experience, and theology can develop in either direction: We can start with the Bible and then apply its teachings to our experience, or start with a question that our experience raises and turn to the Bible for answers. A critical question for any theological proposal is which of the two, the Bible or experience, ultimately norms the other. Which is the final court of appeal? By definition, Christian theology assigns priority to the Bible, so the question for any specific proposal is whether in fact it does so. When we ask this question of Guy and Jones' work here, I find myself suspecting that experience gets pride of place. It is true that they look closely at certain biblical passages, particularly in Jones's case. But both of them seem to accept as a settled fact that same-sex relationships are appropriate for Christians because people find them personally fulfilling. Thus convinced, they turn to the Bible in order to "defuse" the biblical texts that speak against homogenital contact, and to show that such activity does not violate biblical norms for human behavior.

To develop a perspective on human sexuality that is truly biblical, it is important to consult a broad range of biblical evidence on the topic. The Bible contains significant statements about sexuality that don't get much attention in these two essays, and some of them ostensibly support different conclusions. Two of the most prominent passages appear in the Bible's first two stories of creation. According to Genesis 1, the essential purpose of sexual relations is procreation (Gen. 1:26–28); according to Genesis 2, sexual relations meet a profound human need for intimacy (Gen. 2:24). Both accounts support the view that heterosexual monogamy is the divinely ordained framework for sexual relations.

For Grenz in particular, the Genesis accounts are basic to all that follows in the Bible concerning sexuality, including the views of Jesus and Paul. "The Genesis creation stories indicate quite clearly that heterosexuality forms the basis of the dynamic of human sexual bonding from the beginning, an outlook confirmed by Jesus himself." "For Paul…the only proper model of sexual relations is that patterned after the creation story in Genesis 1–2. In keeping with the injunctions of the Holiness Code, Paul concludes that this model is natural, for it alone was instituted by the Creator" (230). There can be only one conclusion: Since the Bible sets forth heterosexuality as God's design for creation, we should not accept homosexuality as normal or as an alternative on the same level.

Guy points out that with contraceptives readily available, procreation is no longer a necessary concomitant of sexual experience. But the fact that sex serves other functions than procreation, and that procreation is now a choice for couples, not an inevitability, does not mean that the procreative potential of sexual activity is irrelevant to its meaning. According to Genesis 2, the relationship is clearly meant to be permanent and to establish a social unit among others in the larger society.

Guy gives physical pleasure and personal preference a prominent place in his approach to sexuality, although he does emphasize that same-sex love is appropriate only in caring, committed relationships. But according to the Bible, there is more to sexual meaning even than that. A meaningful sexual relationship in the biblical sense not only involves more than physical pleasure and personal fulfillment, it is also

Is the Church Ready for Same-sex Sex?

more than a private agreement, however long-lasting, between two people looking to satisfy their physical and emotional needs. The descriptions of sexuality in Genesis 1 and 2 suggest that sexual activity has a social purpose. Sexual relationships, solidified by the emotional bonds that sexual intimacy inculcates, provide the building blocks of a sound society. (In other words, it is the relationship that makes sexual relations important, not the other way around.) Throughout the Bible, sexual activity always has implications for the larger community. As Hays notes, "The New Testament never considers sexual conduct a matter of purely private concern between consenting adults. According to Paul, everything we do as Christians, including our sexual practices, affects the whole body of Christ" (392).

When we look at the range of biblical statements dealing with sexuality, we find a consistent pattern. Consider the New Testament passages that refer to the Genesis expression "one flesh." They indicate that the appropriate setting for sexual activity is a relationship that is permanent (Matt. 19:5), serious rather than casual (1 Cor. 6:16), and characterized by affection and tenderness (Eph. 5:31). But it is also significant that each of these passages upholds heterosexual monogamy. Indeed, while the Bible condemns a number of heterosexual practices—adultery and incest, for example—*all* the passages where it affirms sexual activity refer to heterosexual relations. When we turn to the passages that refer to same-sex relations, another consistent pattern appears. The biblical perspective on them is decidedly negative. Indeed, all the biblical texts that speak of homoerotic activity, though relatively few, "express unqualified disapproval," to use Richard Hays's words.

Jones argues that the trajectory of Paul's theology suggests that the cross of Christ ultimately renders inconsequential, not only divisions between Jew and Greek, slave and free, male and female, but also the division between same-sex couples and heterosexual couples, as well. But Hays's study of Paul's comments on homosexuality leads him to different conclusions. As he reads the New Testament, the division between hetero- and homosexual relationships is not like the distinctions between Jew and Greek, slave and free, male and female. When it comes to slavery and women's subordination, we find internal tensions in the Bible and "counterposed witnesses" that complicate the picture. But not when it comes to same-sex relations. "The New Testament remains unambiguous and univocal in its condemnation of homosexual conduct." It offers "no loopholes or exception clauses that might allow for the acceptance of homosexual practices under some circumstances" (394).

It is often observed that the modern understanding of sexual orientation was unknown in the ancient world, whose inhabitants tended to judge actions, rather than actors. Consequently, they had no way of viewing same-sex relations as the expression of deep personal commitments. This doesn't really change things, according to Hays. "Paul treats *all* homosexual activity as prima facie evidence of humanity's tragic confusion and alienation from God the creator" (389). The fact remains: Whenever the Bible refers to same-sex activity, it condemns it. Whenever it affirms sexual activity, it refers to heterosexual behavior.

What about the Holiness Code? Isn't it obsolete for Christians? Not entirely, Hays suggests. According to Acts 15, Christians were expected to live up to parts of it, including its proscription of fornication (Acts 15:29), so it is reasonable to conclude that its provisions about homosexuality were among them, even though they are not explicitly stated.

For both Hays and Grenz, Romans 1 clearly indicates that homosexuality is a consequence of sin, a manifestation of the fallenness that characterizes the human condition. Consequently, they reject any notion that same-sex relations are an acceptable form of Christian behavior. This does not mean, however, that the church should flatly condemn homosexuality in all its forms. Both accept the view, permeating modern discussions of the topic, that there is a distinction between a homosexual orientation and homosexual behavior. It is generally accepted today that one's sexual identity is a given rather than a choice, the result of complex factors working over time in a person's formative years. Indeed, people often appeal to this concept to justify same-sex relations as the "natural" expression of one's essential sexual identity. Grenz and Hays accept the premise, but reject the conclusion. They agree that people do not willingly choose a same-sex orientation, but they deny that this entitles them to engage in same-sex relations.

The distinction between a same-sex orientation and same-sex genital contact is particularly important to Grenz. He sees a distinct difference between human dispositions and human actions. Many of our dispositions, he contends, are manifestations of our fallen condition and will be restored at the *eschaton*. Sinful actions, however, are a different matter. "The condemnation of God rests not on human dispositions themselves, even though they participate in human fallenness, but on actions that flow from them" (232).

So, even if same-sex relations seem "natural" to someone who is attracted to the same sex by disposition, this doesn't make them morally acceptable. "Ethics is not merely a condoning of what comes naturally," says Grenz. "Our natural inclinations are not a sure guide to proper human conduct, but share in our fallenness." "Even though some researches conclude that males are naturally promiscuous," he notes by comparison, "this supposedly natural inclination does not set aside the biblical ethic of fidelity" (230). I suspect that Guy and Jones would no doubt endorse this in principle, given their emphasis on the importance of loving, committed relationships.

It is important to remember that "personal responsibility is not limited to matters in which we exercise full choice," whether this consists of particular acts or sin in general. We are enslaved to sin and still responsible, whether this results from our personal conscious choices or not. "The Bible…never seeks to excuse persons on the basis of the suggestion that they are not responsible, because they did not consciously choose to be the way they are," Grenz argues. "Rather, the answer the Bible offers is the grace of God becoming active in the midst of our fallenness, failure, and sin" (231).

The question persists, however. Don't the facts of experience simply demand that Christians develop a revisionary interpretation of sexuality, just as the early church revised its understanding of appropriate membership in the Christian community and included Gentiles? Not according to Hays. He admits that the strongest argument for approving same-sex relations in the church is the testimony of individuals who live in stable, loving same-sex relationships and claim to experience the grace of God in them. But, he argues, the analogy breaks down when we examine the way New Testament Christians responded to the conversion of Gentiles. It wasn't just the experience of the Gentiles that convinced them. They carefully examined the Scriptures and discovered a new meaning in the texts about God's saving intentions for all people. In the case of same-sex relationships, the church as a whole has not done this. Instead, the uniform testimony of the church and Christian tradition is that "homosexuality is one among many tragic signs that we are a broken people, alienated from God's loving purpose" (400).

If there is one uncontroversial conclusion we can draw from all this, it is this: There is strong disagreement on the question. On the one hand, there are those like Guy and Jones who argue that same-sex erotic activity is appropriate for Christians within the framework of loving, committed relationships. On the other, there are those like Grenz and Hays who argue that all homogenital contact is unacceptable for Christians, regardless of one's sexual orientation.

With deeply held views on both sides of the issue, where does that leave us? How should the Church today respond to its members who have a same-sex orientation? What should the Church say about same-sex relations and same-sex relationships? Let's conclude by listing some diverse responses. In each case, we will also note a familiar problem that it presents.

1. Same-sex relations are sinful and so is a same-sex attraction. People with a same-sex orientation should seek to reverse it.

Problem. It is widely accepted that sexual orientation is not a matter of choice, and attempts to "change one's orientation" are notoriously ineffective.

2. Same-sex relationships are perfectly natural. They fulfill the essential purpose of sexuality just as well as heterosexual relationships do. Same sex couples are just as capable of sustained, exclusive relationships as heterosexuals. They make just as good parents. They make just as good church members. The Church should welcome into membership people who are involved in loving, committed same-sex relationships.

Problem. The biblical witness uniformly affirms heterosexual relations and relationships and condemns same-sex activities.

3. Although the Church must condemn same-sex behavior, it should not exclude people simply because they have a same-sex orientation. To the contrary, it should welcome them into membership and open to them positions of leadership, with the important proviso, however, that they remain celibate. There are other things the Church should do, as well. It should avoid treating sexual sins as worse than sins of any other type. In particular, the Church should develop a perspective on sexuality that affirms singleness and celibacy as avenues to personal fulfillment. This is especially important in view of the sex-saturated culture we live in, where a lack of sexual activity is widely treated as an enormous deprivation.

Is the Church Ready for Same-sex Sex?

Problem. It is insensitive for naturally heterosexual people within fulfilling relationships to deny the satisfactions they enjoy to those whose same-sex orientation is perfectly natural to them. (In contrast, the Church expects single heterosexuals to remain celibate until they marry.)

4. Homosexuality is not part of the order of things that God intended, and the Church cannot give to same-sex relationships the official approval it gives to heterosexual marriage. Nevertheless, people in committed relationships should not be excluded from Christian fellowship, even if their domestic arrangements fall outside the biblical ideal. Committed same-sex relationships are certainly preferable to promiscuity. Perhaps the Church's approach to same-sex relationships should resemble its attitude toward divorce. It's not ideal, but under certain circumstances, it may be preferable to the alternatives.

Problem. This position will probably satisfy very few people and offend a great many, especially those who find same-sex relationships deeply fulfilling.

5. Hays suggests another possibility that may seem surprising, in view of his forthright objection to same-sex relations. He acknowledges the presence within the Christian community of those whose convictions differ from his. There are "serious Christians who in good conscience believe that same-sex erotic activity is consonant with God's will." In the area of such difficult questions, he argues, "we should receive one another as brothers and sisters in Christ and work toward adjudicating our differences through reflecting together on the witness of Scripture" (401). In other words, let's affirm each other as fellow believers and together pursue a clearer understanding of this difficult issue.

Problem. This seems to fall short of the straightforward witness against same-sex activity that the Bible supports.

Which, if any, of these approaches should Seventh-day Adventists take? There may be some in the Church who still take the first one, but it does not have wide support, at least not anymore. Grenz favors it, but his recommendation notably lacks enthusiasm. Guy and Jones take the second approach, and there may be a number who share it, but they are probably a distinct minority in the Church. The third approach may

Part 4-83

have the widest appeal in the Church, at least in countries where the issue is openly discussed. And though they will leave many people dissatisfied, approaches 4 and 5 might provide a helpful via media. Both fall short of the ringing endorsement that Fritz Guy calls for, but either is certainly preferable to the opprobrium and stigmatization to which lesbians and gays have often been subjected.

In spite of our traditional aversion to same-sex relationships, in recent years we as a church have become more open to the complexity of human sexuality and willing to consider more helpful responses. As we do so, we need to affirm the full humanity of all God's children and treat those who differ with us, in orientation and conviction, as brothers and sisters in Christ.

Questions for Discussion

1. Fritz Guy's theology of sexuality begins with an affirmation of physical pleasure as intrinsic to human experience. How would it affect such a theology if one began with the principle that all human conduct, such as eating and drinking (cf. 1Cor 10:31), and sexual activity as well, should glorify God?
2. According to the first two descriptions of human sexuality that appear in the Bible (Genesis 1 and Genesis 2), sexual activity fulfills two important functions: procreation and personal intimacy. How would a theology of sexuality develop if one gave as much attention to the first as to the second?
3. Fritz Guy rejects the idea that the church should welcome but not affirm people involved in same-sex partnerships. Would such an approach, however, provide a possible via media between the warm affirmation he calls for and the cold rejection that many have received from the church? Is it possible to affirm the value of human beings, to welcome them into fellowship, without approving of their sexual activities?
4. Among Seventh-day Adventists, sexual activity has traditionally been restricted to socially sanctioned as well as personally committed relationships. We have encouraged, if not required, people to wait until marriage to engage in sexual intimacy. When Fritz Guy calls on Christians "to welcome, affirm, and support persons engaged in morally appropriate same-sex relationships," does he mean that formal expressions of commitment are

necessary? Is he perhaps calling for Adventist pastors to perform same-sex weddings?
5. There is a familiar distinction in discussions of sexuality between sexual activity and sexual orientation. The usual argument is that while one's sexual orientation is not a choice, one's sexual activity is, and appropriate sexual activity takes place only in harmony with one's orientation. According to Fritz Guy, however, the moral quality of same-sex intimacy does not depend on sexual orientation. Does this mean that it is appropriate for people whose basic orientation is heterosexual to engage in same-sex love if they choose to do so?
6. While Fritz Guy repeatedly uses the words "caring and committed" to describe appropriate sexual relationships, he does not speak of them as "exclusive," but rather as "non-competitive." Are these two expressions equivalent? If not, his argument seems to allow for sexual activity involving more than two individuals, as long as all the participants are "committed and caring"—committed to the relationship(s) and equally caring for all the others involved. Can two people who engage in physical intimacy as an expression of their love approve of physical intimacy with other people to express love as well? (For example, imagine a trio of sexually intimate people comprising two bi-sexual men and a heterosexual woman, or a polygamous arrangement acceptable to all parties, like the one depicted in the HBO series "Big Love.")
7. At least one of the biblical examples of possible same-sex love Fritz Guy mentions, David and Jonathan, involves someone who was heterosexually active. Does this imply that one can engage in both homosexual and heterosexual relationships without violating the moral criteria he mentions?
8. Given the divisiveness of the issue of same-sex love (cf. the Episcopal Church), does Fritz Guy foresee any way to move toward an open acceptance of homosexual couples among Seventh-day Adventists without fragmenting the Church?

Notes and References

1. It would take an essay at least as long as this one to sift through the terminology employed in the many discussions of this issue. I am sure there are connotations to the various expressions I use that some will find objectionable, and I apologize in advance. It should

be obvious to the reader that this subject is largely outside my expertise. For the most part, however, in different parts of the discussion I follow the lead of the figures whose work I consider, such as "same-sex" and "homosexual," which are taken here as synonymous. One clarification may be helpful. When I speak of "same-sex relations," I have in mind erotic activity between people of the same sex, and when I speak of "same-sex relationships," I'm talking about the larger emotional and social framework in which these take place. This distinction parallels that between "sexual relations," which refers to genital contact of some sort, and "a sexual relationship," which typically refers to some sort of ongoing arrangement. Many people who engage in sexual relations are disconnected from anything that could be called a "relationship."

2. Grenz devotes a chapter to homosexuality in Part 3, "Singleness as an Expression of Human Sexuality," *Sexual Ethics: An Evangelical Perspective* (Louisville, Ky.: Westminster John Knox, 1990), 223–46. Richard B. Hays devotes a chapter to homosexuality in *The Moral Vision of the New Testament* (San Francisco: Harper, 1996), 379–406.

Part Five
Christian Social Perspectives

Part 5 - 2

Christian Sexual Norms Today: Some Proposals

By David R. Larson

There are many ways to insult heterosexual and homosexual men and women today. One of these is to state or imply that it is impossible for us to live sexually responsible lives. Another is to leave the impression that it is unnecessary for us to do so. Both claims are fallacious.

Whether we are heterosexual or homosexual, those of us who are Christians are accountable to ourselves, to each other, and to God for how we sexually think and act. Because our sexual desires and pleasures can be so intense, and because the consequences of enjoying them can be so positive or negative, in this realm of our lives, as in others, it is incumbent upon us to think as clearly and to act as honorably as possible.

This chapter proposes some ethical norms that we Christians can apply to our sexual activities. Those who study military ethics often distinguish between standards by which to determine whether to go to war (*Jus ad bellum*) and norms that pertain once we have decided to take up arms (*Jus in bello*). Although both clusters of ethical guidelines are important, they are different. By way of analogy, this chapter is not about whether we should be sexually active but about how we should conduct ourselves when we are. Greater clarity about this may help us decide whether we should be sexually active in the first place, however.

David R. Larson

The Priority of Relationships

We often hear that in real estate the three most important factors are location, location, and location. The three most important considerations in Christian sexual ethics are relationships, relationships, and relationships. Nothing else matters more, or even as much. The primary question before us is not whether a sexual deed is right or wrong, but whether the relationship of which it is a part is good or bad. Relationships are primary; deeds, though also important, are secondary.

Many of us attempt to discuss the morality of particular sexual acts with little or no regard for the relationships in which they take place. Exploring Christian sexual ethics by starting with such questions is a mistake. This method often leads to answers that perplex more than they persuade, and such outcomes wrongly allow us to impose our sexual likes and dislikes upon others. When sexual violations occur, they take place as deeds within relationships that are deficient or deformed in specific ways. These relationships deserve our primary ethical attention.

One of Philadelphia's magnificent outdoor works of art is Claes Oldenburg's *Kiss*, a gigantic clothespin sculpture that towers several stories above all who view it. Despite its provocative beauty, this statue is unable to tell us whether the encounter it celebrates is ethically honorable because it says nothing about the relationship in which it occurs. Depending upon the goodness or badness of this relationship, the kiss might be ethically right or wrong. When it comes to Christian sexual ethics, relationships count most of all.

Relationships and Love

Most Christians today hold that sexual relationships ought to be characterized by genuine love. To the extent that this is so, we believe that the relationship is honorable; to the degree that it is not, we deem it dishonorable and dangerous.

The conviction that sexual relationships should be characterized by genuine love has not always been believed and practiced, even by those in our Christian heritage. Onan, for example, was condemned because he practiced coitus interruptus instead of impregnating his brother's widow (Gen. 37:1–30).[1] According to the Levirate Marriage Law, he had a duty to help his dead brother's wife conceive, whether or not he

Christian Sexual Norms Today: Some Proposals

felt any particular love for her. Probably this was to give his deceased brother posterity and hence a kind of immortality, and to provide his brother's widow children who could bring her joy and care for her in her old age.[2] Conception was primary, affection secondary.

Hundreds of years later, Martin Luther asked what he should say to a Christian woman who had the misfortune of being married to an impotent man who refused to grant her a divorce. She should give herself to another man, Luther wrote, perhaps her brother-in-law, and attribute the children from this relationship to her husband. He "ought to concede this right to her, allowing her coition with another, since she is his wife in a formal and unreal sense anyway," he wrote.[3] If her husband refuses to allow this, she should feel free to contract another marriage and move to some distant place. "What other counsel can be given to one constantly struggling with the dangers of her own natural emotions?"[4] Satisfaction, not affection, was Luther's primary concern. Although we can identify other instances like these in Scripture and elsewhere, and even though the idealization of romantic love is a relatively recent development, most Christians in our time hold that love should permeate all sexual relationships.

This love is affection for a particular person in all of his or her idiosyncratic individuality. It differs from the type of love about which Diotima instructed Socrates in Plato's *Symposium*.[5] She taught that there should be an ethical progression in which we may begin with love for a specific person but as we mature it becomes love for beauty in general. Perhaps putting her point too severely, it is as though she would have us say to the one we love, "I don't love you, dear; I love the eternal beauty of which you are a partial and passing instance!"

This is not what we Christians have in mind. The kind of love we champion is directed toward someone else as a finite and fallible person with all the joy and sadness that this entails. We do not love someone as though he or she is a moment through which we love timeless excellence. We love this person. We love *him or her*.

The belief that sexual relationships should be characterized by love is relevant to our understanding of the texts in Scripture that condemn homosexual conduct.[6] Specialists in its languages, customs, and historical contexts continue to study the precise kind of activity that each passage rejects, as they should. Does this portion of Scripture condemn homosexual exploitation, unbridled excess, temple prostitution, military conquest, territorial protection, homosexual experimentation by heterosexuals, the exploitative mentoring of young people by prosperous and highly educated adults, or one of a host of other possibilities?

Paul's writings are particularly intriguing in this regard. He condemns male and female homosexual practice in one passage (Rom. 1:1–32) and men wearing long hair in another (1 Cor. 11:2–16), both in large part for being contrary to nature.[7] Whether today we should apply both passages universally, both locally, or either one locally and the other universally is a matter that scriptural evidence—not our preconceived ideas—should decide one way or another. Without compromising the priority of Scripture we should also consult evidence from other areas such as history, science, philosophy, and experience.[8]

Although all of the interpretative verdicts are not yet in, it is already possible to note two things: (1) Scripture everywhere condemns homosexual deeds, and (2) it nowhere addresses those that occur in loving relationships. It is good to know as much as possible about what its authors had in mind; nevertheless, for the purposes of this chapter, it is enough to know this much.

Love as Intense Loyalty

Although the First Testament of Scripture uses several words for *love*, its richest and most distinctive is *chesed*. Variously translated as "graciousness," "mercy," "kindness," loving kindness," "love," "steadfast love," "unrelenting love," and "covenant love," it's significance in Hebrew is so basic and powerful that in English no one word or combination of words fully captures its meaning. Nevertheless, if we must choose only one expression, "intense loyalty" is probably it.[9]

Chesed occurs 270 times in Scripture. The 70 or so times it appears in the Psalms are especially telling because they almost always refer to God's passionate and persistent affection for the people of Israel and, through them, all others. One Psalm, for example, celebrates God's unrelenting love in lines that leaders of worship and their congregations still read responsively. Each recital of one of God's activities is followed by, "for his steadfast love endures forever" (Ps. 136). This love is "fixed, determined, almost stubborn steadfastness." It is "sure love, love unswerving." It encompasses "fidelity, firmness, truth, firm adherence and determined faithfulness to the covenant." It is "the strength, the firmness and the persistence of God's sure love."[10] No theme is more central to Hebrew life and thought.

Christian Sexual Norms Today: Some Proposals

Three famous relationships in Scripture illustrate this kind of love at work. The story of Ruth and Naomi is the account of a widow who left her homeland and settled in a different culture out of loyalty to her mother-in-law. "Do not press me to leave you," she pled, "or to turn back from following you! Where you go, I will go; where you lodge, I will lodge; your people shall be my people, and your God my God" (Ruth 1:15–17). The story of David and Jonathan is about two men who might have fought each other to the death because one was a son of the king and the other a challenger. But David, the shepherd, and Jonathan, the prince, formed an intense friendship that endured despite all odds. After David had become king and Jonathan, the throne's rightful heir, had died in battle, David arranged for Jonathan's crippled son Mephibosheth, to live in the royal household. "I will show you kindness for the sake of your father Jonathan" (2 Sam. 9:7), he declared. The story of Hosea and Gomer is the portrait of a man who persists in loving and caring for his wife despite her flagrant unfaithfulness. Scripture says that Hosea's painful but constant love was like that of the Lord, who "loves the people of Israel, though they turn to other gods and love raisin cakes" (Hos. 3:1).

Covenant is a word Scripture often uses in connection with these relationships. When described as "an agreement enacted between two parties in which one or both make promises under oath to perform or refrain from certain actions stipulated in advance," it sounds much like a modern business contract that specifies minimum requirements legal systems will enforce.[11] Sometimes ancient covenants were this formal and coldly legalistic. More often they were emotionally exuberant promises to be faithful in ways that went far beyond that which was minimally required. In these cases, a covenant was a solemn and emotional promise to be loyal; it was a vow to honor not only the one to whom one makes a vow but also the promises one makes.[12]

Josiah Royce, California's first and foremost native-born philosopher, probably explored the moral meaning and importance of loyalty more thoroughly than any other modern thinker. He depicted it as a supreme moral good, the one from which all others derive and find their significance. "In loyalty, when loyalty is properly defined," he wrote, "is the fulfillment of the whole moral law."[13]

At the outset of his study, Royce defined loyalty as "the willing and thoroughgoing devotion of a person to a cause."[14] Such complete devotion is admirable even when the cause to which it is directed isn't, he held. For example, thieves who are loyal rightly receive more ethical admiration from us than do those who betray each other. Nevertheless, Royce went on to contend in language that echoes Scripture's praise of covenant faithfulness without actually quoting it, loyalty is truest when it is devoted to commendable causes, and the best of these is loyalty itself. We should be loyal to loyalty, he held. "In choosing and in serving the cause to which you are to be loyal, be, in any case, loyal to loyalty."[15]

"Loyalty to loyalty" may sound overly abstract, perhaps even similar to Diotima's teaching, except that Royce put "loyalty" where she spoke of "beauty." Although this may be so, his point seems importantly different. Royce held that in selecting the causes to which we will be loyal we ought to select those that will also aid and further the practice of loyalty in ourselves and others. Anything we do that enhances our own loyalty and makes possible and encourages more loyalty in others is ethically right; everything that doesn't is wrong.

Much like Scripture's praise of covenant faithfulness, Royce held that loyalty is more than the thoroughgoing devotion people can have for each other. It is something of its own, it is an additional factor that includes and sustains those who are loyal to each other. "Loyal lovers," Royce wrote, "are not loyal merely to one another as separate individuals, but to their love, to their union, which is *something more* than either of them, or even of both of them viewed as distinct individuals."[16]

This "something more" is what too many of our sexual relationships lack today, as they have in all generations. Voyeurism and exhibitionism are such cases because by definition each depends upon there being no intense loyalty in the relationship between the parties. The same can be said about coprophilia, necrophilia, pyromania, fetishism, bestiality, frottage, troilism, klismaphilia, coprolalia, pornography, and prostitution. None of the relationships in which these occur embodies anything analogous to God's steadfast love.

Fornication occurs when we intentionally exclude intense loyalty from our sexual relationships. Such relationships alienate one's sexual powers from the rest of one's total self. They alienate one's whole self from the total self of one's partner. These liaisons alienate us from God as well because they are so unlike the steadfast love that God bestows upon each of us.

Adultery is unfaithfulness or infidelity. It is worse than fornication because it more seriously offends what it means to be loyal:

Christian Sexual Norms Today: Some Proposals

The worst epithets are reserved for the sin of betrayal. Worse than murder, worse than incest, betrayal of country invites universal scorn. Betrayal of a lover is regarded by many as an irremediable breach. For the religious, betrayal of God is the supreme vice. The specific forms of betrayal—adultery, treason, and idolatry—all reek with evil.[17]

Fornication is the refusal of intense loyalty; adultery is its destruction. This is why in Scripture adultery is often a metaphor for human perversity in general.

Some recent modifications of Royce's proposals about loyalty helpfully distinguish between its minimal and maximal expressions.[18] At the very least, those who are loyal do not betray each other. Many intensely loyal persons go beyond this and fuse their lives into new social entities that become cells in the body of society without eliminating each person's individuality. This is what we mean when we say that sexual relationships should be characterized by love, and when we specify that, among other things, we Christians understand this love to be intense loyalty.

Love as Equal Respect

When it comes to words for *love*, the Greek term *agape* is as important in the Second Testament of Scripture as is the Hebrew word *chesed* in the First.[19] Its meaning in the Greek language before the time of Jesus Christ is not certain, probably because it was used so infrequently. This makes it all the more surprising that *agape* became so widely identified with the Christian movement. Far more than *philia* (friendship love), *eros* (passion for the true, beautiful, and good), and *epithymia* (sexual urge), it became known as Christianity's distinctive contribution.[20]

Understanding *agape* as "equal respect" is probably the best way to make sense of some of Scripture's commands today:[21] "In everything do to others as you would have them do to you, for this is the law and the prophets" (Matt. 7:12), mandates one. "You shall love the Lord your God with all your heart, and with all your soul, and with all your strength, and with all your mind; and your neighbor as yourself" (Matt. 10:27), declares another. Some refer to these as the Golden Rule and to their negative alternative, "do *not* do unto others as you would *not* that they do unto you," as the Silver Rule. We should not exaggerate the difference between them because they both display the logic of equal respect, however.[22]

This begins with the expressed or unexpressed assumption that we should be logically consistent.[23] It then asserts that when we are healthy we all treat ourselves with respect. We do not always admire what we say and do or always honor the characters we have developed; nevertheless, we value our lives and we protect and preserve them as far as possible. Although we are not necessarily egoistic in ethically unacceptable ways, to this extent we all are self-interested.

The logic of equal respect also requires us to be as honest and accurate as possible about the ways we are similar and different and when these variations matter. When selecting persons to be surgeons, for example, it is vital to notice that some of us can see and that others of us can't, and to select those who can, for example. The difficulty is that we often apply irrelevant considerations. Whether someone who wants to become a surgeon is Occidental or Oriental is not pertinent and should not be taken into account, even though in the past factors such as these have been considered. The person's qualifications should be the only consideration. With regard to treating people with equal respect, the factor that counts most is that we are all human beings. The humanity we share is the most pertinent consideration.

Because there is no ethically relevant difference between one person's humanity and another's, the demands of logical consistency require that we treat others and ourselves with the same kind of respect. To justify any other course of action is to be so irrational that nothing else we say can be taken seriously. A teacher who gives vastly different grades to students who do equally well on a test acts inconsistently and illogically. We cannot defend such conduct.

In its discussion of how husbands should treat their wives, the Letter to the Ephesians offers Scripture's most conspicuous display of the logic of equal respect: "In the same way, husbands should love their wives as they do their own bodies. He who loves his wife loves himself. For no man ever hates his own body, but he nourishes and tenderly cares for it, just as Christ does for the church, because we are members of his body" (Eph. 5:28–30). We often discuss this and other passages from historical and linguistic points of view. We would do well to analyze it from the standpoint of ethics, too.

When we analyze this passage from the point of view of ethics, the first thing we notice is that its line of reasoning depends upon the unexpressed assumption that in our moral thinking we ought to be logically consistent. It then reminds us that, as a matter of fact, all of us, in this case all husbands particularly, actual prize our own lives.

Christian Sexual Norms Today: Some Proposals

Having brought this to our attention, it argues that in loving his wife the husband loves himself, presumably because, for the purposes of this discussion, husband and wife are identical in every ethically relevant way. The conclusion necessarily follows: Because the husband treasures his own life, and because, with respect to the question at hand, there is no ethically pertinent difference between him and his wife, he is obliged to prize her as well. Not to treat her with equal respect would be logically inconsistent.

More than any other thinker since the Enlightenment, Immanuel Kant put the principle of equal respect front and center.[24] One version of his categorical imperative requires us to act so that the principles that inform our actions can be made into universal laws without contradicting themselves. A second version mandates that we treat humanity, whether we find it in others or in ourselves, as ends and never merely as means. In yet another version of his categorical imperative, Kant states that we should act as though we are living in a kingdom in which we are both the ones who make the laws and those who have to obey them. The point of these three versions of Kant's categorical imperative is that logical consistency requires us to treat others as we *inevitably will* them to treat us.[25]

Because the sexual relationship in which rape occurs is the worst and clearest violation of love as equal respect, it deserves our attention. Once again, we begin with the assumption that we should think and act in ways that are logically consistent. We then remind ourselves that we all value our own lives, or in the words of Scripture we do not hate but nourish and tenderly care for them. This means that none of us can consent to be raped because no one can will to experience something that in fact he or she does not will to experience! Furthermore, with respect to this issue, there is no relevant difference between others and us. This makes the conclusion inescapable. To rape someone is to do something that we cannot will to have done to us! If logical consistency is ethically obligatory, as this line of reasoning assumes from the outset, the relationship in which rape occurs is ethically evil.

To the extent that in any specific case they are morally akin to rape, sexual relationships in which a number of other practices take place also deserve our ethical disapproval. These include pedophilia, incest, sadomasochism, polygamy, polyandry, male or female chauvinism, and sexual harassment at workplaces in either of its two recognized forms: unwanted advances and unacceptable environments. It also applies to sexual relationships between professionals and the people they serve:

pastors and parishioners, teachers and students, health care workers and patients, therapists and clients, investment advisors and venture capitalists. Not every sexual relationship that develops in these contexts is morally identical to rape; however, enough of them are that presumptively we should regard them as unacceptable.[26]

Although *agape* is the principle of equal respect, it is also much more:

> *Love is rejoicing* over the existence of the beloved one; it is the desire that he be rather than not be; it is the longing for his presence when he is absent; it is happiness in the thought of him; it is profound satisfaction over everything that makes him great and glorious. *Love is gratitude*: it is thankfulness for the existence of the beloved; it is the happy acceptance of everything that he gives without the jealous feeling that the self ought to be able to do as much; it is gratitude that does not seek equality; it is wonder over the other's gift of himself in companionship. *Love is reverence:* it keeps its distance even as it draws near; it does not seek to absorb the other in the self or want to be absorbed by it; it rejoices in the otherness of the other; it desires the beloved to be what he is and does not seek to refashion him into a replica of the self or to make him a means to the self's advancement. As reverence love is and seeks knowledge of the other, not by way of curiosity nor for the sake of gaining power but in rejoicing and in wonder. In all such love there is an element of that "holy fear" which is not a form of flight but rather deep respect for the otherness of the beloved and the profound unwillingness to violate his integrity. *Love is loyalty*. It is the willingness to let the self be destroyed rather than that the other cease to be; it is the commitment of the self by self-binding will to make the other great.[27]

Marriage, Meaning, and Mercy

If this chapter has been successful so far, we have established that in Christian sexual ethics we should focus primarily upon our relationships. We have also demonstrated that our sexual relationships ought to be characterized by genuine love and that we ought to understand this as intense loyalty and equal respect. Not all of our

Christian Sexual Norms Today: Some Proposals

loving relationships should be sexual, but all of our sexual relationships should be loving. Achieving greater clarity about how we should conduct ourselves when we are sexually active can help us determine whether to engage in such activities at all.

Nothing we have said means that in our developing sexual relationships we should enjoy no physical contact before we privately promise and publicly declare our intense loyalty and equal respect. The guideline of "nothing before" and "everything after" is neither realistic nor wise. Rather, we should strive to calibrate our intensifying intimacies with our developing commitments. "Proportionality," or better yet, "propriety," is the goal. Although there are exceptions, in most cases this process takes months or years, not days or weeks.

Genuinely loving heterosexual and homosexual relationships exist. This does not mean that they perfectly embody intense loyalty and equal respect but that people in them accept this norm as their goal and realize it to a considerable degree. Some speak of "the homosexual lifestyle" as though all homosexuals arrange their lives in the same way. This is not so. Just as there is no one heterosexual lifestyle, there is no single homosexual way of life. Violations of love as intense loyalty and equal respect occur in both groups, as do their intended and actual fulfillment. We should not ask whether to allow loving heterosexual and homosexual unions to exist; they already do. Everything we say from here on out must begin with this fact and stay riveted to it.

We should acknowledge that these relationships exist. We should do everything we can to sustain them and to support people who are in them. We should encourage and enable these persons to contribute to the church and to society instead of exhausting all their resources on themselves. We should prevent others from abusing or violating them and discipline those who do. We should do all we can with voice and vote to make sure that they enjoy the rights and duties that all citizens possess. We should expect them to behave responsibly, as we do all others.

We should also find ways to honor them in appropriate Christian ceremonies. Whether we should refer to all of these relationships as "marriages" is an important question that we can successfully answer only in specific contexts.[28] Using one word has the advantage of highlighting the value we place on both heterosexual and homosexual loving unions. In many places today, the costs of doing this would outweigh the benefits, however.

David R. Larson

Over time, we have changed the meanings of words, sometimes surprisingly, and the world will not stop spinning if we do this again. We once used the word *nurse* for women who breast feed infants. We expanded its meaning to apply to those who take care of children more generally. We sent women into war zones, each as a "nurse" who helped and comforted wounded and dying soldiers. Today in many medical centers we have male "nurses" whom most patients respect and appreciate, even though their titles, which are not literally accurate, might have offended previous generations.

We changed the meaning of the word *fellow* in similar ways. We used it at first for "man" or "boy." We then applied it to some advanced scholars, appropriately enough because virtually all of them were males. The idea of a woman "fellow" makes no more literal sense than does a male "nurse." We comfortably use both titles, however.

This shows that, although today we usually reserve the word *marriage* for heterosexual unions, in principle there is no reason why this must always be so. Nevertheless, in fact we changed the meaning of "nurse" and "fellow" and other words slowly, locally, unevenly, and freely. It is doubtful that we could have increased the spread of these transformations by forcing them.

A complicating factor is that some heterosexuals and homosexuals do not want to apply the word *marriage* to their loving sexual unions, and others are ambivalent about it. For them, the word refers to an institution that long exploited women and children and they want to forge ways of interacting that are healthier for all. Instead of transforming the meaning of "marriage," they prefer to abandon this term in favor of others that do not possess all of its negative connotations.

Another difficulty is that there is no consensus among Christians today how to understand theologically the homosexual orientation. Some regard it as part of God's good creation, another expression of the variety in all things that God obviously prefers. Others see it as an aspect of our broken world with which we must all cope as well as possible. Still others stake out a third position, one that contends that the homosexual orientation may not represent God's primordial intention but that it is a blessing in our less-than-perfect world. We see this, they hold, in the ways homosexuals often enrich all of our lives precisely because of their orientation, not despite it. Such questions strike many other Christians as confusing, frustrating, and ultimately of no practical value no matter how we answer them.

Christian Sexual Norms Today: Some Proposals

Yet another complicating factor is that on this issue many Christians appear to have backed themselves into a conceptual corner without realizing it. One stance is consistent. It holds that human sexual intimacy has two proper purposes, unitive and procreative, which we should never intentionally separate. Largely for this reason, it rejects both artificial contraception and homosexual marriage as unnatural. The opposite position is also consistent. It also affirms these two purposes but holds that it can be morally acceptable to separate them intentionally. It therefore approves of both artificial contraception and homosexual marriage as equally natural. The third position appears to be inconsistent. It holds that sexual intimacy has two purposes, unitive and procreative, which we may legitimately separate. Nevertheless, it splits the difference between the first two stances by condoning artificial contraception as natural and condemning homosexual marriage as unnatural. Some claim that on its own premises this third position should reach the opposite conclusions, that artificial contraception is unnatural because it *intentionally* separates the unitive and procreative purposes, whereas homosexual marriage is natural because it *foresees* this outcome but *does not intend* it.[29]

These are not the kinds of questions that we can answer swiftly and simultaneously for Christians around the whole world. This is why we should focus upon our moral certainties rather than our moral perplexities. This is also why it makes sense to honor the principle of subsidiarity.[30] This guideline, which applies in church leadership as well as in government, business, academia, military life, and other settings, encourages us to answer questions at the lowest effective level of administration. Ignoring this principle can transform a local problem into regional, national, or even global discord. Christian leaders should establish broad guidelines and leave their implementation up to those who are nearest to the people.

Some political and religious leaders wrongly distract us from their destructive policies by vociferously attacking any changes in the meaning of words such as *marriage*. Their policies are widening the gap between the rich and poor. They are plunging us into military conflicts all over the world. They are allowing our roads, bridges, schools, and libraries to deteriorate. They are preventing us from making certain that each citizen has access to basic health care without bankrupting the system. And they are damaging our natural environments, leaving them less vibrant for subsequent generations. These politicians are able to implement such policies without our unified objections partly because they successfully divert our attention to other things like the proper meaning of words like *marriage*, something that will evolve on its own in any case. We should not let them do this.

Whether or not we call them "marriages," genuinely loving heterosexual and homosexual relationships are difficult to establish and maintain. In varying ways and degrees we all know what Paul meant when he wrote that sometimes he did what he did not want to do or did not do what he wanted. It is easier to intend something than to accomplish it, he rightly observed (Rom. 7:14–25). But we should remember that Paul also said that there is no condemnation for those who are in Christ Jesus (Rom. 8:1–8). He was talking about God's mercy, which arrives each moment as divine forgiveness and moral power. We can experience God's mercy without being in loving sexual relationships. We cannot long last in such unions without it.

In the final analysis, the Christian moral life is not primarily a matter of obeying rules or achieving goals. These are important, but not ultimately so. To be a Christian is to respond favorably again and again to God's steadfast love, which endures forever.[31] The gospel is first, the law second.

Analogously, in our relationships with each other, acceptance should precede confrontation. We all need both. But if we do not know that others truly value us and desire our best good, we are unable to welcome the changes they recommend. Some say that acceptance plus confrontation yields positive transformation.[32] The actual recipe calls for at least a dozen helpings of acceptance for each portion of confrontation. God loved us while we still were sinners (Rom. 5:8); this is how we should treat each other!

Questions for Discussion

1. The Bible says nothing bad about the practice of slavery and nothing good about homosexual deeds. We have moved beyond (not against) Scripture in the first case. Should we do so in the second one as well?
2. What other passages in the Old Testament portray love as "steadfast loyalty"? What other portions of the New Testament depict it as "mutual respect"?
3. Do you think it is a good idea to expect Christian heterosexuals and homosexuals to live with the same sexual rules?

Christian Sexual Norms Today: Some Proposals

4. When we say that some practice is either "natural" or "unnatural", precisely what do we mean?
5. Paul says that heterosexual men and women should get married instead of "burning" with sexual passion. Does this apply to homosexual Christians, too?

Notes and References

1. All scriptural quotations are from the New Revised Standard Version.
2. Wrongly identifying his misdeed, many people over the years have equated "Onanism" with masturbation. The story of Onan is actually about a different issue: a man's refusal to honor his deceased brother, to guarantee his posterity, and to provide for his widow's social and economic needs when there were no other support systems.
3. John Dillenberger, ed., *Martin Luther: Selections from His Writings* (New York: Anchor/Double Day, 1961), 337.
4. Ibid., 338.
5. Seth Benardete, ed. and trans., *Plato's Symposium* (Chicago: University of Chicago Press, 2001).
6. Gen. 19: 4–11; Judges 19: 1–30; Lev. 18:22 and 20:13; Rom. 1: 16:32; and probably 1 Cor. 6: 9; and I Tim. 1:10.
7. Appeals to "nature" can be perplexing in our time as well. People attempt to discern what is "natural" by consulting their proclivities, conducting surveys, reviewing history, doing cross-cultural studies, performing scientific experiments, and so forth. These approaches are often less than satisfactory because they do not provide a conceptual bridge between how things are and how they ought to be. Classical natural law theories did not have this problem to the same degree, for at least two reasons. One of these is that they openly declared that we should act in harmony with true human nature, something we cannot discover simply by looking around or within. The other is that using philosophical and theological resources they were able to describe true human nature in ways that many people found persuasive because it fit within their widely shared worldview. Although many deny this, all natural law theories say something like this: "Given such and such a worldview, this is natural and that is unnatural." Appeals to what is "natural" are therefore often placeholders for more

comprehensive assertions. In many societies today, there is little consensus about these larger issues.
8. The Copernican Revolution prompted us to understand some passages of Scripture differently. So did the Great Disappointment of October 22, 1844, when Jesus Christ did not return to earth in glory as the Millerites' understanding of Scripture's prophecies had led many to believe. Experience has also taught us to be more cautious about picking up snakes and drinking poison than some endings of the Gospel of Mark seem to advocate. In no case did Scripture or our value of it change; in each case our understanding of how best to understand and apply it to our own lives did.
9. E. M. Good, "Love in the OT," in George Arthur Buttrick, *The Interpreter's Dictionary of the Bible* (New York: Abingdon, 1962), 3:164–68; and Katherine Doob Sakenfeld, "Love (OT)," in David Noel Freedman, ed., *The Anchor Bible* (New York: Double Day, 1992), 4:375–80.
10. From Norman H. Snaith, *The Distinctive Ideas of the Old Testament* (Philadelphia: Westminsters, 1946), in Paul Ramsey, *Basic Christian Ethics* (Louisville: Westminster/John Knox, 1993), 5.
11. George E. Mendenhall and Gary A. Herion, "Covenant," in Freedman, *Anchor Bible*, 1:1179.
12. For discussions of the current differences between "codes," "contracts," and "covenants," please see William F. May, *The Physicians Covenant: Images of the Healer in Medical Ethics*, 2d ed. (Louisville: Westminster John Knox, 2000); and idem, *Beleaguered Rulers: The Public Obligation of the Professional* (Louisville: Westminster John Knox, 2003).
13. Josiah Royce, *The Philosophy of Loyalty* (New York: Macmillan, 1908), 16, 17.
14. Ibid..
15. Ibid., 121.
16. Ibid., 20.
17. George P. Fletcher, *Loyalty: An Essay on the Morality of Relationships* (New York: Oxford University Press, 1993), 41.
18. Ibid., 41–77.
19. G. Johnston, "Love in the NT," in George Arthur Buttrick, ed., *The Interpreter's Dictionary of the Bible* (New York: Abingdon, 1962), 3:168–78; William Klassen, "Love (NT and Early Jewish

Christian Sexual Norms Today: Some Proposals

Literature)," in Freedman, *Anchor Bible Dictionary*, 4:381–96; and Ethelbert Stauffer, "Agapao," in Gerhard Kittle, ed., *Theological Dictionary of the New Testament*, Geoffrey W. Bromily, trans. and ed. (Grand Rapids, Mich.: Wm. B. Eerdmans, 1964), 1:21–55.

20. Debating whether *agape* is altruistic and *eros* and other forms of love are egoistic is not the best use of our time because this controversy rests upon the assumption that at bottom we are distinct individuals related to each other only externally and contingently. The opposite is actually the case. Our relationships are internal and necessary, such that no one can be who he or she is in total isolation from others. Therefore, it matters little whether initially we aim our love at ourselves or others because, if it is genuine, eventually it will benefit both. We are not grains of sand, but threads in a tightly woven fabric. If we change one of us, we modify all of us. The claim that *agape* is wholly altruistic has especially negative consequences for Christian sexual ethics. After all, if *agape*, the distinctive form of Christian love, necessarily rejects our intense desires to receive as well as give sexual pleasure, very few of us can be Christians, or even want to be. Following Jack W. Provonsha's lectures at Loma Linda University, it seems best to depict *agape* as a sun, with the other forms of love circling it like planets, thereby emphasizing that they are all valid and valuable providing in their proper orbits they are centered on and controlled by *agape*.

21. Gene Outka, *Agape: An Ethical Analysis* (New Haven: Yale University Press, 1972), pp. 7–54. Whereas Outka uses "equal regard," this chapter employs "equal respect" in hopes that its connotations are stronger.

22. The principle of generic consistency, "Act in accord with the generic rights of your recipients as well as of yourself," is expounded with no appeals to religious authorities in Alan Gewirth, *Reason and Morality* (Chicago: University of Chicago Press, 1978); and Edward Regis, Jr., ed., *Gewirth's Ethical Rationalism: Critical Essays with a Reply by Alan Gewirth* (Chicago: University of Chicago Press, 1984). This appears to be yet another occasion in which religious conviction and secular reason point in the same direction.

23. As developed in this chapter, the logic of equal respect does not commit the naturalistic fallacy by claiming that from nothing but a neutral description we can deduce an ethical prescription. To the

David R. Larson

contrary, it begins with the *prescriptive* assertion that it is *ethically* obligatory to be logically consistent, even though this is not always stated explicitly. This is the major premise; the minor premise is that the guiding principle of some deed is not consistent with itself. A necessary conclusion follows. It is that this act is therefore ethically wrong. This major premise is incapable of absolute proof. Nevertheless, it has the advantage of not assuming too much initially. The approach in this chapter assumes so little ethics at the outset that it is difficult to imagine anyone objecting. If someone actually contends that we have no ethical obligation to be logically consistent, it is difficult to take him or her seriously. Taking that position at face value would require us to agree that even the statement that logical consistency is ethically dispensable need not be consistent with itself. This seems to get us nowhere.

24. Immanuel Kant, *Groundwork for the Metaphysics of Morals*, Allen W. Wood, ed. and trans. (New Haven: Yale University Press, 2002).
25. The "Golden Rule," or what this chapter calls "the logic of equal respect," makes a point that is logical, not psychological. It does not mean that we should treat other people as we would like them to treat us. This meaning is too subjective. The point is that we should treat others as we inevitably will to be treated ourselves. This is more objective.
26. For the role of presumptions in Christian ethics, please see J. Philip Wogaman, *A Christian Method of Moral Judgment* (Louisville: Westminster John Knox, 1997).
27. H. Richard Niebuhr, *The Purpose of the Church and its Ministry* (New York: Harper and Row, 1956), 35.
28. Please see Andrew Sullivan, *Same-Sex Marriage: Pro and Con: A Reader* (New York: Vintage Books, 2004); and Marvin Mahan Ellison, *Same-Sex Marriage? A Christian Ethical Analysis* (Cleveland: Pilgrim, 2004).
29. The longstanding principle of double effect in Christian ethics distinguishes between outcomes that are "intended" and those that are "merely foreseen." Setting aside some important technicalities, this principle says that when one action has two inescapably linked outcomes, one ethically acceptable and the other ethically unacceptable, the deed may be done if and only if we exclusively intend the ethically acceptable effect. One way to tell whether a certain action qualifies is to ask whether we would eliminate the

Christian Sexual Norms Today: Some Proposals

ethically unacceptable outcome if we could. A surgeon foresees that he or she will leave a scar but does not intend to do this, as evidenced by the efforts made to make the scar as small and invisible as possible. A surgeon who makes no attempt to minimize the size and visibility of scars may be suspected of intending to leave them. This analogy fits our discussion almost perfectly because many homosexual couples foresee that they will have no biological children, but that they do not intend this is exhibited by their various attempts to adopt children.

30. For a discussion of the principle of subsidiarity in Christian ethics, please see J. Philip Wogaman, *A Christian Method of Moral Judgment* (Louisville: Westminster John Knox, 1997).
31. H. Richard Niebuhr, *The Responsible Self: An Essay in Christian Moral Philosophy* (New York: Harper and Row, 1963).
32. Howard Clinebell wrote this formula on a whiteboard for his students in pastoral psychology at Claremont School of Theology in the 1970s.

Ministering to Gays within the Church Community: A Pastoral Perspective

By Mitchell F. Henson

The year was 1953. I was ten and a member of the local Pathfinder Club in Greensboro, North Carolina, that met each Sunday evening in the basement of a church member's home. There we learned to march; there we learned to salute; there we learned to stand in military formation and snap to attention. We earned badges in weaving, knot tying and cooking, and basic survival techniques. Several of our Pathfinder leaders were veterans of the Korean and Second World Wars. And so our Pathfinder Club had a military emphasis.

On one camping trip, we were taken into the woods and shown a stream. There were some small, wiggly creatures that looked very much like small lizards. They were called salamanders, and we were told that having salamanders in the stream was a good indication that the water was safe to drink. "If it's safe enough for them, it's safe enough for you." It would be many years before I came to understand how important these words were—not only for survival in the woods, but also for survival in the church!

On February 1, 1960, in the Woolworth store on Main Street, several young men and women moved from one section of the store to stage a sit-in at the soda fountain, where only whites were allowed. Historically, that sit-in at Woolworth's became almost as important as Rosa Parks's sit-down on the bus, December 1, 1955, and as significant

Mitchell F. Henson

as the march on Montgomery, Alabama, March 7, 1965. These were historic events in the racial struggles of the 1950s and 1960s.

Meanwhile, on State Street, the Seventh-day Adventist Church met each Sabbath morning, and not one word was mentioned from the pulpit about these momentous events. We were waiting for Jesus to come. It was our obsession. It was our goal. It was our mission. It was our calling. We had no time for earthly concerns such as equality and justice. We were only strangers on the earth. Our home was in heaven, and we were interested in getting there as soon as possible!

This was the lens I looked through as I saw the world around me from ages nine to eighteen. I knew that man would never walk on the moon, because God would never allow the "sin of this planet" to spread throughout his universe. I knew that time would not last long enough for me to become sixteen years of age and drive a car. All of these things I knew, because I was taught them, and because I believed them.

All through my theological training, first at Southern Missionary College and later at Columbia Union College, issues of social justice were never addressed. There was only exegesis of biblical texts, an effort to understand and defend the writings of Ellen White, and, of course, an obsession with the signs of Christ's soon coming.

It was at the Seventh-day Adventist Theological Seminary that we first began to look at social issues. There were blacks at the seminary who said the church could never really be baptized with the outpouring of the Holy Spirit as long as there was a separation between brothers and sisters. There were non-Adventist speakers who came to talk to us: Anthony Campolo challenged us to look up from our books and look around at individuals, situations, and circumstances in our environment. Some of our professors, such as Roy Branson and Harold Weiss, also encouraged us to do this. Still other instructors and guest speakers insisted that these were views of a "social gospel," and as such were a distraction to God's "Remnant Church" and should not occupy our time or attention.

Although Scripture is replete with "social gospel" examples such as "inasmuch as ye have done it unto the least of these, ye have done it unto me," each generation of Adventists must somehow try to incorporate the social aspects of Christianity into a theology of Adventism. This will of course be a struggle, but it is a struggle rich with insights, and it demands courage, compassion, and a continual reevaluation of our theology, our praxis, and our view, both of the

Ministering to Gays within the Church Community

world and of what it means to be a remnant people.

In 1984 I went to the Glendale City Seventh-day Adventist Church in Glendale, California, as an associate pastor. I had been a senior pastor for a number of years. I had enjoyed that experience, but felt I wanted to gain additional education. I also wanted to step back and take another look at what ministry was all about. And so began seven wonderful years at Glendale City Church as an associate.

Some time in the early 1980s we became aware, in our staff meetings, of discussions about certain young men who were beginning to attend our church. During this time AIDS was becoming an epidemic in America. We would get calls asking if we would be willing to minister to, or visit, or at times to bury young men who had died of AIDS.

As Senior Pastor Rudy Torres tells the story, one day a young man, Carlos Martinez, came to our church and "came out" to a Bible study group. He indicated that he had contracted AIDS, but he believed that God continued to love and care for him. Soon Carlos was in the hospital. Torres and I visited him, and in the course of those visits we had numerous conversations with nurses and other attendants. We found there were many young men in the hospital who, when it was discovered they had AIDS, lost all church affiliation. As we continued to minister to Carlos and others, we became known as pastors willing to reach out to young men facing an illness that, at that time, was considered inevitable death.

It was during this time that I began to work through the prejudice that I held in my heart toward gays and homosexuality in general. I knew that, according to my understanding of Scripture, no homosexual would be in the Kingdom of God; yet here were young men reaching out to us in their time of need. The gratefulness that they and their families showed us moved my heart and forced me to reevaluate my beliefs. I began to understand God's grace, forgiveness, and acceptance at a deeper level. After burying eight or ten of these young men, I realized that for me ministry would never be the same again.

Let me be very specific as to why Glendale City Seventh-day Adventist Church continues to minister to all who come. I believe the attitude that existed toward blacks in the church when I was a young man exists today toward homosexuals. It's not that we don't allow them to attend (as long as we "don't know who they are"). It's not that we might not even encourage them to become members (as long as they declare celibacy). But we certainly would not want their considerable talents to be used or put them into positions of leadership knowing they are gay. We might find ourselves in embarrassing situations, trying to explain to conservative activists and those who seek to "protect the reputation of the church" how we can maintain high standards while accepting and allowing homosexuals to be actively involved.

I believe many younger members of our churches are waiting to see how we handle this important issue. Are we going to develop a better understanding of the Holy Spirit's ministry? Are we going to leave it in *his* hands to comfort and guide people into a better understanding of God's will for their lives? Are we going to actualize the words of Christ, "whosoever will, may come unto me"? At times, our determined efforts to change people socially betrays a weak belief in the wooing, changing power of the Holy Spirit, who continues to work in the lives of individuals long after they have become church members and leaders.

The black hole of Christian theology is the subject of sexuality. Old Testament Scripture is abundantly clear that sex is for procreation. In the New Testament, Paul warns that it would be better to "marry than to burn" (meaning "burn with passion"), because time is short. In recent years, as we have incorporated the understandings of psychology (including the need for intimacy and personal contact) into our teaching about sexuality, and since technology has provided us with easy and noninvasive ways of interrupting the natural procreation process, I think we can safely say that, in the Western world at least, 99 percent of all sexual activity, both marital and extramarital, is for other than procreative purposes. Yet many Christians continue to interpret Scripture referring to sex, intimacy, and marriage in traditional ways.

As heterosexuals, we have expanded the biblical meaning to include sex for pleasure and intimacy, but we have stopped short of understanding sexuality in a broader sense—not just genital stimulation or procreation, pleasure, and intimacy, but sexuality as a statement of who I am as a human and how I relate to life as a sexual being. Perhaps we have avoided this because of the loaded connotation of the word *sex*; or perhaps we have simply not studied it carefully because "time is short," and we have more pressing matters. Nonetheless, as time continues, we find ourselves increasingly challenged to revisit and define more clearly our views on sexuality, singleness, celibacy, celibacy in marriage, and a wide range of sexual behaviors and mores that continue to be practiced in our culture.

Ministering to Gays within the Church Community

I wish to address some of the myths that continue to be part of the Christian community's vocabulary. Individuals have called our church, asking why gays are allowed to attend. Callers have used phrases such as "gay lifestyle" and "living in sin," and Change Ministries have used these phrases as a challenge to our practice of open and inclusive worship.

The first phrase I wish to address is "the gay lifestyle." In the heterosexual community, this phrase has become a euphemism for certain specific sexual practices, which I will not explicitly discuss here, other than to note that heterosexuals practice *all* of the sexual practices included in the so-called "gay lifestyle," and on a rather regular basis! I will briefly mention some statistics readily available on the Internet (see, for example, *Mademoiselle Magazine*, Dec. 1993). Oral and anal sexual contact between heterosexual adults is quite common, with 88 percent of men and 97 percent of women reporting these practices.

Or, put in another, more "palatable" way, it is sexual activity that has absolutely no chance of fulfilling the biblical injunction of being "fruitful and multiplying the earth." As a pastor, when I am challenged with individuals who accuse others of practicing a "gay lifestyle," I realize that these calls come from people who are simply uninformed about the whole continuum of human sexual expression. And, as any pastor knows, I have neither responsibility nor permission to inquire specifically about church attendees' intimate sexual behaviors. But many "Christians" persist, believing that they are somehow standing for the principles of conservative Christianity by throwing the phrase "gay lifestyle" around in a rather wanton manner.

Let me tell you what I've learned as a pastor in my association with the gay members who attend my church. There is no more a gay lifestyle than there is a black lifestyle, a Protestant lifestyle, a Catholic lifestyle, or even a Seventh-day Adventist lifestyle. Now, of course, you will recognize immediately that each of these groups has certain behaviors that are unique to them. But do these unique aspects qualify as a lifestyle? I think not!

As homosexuality has become more publicized in the media and more support organizations have been established, increasing numbers of individuals feel freedom to "come out" and declare their homosexuality. Yet most sociological studies indicate the level of homosexuality in typical societies has remained relatively constant for hundreds, even thousands of years. It cannot be then, as some would

Mitchell F. Henson

assert, a disease that can be caught, or some kind of political movement to be recruited and joined, or even some kind of abhorrent religion determined to proselytize and gain new congregants. I will readily acknowledge, however, that some people are quite vociferous in their support of homosexuality…and of heterosexuality, and of celibacy. In other words, there's no particular way, if we're honest, to categorize gays in this way. Categorizing people into lifestyles allows us to hold prejudice while claiming to uphold principles.

- There are gays who have chosen not to acknowledge their sexual definition. They are still "in the closet."
- There are gays who are "out" but choose, for personal reasons, to remain celibate. They may or may not be married and living in "heterosexual" relationships.
- There are gays who are "out" and in the gay community only, and who live wanton lives, going from relationship to relationship to relationship—just as we find in the heterosexual community. Most of the biblical texts that challenge sexual exploitation by gays refer to this group. We refer to heterosexuals who act these ways as fornicators, prostitutes, or whores. But rarely do we exclude them from Christian worship. In fact, most ministers go to great pains to make sure that we understand that Jesus was friends with just such people! He ate with them. He preached to them. He loved them!
- And finally (and this is by no means a complete picture of the varied lives of gays), there are those in committed relationships, living in mainline heterosexual communities. Sometimes they're seen as the creative individuals on the block, the artistic people, and they often carry on full and rich lives. They have a wide range of friends within the gay and straight communities.

In other words, there is a wide range of lifestyle expression by gays. In communities that are more accepting, they may be more visible.

Another myth I have discovered in my pastoral work is that gays are theologically liberal. Some of the most conservative Christians in my community, those familiar with Ellen White, who use Bible proof texts as a basis for their beliefs, are my gay church members! They often express how much they wish for the soon coming of Jesus. They long for a place where there are no walls of separation, no condescending smiles, no shallow "good to see you" welcomes, which are often quickly retracted when members find out who they really are. One interesting fact is that, on communion Sabbaths, most of the gays

Ministering to Gays within the Church Community

in my congregation attend and participate.

Most Adventists know that there is notoriously weak attendance by heterosexuals on communion Sabbath. Some have conjectured that the reason is because we practice the ancient ritual of foot washing. Many pastors have attempted to update the service by surrounding it with love feasts, family communions, and other innovations to try and make it more appealing. I remember recently sitting on the back pew with my wife as the elements were served. All around me, young men and women reached out and accepted with eagerness these emblems of our Lord's body. Tears came to my eyes as I realized that this was one of the few churches, probably one of the very few Seventh-day Adventist churches, where they would be allowed to accept these emblems or at least to accept them eagerly and joyfully. What a privilege it was to be in that service on that day!

Another myth I wish to deal with is that of "living in sin." This one, of course, has great energy for those who wish to take church action and discipline individuals who may not fit our social or ecclesiastical norms. It is often used against those divorced for "nonbiblical" grounds or those living with someone to whom they are not legally married; and it's often the language used when referring to homosexuals. But when we look carefully at the idea of living in sin, through the eyes of Scripture and Christ, we begin to realize that each one of us, at every moment, in some sense is living in sin.

Now I don't wish to twist words here. I understand the concept of living in sin, as discussed in the *Seventh-day Adventist Church Manual*. It has to do with living in a way that flaunts church doctrine or brings reproach on the denomination. It has been my experience, however, that the reproach brought on the church by prejudice against gays does greater damage than any reproach that stems from their attendance. People in the community, especially unchurched individuals, expect the church to be a place where people are accepted. They have heard us call it a hospital for sinners! They believe that if someone desires to attend church, they should be allowed to do so. Sadly, however, there are too many who have a story of someone whom a church has hurt, seeking to uphold the standard of sinless living by trying to weed out those "living in sin."

I am well aware of the rules in the *Church Manual* against homosexuality. And I can truthfully say there are no individuals in my church who have asked to be accepted into church membership just because they are homosexual. Heterosexuals and homosexuals alike

Mitchell F. Henson

request church membership because they find the church to be a warm and loving place where they can grow in Christ. Understanding our lives through grace means that we all acknowledge we are constantly living in sin and need the fellowship of the "saints" to help us cope with this sinful world.

In all my years of pastoring a church with gay members, never has a gay Christian asked me to endorse any kind of behavior or lifestyle. If one were living a life intended to be an affront to the church—one that was hostile, arrogant, or hurtful—that *attitude* would be at least as destructive as the *behavior*. And that *attitude* would need to be confronted. In other words, living in sin is more than a sinful act: it's a sinful attitude, a hurtful attitude, a destructive attitude, an arrogant attitude, a rebellious attitude. That attitude should be confronted for the protection of the body of Christ.

Of all the experiences I have had with gay men who have wished they could change, but were unable, one stands out in my mind. I will make only general references here to this individual since some of you may remember him when he held a prominent position in the church. He lost everything when it was discovered that he was gay. Being forced out of his profession, he became involved in some angry, dysfunctional, sexual relationships where he unfortunately contracted AIDS. During this time of despair, he somehow heard of Glendale City Church and came to visit me. Here was a man that I had known years before—articulate, intelligent, educated, and creative—now destitute and completely sick, a mere shadow of the man I had previously known. We talked a bit. I of course prayed and empathized with him, and I gave him some money for a bus ticket.

Several months later, I received a letter, which I still have. The letter said, "When you receive this letter, I will already be dead from an overdose of medication that I've been saving. I gave up my position in the university because I could no longer live a life that was a lie. And now, I have decided to take my life because I find that my life no longer has meaning." I thought to myself, as I think to myself even today, what an honest man. What a tragically honest man! I'm not blaming anyone for the circumstances he found himself in, but neither am I blaming him. To see someone who had once flown so high reduced to an almost less-than-human position was an experience I have promised God I will never forget, and will never knowingly be a part of.

Perhaps many of you remember the television program *The*

Ministering to Gays within the Church Community

Twilight Zone. Back in the 1950s and 1960s it was one of the most popular TV shows. I wish to cite a portion of one of the classic episodes. As the scene opens, we see a body lying in a hospital bed, face swathed in bandages, with only a slit for the mouth. I would like to introduce to you Janet Tyler, patient number 307, who has returned for her eleventh treatment. The bone structure of her face is such that plastic surgery is not the treatment of choice. Her physicians have chosen injections of various kinds, including thyroid treatments, to no avail. Now she waits expectantly, yet with dwindling hope, that this final procedure will affect change so she will no longer feel like a freak of nature. She is a young woman alternating between despair and wistful hope for a better life for herself. The nurse gently eases the thermometer into her mouth through the narrow opening. It's time to read the patient's vital signs—temperature, blood pressure, and pulse. And Janet speaks:

> "What about today? What is it like outside? Is it beautiful?"
> "It's nice," says the nurse.
> "When will they take the bandages off?" Janet asks, through muffled tones, inside her gauzed tomb.
> "Soon," says the nurse. "Honey, why don't you rest? You've been through a lot."
> And Janet continues to no one in particular, "It's pretty bad, isn't it?"
> "I've seen worse," said the nurse.
> "No, it's pretty bad. I don't know how much more I can take. Eleven treatments. The government insurance has notified me that this is the last treatment they will pay for. Ever since I was a little girl people have turned away from me in disgust. I remember when I was only a child, another little girl—I thought a friend of mine—looked at me and screamed and ran away. I've never wanted to be beautiful, to look like a painting, or be some movie star; I just wanted to look like everybody else. I just wanted to be normal."
> "Get some rest, honey. Tomorrow the doctors will come, and then we will see."

Throughout the film, the camera angles are always at the eye level of Janet Tyler, as if looking through her eyes. We never get a look at the physicians; there is never a frontal shot of the nurses or any of the attendants. Their faces are always shrouded, either in shadows,

Mitchell F. Henson

cigarette smoke, screens, furniture, or some cloth object. "All of this was done," said the producers, "to heighten the curiosity of those of us who were watching. It built mystery, intrigue, and anticipation." Finally, when the gauzes are removed, we are shocked! Revealed is a woman of stunning beauty. Surely the procedure has worked this time! Surely she will be pleased. She is handed a mirror but shrieks in horror. Throwing the mirror against the wall, she runs wildly down the dark, shadowed corridors of the hospital. The camera backs away, and only then do we see the faces of the caregivers. They all look like pigs—horrible, misshapen, and grotesque.

The film ends with these words by Rod Serling: "Now the question comes to mind, Where is this place? And when is this time? Where ugliness is the norm, and beauty the deviation from that norm?" And I will add, what about the church? What about your church? What should be our attitude and posture toward those who are gay? Are they included in Jesus' statement, "Whosoever"? Can you be sure that the change you demand for another will be an improvement? Playing God may be the ultimate blasphemy!

I am a pastor, and as a pastor I have served various churches for more than thirty years. Throughout that time, I have sought to be faithful to the call of God. I have fallen far short of that desire, but it still burns in my soul; and the difference between what I want to be and what I actually know myself to be gives me the blessed grace to accept others. All the spiritual, emotional, and psychological surgery I have had has not made me someone else. Underneath it all, I am still myself—a better me, I hope, and certainly a more caring and less judgmental me. For I can see through my own relationships and my struggles with my own demons how hard—how impossible, in fact—it is to become someone else. So I've had to settle for the person that I am now, with daily effort and prayer to be the best me that I can. But grace, sweet grace, saving grace, assures me that at all times, this side of heaven, I am accepted by God, saved by Christ's blood and assured of eternal life. That acceptance, that love, that assurance, that spiritual continuity, woos me to be a better servant, husband, father, grandfather, friend, and, yes, pastor.

Struggles? Yes. Disappointments? Yes. Heights? Yes. Depths? Oh yes. But nothing, not one thing, says Scripture, shall be able to separate me, shall be able to separate you, shall be able to separate us from the love of God, as it is in Christ Jesus. With that inclusive statement, I rest my ministry in the hands of Jesus who said, "Whosoever."

Ministering to Gays within the Church Community

Questions for Discussion

1. How many gays do you personally know? Gay Christians?
2. What's the worst thing about being gay? Is there any good thing about being gay?
3. Do you believe a gay person should remain celibate, if he or she is going to be a Christian and join a church? Do you believe non-married heterosexuals should remain celibate? Do you see a difference between the two? If so, explain
4. Should the church provide training for its pastors about how to dealing in a caring way for its gay members and their families?.

Public Policy Issues Involving Homosexuality

By Mitchell A. Tyner

Homosexuality—more particularly, the status of homosexuals and their relationships before the law—has become one of the most confrontational, divisive topics of our time, both politically and theologically. Numerous writers have identified well over one thousand instances where homosexual couples are denied the rights and privileges available to heterosexual couples, and this revelation has lead many to advocate the legal recognition of homosexual marriage or the functional equivalent thereof. Their efforts, in turn, have produced the most vociferous backlash from those who argue that to do such a thing will be to remove the moral underpinnings of American society. Other writers have described the nonmarriage-related inequality of homosexuals in current society, involving such issues as the nonprotection of homosexuals as a suspect category, leading to denial of protection in such fundamental rights as employment and housing.

Recently, numerous jurisdictions have moved significantly toward legal equality for homosexual, including listing sexual orientation as a protected category in local or state human rights statutes and recognizing homosexual marriage or domestic partnerships. The most significant judicial move was the 2004 decision of the U.S. Supreme Court in *Lawrence vs. Texas*, which ruled that antisodomy laws could not be applied to homosexuals. In the *Lawrence* ruling, the Court

Mitchell A. Tyner

overruled its infamous previous decision in *Bowers vs. Hardwick* and recognized the existence of a right to privacy in sexual matters.

Legally, this movement continues apace, as several states and nations enact protective statutes. It is not the purpose of this discussion to address the current legal and political realities, as others have done so admirably. The conference that gave rise to this book addressed homosexuality in the Seventh-day Adventist context, and this chapter continues in that vein. Previous speakers have addressed the questions of how Seventh-day Adventists, both corporately and individually, should understand the phenomenon of homosexuality in Scripture, the existence and experience of Seventh-day Adventist homosexuals, and the responsibilities of both the church and its members to them. That leaves a further question: How do we, corporately and individually, relate to the religio-political questions involving homosexuality that are currently producing so much heat and so little light? What are the considerations that should be involved in the formation of an Adventist response to such public issues? This chapter looks at four, the first two scriptural and timeless, the last two more contemporary. The list is not exhaustive; it should include but is not limited to the following.

1. Does the Proposed Position Maximize Human Freedom?

To be faithful to Scripture, our positions on public policy issues should work to maximize human freedom to the highest appropriate level. Arguably, the most revealing Scripture passage that involves freedom is not the little horn or Revelation 13, but Luke 15, the passage we refer to as the story of the Prodigal Son, although it might better be called the story of the Waiting Father.

A young man, raised on an affluent but remote farm went to his father and said "Dad, I'm bored. I'm tired of living way out here. I want to experience the world for myself; I want to go to the big city; I want to do my own thing. And Dad, I want you to give me an advance on my inheritance to finance the trip."

Nothing in either Jewish or Roman law gave the father any obligation to grant that request, but he did. The son left, wealth in hand, and headed for the bright lights. As long as the money lasted, so did his social status. But soon he found himself in a descending socioeconomic spiral. His money gone, he was forced to earn his livelihood by doing something most hateful to a young Jew: feeding hogs. He awoke one

Public Policy Issues Involving Homosexuality

morning in the pigpen, looked around him, and said, "What a miserable state of affairs! What a genuine wreck I have made of my life."

To put this story in Seventh-day Adventist terms, imagine a young man from a farm in the eastern Montana who, having gone to New York, awakens in a drug-induced stupor in one of those neighborhoods you don't want to enter at night. He has been making his living dealing drugs. He awakens and thinks, "This is Sabbath morning. Mom and Dad are in church, and look at me. Look how far I've come."

The Bible simply says, "He came to himself." He realized his position. He looked around and said, "I have ruined my life, I have nothing: nowhere to sleep, no means of support, nothing to eat, and I can't go home. I've had my share of the family wealth and I've squandered that. It's gone. Even my dad's hired hands out there on the farm are better off. I ought to go home and just ask Dad to hire me."

He sat there in the mud and composed the speech he would offer his father. He would say, "Father, I have sinned before you and before God. I am no longer worthy to be called your son—just hire me and let me live out in the bunkhouse with the hired hands." With that, he started home.

Imagine the father, sitting on the veranda of one of those old farm houses—the kind with the long porch that ran the width of the house. The family sat there in the evening catching the cool breeze, talking about the weather, the crops, and family news.

The father has been sitting there every afternoon since his son left. He's never given up on his son's return. Then one day, far off down the road, he sees a pathetic figure limping along. He's lame, he's ill-kempt, and he's dirty. But the father immediately recognizes him as his son. The father doesn't wait for the son to come to him. Instead, the father hurries off the porch, down the path, through the gate, and down the road to meet his son. As they meet, the son begins his prepared speech of contrition: "Dad, I've blown it, I'm not worthy to be called your son...." and he never gets to finish the speech.

It's as though the father said, "Son, I know, I understand. We'll talk about that another time. For now, all that matters is that you're home. Come inside, we'll celebrate your return!" With that, he covered this filthy figure with his best cloak, put a ring on his finger, and led him to the house, where the celebration began.

The older son heard the sound of the celebration and asked one of the hired hands what was happening. He was told, "Your brother's back and your father's throwing a party." But the older brother refused to join the celebration.

Mitchell A. Tyner

Eventually, the father came to him and said, "We're celebrating your brother's return—come in and join us!"

The elder brother said, "Look, Dad, I've been with you all these years. I have obeyed your every command. I have done everything you have asked but you never threw a party for me. Now this son of yours comes home after wasting your money and his life and you expect me to celebrate? Why should I?"

Notice that the elder brother was factually correct, which merely shows that one may be quite correct but very wrong as to the correct interpretation and application of those facts. Notice also that the elder brother referred to "your son," not "my brother."

The father replied, "Your brother was lost, and has been found; he was dead and he is alive to us again. It is proper that we celebrate!"

Who was right in that story, the father or the son? The father, of course. The father represents God, our Father. The son represents us, for each of us has at one time or another wandered away from our spiritual home.

Why did the father let that happen? The father could have prevented it. He didn't have to give his son the money, but he did. It can even be alleged that by funding the journey of the prodigal, the father aided and abetted prodigality. Why? Because the father was more interested in his son than in his money. Because ultimately he was interested in his relationship with his son. Because he wanted a relationship with his son that was possible only when the son was ready to enter into it voluntarily. The father would not force his son to stay at home. He would not be satisfied with coerced obedience.

Isn't that a marvelous parable of our heavenly Father! Our Father put such a high value on his relationship with us that he paid the price of Calvary to avoid coercing us. He could have forced us to stay at home with him, and no one could have faulted him for doing so. But he will not be satisfied with coerced obedience. Yes, he's interested in our conduct. But when we come back to him, he doesn't say, "All right, before you come in the house let's talk about that time in the pigpen. Let's talk about what you did, let's talk about the money you wasted, let's get all of this straightened out." No, he puts his robe of righteousness around us and says, "Come inside. The party is ready to start—in your honor."

Here is a parable that illustrates an important facet of the great controversy between good and evil, a key historic Adventist teaching. God could have created us in such a manner that we could not have

Public Policy Issues Involving Homosexuality

sinned. He didn't, because he wanted a relationship with us based on our choice to establish it. He refused to coerce us. But doing that cost him dearly. It cost him the life of his son at Calvary, paid so that we could relate to him freely. Every man, woman, boy, and girl is free to relate to God freely, according to his or her conscience, not someone else's.

What are we to learn from this story? First, that God put a tremendous value on freedom. He could have prevented Calvary, but didn't, because he would not coerce our obedience. Second, we have no business, like the older brother, being more judgmental with each other than our Father is with us. Third, we have been given an example that speaks to our own attitudes and actions: If God went to that length to not coerce us, then how dare we, his children, coerce each other?

2. Does the Suggested Position Maximize Equality?

Again, to be faithful to Scripture, our positions on public policy issues should work to maximize human equality to the highest appropriate level.

Consider the Gospel of Luke, chapter 10. Jesus was confronted with a questioner—a lawyer, a young scholar of religious law who had heard of Jesus and wanted to put Jesus' teaching on the record. The dialogue went something like this:

Lawyer: "Rabbi, what shall I do to inherit eternal life?"

Jesus: "What do you read in the law?"

Lawyer: "You shall love the Lord your God with all your heart, with all your strength, and with all your mind, and your neighbor as yourself."

Jesus: "You read well. Now go and do that and you will live."

When confronted with an unwanted answer, one may acquire at least a little wiggle room by seeking to define further one or more terms used in the answer. So the lawyer replied, "And just who is my neighbor?"

Knowing that his questioner was not amenable to a direct answer, Jesus chose to answer indirectly, through a story, the Parable of the Good Samaritan.

"A certain man," said Jesus, "went down from Jerusalem to Jericho." Mr. Anonymous chose a narrow, twisting mountain road that descends rapidly from the Judean hills to the Dead Sea Valley. It is a dangerous route today, and surely was much more so in Roman times.

Mitchell A. Tyner

During the course of his journey, Mr. Anonymous was mugged: He was attacked by thieves, assaulted, stripped of everything of value, and left for dead.

Jesus then presented his audience with an interesting procession of observers. First to come on the scene was a priest, clergy, one trained to identify with and alleviate human need. True to his calling, he viewed the wounded man and thought, "This is terrible! This man has been wounded through no fault of his own, yet here he lies." But he quickly caught himself before his empathy got him into trouble. He thought, "The thieves who did this may still be nearby. They could well do the same to me. And after all, my first responsibility is to my family and to my ministry. This man is part of neither. I don't know him and I don't owe him! If I am injured or killed, who will care for them? Surely the proper and prudent thing for me to do is to go on and report this to the authorities. And besides, I'm carrying a month's tithe from all the local congregations down to the National Bank of Jericho for deposit. We can't risk losing that."

Having armed himself with good excuses, he passed by the wounded man. But he did not pass by too closely—so close that he would have to look in the man's eyes and sense his pain. Instead, he passed by on the far side, evidence that the pacification of his conscience was not working all that well.

Next came a Levite. Here was another man trained much like the priest. He, too, was taught to be a shepherd of the flock, but he was not serving in a direct pastoral role. Perhaps in modern parlance we could call him a religious bureaucrat, a denominational administrator. The Levite also reacted as trained. He, too, saw the injured man and began to empathize. But his mind wandered a bit: "This is awful! We must regain control of our streets and put these criminals away where they belong!" As he worked himself up on the subject of the shortcomings of the criminal justice system, he also began to sense the priest's predicament: "They could do the same to me." And he also reasoned his way out of that bind: "I'm going down to Jericho to deliver an address on the ethical treatment of strangers. If I stop here, I help only one person. But if I go on, my lecture could be the start of a whole new Good Samaritan Society in Jericho. Surely, the responsible thing is for me to proceed." And so, for the sake of giving a lecture on loving others, he left his neighbor to languish in pain and distress. He followed the priest's detour and passed by on the far side.

And then came a Samaritan. Why did Jesus choose a Samaritan for

Public Policy Issues Involving Homosexuality

this role? Perhaps it was because he well knew the reaction of his questioner to such a person. Samaritans were the outcasts of the day. Public opinion was that they were not pure Jews; they came from an inferior stock, inferior social position, an inferior education. They could not be trusted. If we had passed through the streets of Jerusalem, we might have overheard conversations in which it was said, "You can't trust those Samaritans. They'll lie and cheat and steal. They'd rather draw welfare than work for a living. Best to have nothing to do with them for your own safety." If the injured man had known a Samaritan was approaching, he probably would have shuddered in anticipation of further harm.

But the Samaritan stopped, the only one of the three observers to do so. He stopped to give aid to someone who otherwise might have despised him.

The Samaritan's reaction was neither ivory tower theory nor mere emotional response. He methodically poured oil and wine (the only cleansing/disinfecting agents available to him) into the injured man's wounds, bound them, put the man on his pack animal, and took him to the nearest inn. Before leaving, he said to the innkeeper, "take care of him, and when I return I'll settle the cost with you." The Samaritan disregarded the threats to his own safety that had been correctly noted by the priest and the Levite. He just acted, on behalf of someone very much not like him.

At this point, the dialogue between Jesus and his interrogator resumed.

Jesus: "Now, which of these three do you think acted as a neighbor to the injured man?"

Lawyer: "Obviously, the one who stopped to help."

Jesus: "Exactly. Go and do likewise."

Isn't it interesting what Jesus did *not* say to the lawyer? He did not say to him, "Go and study the scrolls. When you can properly and coherently exegete the prophecies and explain Ezekiel's vision of the wheels within wheels, then come back and we will discuss you future course of action." Jesus spoke nothing of what the questioner should know or believe, only of what he should *do*. He spoke not of orthodoxy, but of orthopraxy. He simply said, "Go and *do* likewise."

Four characteristics of the Samaritan's response bear emulation. First, it was a *caring* response. The Samaritan obviously cared enough about the injured man's predicament to endanger himself in order to help. The act of not taking the detour mapped out by the preceding observers was motivated by recognition of the value of another human in need—in other words, *caring*.

Second, it was an *involved* response. It is all too easy for moderns to trust groups— relief groups, state agencies, religious organizations—to react to human need while we comfortably sit back and make donations of a bit of money and a bit of time. The Samaritan put far more than that into the project.

Third, it was a *committed* response. The Samaritan not only bound the wounds of the victim, he also volunteered to underwrite his care for an indeterminate period. Now that's commitment!

Fourth, it was a *relevant* response. The Samaritan could have continued on his way, and on arrival in Jericho sought to convene a council on the causes and remedies for highway crime. Not a bad thing in itself, but not relevant to the man lying in the road. Rather, the Samaritan got immediately involved, and he did what needed to be done at that moment. He acted relevantly.

Perhaps most importantly for this discussion, all of this was for someone with whom the Samaritan would have been in profound disagreement theologically, politically, and otherwise. There was no pondering of theological convergences, of historic ties, of cultural affinities. There was no consideration of public opinion or of the opinion of other Samaritans, no mapping of potential geopolitical consequences. The Samaritan did not see a Jew (or an Edomite, or a Roman or Greek, or whoever the victim was), he just saw a person in need and recognized that he had the ability to meet the need.

How does this story inform our response to such questions as equal rights for homosexuals—or anyone else? It says that our response must be caring, involved, committed, and relevant. It must not be deterred by the approbation of many for the object of our care, or by the potential threat to our own standing. We must be prepared to evenhandedly aid those for whom we can be of service, regardless of their agreement—or lack thereof—with our beliefs and interpretations. How could such considerations ever lead us to deny equal rights to homosexuals, or anyone else?

In the current context, a consideration of the interrelationship of freedom and equality is necessary, for equal rights not infrequently act as a restraint on freedom. We do not exercise our freedom in a vacuum, but in the context of social relationships. As the apostle Paul said, "None of us lives to himself." Paul also observed, "All things are lawful to me, but all things are not expedient." A responsible exercise of our freedom always considers the effect of our actions on the rights and needs of others.

Since the late 1990s, there has been, within the church-state community, a running discussion concerning whether or not sincere religious belief should constitute a valid defense to a charge of violating the equality rights of others. The question arose in this fashion. In 1990, in the case of *Employment Division, Department of Human Resources of Oregon vs. Smith*, the U.S. Supreme Court severely cut back the reach of the Free Exercise Clause of the First Amendment to the U.S. Constitution. One result was the formation of a broad coalition that sought legislation to moderate the damage done to religious freedom. This brought about the passage of the Religious Freedom Restoration Act (RFRA) in 1993. The Court responded a few years later, in *Boerne vs. Flores*, by ruling RFRA inapplicable to the states. The coalition then prepared a bill known as the Religious Liberty Protection Act (RLPA). RLPA never got off the ground. It foundered on the question of religious belief as a defense. One side said, "If religious belief is not included in the bill as a legitimate defense, we will leave the coalition."

The other side said, "If religious belief *is* recognized as a defense, we will leave the coalition." The coalition then foundered.

What was this discussion really about? Homosexuality. The question was whether a sincerely held religious belief that one should not employ or rent to homosexuals should be a valid defense to a charge of violating protected rights. Difference of opinion on that question is so deeply held that it has prevented the religious community from achieving broad-based protection for free exercise of religion since that time.

How do we answer that question? Should our religious beliefs allow us to discriminate? When we put the question in the context of race, the answer is clear for most people: Just because a person sincerely believes that he or she should not hire or rent to a person of color should not relieve him or her of the duty of nondiscrimination. In this instance, the equality rights of one person trump the religiously motivated practice of the other. Few will argue against that position—until they recognize that it cannot be distinguished on any principled basis from the question of equality rights of homosexuals. It simply comes down to the fact that one is generally accepted in our society and the other is not—yet. Surely our response to such questions should maximize both freedom and equality, properly balancing the two, rather than merely reflecting popular opinion.

Mitchell A. Tyner

3. Is the Proposed Position Informed by Our History?

To be responsible, our positions on public policy issues should take cognizance of the applicable lessons found in our own history. We have experience with the negative results of efforts by well-meaning people to enact their views and religious convictions into law. Consider the effects of the national Sunday law drive of the late-nineteenth century.

In 1888, Senator H. W. Blair of New Hampshire sponsored a Senate bill (N. 2983) to promote Sunday observance as a day of worship. Blair's bill (and a similar one in 1889) was defeated, at least in part due to the five hundred thousand signatures secured against it by the then-tiny Seventh-day Adventist Church, spurred on by the enthusiasm of A. T. Jones, among others. The national bill was stopped, but the effort to enforce Sunday observance was not. Rather, the scene of activity shifted to the states.

During 1895 and 1896, at least seventy-five Seventh-day Adventists were prosecuted in the United States and Canada under state or provincial Sunday laws. Some were fined; a few were acquitted or were lucky enough to have their cases dismissed. But 28 served jail terms, aggregating 1,144 days: almost 3-1/2 years in total.[1] Such prosecution was not happenstance or just a small part of a broader picture of thousands of Americans arrested for a wide variety of Sunday activities. To the contrary, it was a matter of selective enforcement. Those prosecuted were targeted not just for their conduct, but for the reason behind it.

Perhaps the most significant of these cases was that of R. M. King of Obion County, Tennessee.[2] King had farmed in the community for twenty years and was held in high esteem by his neighbors, although they disagreed with the practice he followed as a Seventh-day Adventist of tilling his fields on Sunday. His neighbors tried to persuade King not to work on Sunday, but he resisted. Finally, "they insisted that he must keep Sunday and not teach their children by his example that the seventh day is the Sabbath and if he did not comply with their wishes he would be prosecuted." King was subsequently arrested for working in his fields on Sunday, June 23, 1889. On July 6, Obion County Justice J. A. Barker found King guilty as charged and fined him a total of $12.85. Since King refused to stop Sunday work, his neighbors had him indicted by a grand jury for virtually the same offense.

Judge Swiggart and a jury heard the matter in Troy, Tennessee, on March 6, 1890, Attorney General Bond appearing for the state and

Public Policy Issues Involving Homosexuality

Colonel T. E. Richardson for King. The charge was that King's repeated Sunday breaking constituted a public nuisance—a charge that opened the way to a harsher penalty than did mere violation of the Sunday law. The jury heard five witnesses for the prosecution and one for the defense. It deliberated only half an hour before returning a guilty verdict and assessing a fine of seventy-five dollars. The judge denied a motion for a new trial and warned that King and his ilk must obey the law or leave the country.

Colonel Richardson appealed on King's behalf to the state supreme court, which in 1891 merely affirmed the trial court without opinion. Then Richardson, joined by Donald M. Dickinson, U.S. postmaster general from 1888 to 1889, appealed to the United States Circuit Court for the Western District of Tennessee.[3] Their theory on appeal was a new one: Since no previous case recognized habitual Sunday breaking as a public nuisance and no state statute described it as such, to convict King for such activity constituted denial of the due process and equal protection of law as guaranteed by the Fourteenth Amendment to the United States Constitution. Significantly, they also argued that he had been denied the religious freedom guaranteed him by the First Amendment religion clauses.

On August 1, 1891, Judge Hammond rendered his decision. He acknowledged:

> By a sort of factitious advantage, the observers of Sunday have secured the aid of the civil law, and adhere to that advantage with great tenacity, and in spite of the clamor for religious freedom and the progress that has been made in the absolute separation of church and state, and in spite of the strong and merciless attack that has always been ready, in the field of controversial theology, to be made, as it has been made here, upon the claim for divine authority for the change from the seventh to the first day of the week.[4]

Nevertheless, the state court decision was sustained. Was it proper to define such conduct as a public nuisance? It was, said Hammond, if a state court said so. A federal court would not second-guess a state court on the meaning of that state's law. Hence, no deprivation of due process existed. King also lost on his First Amendment claims, said Hammond, because that amendment did not apply to the states. According to the decision, "the Fourteenth Amendment of the Constitution of the United States has not abrogated the Sunday laws of the states, and established religious freedom therein. The states may establish a church or creed...."[5]

Upon that point, King's lawyers appealed to the U.S. Supreme Court in the fall of 1891, asking the Court to clarify whether the Due Process Clause of the Fourteenth Amendment made First Amendment guarantees binding upon the state.[6] It was a strategy used successfully by Jehovah's Witnesses in 1940.[7] If the Supreme Court had adopted that theory in 1891, the course of Sunday legislation, and indeed all religion clause jurisprudence, would have been different. But the Court did not have the opportunity to rule on the question: R. M. King died on November 12, 1891, before his case came before the Court.

The 1890s may have been the high-water mark in the prosecution of Sabbatarians, but the flood did not recede immediately. As the tide of fundamentalism rolled toward its crest about the time of the famous Scopes trial, it carried with it a continuing volume of such prosecutions.[8] Well into the twentieth century, as America experienced increasing industrialization and urbanization, with the concomitant rise of secularism and liberal thought, the pattern continued—and not just in the rural South. In 1923, three Seventh-day Adventists were arrested in Massachusetts and fined for painting the interior of a house on Sunday in order to get it ready for occupancy the next day. In 1932, a deputy sheriff of Washington County, Virginia, arrested two Seventh-day Adventists for Sunday work: one, a crippled mother who walked on crutches, for washing clothes on her own premises, and, the other, a man who donated and hauled a load of wood to a church to heat it for religious services.

As late as 1938, a Massachusetts storekeeper was arrested for selling fresh eggs on Sunday, at a time when it was legal to buy cooked eggs, beer, and liquor, and to attend sports events and movies on the same day.[9]

Beginning in 1940, a line of U.S. Supreme Court cases established that the First Amendment, including the religion clauses, had indeed been made applicable to state and local governments via the Fourteenth Amendment, thus opening the door to Sunday-law challenges based on those clauses, and in 1961 those challenges found their way to the Court. The questions raised in R. M. King's case in 1891 would finally be answered by the high court seventy years later. It's just as well that King didn't live to hear the answer: Sunday laws were upheld as no longer religious in nature. That claim would have been impossible to make with a straight face in 1891.

Public Policy Issues Involving Homosexuality

The point? That Adventist activism of an earlier day averted two bills in Congress, and came very close to producing a fundamental change in the law, one that the Court might have reached a half-century earlier but for the death of R. M. King. Not until 1963, in the case of *Sherbert vs. Verner*, did the Court accord religious belief and practice the protection it deserves. And Adele Sherbert was also a Seventh-day Adventist! Our own history should teach us what we can accomplish in the area of human rights when we put sufficient resources into the effort.

Another case in point was that of Day Conklin of Big Creek, Forsyth County, Georgia, who in March 1889 was arrested, tried before a jury, and fined twenty-five dollars and costs, amounting in all to eighty-three dollars. His offense: cutting wood near his front door on Sunday, November 18, 1888. Attorney William F. Findley later gave the following recollection of the case:

> One of these Seventh-day Adventists was tried over here in Forsyth County, and I think there never was a more unrighteous conviction. There was a man named Day Conklin, who was moving on Friday. He got his goods wet on Friday, and it turned off cold. On Saturday he went out and cut enough wood to keep his family from freezing. On Sunday, he still hadn't his things dry, and it was still as cold as it had been on Saturday. He still cut enough wood to keep his family warm, and they convicted him for doing this. I say that is an outrage, an unrighteous conviction, for he was doing the best he could. One of the jurymen told me that they did not convict him for what he had done, but for what he said he had a right to do. He said he had a right to work on Sunday.[10]

Notice, "we convicted him because he said he had a *right*." In reality, Conklin was convicted because he claimed that his religious practice was of equal dignity and deserved the same respect and protection as that of the majority. His real crime was to claim equality.

Today, much of the resentment of homosexual claims for equal rights at bottom is resentment of a claim of equality. "They have the temerity to claim that they are our equals." In the homosexual marriage debate, many are willing to approve some arrangement that affords homosexuals all or most of the rights pertaining to marriage, as long as it is called something else—as long as there is not a claim of equality! That is sadly reminiscent of the fate of Day Conklin.

Mitchell A. Tyner

Our own history teaches us that when even sincere, well-meaning people seek to use the law to enforce their views of morality on others who do not share those views, bad things happen to good people. That lesson, coupled with an awareness of the potency of our advocacy, rightly motivated and focused, should place us in the front lines of those who defend equality rights today.

4. Is the Proposed Position in the Best Interest of the Church?

Certainly the best interest of the church is a valid consideration. None will wish to jeopardize the church by advocating, in its name, a particular position. Some will argue that the best interest of the church is served by keeping a low profile on social and political issues. They will cite Ellen White's advice that the church in the South should remain segregated, at least for the time, and that we should not publicly oppose Bible reading in the public schools. Those statements must be read and understood in the context of a time in which the church was fragile and vulnerable. Public opinion was such that advocacy on those issues would have cut off almost all avenues of witness.

Is that true today? Would advocacy on behalf of equality rights for homosexuals negate the ability of the church to witness to society? In contrast, will continued silence on the issue negate our ability to communicate with thinking people who espouse a principled view of the matter? Our society is no longer monolithic on these issues; we do not face a situation analogous to the times in which Ellen White wrote.

> More fundamentally, how can it ever be in the church's interest to act other than in accordance with scriptural counsel and instruction? The Bible clearly tells us that God puts a tremendous value on human freedom. Our divinely given example is one who rendered aid where it was needed, not as a "respecter of persons." Our own history shows the dangers that follow the legislation and imposition of religious beliefs and religiously based moral convictions on those who do not share them. To act on these principles is in the best interest of the church. Indeed, to fail to do so would be an indictment of the church, an irresponsible neglect of its best interest.

Public Policy Issues Involving Homosexuality

Questions for Discussion

1. What are the proper lessons to draw from the Adventist experience in the 1880s?
2. Should Christians seek to outlaw conduct they believe to be biblically banned?
3. Should Christians defend the rights of those who advocate practices they find morally objectionable?
4. What are the proper limits of the free exercise of religion?

Notes and References

1. Quoted in William Addison Blakely, *American State Papers*, 4th rev. ed. (Washington, D.C.: Review and Herald , 1949), 514.
2. *In Re King,* 46 P. 905 (U.S. Cir. Ct., West Tenn., Aug. 1, 1891).
3. Now known as the United States District Court for the Western District of Tennessee.
4. *In Re King*, quoted in Blakely, *American State Papers*.
5. Ibid.
6. Robert M. King vs. W.L. Jackson, Sheriff of the County of Obion, State of Tennessee, United States Supreme Court docket number 14912; Appeal from the United States Circuit Court for the Western District of Tennessee, filed October 23, 1891; United States National Archives, Record Group 267, M216, Roll8, page 16005
7. *Cantwell vs. Connecticut*, 310 US 296 (U.S. Supreme Court, 1940).
8. *Scopes vs. Tennessee*, 289 SW 363 (Tenn. Sup. Ct. 1927).
9. Blakely, *American State Papers,* 508.
10. Ibid., 488–91.

Love, Subsidiarity, Equality, and Inclusiveness

By Gary Chartier

Larson: Love and Subsidiarity

David Larson has written a characteristically graceful and thoughtful essay about Christian sexual morality. He has said many useful and provocative things. I want to focus on two: his claim that intense loyalty is a moral requisite for sexual relationships and his suggestion that the principle of subsidiarity should inform judgments about ecclesial responses to disputes about the status of lesbians, gays, and bisexuals.

Love

Larson identifies two aspects of love that ought to be exhibited by morally appropriate sexual relationships: love as intense loyalty and love as equal respect. Love as equal respect is a fundamental principle of morality, embodied in the Golden Rule.[1] Larson helpfully elaborates this principle.

Larson's arguments regarding love as intense loyalty are not so persuasive, however. He helpfully distinguishes our view of erotic love as concerned with one's partner in her or his particularity and as concerned with sharing the whole of life rather than simply sexual pleasure (or, for that matter, child-rearing or household chores). I think it is clear that erotic love as he has described it is a great good.[2] A free self-gift, effected through a promise, such love offers liberation from isolation, fear, insecurity, and loneliness; validation, self-knowledge, and self-esteem; dignity, security, trust, self-respect, and self-acceptance; the possibility of discerning more clearly the beauty, vulnerability, and value of all things; and the opportunity for delight, challenge, stimulation. and self-transcendence.[3] Committed love "is transformative"—liberating, empowering, ennobling.[4]

It does not follow, however, from the premise that such love is a great good that it is a morally necessary context for sexual interaction. Larson gracefully outlines biblical images of covenant love. But these images, although they point clearly and powerfully to the worth of such love, do not on their own establish that it is morally required as a setting for sexual expression. Larson rightly notes that some kinds of sexual relationships lack the sort of intense loyalty Josiah Royce describes. But he fails to provide us with a plausible rationale for supposing that all such relationships should be marked by this kind of loyalty in the first place.

Sexual relationships from which a suitable level of commitment is lacking "alienate one's sexual powers from the rest of one's total self," Larson says. "They alienate one's whole self from the total self of one's partner. These liaisons alienate us from God as well because they are so unlike the steadfast love that God bestows upon each of us." But why, precisely, do they do this? Larson does not say.

Obviously, a sexual relationship not marked by complete commitment is one in which the partners are not as present to each other as they would be were they maritally committed. As a result, they miss out on the goods that can come only with marital commitment. But what follows from this? They experience other goods, and perhaps avoid what they see as serious risks. Some further premise is required to warrant the conclusion that they wrong each other or themselves simply by not experiencing as much good (of one sort) as possible.

I am not sure what it means to "alienate one's sexual powers from the rest of one's total self." Larson seems to suggest, by using this phrase, that a complete self-gift, which should be forthcoming in sex, is absent when suitable commitment is lacking—and that this is something that both divides oneself and invites a similar self-division on the part of one's partner. But this conclusion only follows if—emotionally or semiotically—sex would necessarily convey a complete self-gift absent someone's decision not to give fully of her- or himself.

Love, Subsidiarity, Equality, and Inclusiveness

And I have doubts about this premise.

Sex can certainly foster attachment and intimacy. This means that people who become sexually involved increase the likelihood that they will be hurt if they are rejected by their sometime partners. This is obviously one of several good reasons for honesty and promise keeping in the context of sexual relationships. But it does not follow that sex ordinarily communicates or creates *total* commitment. Different people feel and believe and communicate different things when they are sexual. Although sex, as a "natural symbol," is apt for the communication of a delimited range of meanings related to intimacy, it does not follow that the *same* meaning is borne by every sexual act. The notion that such acts carry an *inherent* meaning—total self-bestowal—with which sex outside the framework of marital or quasi-marital commitment is in conflict treats sexual acts and relationships as uniform in a way I believe they are not.

Although commitment does protect people's vulnerability to each other, a vulnerability sex can accentuate, different sexual experiences and relationships can give rise to different sorts of vulnerability. And we often think in other contexts, in any case, that people do not wrong themselves or others when they accept significant risks. Further, great personal intimacy *without sex* can give rise to comparable vulnerability without being the object of censure by opponents of sex outside the context of marital commitment.

Someone might also argue for a position like Larson's by suggesting that being sexual only within the context of marital or quasi-marital commitment would help to ensure that sex fostered intense bonding between people and thus served the cause of solidifying and stabilizing erotic relationships. This argument seems plausible as far as it goes: limiting sex to marriage or quasi marriage could indeed have this effect. But the fact that a particular policy will serve to increase some good does not show that not following this policy is wrong. We do not have a duty to maximize the good (assuming, indeed, as I deny, that this is a coherent injunction). If we do have a duty to seek flourishing and fulfillment, and not merely the avoidance of harm, it does not follow that we must all seek the same *kind* of flourishing and fulfillment, that we must all pursue perfection in the same regions of our lives.

Only if sex outside the framework of commitment leads to self-alienation and alienation between partners does Larson's final point, that it leads to alienation from God, follow plausibly. It will be morally relevant that sex outside the framework of suitable commitment is "unlike the steadfast love that God bestows upon each of us" only if it is harmful, which I have argued that it need not be, or if it embodies less good of a relevant sort than it might, and we are obligated to maximize the good—which again it seems implausible to suppose that we are.

"Many intensely loyal persons," Larson observes, "fuse their lives into new social entities that become cells in the body of society without eliminating each person's individuality. This is what we mean when we say that sexual relationships should be characterized by love, and when we specify that, among other things, we Christians understand this love to be intense loyalty." Again, the image Larson paints here is attractive. But who are "we" who imply that sexual relationships should all be characterized by intense Roycean loyalty? Such loyalty is a great good, but Larson has not demonstrated that its absence, without more, renders sexual relationships morally deficient.

Subsidiarity

The principle of subsidiarity holds, roughly, that a decision should not be made at a higher level of an organization or community when it can be made at a lower level—a level closer to those directly affected by it. This principle seems intuitively plausible as a matter of both efficiency and justice. Larson suggests that this principle should affect our resolution of disputes regarding same-sex sex and same-sex marriage. This seems right, if it means that a range of institutional mechanisms and political strategies are appropriate for achieving just ends, or if it means that a range of possible ends will be compatible with the demands of justice.

However, Larson suggests that several specific questions "are not the kinds of questions that we can answer swiftly and simultaneously for Christians around the whole world," and that these questions can finally be addressed satisfactorily at the local level. Here I am not persuaded. He seems to have in mind at least three questions: what conclusions we should reach about the sources and status of same-sex sexual desires; whether any responsible sexual relationship must be open to procreation; and whether *marriage* provides the proper institutional framework within which to honor same-sex relationships. All three ultimately require resolution beyond the local level.

An answer to the first question that treats same-sex erotic desire as

Love, Subsidiarity, Equality, and Inclusiveness

a sign of brokenness—as a deficiency, even if one we must accept—will send the message, wherever it is heard, that same-sex erotic desires give those who experience them reason to be ashamed. Certainly it will not do for "Christian leaders…[to] establish broad guidelines [for the resolution of this sort of question] and leave their implementation up to those who are nearest to the people." It is rarely helpful for church authorities to impose solutions to knotty problems on those they serve. But ultimately, the question whether some members of a Christian community should regard themselves as suffering from an impairment or handicap simply because they experience same-sex erotic desires (and certainly if they act on those desires) is a question regarding the inclusiveness of the church that is too important to be answered in a variety of ways. Imagine a similar claim—that having dark skin is a regrettable consequence of Noah's curse on Ham—not part of God's creative plan for humanity, but "an aspect of our broken world with which we must all cope as well as possible." I do not believe a responsible Christian community could make it a matter of local choice whether a marginalizing theological position of this kind could be propounded.

The same is true of the question of the moral link between sex and openness to procreation. The conclusion that there is such a link, and that because it obtains same-sex sex is wrong, would obviously have substantial consequences for same-sex erotic relationships in church communities throughout the world. It will not do, I think, to suggest, again, that this is the sort of thing that can be resolved locally. For at the end of the day, in communities that accept the necessity of linking sex with openness to procreation, the message will be clear that some people are grievous sinners because of their erotic relationships.

Subsidiarity doesn't offer a satisfactory solution to the dispute over recognizing same-sex marriages, either. It is certainly right that some same-sex couples have doubts about the institution of marriage, and they should be free to structure their lives and celebrate their unions as they see fit. It makes sense then to let a thousand flowers bloom. But we cannot ultimately regard as just a model in which same-sex couples wishing to marry are permitted to do so in some environments but not in others. For the *option* of same-sex marriage sends a clear message: that same-sex couples are welcomed in our communities on an equal basis with different-sex couples. The denial of this option sends a similar message: that persons in same-sex relationships are, at best, second-class church members. We would not treat it as appropriate for some local communities within our church family to use an irrelevant characteristic, ethnicity, as basis for determining whether a couple's relationship should be solemnized and celebrated. We cannot proceed as if gender *is* a relevant characteristic when there is no rational basis for doing so.

Again, different political environments may require the use of different political strategies to achieve justice and inclusiveness. But the ultimate aim of those who seek these goals in the church cannot and should not be an environment in which fairness and inclusion are evident in some places but not in others. The church as a whole must be a community in which God's love and justice are embodied.

Tyner: Equality Before God and Under Law

Mitch Tyner has offered a clearly argued and helpful analysis of public policy issues related to lesbians, gays, and bisexuals from a Christian, and specifically Adventist, perspective. I particularly appreciate his blunt equation of discrimination based on race and discrimination based on sexual identity. His willingness to characterize such discrimination as equally troubling seems exactly right. For in both cases discrimination in housing, employment, the provision of public benefits, and other areas of life reflects no reasonable concern that can be specified apart from false empirical or normative beliefs.

For instance: nondiscrimination against lesbians, gays, or bisexuals might be thought to render the sexual abuse of children more likely. In fact, though, the odds that any individual, whether straight or gay, will abuse a child sexually are very small. There is no reason to believe that, simply because someone is lesbian, gay, or bisexual, he can be presumed to be a pedophile, or that he will be any less caring or respectful than a straight person in his relations with children.[5] Treating consensual lesbian, gay, or bisexual relationships as legally equivalent to straight ones offers no more license for abusive behavior to lesbian, gay, or bisexual pedophiles than accepting straight sex as appropriate does to straight pedophiles.

Some people might suppose, perhaps, that children would be harmed by social tolerance for lesbians, gays, and bisexuals in another way: they might be more inclined to take on such persons as sexual role models and thus to engage in same-sex sexual behavior themselves. But this argument assumes that there is something wrong with such behavior—which is just the point at issue. Even if people

Love, Subsidiarity, Equality, and Inclusiveness

generally adopted same-sex sexual lifestyles by imitation (and there is of course great doubt that this is the case), or if public tolerance for such lifestyles made it more likely people would express same-sex desires they might otherwise repress, there would be nothing wrong with creating circumstances that disposed them to do so, presuming there was nothing wrong with being lesbian, gay, or bisexual or engaging in same-sex sex, in the first place.

It is especially daring of Tyner to equate the desire of lesbians, gays, and bisexuals to be identified as equal members of the community, of comparable dignity with straights, with the similar desire by Christians who observe the Sabbath on Saturday to be treated as equal in status with Christians who observe the Sabbath on Sunday. Tyner rightly notes that Adventists understand what it means to be members of a disfavored minority, and rightly suggests that Adventists should use this understanding to inform their responses to the concerns of lesbians, gays, and bisexuals.

I would argue for only one addition to Tyner's excellent set of policy proposals: an explicit recognition that the principles of freedom and equality he so passionately defends must apply to the church itself as a matter of law. I think it would be a natural reading of Tyner's argument to conclude that the church should apply these principles to its own activities as an expression of its basic principles. But I think there is a case to be made that religious communities should be actively discouraged from engaging in egregious discrimination just as other private associations may be.[6] I suspect there is no value in being doctrinaire here: it might well be reasonable to permit a religious organization that maintains, incorrectly, that there is something wrong in principle with same-sex sex to employ as pastors persons whose conduct is consistent with its official discriminatory position, just as a white supremacist religious movement need not be required to employ pastors of African descent. But there is a much stronger case to be made for the view that religious belief not be allowed to serve as a defense to charges of discrimination where nonpastoral employees, or issues quite unrelated to employment (the discipline of students, say), are concerned.

There is, of course, reason to be very nervous about state interference in the operations of religious communities, and I think Tyner and others could sensibly be nervous about imposing antidiscrimination rules on churches, synagogues, mosques, and temples. If I am willing to take the risk, it is because I think discrimination is so unequivocally repugnant that it deserves the community's most uncompromising sanction, and that responsible religious communities have nothing to fear from the expectation that they will treat everyone with inclusive respect and love.

Henson: Inclusive Ministry, Nature, and Experiments in Living

Henson's remarkable public ministry to lesbians, gays, and bisexuals has been unprecedented among Adventists. His essay overflows with compassion and spiritual insight. He offers a moving and evocative narrative that highlights the ways in which the experience of ministry can drive changes in theology. He rightly notes that, if we abandon the view that sex is morally appropriate only when it is intended to be procreative, we will find it difficult to defend with any credibility the view that same-sex sex is wrong. And he clearly recognizes that the reevaluation of our thinking about same-sex relationships cannot occur in isolation from our reconstruction of norms regarding sexual behavior more generally. I like Henson's piece very much: its warmth, its theological good sense, its humane pastoral sensibility are all memorable and appealing. It must be a real gift to be a member of Henson's congregation. I want to offer only three comments related to what he says.

About "living in sin": Henson's observations about the use of this loaded phrase are apt and helpful. Even if people involved in same-sex sexual and romantic relationships *were*, in virtue of doing so, sinful, this would hardly justify treating them differently from all the other sinners the church is intended to nourish and heal. There would still be good reason to think that the church should embrace and welcome them. However—and I have no reason to think that Henson disagrees—same-sex sexual relationships that are not exploitative, unfair, or uncaring do *not* qualify as sinful. So it is surely crucial to emphasize, when we say that we are all sinners and that the church is (or should be) designed for all of us, that people are not sinners *just because* they are involved in same-sex sexual relationships. (Henson's own practice of ministry makes it evident, I think, that he knows this.)

About "nature" and sexual orientation: Henson may be right that "most sociological studies indicate the level of homosexuality in typical societies has remained relatively constant for hundreds, even thousands, of years." (I am unsure what makes a society "typical."

Love, Subsidiarity, Equality, and Inclusiveness

Would classical Athens count?) But we should be clear that whether he is right about this or not cannot finally determine what we say about same-sex sexual relationships. Whether sexual orientation (which seems in any case to fall along a continuum rather than to divide into neat, binary categories) is rooted in biological constants is irrelevant to its moral status. If we had good reason on other grounds to regard same-sex sexual behavior as wrong, then perhaps it might be the case that biological disposition might give people a legitimate excuse for engaging in what would otherwise be bad behavior. But if there are no such grounds—as it seems to me that there are not (many of the contributions to this volume provide us with good reason to agree)—then people involved in such relationships need no excuses. (And to be clear, Henson does not suggest that they do.)

About Henson's typology of same-sex lifestyles: he is surely right that betrayal and calloused abandonment are deeply wrong. No one who affirms that God is faithful even when we are faithless can see either as appropriate. But Henson's typology explicitly identifies only celibacy, marriage, and exploitative irresponsibility as possibilities for people who find same-sex sexual relationships appealing. To be sure, he explicitly notes that there are other options: and it seems to me that this is right, that the continuum contains a broad range of possibilities. There are, for instance, sexual relationships that are not exploitative or manipulative but that are open-ended, perhaps explicitly short-term, and not necessarily exclusive. And there are marriages and other long-term partnerships in which the partners are committed, in which they share and build a common identity and a sense of "we," in which they delight in and desire and care for each other, but in which one or both partners may be free to be sexual with others.[7] These arrangements seem to me to be unnecessarily risky, but that doesn't mean that reasonable people can't disagree about this or that there is nothing to learn from these relationships. Lesbians and gays have explored a range of possible relational configurations. Those of us who desire different-sex sexual and romantic relationships can learn from their experiments in living (without always concluding, of course, that a given model is appropriate or wise).

Conclusion

Larson, Tyner, and Henson deserve our thanks for pressing the church toward fairness and compassion. I would not want any questions I have raised to obscure my fundamental appreciation for the decency and sensitivity all of them have exhibited. An Adventism that adopted the moral, political, and spiritual stances they have recommended and modeled would have made giant strides toward becoming the kind of community—just, open, caring—Larson, Tyner, Henson, and I agree it can and should be.

Questions for Discussion

1. Is erotic love a great good, as Chartier and Larson both suggest, or is it overrated?
2. Why do you believe Larson says that sexual relationships not marked by comprehensive commitment are alienating? Do you believe he's right? If so, in what circumstances?
3. How important is sexual bonding between people? Can romantic and erotic relationships exist if such bonding is relatively tenuous?
4. How should we decide which questions are appropriately answered by the global church and which by local entities? Are there questions a particular denomination should wait to answer until Christians as a whole have answered them?
5. Should anti-discrimination laws and regulations apply to churches, or should churches have a freedom to discriminate that other entities don't have?

Notes and References

1. Compare John Finnis, *Natural Law and Natural Rights* (Oxford: Clarendon Press of Oxford University Press, 1980), 108; John Finnis, "Commensuration and Practical Reason," *Incommensurability, Incomparability, and Practical Reason*, ed. Ruth Chang (Cambridge, Mass.: Belknap Press of Harvard University Press, 1997), 227–32.
2. See William Jankowiak, ed., *Romantic Passion: A Universal Experience?* (New York: Columbia University Press, 1995); Anthony Giddens, *The Transformation of Intimacy: Sexuality, Love and Eroticism in Modern Societies* (Cambridge, Eng.: Polity, 1992); Ferdinand Mount, *The Subversive Family: An Alternative History; of Love and Marriage* (New York: Free Press, 1992); Robert C. Solomon, *About Love: Reinventing Romance for Our Times* (New York: Touchstone-Simon, 1988).

Love, Subsidiarity, Equality, and Inclusiveness

3. So Judith S. Wallerstein and Sandra Blakeslee, *The Good Marriage: How and Why Love Lasts* (New York: Warner 1995).
4. Ibid., 334.
5. Kurt Freund, Robin Watson, and Douglas Rienzo, "Heterosexuality, Homosexuality, and Erotic Age Preference," *Journal of Sex Research* 26, no. (Feb. 1989): 107–17; Kurt Freund and Robin Watson, "The Proportion of Heterosexual and Homosexual Pedophiles among Sex Offenders against Children," *Journal of Sex and Marital Therapy* 18, no.1 (spring 1992): 34–43; David J. Kleber, Robert J. Howell, and Alta L. Tibbits-Kleber, "The Impact of Parental Homosexuality in Child Custody Cases: A Review of the Literature," *Bulletin of the American Academy of Psychiatry and the Law* 14, no. (1986): 81–87; Minnie M. Whitehead and Kathleen M. Nokes, "An Examination of Demographic Variables, Nurturance, and Empathy among Homosexual and Heterosexual Big Brother/Big Sister Volunteers," *Journal of Homosexuality* 19, no. 4 (1990): 89–101; Margaret Schneider, "Educating the Public about Homosexuality," *Annals of Sex Research* 6, no.1 (1993): 57–66.
6. Compare Brian Barry, *Culture and Equality* (Cambridge, Eng.: Policy, 2000), for a nuanced discussion of discrimination by religious organizations and potential legal responses.
7. See, for instance, Didier Eribon, *Michel Foucault*, trans. Betsy Wing (Cambridge, Mass.: Harvard University Press, 1991), 141; David Macy, *The Lives of Michel Foucault: A Biography* (New York: Pantheon 1993), 145–46; "Conversation," *Werner Schroeter*, ed. Gerard Courant (Paris: Cinematheque/Institut Goethe, 1982), 43, quoted in Eribon, *Michel Foucault*, 141–42. That relationships like that of Foucault and his partner, Daniel Defert, need not be unfair or uncaring doesn't mean that it is wise to structure relationships as they did. I am inclined to think that it is not. Compare Hugh and Gayle Prather, *I Will Never Leave You: How Couples Can Achieve the Power of Lasting Love* (New York: Bantam, 1996).

Contributors

Sherri Babcock
Consulting Engineer
Pickerington, Ohio

Gary Chartier
Assistant Professor of Law and Business Ethics
La Sierra University
Riverside, California

René Drumm
Chair and Professor of Social Work and Family Studies
Southern Adventist University
Collegedale, Tennessee

Bonnie Dwyer
Editor, *Spectrum Magazine*
Roseville, California

David Ferguson
Financial Consultant
Glendale, California

Aubyn Fulton
Professor of Psychology
Pacific Union College
Angwin, California

Roy E. Gane
Professor of Hebrew Bible and Ancient Near Eastern Languages
Andrews University
Berrien Springs, Michigan

Carrol Grady
Freelance Writer; Founder and Host, Someone-to-Talk-to.net Web site
Snohomish, Washington

Fritz Guy
Research Professor of Philosophical Theology
La Sierra University
Riverside, California

Contributors

Mitchell F. Henson
Senior Pastor
Glendale City Seventh-day Adventist Church
Glendale, California

John R. Jones, Associate Professor of New Testament Studies and World Religions
La Sierra University
Riverside, California

Ben Kemena
Chief of General Medicine and Faculty Hospitalist
University of Colorado, Denver

David R. Larson
Professor of Religion
Loma Linda University
Loma Linda, California

Ronald Lawson
Professor of Sociology
Hunter College
City University of New York

Leif T. Lind
Former Missionary and Seventh-day Adventist Minister
Europe, Africa, and North America

Richard Rice
Professor of Religion
Loma Linda University
Loma Linda, California

Catherine Taylor
Licensed Clinical Social Worker
Springfield, Vermont

Mitchell A. Tyner
Former General Counsel
General Conference of Seventh-day Adventists
Silver Spring, Maryland

Harry Wang
Clinical Professor of Psychiatry
University of California, Davis

Indexes

Scripture Index

Genesis P3-50, P3-79, P3-81, P4-31, P4-52, P4-78, P4-79; 1 P4-37, P4-79, P4-84; 1–2 P4-64; 1:26–28 P4-78; 1:28 P1-45, P4-53; 1:30 P3-78; 19 P4-4, P4-31, P4-66; 19:4–11 P5-17; 19:4–11 P4-51; 2 P4-78, P4-79, P4-84; 2:18 P1-17, P1-45, P4-49; 2:23–24 P4-56; 2:24 P2-20, P4-78; 2:7 P4-44; 25 P3-77; 3:16 P4-48; 37:1–30 P5-4; 4:1 P4-55; 6 P4-31; 9:20–27 P4-61
Exodus: 17:14–16 P4-62; 20:14 P4-47; 20:17 P4-61; 21:17 P4-62; 21:5–6 P4-53; 31:15 P4-61
Leviticus: 11:44 P4-32; 12–13 P4-66; 17–26 P4-4, P4-74; 17–20 P4-68; 17–27 P4-66; 17:10–16 P4-4; 18 P4-32, P4-65, P4-66, P4-67, P4-68; 18:22 P3-21, P4-4, P4-31, P4-32, P4-35, P4-52, P4-64, P4-66, P4-67, P4-68, P4-70, P4-74, P5-17; 18:6–18 P4-4; 19:11 P4-65; 19:19 P4-4; 19:27 P4-4; 20 P4-65, P4-66, P4-67, P4-68; 20:13 P4-4, P4-31, P4-32, P4-35, P4-52, P4-64, P4-66, P4-67, P4-68, P4-70, P4-74, P5-17; 20:26 P4-5; 20:7–21 P2-34; 20:9 P4-62; 24:8 P4-67
Numbers: 15:32–36 P4-61, P4-67; 28:9 P4-67; 31:26–47 P4-53
Deuteronomy: 22:9–11 P4-32; 25:19 P4-62; 29:22 P4-31; 32:32 P4-31
Joshua: 6:17, 21 P4-62
Judges: 19 P4-4, P4-66; 19: 1–30 P5-17; 19:11–13 P4-66; 19:22–25 P4-52; 19:22–24 P4-66; 19:29 P4-66
Ruth 1:15–17 P5-7
1 Samuel: 18:3 P4-54; 20:30 P4-54
2 Samuel: 1:27 P4-54; 9:7 P5-7
Psalms: 136 P5-7
Proverbs: 16:5 P4-32; 3:22 P4-32; 6:16 P4-32
Isaiah: 1:9–10 P4-31; 13:19 P4-31; 14:12 P3-80; 58 P3-76, P3-82; 62:5 P4-46
Jeremiah: 49:18 P4-31
Lamentations: 4:6 P4-31
Ezekiel P4-59, P5-41; 16:46 P4-31; 16:50 P4-31; 34 P3-76, P3-82; 48–49 P4-31; 53 P4-31; 55–56 P4-31
Hosea 3:1 P5-7
Amos: 4:11 P4-31
Zephaniah: 2:9 P4-31
Matthew: 10:15 P4-31; 10:27 P5-9; 11:23–24 P4-31; 11:8 P4-8; 19:12 P4-33, P4-55; 19:19 P1-48; 19:4–6 P2-20, P2-34; 19:5 P4-79; 23:24 P4-57; 26:33–35 P4-9; 5:3–12 P1-28; 6:10 P4-58; 6:17–48 P4-53; 7 P1-55; 7:12 P4-47, P5-9; 7:5 P4-59; 8:5–13 P4-33, P4-54
Mark: 2:27 P4-31
Luke: 1:37 P4-70; 10 P5-39; 10:12 P4-31; 12:57 P4-42; 17:29 P4-31; 22:33–34 P4-9; 26:39 P4-44; 7:1–10 P4-33, P4-54; 7:25 P4-8
John: 1:14 P4-44; 10 P3-76, P3-81; 15:17 P1-55; 16:12–13 P4-30; 2:10 P4-30; 4:51 P4-33; 8:11 P4-71; 8:7 P4-57; 9:1–3 P1-25
Acts: 15 P4-67, P4-80; 15:20 P4-

Scripture Index

34, P4-68; 15:29 P4-68, P4-80; 21:25 P4-34; 29 P4-34; 8:26–40 P4-33, P4-54
Acts of John: 2:279–82 P4-11
Romans: 1 P4-12, P4-15, P4-17, P4-18, P4-23, P4-69, P4-74, P4-80; 1: 16:32 P5-17; 1:1–32 P5-6; 1:16 P4-30; 1:16–17 P4-12; 1:17 P4-30; 1:18 P4-12, P4-13, P4-30; 1:18–23 P4-12, P4-13; 1:18–32 P4-12, P4-21, P4-75; 1:19–31 P4-33; 1:23 P4-69; 1:24 P4-12, P4-13, P4-69; 1:24–25 P4-13; 1:24–27 P2-34, P4-12, P4-18, P4-65, P4-68, P4-69; 1:24–25 P4-13; 1:24-27 P4-68; 1:25 P4-39, P4-69; 1:26 P4-12, P4-19, P4-37; 1:26, 27 P1-24; 1:26–27 P4-13, P4-37, P4-39, P4-52, P4-64, P4-74; 1:27 P4-17, P4-36, P4-39; 1:28 P4-12; 1:28–31 P4-39; 1:28–32 P4-13; 1:28–32 P4-13; 1:29–31 P4-69; 1:32 P4-39; 11:21 P4-37; 11:24 P4-37; 12 P3-80; 13:13 P4-12, P4-33; 14 P4-69; 14:14 P4-26, P4-75; 14:5 P4-27; 2 P4-19; 2:1 P4-18; 2:14 P4-37; 24 P4-37; 27 P4-37; 3 P4-12; 3:2 P4-39; 3:21–26 P4-12; 3:21f P4-19; 3:22–24 P4-17; 3:9 P4-39; 4 P4-69; 5:8 P5-16; 7:14–25 P5-16; 8:1–8 P5-16; 8:37 P4-9; 8:38–39 P4-9; 9:4 P4-39; 9:5 P4-39
1 Corinthians: 1:11 P4-71; 1:26–28 P4-10; 10 P4-7, P4-33; 10:31 P4-84; 11 P4-33; 11:14 P4-37; 11:14, 15 P4-37; 11:2–16 P5-6; 11:23–29 P4-10; 11; 6:9 P4-7; 12 P3-80; 13 P4-30; 13:11, 12 P1-14; 15:39–41 P4-31; 2:2 P4-33; 5 P4-65, P4-66, P4-70; 5:1 P4-69; 5:10 P4-8, P4-33; 5:11 P4-8; 5:9 P4-7; 6 P4-7, P4-9, P4-70; 6: 9 P5-17; 6: 9–10 P4-71; 6:11 P4-26; 6:12–20 P4-42; 6:16 P4-79; 6:19 P4-30; 6:9 P4-7, P4-11, P4-33, P4-68; 6:9, 10 P1-24; 6:9–10 P4-8, P4-52; 6:9–11 P2-34; 7 P4-28; 7:1–7 P4-15; 7:29 P4-15; 7:6–9 P4-10; 7:9 P1-17; 8 P4-69; 8:4 P4-37; 8:7 P4-27
2 Corinthians: 11:5; 12:11 P4-10; 12:20 P4-33; 6:6 P4-33
Galatians: 2:15 P4-37; 23 P4-33; 3 P4-6; 3:28 P4-33, P4-67, P4-68; 4:1–11 P4-26; 4:8 P4-37; 5:1 P4-29, P4-33; 5:13 P4-6; 5:16 P4-15; 5:16–24 P4-33; 5:19–21 P4-33; 5:22 P1-28, P3-80, P4-33; 6:2 P1-48
Ephesians: 2:3 P4-37; 4 P3-80; 5:22–24 P4-48; 5:25 P4-49; 5:26–27 P4-49; 5:28–30 P5-10; 5:31 P4-79; 5:5 P4-34; 6:12 P4-9; 6:5–9 P4-53
Philippians: 16 P4-53; 4:13 P4-70; 4:8 P4-33
Colossians: 2:14 P4-41; 2:17 P4-41
1 Thessalonians: 4:4–5 P4-59
1 Timothy: 1:10 P4-7, P4-11, P4-52, P4-68, P5-17; 1:9 P4-33; 10 P4-33; 6:11 P4-33
2 Timothy: 3:2–5 P4-33
Hebrews: 1:1–4 P4-53; 12:16 P4-34; 13:14 P4-34; 13:8 P4-30; 4:15 P4-42, P4-45; 5:11–14 P4-42
1 Peter: 3:18 P4-44; 4:4 P4-44
2 Peter: 2:6 P4-31
2 John: 7 P4-44
Jude: 6–7 P4-31
Revelation: 11:8 P4-31; 21:6 P3-79; 21:8 P4-7; 22:15 P4-7

B-5

Judicial Index

Boerne vs. Flores P5-43
Bowers vs. Hardwick P2-27, P5-36
Cantwell vs. Connecticut P5-49
Employment Division, Department of Human Resources P5-43
General Conference of Seventh-day Adventists vs. Kinship International, Inc.
   P3-41
Lawrence vs. Texas P2-28, P3-44, P5-35
Romer vs. Evans P2-28
Scopes vs. Tennessee P5-46, P5-49
Sherbert vs. Verner P5-47

Subject Index

A

Abnormal P2-7, P2-10, P2-21, P4-55
Abomination P4-4, P4-66, P4-74
Abraham P3-76, P3-77, P3-79; Hagar and P3-77
Absolute truth P1-4, P1-6
Abuse P3-41, P3-45, P3-81; as factor in "cure" P2-17; change and P3-25; Cook and P3-39; drug P3-59; sexual P1-5, P1-9, P1-19, P3-19, P3-81, P4-29; childhood P1-9, P2-15, P3-9, P5-56; substance P1-46, P2-48; youth and P2-37, P2-38, P2-51
Academy P1-6, P1-32, P1-32–P1-33, P1-36, P2-37
Acceptance P4-80, P5-12, P5-16, P5-25–P5-26, P5-28, P5-32; Bible and P4-78; church P1-12, P1-22, P1-54, P3-22–P3-24, P3-35, P3-48, P3-54–P3-57, P5-29–P5-30; God's P4-54; Hellenism's P4-30; in Adventist schools P3-16–P3-17; self P1-7, P1-35, P3-11, P3-14, P3-16, P5-52; after Quest P3-39; self, denial P1-16; youth and P3-53
Acquired Immune Deficiency Syndrome. *See* AIDS
Adam P4-44, P4-54
Adams, Roy P3-50, P3-72
Addiction P1-25; drug P2-24
Adikia P4-13, P4-18
Adolescence P2-35–P2-36, P2-37–P2-39
ADRA. *See* Adventist Development and Relief Agency
Adulterer P4-7, P4-8
Adultery P1-47, P4-12, P4-65, P4-68, P4-79, P5-8–P5-9; grounds for divorce P3-59
Adventist Development and Relief Agency P3-63
Adventist News Network P3-45
Adventist Review P3-35, P3-39, P3-50, P3-54, P3-59
Adventist schools P1-35–P1-55
Adventist Today P3-51, P3-52
Agapaic love P4-26, P4-28
Agape P5-9, P5-12, P5-19
AIDS P2-13, P3-59–P3-64; activists P3-60–P3-61; death from P1-36; in 1980 P2-13, P2-27; ministering to patients P5-25; SDA and P3-60, P3-61–P3-64, P5-25
Akatharsia P4-13, P4-18, P4-32
Akman, J. P2-42
Alienation P2-22, P2-37, P4-80, P5-53; from Church P1-47–P1-50
Allen, L.S. P3-26
Altruistic love P5-19
American Academy of Pediatrics P2-16, P2-21
American Bar Association P2-16, P3-30
American Civil Liberties Union P3-53
American Civil War P2-5
American Counseling Association P2-21, P2-22
American Medical Association P2-16, P2-21, P2-22

B-7

Subject Index

American Psychiatric Association P2-34–P2-35, P3-30; homosexuality: as disorder P2-9; as illness P2-12, P2-25, P2-32–P2-35, P2-34–P2-35; as normal variant P2-16, P2-21, P2-26, P2-49–P2-50; reparative therapy P2-22; same-sex marriage and P2-29
American Psychological Association P2-22, P2-34, P3-30; homosexuality as normal variant P2-16, P2-21
Anderson, Ben P3-48
Anderson, Inge P3-47, P3-71
Andreasen, M.L. P4-40
Andrews University P3-32, P3-33, P3-53, P3-61; Kinship International mailing P3-37; president's arrest P3-38
Andrizou P4-9
Anger P1-43, P2-37, P3-80, P4-49
Animals P3-76, P4-13, P4-15; crossbreeding of P4-4; homosexuality in P1-40, P2-32; lying with P1-26
Annual Council P2-20, P3-32, P3-38, P3-51, P3-61; statement on homosexuality P3-43
Anxiety P1-44, P2-21, P2-22, P2-37, P2-48, P2-50, P3-81
Arndt, William F. P4-33, P4-34
Arousal P2-12, P2-16, P2-18, P4-55
Arrested development P2-31
Arsenokoitai P4-8
Arsenokoites P4-7, P4-68; as exploitation P4-11–P4-12; historical context P4-10–P4-12
Aschemosune P4-17, P4-18
Asebeia P4-13, P4-18
Asylums P2-9, P2-10, P2-24
Athenaeus P4-36
Atimazestha P4-18
Atimias P4-18

Atlantic Union College P1-4
Atlantic Union Conference P3-44
Attraction P1-35, P1-40, P2-18; continuum P2-30; genetics and P2-17; heterosexual P4-16; same-sex P1-17, P2-31, P2-36, P3-9, P4-16, P4-82; after the "cure" P1-41, P2-9
Augustine P4-36, P4-45, P4-59
Autarcheia P4-15
Aversion therapy P1-41, P2-22
Avondale College P3-31

B

Babcock, Sherri P1-3–P1-14, P1-54
Bagemihl, Bruce P1-51
Bailey, D. Sherwin P4-31
Bailey, J. Michael P2-14, P2-27
Bailey, J.M. P3-5, P3-26
Bailey, Michael P1-50
Baker, Delbert W. P3-73
Balch, David P1-51
Barker, Justice J.A. P5-44
Barr, James P4-35
Barry, Brian P5-61
Baumeister, R.F. P3-27
Bayer, R. P2-41, P2-42
Beach, Frank P2-32, P2-41
Beard, George P2-24
Beautrais, A. P2-43
Behavioral therapy P2-13
Behrens, Lyn P3-53
Bem, D.J. P3-5, P3-26
Benton, Elvin P3-69
Benton, Josephine P3-69
Berger, Edmund P2-10, P2-25
Beson, Wayne P1-51
Bestiality P2-4, P4-55, P4-65, P5-8
Betrayal P5-9
Bettencourt, Troix P2-44
Bias P2-22, P2-23, P2-33, P2-40, P2-51, P4-51; youth and P2-29, P2-36

B-8

Subject Index

Bible P2-20, P3-34, P3-43, P4-74, P4-77–P4-80, P4-81, P5-48; prohibitions in P4-4
Biblical criteria P4-64
Biblical interpretations P3-17, P3-20–P3-21, P4-23–P4-24, P4-24–P4-25
Biblical proscriptions P4-51, P4-64
Biblical Research Institute P3-36
Biblical wording: changes of P4-8
Bieber, Irving P2-10, P2-26, P2-31, P2-41, P3-27
Bigotry P2-3, P2-16, P2-18
Biological basis P1-39, P2-3–P2-44, P2-4, P2-45–P2-49, P3-4
Biological continuum P3-4, P3-76
Biological factors P3-4
Birth order, homosexuality and P1-39
Bisexuality P4-23, P4-49, P4-71, P4-75; definition P2-30, P3-7; Freud on P2-31
Blair, Senator H.W. P5-44
Blake, Christopher P3-48, P3-71, P3-73
Blakely, William Addison P5-49
Blakeslee, Sandra P5-61
Blanchard, R. P1-51
Blass, F. P4-36
Body of Christ P4-22, P4-77, P4-79, P5-30
Body structure P2-14, P2-18
Bogaert, A.F. P1-51
Bondage P2-4, P4-26, P4-29
Bonding P1-16, P1-28, P4-46, P4-78, P5-53
Boswell, John P4-36
Bouchard, Robert P3-72
Boyfriend P1-5, P3-49
Bradford, Charles P3-29, P3-75, P3-82
Brain, structural differences of homosexuals P2-27
Branson, Roy P5-24

Brawley, Robert L. P1-51, P4-34
Breasts P3-4
British Medical Association P2-11, P2-26
British Union Conference P3-45
Bromily, Geoffrey W. P5-19
Brothers, study of homosexual P2-15
Bryant, Anita P3-30, P3-67
Bullies P2-39, P2-51, P3-81
Bush, George H. W. P3-60
Bussey, Barry P3-50, P3-72
Buttrick, George Arthur P5-18

C

Cabaj, R. P2-41
California Protection of Marriage Initiative P3-44
Campolo, Anthony P1-51, P5-24
Capital punishment P3-30, P4-61, P4-67
Caring Church P3-60, P3-64
Caring church P3-29, P3-75, P3-79, P3-82
Casey, Fred P3-73
Cason, Virginia P1-50
Cass, Virginia P2-42
Castration therapy P2-7, P2-16, P2-24
Casual intimacy P4-46, P4-79
Casuistry P4-20, P4-70
Categorical imperative P5-11
Catholics P3-44; Paul Grady P1-42–P1-45
Causes of homosexuality P1-38–P1-40, P2-14–P2-15, P2-27, P2-46–P2-52
Celebration of Covenant P1-10

B-9

Subject Index

Celibacy P1-9, P1-28, P3-35, P3-43, P3-47, P3-79, P3-80, P5-28, P5-59; after reparative therapy P2-17; before marriage P3-54; commitment to P3-55; enforced P2-12; eunuch P4-53; for personal fulfillment P4-82; SDA and P2-19, P3-45, P3-48, P3-51, P5-25
Cellular biology P2-4
Ceremonial law P3-21, P4-4, P4-20, P4-28
Ceremonial observance P4-27
Ceremonial purity P4-5, P4-26–P4-27, P4-67, P4-75; contaminating P4-5
Change programs P1-19, P1-40–P1-42, P3-17, P3-25, P3-37–P3-41; church referrals P2-48; failures of P3-65, P3-81
Change therapies P2-3
Chartier, Gary P3-52, P5-51; publication P3-72
Chase, Cheryl P1-51
Chauvin, E. P2-43
Chauvinism P5-11
Chesed P5-6, P5-9
Children P2-16
Chinese Psychiatric Association P2-12
Choice P2-3, P2-4, P2-7, P2-45–P2-46, P3-47, P4-82; Christianity and P1-55; conscious P2-13, P2-18; homosexuality and P3-25; homosexuality as P2-18, P2-47, P4-16; sexual orientation as P3-8
Christian imperative P4-57–P4-58
Christianity Today P3-40
Chromosomes P2-15, P3-76
Church: alienation from P1-47–P1-50
Church involvement: ambivalent P1-12

Church Manual P3-36, P3-42, P3-43
Church membership P1-23, P1-54, P3-15, P3-22, P3-79, P4-82, P5-29; international P3-57
Church-related employment P3-14–P3-82
Civil marriage P2-17
Civil rights P3-30, P3-52, P3-65; 1960s P2-33, P3-30; APA and P2-29; Colorado and P2-15; homosexual agenda P3-50; rolling back P3-40
Civil union P2-28, P3-44, P3-45
Clinebell, Howard P5-21
Closet P5-28. *See* Coming out
Cobb, John B. Jr. P4-62
Cognitive dissonance P2-36
Cognitive functioning P3-5
Colopinto, John P1-51
Colorado for Family Values P1-40, P3-40
Columbine High School P2-17
Coming out P1-19–P1-20, P5-27–P5-28; at work P1-21–P1-22, P3-14–P3-82; in the Adventist world P3-10–P3-15, P3-53; reactions to P1-20–P1-21; to extended family P1-23–P1-25, P1-26; to family P2-38, P3-11–P3-13; to friends P3-14; to parents P1-7; to self P2-35, P3-11; to spouse P1-19–P1-20, P3-13
Commie P2-9
Commitment P3-46, P4-26, P4-46, P4-47, P5-52, P5-53; as sin P1-47; integration of sexual orientation P2-36; sex and P5-51–P5-54; to celibacy P3-55; to God P3-78, P3-80
Communist P2-9
Complexities P3-51
Complexity P4-77, P4-84

B-10

Subject Index

Comstock, Gary David P4-40, P4-41, P4-61
Conceptual horizons P4-23
Confusion P2-21, P3-11, P3-65, P4-29, P4-80
Congregation P1-54, P3-54–P3-57, P4-58
Conklin, Day P5-47
Connoley, John Tyler P4-61, P4-62
Conservative Adventists P3-35, P3-47, P3-51, P3-53, P3-56, P3-77; gay P3-38
Conservative Christianity P5-27
Conservative Christians P3-31; AIDS and P2-13; conversion therapies and P2-47; discrimination and P3-30–P3-31; gay P5-28; violence P4-57
Conservative churches P1-17, P1-42, P1-55, P3-38, P3-44
Conservative organizations P2-21
Context: Christian P4-20; civil P3-30–P3-31; cultural P4-51, P4-66; for sexual interaction P5-52; influencing churches P3-65; interpersonal P4-48; meaning from P4-11; of a faith community P4-28; of APA 1973 policy change P2-12; of Bible P1-9; of biblical revelation P4-50; of Catholicism P1-43; of Leviticus 18:22 P3-21; of loving relationship P4-47, P4-64; of loving same-sex relationships P4-3, P4-6, P4-19, P4-24, P4-25–P4-26, P4-27, P4-28; of nineteenth century P2-4; of Romans 1 P4-68, P4-76; of romantic love and sexuality P4-43; of social relationships P5-42; of the Christian Church P4-67; religious P3-30–P3-31; SDA P3-75, P5-36, P5-48; social P4-68

Continuums: attraction P2-30; biological P3-4, P3-76; emotional and cognitive P3-6; gender P3-5; Relationship P5-59; Sexual preference P1-42, P3-6, P3-6–P3-7, P3-76, P4-50
Contraception P4-50, P4-78, P5-15
Contrary to nature P4-15–P4-17, P4-50, P4-54–P4-55, P4-68, P5-6
Conversion therapy P2-21, P2-23, P2-47. *See also* Therapies
Cook, Colin P1-19, P1-40, P1-51, P3-17–P3-19, P3-37–P3-41; emergence of P3-32; failures of P2-17
Copernican Revolution P5-18
Coprolalia P5-8
Coprophilia P5-8
Cotton-Huston, Annie P2-53
Counseling P1-9, P1-41, P2-21, P2-51, P3-34
Counselor P3-35, P3-37, P3-46; Colin Cook P1-19, P3-19; sexual abuse P1-40, P3-80
Countryman, L. William P4-32, P4-39, P4-40, P4-59
Courtney, K. P2-27
Covenant P1-10, P4-52, P5-6, P5-7; faithfulness P5-8; love P5-52; marriage P3-47, P3-77
Cox, James P3-68
Cranston, K. P2-43
Creatio ex nihilo P4-44
Creation P2-20, P3-50, P4-19–P4-20, P4-44, P5-14; God's relationship to P4-45
Cress, John P3-49, P3-71
Crick, Francis P2-7
Cultic impurity P4-75
Cultural context P1-38
Culver, Virginia P3-70
Cure P3-19, P3-33

B-11

Subject Index

Curing homosexuality P1-40–P1-42, P2-8, P2-22, P2-25, P2-26, P2-28, P2-31–P2-32, P2-34, P3-17–P3-19, P3-25; behavior modification P2-16; castration as P2-7; failures of P3-6; healthcare professionals on P2-21–P2-23; negative side effects of P2-48; psychoanalysis P2-10

D

Dain, H.J. P3-27
Daniel, F.C. P2-24
Darwin, Charles P2-5, P2-7, P2-24
Dating P1-5, P1-6, P1-7, P1-9–P1-10; as denial P2-36
D'Augelli, A. P2-44
D'Augelli, D. P2-42
David P3-77, P4-52, P4-74, P5-7
Davidson, Richard P4-71, P4-72
Davis, Gray P3-44
Day of Judgment P1-50
Debrunner, A. P4-36
Defense of Marriage Act P3-45
Defert, Daniel P5-61
Degeneracy P2-5, P2-6, P2-10, P2-24, P2-31, P2-52; pyramid P2-5, P2-6, P2-7, P2-8, P2-15, P2-18, P2-48–P2-49
Denver Post P3-40
Depravity P4-13, P4-13–P4-14
Depression P1-44, P2-50, P3-34, P3-81; gay youth and P2-37; reparative therapy and P2-22, P2-48
Desires P4-45, P4-54; eliminating P2-20–P2-23, P2-24; fleshly P4-15; for companionship P1-45–P1-47; natural P4-16; pleasure and P4-47, P5-19; sexaul P5-57; sexual P2-15, P4-47, P4-70, P5-3, P5-54–P5-55, P5-59
Desperation P1-7, P1-34, P4-70
Desroches, Frederick J. P3-27

Deviant philosophy P3-35
Deviants P2-9, P2-24
Differentness, God's acceptance of P3-76–P3-77
Diagnostic and Statistical Manual of Mental Disorders. See DSM
Diamond, L.M. P3-26
Diaz, Eunice P3-60–P3-61, P3-74
Dickinson, Donald M. P5-45
Dilemma P1-15, P1-38
Dince, P.R. P3-27
Diotima P5-5, P5-8
Discrimination P2-33, P2-40, P3-30, P4-74, P5-43, P5-56–P5-57; Christian churches P3-30; church employment and P5-57; civil unions and P3-45; homosexuals P3-30; Loma Linda University P3-53; religious beliefs and P5-43, P5-57–P5-58; to protect children P5-56
Disfellowship P1-3, P1-48, P1-49, P3-55, P3-56, P3-58, P4-65
Divorce P5-5, P5-29; Colin Cook P3-41; homosexuality as grounds P3-32, P3-59; SDA attitude P4-83
Dobson, James P3-40
Doll, L.S. P3-27
Domestic partnership P3-44, P3-45, P4-83, P5-35
Dominion P3-76
Doob, Katherine P5-18
Dorner, Gunther P2-12, P2-26
Double effect principle P5-20
Double minority P2-37
Douglas, Mary P4-32, P4-59
Downey, J. P2-41, P3-6, P3-26
Dreams P1-17–P1-18, P3-6
Drug abuse: as factor in "cure" P2-17
Drug therapy P1-41
Drumm, René P3-3–P3-27, P3-75–P3-82

Subject Index

DSM P2-21, P2-33; I P2-32; II P2-32; III P2-34, P2-35; III-R P2-35; IV P2-35, P2-49
Dudley, Carl S. P4-42
Dwyer, Bonnie P1-53–P1-55
Dyke P2-39

E

Early Teens P1-53
Easton, Derek P3-73
Ebertz, L. P3-26
Eden P3-75, P3-78
Effeminate P2-8, P2-25, P3-5, P3-7, P4-9. *See also* Sissies
Egalitarianism P2-5, P4-47, P4-54
Ego-dystonic homosexuality P2-34
Egoistic love P5-19
Elder, Harvey P3-60, P3-61, P3-62, P3-64, P3-72, P3-74
Electric shock therapy P2-25
Electro-convulsive therapy P2-9, P2-25
Ellis, Havelock P2-24
Ellis, L. P3-26
Embarrassment P3-24, P3-60, P5-26
Emetics therapy P2-8, P2-25
Emotional and cognitive continuum P3-6
Emotional functioning P3-5
Enlightenment P2-5, P2-6, P2-12, P5-11
Enoch P4-31
Environment P2-14, P2-15, P3-75; blaming P3-79; Eden P3-78; gender identity and P1-39; Genesis P4-52; in utero P2-47; natural P5-15; political P5-56; SDA P2-52, P3-79, P5-24; sexual identity and P1-42; shaping behavior P2-46; unaccepting P2-22, P5-11; violent P2-50–P2-51
Episcopal Church P3-30, P3-50

Epithymia P5-9
Epstein, Robert P1-51
Equality P5-35, P5-39–P5-43, P5-56–P5-58; crime to claim P5-47–P5-48; in loving relationships P4-28; Jew/gentile P4-7, P4-67; love and P5-12; SDA and P5-24
Eribon, Didier P5-61
Eros P4-46, P5-9, P5-19
Eschaton P4-80
Esther P3-77, P3-79
Estrogen P3-4
Ethically irrelevant considerations P5-10
Ethics P2-46, P3-66, P4-3, P4-24, P4-81, P5-10–P5-12; guidelines P2-16; military P5-3; of interpretations P4-24–P4-25; sexual P5-4, P5-12, P5-19; sexual activities and P5-3–P5-21
Eunuch P4-53
Eva, Duncan P3-33, P3-37, P3-68, P3-69
Evangelicals P1-41, P2-18, P3-31, P3-40
Eve P4-49, P4-54
Exhibitionism P5-8
Exorcism P1-41
Experimentation P2-5, P2-6, P2-8, P5-5
Exploitation P4-11, P4-12, P4-26; homosexual P5-5; marriage and P5-59; marriage as P5-14; Quest Learning Center P3-65; sexual P3-34, P5-28
Extramarital sex P2-4, P3-43, P4-52, P5-26

F

Fag P1-35, P1-36, P2-9, P3-14
Faggot P2-39, P3-81

B-13

Subject Index

Faith P1-41, P3-66, P4-75; challenge to P3-37; cured by P3-39
Faithfulness P3-34, P3-54, P4-26, P4-28; covenant P5-8
Family P1-3, P2-14, P2-38, P3-51; coming out to P3-14; desire for P3-9; desire for a P3-18; Kinship as P3-21–P3-22; life P3-9
Family Research Council P1-45, P1-52
Fantasies P3-6, P3-24
Fantasy play P3-5
Far Eastern Academy P1-33, P1-35
Farag, Saleem P3-62, P3-63, P3-74
Father: absent P2-10, P2-25; detached P2-14, P2-27; dominant P3-9; homosexuality and P2-32
Faulkner, R. P2-43
Fear P1-19, P1-36, P3-14; for personal safety P3-8; harassment and P1-36; holy P5-12; of exposure P1-7; of heterosexuality P2-32; parental P1-34–P1-35
Feminine virtues P1-28
Fergusson, B. P2-43
Fernandez, M. P2-43
Fetishism P2-32, P5-8
Finnis, John P5-60
Fiorenza, Elizabeth Schüssler P4-41
First Amendment P5-43, P5-45, P5-46
First love P1-7
Fisher, B. P2-42
Fletcher, George P. P5-18
Fliers, E. P2-27
Focus on the Family P2-17, P3-40
Folkenberg, Robert P3-42–P3-43, P3-62, P3-70
Ford, Clellan P2-32, P2-41
Ford, Desmond P3-68
Foreseen outcome P5-15, P5-20
Fornication P4-80, P5-8, P5-9
Foucault, Michel P4-41, P5-61

Fourteenth Amendment P5-45, P5-46
Freedman, David Noel P5-18, P5-19
Freedman, M. P2-41
Freedom P4-29, P5-36–P5-39; Paul on P4-6; religious P3-46, P5-43, P5-45–P5-47; to come out P5-27; versus license P4-6
Freud, Sigmund P2-5, P2-6, P2-8, P2-11, P2-24, P2-25, P2-31–P2-35, P2-41
Freund, Kurt P2-25, P5-61
Friedman, R. P2-41, P3-6, P3-26
Friedman, R.C. P2-14, P2-27
Friends: Biblical P5-7; coming out to P1-35, P3-14; gay youth P2-35, P2-37; Jesus P5-28
Frottage P5-8
Fruits of the Spirit P3-80
Frustration P2-9, P3-9
Fryer, John P2-33
Fulton, Aubyn P2-45–P2-52, P3-51, P4-60; publication P3-72
Fundamentalists P2-17–P2-18, P3-31, P3-44, P5-46
Furnish, Victor Paul P4-36, P4-37, P4-39

G

Gagnon, Robert A.J. P4-37, P4-39, P4-40, P4-61
Gane, Roy P4-71, P4-72
Garafalo, R. P2-43
Gay liberation movement P2-33
Gay lifestyle P5-13, P5-27–P5-28
Gay marriage P2-17 *See also* Same-sex marriage.
Gay Pride Day P2-12
Gender continuum P3-5
Gender identity P2-30, P3-4
Gender role P2-30, P2-36, P3-4, P4-5
Gene sequences P2-3

Subject Index

General Conference P1-10, P1-28, P1-49; 1985, statement on homosexuality P3-36; 1994, speaking to homosexual gatherings P3-42; 1999 statement P2-20; 2005, welcoming church vision P3-29; AIDS Committee P3-61, P3-62; divorce rules P3-32; DOMA and P3-45; first national Kampmeeting P3-34; homosexuality and divorce P3-59; Kampmeeting recommendation P3-35; Kinship countermaterials P3-37; Kinship International and P3-66; Quest Learning Center and P3-37, P3-39; reaction to coming out P1-20–P1-21; vs Kinship P3-41

General Conference Administrative Committee P3-42, P3-43, P3-45; affirmation of marriage P3-43

General Conference Health Department P3-61, P3-63

Generic consistency principle P5-19

Genes P2-7

Genetic code P2-5

Genetic predisposition P2-15

Genitalia P2-12, P2-27, P3-4, P4-55

Gewirth, Alan P5-19

Gibson, P. P2-43, P2-44

Giddens, Anthony P5-60

Gifts of the Spirit P3-80, P3-81

Gingrich, F. Wilbur P4-33, P4-34

Girlfriend P1-5, P1-32, P3-9, P3-14

Glendale City SDA Church P5-25, P5-30

God: acceptance of P3-48; accountable to P4-63, P5-3; alienation from P5-53; ask to change P1-5, P1-17, P1-32, P1-33, P1-35, P1-38, P1-41, P3-8–P3-9, P3-17, P3-32; call of P5-32; character of P1-8, P1-24, P5-6, P5-8, P5-52; children of P3-45; coercion, lack of P5-39, P5-48; Creator P1-26, P1-45, P2-18, P3-78, P4-45, P4-64, P4-78, P5-14, P5-55; dedicate to P1-7; differentness acceptance by P3-76–P3-77; direction from P3-20; equality before P4-67; faithfulness of P5-59; gift/talent from P1-22, P3-80; grace/mercy/love of P1-31, P1-48, P1-50, P1-54, P2-20, P3-43, P3-58, P4-69, P4-81, P5-16, P5-25, P5-56; holiness before P4-4; humor of P1-10; incarnation of P4-54, P4-56; intention of P4-58; judgment of P1-18, P3-29, P3-59, P3-62, P3-82; peace with P1-27; power to change P3-37; rejection by P2-37; relationship with P1-13, P3-76, P3-77; talk to P1-6; trust P1-42

God's withdrawal P4-14

God's wrath P4-12–P4-13, P4-30

Gold, Ronald P2-34

Golden Rule P4-47, P5-9, P5-20, P5-51

Gomer P5-7

Gonsiorek, J. P2-41

Good, E.M. P5-18

Good Samaritan P3-75, P5-39–P5-41, P5-39–P5-42

Goreen, L. P2-27

Gorski, R.A. P3-26

B-15

Subject Index

Gospel P2-48, P3-37, P4-53, P4-57; authentic miracle P4-70; imperative P3-49; imperatives P2-52; John's P4-30; Luke P5-39–P5-41; Mark P5-18; Paul P4-6–P4-7
Grace P1-11–P1-12, P4-75
Grady, Bob P1-32, P1-33
Grady, Carrol P1-31–P1-55, P1-54, P3-25, P3-46, P3-50, P3-71; publication P3-72
Grady, Paul P1-31–P1-55, P1-54
Graf, Karl Heinrich P4-32
Grant, Robert M. P4-35
Gray, E. P3-27
Great Disappointment of 1844 P5-18
Greco-Roman thought P4-13, P4-14–P4-17, P4-16, P4-68; dualistic assumptions of P4-9; gender assumptions P4-19; on bisexuality P4-75; on vice/virtue P4-7; Pauline vice lists P4-68
Greeks P4-16; on bisexuality P4-23
Green, Richard P2-13, P2-14, P2-27, P2-47
Greenfield, L.A. P3-27
Grenz, Stanley P4-62, P4-77, P4-78, P4-80, P4-81, P4-82, P4-83, P4-86
Grief P1-34, P4-49
Gross, Terry P2-43
Guiding principle P1-13
Guilt P1-34, P1-41, P2-21, P3-31, P3-34, P4-18; Quest Learning Center P3-38
Guy, Fritz P3-59, P3-73, P4-66, P4-73, P4-74, P4-77–P4-78, P4-78–P4-79, P4-81, P4-83, P4-84–P4-85; response to P4-64–P4-65, P4-70–P4-71

H

Hallock, Larry P3-68
Hamer, Dean P2-15, P2-27
Hammond, Ella P1-50
Handysides, Alan P3-63, P3-64, P3-74
Happiness P1-46, P2-22, P5-12
Harassment P1-35–P1-37
Haskell, Stephen P1-4
Hausman, K. P2-41
Hays, Richard B. P4-40, P4-77, P4-79, P4-80, P4-81, P4-82, P4-83, P4-86
Healing ministry P3-37
Heaven P1-37, P3-75, P3-76, P3-82, P5-24
Hebraic heritage P4-5
Hebrew Bible P4-52
Hegstad, Douglas R. P3-73
Hell P1-15, P3-58
Hellenistic P4-5
Helminiak, Daniel P4-36, P4-37, P4-39, P4-40
Hendershot, Vernon P3-31
Henson, Mitchell P5-23–P5-32; response to P5-58–P5-60
Herick, Gregory M. P2-53
Herion, Gary A. P5-18
Hershberger, S. P2-44
Heye, Bekele P3-62, P3-74
High school P2-39
Hilgert, Earle E. P4-42
Hiltner, Seward P4-32
Hirshfield, Magnus P2-7, P2-24
Historical context P4-76, P5-5–P5-6; Arsenokoites P4-10; Holiness Code P4-4–P4-5; Malakos P4-8–P4-10; Romans 1 P4-12
HIV testing P2-27; youth and *See also* AIDS.
Holiness Code P4-4–P4-5, P4-66–P4-68, P4-74, P4-78, P4-80; impurity in P4-70; morally binding P4-19
Holland, Chris P3-72
Holtz, Duke P3-48

Subject Index

Holy Spirit P1-4, P1-50, P3-81, P4-45, P4-70, P5-24, P5-26
Homeless youth P2-38
Homo sapiens P4-46
Homo symbolicus P4-46
Homoerotic practice P4-12, P4-16–P4-17, P4-68, P4-79; P4-30
Homogenital sex P4-21, P4-22, P4-82; as ceremonial observance P4-76; Biblical texts P4-78; false religion and P4-17; Greco-Roman view of P4-68; Jews on P4-18; Paul on P4-20; Plato on P4-15–P4-16
Homophobia P2-26, P3-59, P4-56
Homosexual deeds P5-6, P5-16
Homosexuality: American Psychiatric Association P2-32–P2-35; as illness P2-30; as self-indulgence P4-10, P4-75; as social threat P4-56; Biblical condemnation of P4-51–P4-54, P4-76; Biblical understanding of P4-22, P4-23; in animals P1-40; levels of across time P5-27; myths about P5-27–P5-29; placement in Paul's vice list P4-14; pre-Christian view of P4-21–P4-22; SDA reaction to P1-10, P1-22–P1-23, P1-25–P1-26; separate from other inversions P2-4; theological understanding of P5-14; theoretical causes of P1-38–P1-39
Homosexuals: conservative P5-28–P5-29; possible instances in the Bible P4-52–P4-54; relating to P3-24–P3-26; SDA attitude toward P5-25–P5-26
Homosexuals Anonymous P3-38, P3-39
Hooker, Evelyn P2-12, P2-16, P2-26, P2-32, P2-33, P2-40, P2-41; on mental illness P2-11
Hopkins, Gary L. P3-73

Hopp, Joyce P3-73
Hormone treatment P2-12, P2-16, P2-25, P2-27
Hormones P1-39, P1-40, P2-14, P3-4, P3-76; homosexuality and P2-12, P2-13–P2-14; prenatal P2-26
Horwood, L. P2-43
Hosea P4-59
Howell, Robert J. P5-61
Human freedom P5-36–P5-39
Human Genome Project P2-6, P2-17, P2-28
Humana, Charles P4-62
Humiliation P1-31, P1-34, P3-31, P4-52
Humphreys, Laud P3-27
Husband P4-28, P4-49, P5-5, P5-10–P5-11

I

Identity: assumption P2-36; confusion P2-36; cultic P4-4–P4-5, P4-6–P4-7; formation P2-36
Idolatry P4-12–P4-13, P4-17, P4-26; deliverance from P4-26
Illness: homosexuality as P2-9
Immature fixation P2-31
Immoral behavior P4-55
Immorality: HIV/AIDS P3-60; school dismissal P3-53; sexual P4-68, P4-69; Sodom and Gomorrah P4-51
Impropriety P1-40
Impurity P4-13
IMRU? P3-21
Incest P4-65, P4-79, P5-11; as factor in "cure" P2-17; degeneracy P2-5; in Africa P3-63
Injections: hormone P2-9, P2-13, P2-16; progesterone P2-12, P2-26
Insanity P2-31

B-17

Subject Index

Insight P3-32–P3-33, P3-48, P3-49, P3-55
Intended outcome P5-15, P5-20
Intense loyalty P5-12–P5-13, P5-51, P5-52, P5-54
Internal gland secretions P2-7, P2-24
Interpretation P4-77; clobber texts P1-38; criteria P4-64; curse of Genesis P4-48; literal P3-47; Prodigal son P5-38; revisionary P4-81; through conversation P4-25–P4-26; traditional P3-3, P3-21, P3-31, P3-33, P4-51
Intersex individuals P1-39–P1-40, P3-4
Intimacy P1-46
Inversion P2-4, P2-30

J

Jacobs, Bob Earl P3-70
Jankowiak, William P5-60
Japenga, A. P3-70
Jenny, Carole P2-15, P2-28
Jesse P4-53
Jessel, David P1-51
Jewish perspective P4-17
Jews P4-6–P4-7, P4-12–P4-13, P4-16–P4-19; as degenerates P2-24; divine grace and P4-21; equality and P4-67; on heterosexuality P4-23; Samaritans P5-41; social degeneracy and P2-6; von Krafft-Ebing and P2-5, P2-24
Johns Hopkins University P1-39
Johnsson, William P3-50, P3-72
Johnston, G. P5-18
Johnston, Robert M. P3-72
Jokes P1-47, P2-38, P3-56
Jonathan P4-52, P4-74, P5-7
Jones, John P4-3–P4-30, P4-61, P4-73, P4-74, P4-75, P4-77, P4-79, P4-81, P4-82, P4-83; response to P4-63, P4-64, P4-65–P4-71
Jones, Stanton L. P4-39, P4-40
Jus ad bellum P5-3
Jus in bello P5-3
Justice P1-49, P2-52, P3-30, P5-54, P5-56; SDA and P5-24

K

Kakia P4-18
Kampmeeting P3-42
Kant, Immanuel P4-59, P5-11, P5-20
Kelsey, Barbara P4-60, P4-62
Kelsey, Morton P4-60, P4-62
Kemena, Ben P2-3–P2-44, P3-53; response to P2-45–P2-49, P2-52
Kerbeny, Karoly Maria P2-23
Keys, D.P. P3-27
King, R.M. P5-44–P5-46, P5-49
KinNet P3-21, P3-22
Kinsey, Alfred P1-42, P2-10, P2-25, P2-32, P2-41
Kinship Connection P1-10, P3-41, P3-54
Kinship International P3-41, P3-42
Kinship Kampmeeting P1-49, P3-33–P3-35, P3-36–P3-37, P3-38, P3-51, P3-54
Kirby, M. P2-42
Kittle, Gerhard P5-19
Kitzinger, C. P3-27
Klassen, William P5-18
Klawans, Jonathan P4-72
Kleber, David J. P5-61
Klismaphilia P5-8
Klostermann, August P4-32
Knight Amendment P3-43
Koranteng-Pipim, Samuel P3-51, P3-72
Krajeski, J. P2-33, P2-41
Kruks, G. P2-44

Subject Index

Kubo, Sakae P3-68
Kulkin, H. P2-43

L

La Sierra College P1-32
La Sierra University P3-52
LaHaye, Tim P1-41, P1-51
Lake, Kirsopp P4-34
Lamberg, L. P2-42
Larson, David P3-36, P5-3–P5-16; response to P5-51–P5-56, P5-59
Lawson, Ronald P1-51, P3-29–P3-66; response to P3-75–P3-82
Left-handedness P2-3, P2-11, P2-18, P4-48, P4-55
Legal issues P5-35–P5-36
Lenzer, J. P2-42
Lesbians P1-3–P1-13, P2-14–P2-15, P2-39, P3-5, P3-7, P4-68; church membership P3-22; covert P3-55; diethylstilbestrol P2-12, P2-26; frequency of P2-25; La Sierra University and P3-52; Otoacoustic emissions P2-28; the Bible on P4-4
LeVay, S. P2-14, P2-27, P3-26
Levirate Marriage Law P5-4
LGBT P2-30, P2-38, P2-40, P2-51–P2-52
Liberal churches P3-30
Libido P2-14, P2-16, P2-18
Liebman, Samuel P2-8, P2-25
Lifestyle P4-71, P5-27–P5-28, P5-30; Christian P3-37; gay P1-19, P1-23, P1-26, P2-52, P3-35, P3-59, P4-70, P5-13, P5-57; heterosexual P5-13; promiscuous gay P1-36, P1-41; same-sex P5-59; self-indulgent P4-75
Lind, Leif P1-15–P1-29, P1-54–P1-55
Living in sin P5-27, P5-29–P5-30, P5-58

Lobotomy P2-8, P2-11, P2-25, P2-26
Logic of equal respect P5-9
Logical consistency P5-10–P5-12
Loma Linda University P2-29, P3-36, P3-53, P3-54, P5-19; Medical Center P3-59
Londis, James P3-33, P3-68
Loneliness P1-5, P1-7, P1-8, P1-46, P3-80, P5-52
Loss P1-35, P4-70
Love P1-48, P2-34, P4-46; as loyalty P5-6–P5-9; as respect P5-9–P5-12; as sin P1-47; challenges of P1-54; Christian P5-5–P5-6; God's P3-77–P3-78; health and P1-46; husbands and P4-49; Jesus's P2-20; lack of P2-19; Larson on P5-51–P5-54; marriage and P1-45; parental P1-7, P3-12–P3-13; personal P5-5; relationships and P5-4–P5-16; sexual relationships and P5-5; "the sinner" P3-66
Loving P4-52; community P1-54, P2-52, P3-56; companionship P4-45; conversation P2-45; God P2-19; home P5-30; kindness P5-6
Loving relationships P4-24–P4-28, P4-47, P4-64, P4-70, P4-81–P4-82; Church and P4-82; difficulty with P5-16; Paul P4-76, P4-77; Scripture P5-6, P5-13
Loyalty P5-6–P5-9, P5-8, P5-12, P5-12–P5-13, P5-51–P5-54
Luther, Martin P5-5, P5-17

M

Macy, David P5-61
Maher, Bridget E. P1-52
Mairs, Nancy P4-62
Malakoi P4-8, P4-10

B-19

Subject Index

Malakos P4-7, P4-9. *See also* malakoì; as male homosexual behavior P4-10; historical context P4-8–P4-10
Male bonding P1-16
Male dominance P4-56, P4-57
Marcus Aurelius P4-34
Marriage P1-17, P4-48–P4-49, P5-12–P5-16, P5-14; affirmation of P3-43; as "cure" P3-25, P3-34; benefits of P1-45; changing views of P3-77; church and P4-83; constitutional amendment P3-31; covenant of P3-47; gays and P3-79, P3-80; homosexual P5-13; laws P3-43–P3-44, P3-46, P3-50, P3-52; Martin Luther on P5-5; meaning and purpose of P1-45; meaning of P5-12–P5-16; Paul on P4-15, P4-27, P4-45; politicians and P5-15; same-sex P5-55; traditional P4-56
Martin, C. P2-41
Martin, Dale B. P4-34, P4-35
Masculine virtues P4-9
Masochism P2-10, P2-25
Masturbation P2-4, P2-24, P5-17
Max, Louis P2-8, P2-25
May, William F. P5-18
McFadden, Dennis P2-28
McLarty, John P3-51, P3-72
McLoughlin, Kate P3-71
McLoughlin, Michael P3-70
McNeill, John J. P4-31, P4-35
Mendel, Gregor P2-7
Mendenhall, George E. P5-18
Mental disorder P2-21, P2-45, P2-49–P2-50, P2-51, P3-30; AMA on P2-22; APA on P2-9, P2-25; DSM P2-32; mental health professionals P2-21, P2-29
Mental illness P2-16, P2-34, P2-34–P2-35, P2-52
Mephibosheth P5-7

Message P3-59
Metropolitan Community Church P3-20, P3-52
Milgrom, Jacob P4-67, P4-70, P4-72
Military P2-9, P2-25
Miner, Jeff P4-61, P4-62
Ministering P2-20, P3-33, P3-56–P3-57, P3-58, P3-63, P5-25–P5-26
Ministers P1-15, P5-28
Ministry P3-49, P3-50
Ministry Magazine P1-19, P3-18, P3-37, P3-39
Missionaries P1-4, P1-15, P1-31, P3-10
Moberly, Elizabeth P1-41, P1-51
Moir, Anne P1-51
Money, John P1-39, P2-12, P2-26, P2-41
Moral criteria P4-65; for sexual intimacy P4-47, P4-64; for sexual relationships P4-52; of sexual intimacy P4-48; practical implications of P4-47
Moral evil P4-13, P4-75
Moral impurity P4-67
Moral law P4-20, P4-65, P4-68, P5-7
Moral quality P4-26–P4-27, P4-43, P4-74
Morality P4-20, P4-28, P5-48; P2-49, P4-26; HIV/AIDS P3-62; legislating P3-46; sexual P4-25, P4-55, P5-4, P5-51
Mosaic laws P4-65
Mostert, Thomas P3-43, P3-52, P3-72
Mother: castrating P2-14, P2-27; domineering P1-27, P2-10, P2-25, P2-26, P3-9; homosexuality and P2-32
Mount, Ferdinand P5-60
Moyer, B. P2-42

B-20

Subject Index

Murder P2-46, P4-14, P4-69
Musvosvi, Joel P3-62, P3-74
Mutuality P4-26, P4-28, P4-55, P4-74
Mwansa, Pardon P3-64
Myths P3-7, P3-7–P3-9, P3-25, P5-27–P5-29

N

Naomi P5-7
National Association of School Psychologists P2-21, P2-23
National Association of Social Workers P2-16, P2-21, P2-23, P2-34
Natural law P4-15, P4-19, P4-75
Natural order P4-14, P4-16
Nature P2-15, P2-46–P2-47, P4-16, P5-58
Nazi Germany P2-5, P2-6, P2-8
Necrophilia P4-55, P5-8
Negroes P2-5, P2-8
Nelson, James B. P4-59, P4-60
New Testament P4-5, P4-7, P4-20, P5-26; arsenokoites P4-11; gender assumptions in P4-19; malakos P4-8–P4-9; normative principles P4-52; on sexual conduct P4-79–P4-80; Pauline references P4-51
Niebuhr, H. Richard P5-20, P5-21
Nineteenth century P4-50, P4-76, P5-44
Nixon, Richard P2-11
Nixon, Robert P3-36
Nokes, Kathleen M. P5-61
Non-Adventist P1-10, P3-19, P3-48, P3-49, P5-24; homosexuals P3-24; partners P3-48
Nondiscrimination P2-23
Nongender-typical behavior P1-34
Normal P2-7, P2-10, P2-24; desire to be P1-38; Hooker on P2-11
Norms P3-8; Biblical P4-78; cultural P4-16, P4-28; ecclesiastical P5-29; gentile P4-7; sexual P4-5, P4-6, P4-19, P5-3–P5-16, P5-58
North American Division P3-35
North New England Conference P3-44
North Oshawa Church P3-56
Nurture P1-39, P2-5, P2-15, P4-44; spiritual P3-33
Nurturing: homosexual relationships P3-36; pastors and P3-81; relationship with God P1-13; same-sex relationships P4-57; SDA Kinship P3-66; SDA Kinship and P3-48; under dominion P3-76

O

Obsatz, Sharyn P3-73
Oedipal conflict P2-31
Old Testament P5-26
Oldenburg, Claes P5-4
Onan P5-4, P5-17
One flesh P2-20, P4-79
Ontario Conference, 2006 P1-54
Orgasm P4-45
Orientation, sexual: biological basis P2-3–P2-4; changing P2-20–P2-23, P3-17; components of P3-3–P3-6; concept of P2-4–P2-19; definition P2-30; determinants of P2-45–P2-49; myths P3-7
Origen P4-62
Ornish, Dean P1-46, P1-52
Otoacoustic emissions P2-28
Outka, Gene P5-19

P

Pacific Union P3-40
Pacific Union College P1-33, P3-53

B-21

Subject Index

Pacific Union Conference P3-43, P3-52
Pagan P3-21, P4-17, P4-52, P4-76
Paine, N. Emmons P2-24
Para phusin P4-15, P4-17, P4-19, P4-37
Paradise Valley, California P1-32
Parental relationships P1-41, P2-14, P3-9
Parental response P1-3, P1-35, P2-50, P3-11–P3-13, P3-24–P3-26; negative P2-13–P2-14; support for P1-48–P1-49
Parents P1-11, P1-37–P1-38; gays as P1-11, P1-12, P2-16
Parks, Rosa P5-23
Partners P1-27, P3-48; church and P3-23, P3-49, P3-56; family and P3-12; Loma Linda University and P3-54; multiple sex P3-63, P3-64
Pasanen, Edward P2-28
Passion P4-14, P4-15, P5-9, P5-17, P5-26; Augustine on P4-45; degrading P4-74; fleshly P4-10
Pathfinder Club P5-23
Pathological P2-11, P2-23, P2-31, P2-33
Pathology P2-16, P2-18, P2-30, P2-50
Patterson, C. P2-42
Pattison, E.M. P3-26, P3-27
Pattison, M.L. P3-26, P3-27
Paul P4-6–P4-30, P4-7, P4-8, P4-9, P4-10, P4-12, P4-18, P4-20, P5-16, P5-26, P5-42–P5-43; fleshly desires P4-15; pre-Christian view of homosexuality P4-21–P4-22; Romans 1 P4-12–P4-19; two levels of depravity P4-13, P4-75
Pauline vice lists P4-7–P4-12, P4-14, P4-18, P4-68

Paulk, John P2-17
Paulsen, Jan P1-49, P1-52, P3-29, P3-45, P3-63, P3-64, P3-67, P3-71, P3-79, P3-82
Pausanius P4-42
Payne, Leanne P1-41, P1-51
Peace P1-27, P1-47, P3-17, P3-18, P4-71
Pearson, Michael P3-67
Pederasty P4-15, P4-16, P4-17, P4-23
Pedophilia P2-4, P2-15, P2-32, P4-55, P5-11, P5-56
Penis P1-39, P3-4, P3-5, P4-65
Percie, G. P2-43
Persons with AIDS. *See* PWA
Perversion P4-50, P4-75
Peterson, Kelli P2-43, P2-44
Pfaelzer, Mariana P3-42
Philia P5-9
Philip P4-53
Philo Judaeus P4-16, P4-33, P4-37
Phusikôs P4-16
Phusis P4-16
Physical pleasure P4-44–P4-45
Physicality P4-44
Pierson, Robert P3-67
Pilkington, N. P2-44
Pillard, Richard P2-14, P2-27
Piner, Kenneth Edward P3-70
Pinko P2-9
Plato P5-5; on homogenital sex P4-15; self-indulgence P4-14
Pleasure: legitimacy of P4-15; physical P4-44–P4-45, P4-44–P4-46, P4-45, P4-46–P4-47, P4-47, P4-74, P4-78
Plethmysography P2-12
Plutarch P4-36
Political climate, 19th century P2-5
Political correctness P3-50, P4-70
Politicization of homosexuality P2-9
Politics P2-49–P2-50, P5-15
Polkinghorne, John P4-62

Subject Index

Pollard, Leslie N. P3-73
Polyandry P5-11
Polycarp P4-9, P4-34
Polygamy P5-11
Pomeroy, M. P2-41
Poneria P4-13, P4-18
Porneia P4-26
Pornography P1-47, P5-8
Pornos P4-7
Porter, Harold G. P1-48
Potter, La Forest P2-8, P2-25
Prather, Gayle P5-61
Prather, Hugh P5-61
Praying P2-51, P3-17, P3-34, P4-70; for change P1-17, P1-32, P1-35, P1-37–P1-38, P1-41, P1-42, P2-19, P3-8–P3-9, P3-17, P3-24; for forgiveness P1-18; for guidance P3-20; for understanding P1-6; honestly P3-79
Pre-Christian sources P4-17, P4-18, P4-21–P4-22, P4-68
Predictive markers P1-34, P2-13, P2-18
Prejudice P2-16, P2-18, P2-50, P3-30, P4-50
Premarital sex P1-17, P2-4
Present truth P1-4, P1-8
Primates P2-32
Principles P4-52, P4-74, P5-57
Prison P2-6, P2-9, P2-24, P2-25, P3-58
Procreation P2-4, P4-14–P4-15, P4-45, P4-54–P4-55; contraception and P4-50–P4-51, P4-78; Genesis on P4-52; openness to P5-55; sex and P4-54–P4-55; sex in Old Testament P5-26; sexual intimacy and P5-15
Prodigal son P5-36–P5-39
Progesterone P2-12, P2-14, P2-26
Propriety P5-13
Prostitution P2-4, P3-13, P3-21, P5-8, P5-28; in vice lists P4-12; male P4-8, P4-16, P4-17; temple P3-34, P4-23, P4-52, P5-5
Protestants P2-5, P3-44, P3-46, P4-45
Provonsha, Jack W. P5-19
Psychiatry P2-30–P2-35, P2-45, P2-49–P2-50
Psychoanalysis P2-10, P2-25, P2-31
Psychosexual development P2-31
Psychosocial issues P2-37
Puberty P1-32, P1-40, P2-36, P3-6, P3-10
Public issues, criteria for addressing P5-36–P5-48
Punishment P2-4, P2-24
PWA P3-59–P3-64

Q

Quaker tradition P1-11
Queer P1-35, P2-39
Quest Learning Center P3-17–P3-19, P3-37–P3-41, P3-41; failures of P3-47, P3-48, P3-81

R

Racism P2-5
Radiation therapy P2-8, P2-25
Rado, Sandor P2-31–P2-32
Rae, Walter P3-69
Ramsey, Paul P5-18
Rape P1-5, P1-47, P2-4, P3-34, P3-63; Abraham's guests P4-51, P4-66; gang P4-66; Levite's concubine P4-51; respect and P5-11; sex as P4-57; sexual behavior changes and P2-15
Reading, Pennsylvania P3-17–P3-18, P3-33, P3-37, P3-38
Realization of homosexuality P1-6, P1-16

B-23

Subject Index

Regis, Edward Jr. P5-19
Reign of Christ P4-25, P4-63
Reinach, Alan P3-43, P3-44, P3-45, P3-52, P3-71, P3-72
Rejection P3-3, P3-23, P3-24, P3-31, P3-65; alienation and P3-47; church and P1-48, P1-49; communicating P4-57; self P3-34, P3-38; youth and P2-37
Relationship continuum P5-59
Relationships P3-76, P4-23, P4-46–P4-48, P5-28, P5-59; Biblical view of P3-43; ethics of P4-81; God and P3-78; health and P1-46; incestuous P4-65; lesbian P1-10–P1-13; love and P5-4–P5-16; loving, same-sex P4-4, P4-19, P4-24–P4-28; parental P3-9; peer P2-35; priority of P5-4–P5-16; same-sex P4-57–P4-58, P4-73–P4-74, P4-76–P4-84; Sherri Babcock P1-8, P1-10–P1-12
Religion P4-17, P5-28, P5-43, P5-45, P5-46; change as good P3-17; Seventh-day Adventist P3-42; sexual orientation and P2-45; threats to P3-50
Religious convictions as law P5-44–P5-48
Religious Freedom Restoration Act P5-43
Religious Right P3-31, P3-40, P3-44, P3-45, P3-65
Remafedi, Gary P2-16, P2-27, P2-44
Remnant P1-4, P3-81, P5-24–P5-25
Reparative therapies P1-42, P1-44, P2-20–P2-23, P2-28; failures of P2-17
Research P1-39, P2-7–P2-8, P2-32; 1990s P2-14–P2-15; after Stonewall P2-12; Hooker P2-11; Kinsey P2-10; pedophilia P2-15–P2-16; sissies P2-13–P2-15
Respect P4-25, P5-9–P5-12
Responsible lives P5-3
Richards, H.M.S. P1-50
Richards, Kevin G. P3-74
Richardson, Colonel T. E. P5-45
Ricoeur, Paul P4-60
Rienzo, Douglas P5-61
Right-handedness P2-11, P4-48
Ritterskamp, R. P2-44
Ritual impurity P4-67
Ritual observance P4-26–P4-28
Ritual purity P4-4
Robinson, D.A. P1-4, P1-51
Robinson, Gene P3-50
Rogers, Jack P4-61
Rohr, Richard P4-62
Roman Catholic Church P2-18, P2-28
Rosler, Ariel P2-28
Rotheram-Borus, M. P2-43
Royce, Josiah P5-7–P5-8, P5-18, P5-52
Ruth P3-77, P3-79, P5-7

S

Sabbath P1-11, P1-26, P3-46, P3-50, P5-57; commandment P3-76; communion P5-28–P5-29; Decalogue and P4-20; problem texts on P1-18; R.M. King and P5-44
Sabbath School P1-4, P1-53, P1-54, P3-10, P3-60; discussions P1-13; teaching P1-22, P3-23
Sacks, Jonathan P1-31, P1-50
Sadness P1-35, P5-5
Sadomasochism P4-55, P5-11
Safety P2-12, P2-52, P3-8, P3-78, P4-47
Sakenfeld, Katherine Doob P5-18

Subject Index

Same-sex attraction P2-36
Same-sex marriage P3-45, P3-50, P5-55; APA and P2-29; APA on P2-29, P2-39; church opposition to P3-43–P3-44; Massachusetts P3-30
Same-sex sex: cultic identity and P4-5; heterosexual males and P3-7; Paul's lack of moral language about P4-14
San Francisco Central Adventist Church P3-47
San Francisco Central Church P3-56
Satan P1-24, P1-38, P2-40
Satinover, Jeffrey P2-28
Savin-Williams, R. P2-44, P3-26
Scanzoni, Letha Dawson P4-59
Scarone, Daniel P3-73
Schneider, Margaret P5-61
Schools P2-50–P2-51; Adventist P3-15–P3-17, P3-52–P3-54; bullying P2-38–P2-39, P2-51–P2-52; harassment P1-35–P1-37
Schroeder, Michael P2-17, P2-28, P2-48, P2-53
Schroeter, Werner P5-61
Scripture P4-22, P4-51–P4-55, P5-5–P5-6, P5-6–P5-7; Christian principles of P4-28; covenant in P5-7; faithfulness in P5-8; legitimacy of thought P4-23–P4-24; love in P5-9; marriage and P3-43; relevant to all relationships P4-28; respect in P5-10
Scroggs, Robin P4-33, P4-34, P4-35, P4-37
Scruton, Roger P4-62
SDA: advocacy P5-48; position on homosexuality P2-50; position on homosexuality, 1999 P2-20; reaction to homosexuality P3-22–P3-24

SDA Kinship International P1-8, P1-9, P3-21, P3-30, P3-32, P3-33–P3-37, P3-35–P3-37; acceptance from P1-49; growth of P3-48, P3-57; improvement for young gays P3-65–P3-66; in Uganda P3-58; Insight article P3-49; law suit P3-42
Self-acceptance P1-7, P1-35, P3-11, P3-14, P3-16, P5-52; after Quest P3-39; denial P1-16
Self-alienation P5-53
Self-rejection P3-34, P3-38
Sensitization P2-36
Separation-individuation P2-35
Septuagint: Sirach: 23:17 P4-34
Serling, Rod P5-32
Seventh-day Adventist Church Manual P5-29–P5-30
Seventh-day Adventist Theological Seminary P3-33, P5-24
Sex: for pleasure P4-14–P4-15; nonprocreative P5-26, P5-27
Sex-typed behavior P3-5
Sexual abuse P1-5, P2-28, P3-19
Sexual behavior, sexual orientation and P3-7
Sexual complementarity P4-55
Sexual conduct P4-5
Sexual harassment P5-11
Sexual identity formation P2-36
Sexual intimacy: bonds from P4-46–P4-47; moral criteria and P4-47–P4-48; moral quality of P4-48–P4-51; purposes of P5-15
Sexual inversion P2-24, P2-30
Sexual mores, up to 1840s P2-4
Sexual orientation P2-30, P3-3; formation, myths about P3-7–P3-9
Sexual preference P3-6, P3-6–P3-7, P4-74

Subject Index

Sexual preference continuum P1-42, P3-6, P3-6–P3-7, P3-76, P4-50
Sexual proportionality P5-13
Sexual relationships: between unequals P5-11; love and P5-5, P5-5–P5-16, P5-12; without love P5-4–P5-5
Sexual sadism P2-33
Sexuality: intrinsic goodness of P4-45–P4-46
Shame P4-18, P5-55; Adventists' P3-31; from harassment P1-36; HIV/AIDS and P3-61; Jonathan and P4-53; parental P1-34–P1-35
Shameful P4-14, P4-51
Shameless P4-14, P4-16–P4-17, P4-74
Sharp, H.C. P2-24
Shidlo, Arial P2-17, P2-28, P2-48, P2-53
Shidlo, Ariel P2-53
Sibyllene Oracle: 2:70–77 P4-11
Siker, Jeffrey S. P4-35, P4-36, P4-41
Silver Rule P5-9
Sin P2-45–P2-47, P2-48, P4-70, P4-80, P4-81; betrayal P5-9; crisis of faith P1-37–P1-38; deliverance from P4-26; gentile P4-69; nonprocreative sex as P2-30; sex as P4-45–P4-46; sexual P3-31–P3-32; treatment of gays P2-51; uncleanness or P4-19–P4-20
Sinful P1-54, P2-36, P2-46–P2-47, P4-64, P4-82; actions P4-80; choice P1-48, P2-15, P2-16; desire for companion P1-45; homosexual activity P3-49; love P1-47; Paul P4-12, P4-18, P4-20, P4-22; same-sex behavior P3-24

Sissies P1-32, P2-13–P2-14, P2-27, P3-5
Situational ethics P4-29
Sklar, Jay P4-72
Slavery P2-5, P4-52, P4-79
Sligo SDA Church P3-33, P3-59
Smith, Sandy P1-5
Smoot, Grady P3-32
Snaith, Norman H. P5-18
Social degeneracy P2-5–P2-6
Social gospel P5-24–P5-25
Social issues P5-24, P5-24–P5-25
Social justice P1-12, P5-24
Sociocultural differences P4-6
Socrates P5-5
Sodom P4-4, P4-51
Sodomite P4-33
Softness, in early Christian times P4-8–P4-10
Solomon, Robert C. P5-60
Sophie, J. P2-42
Sorrow P1-34, P1-35, P3-34
Sorum, Jonathan P3-72
Southern Adventist College P3-36
Southern Adventist University P3-53
Spangler, Robert P3-69
Spectrum P1-18, P1-54, P3-38, P3-51, P3-52
Spiritual P1-11, P2-19, P4-44, P4-57; growth P4-26; home P1-12–P1-13, P3-56; maturity P4-27
Spirituality P3-75, P3-82, P4-44
Spitzer, Robert P1-42, P2-34, P2-47, P2-53
Spouse P3-13–P3-15, P3-32
Springett, Robert P3-36; P3-69
Srnec, J. P2-25
State interference P5-57
Stauffer, Ethelbert P5-19
Steadfast love P5-6, P5-8, P5-16, P5-52, P5-54
Steed, Lincoln P3-50, P3-72
Stein, T. P2-41

Subject Index

Stereotypes P1-34, P2-30, P3-23
Stoller, R. P2-42
Stonewall Riots P2-11–P2-12, P2-26, P2-33
Struggling with homosexuality P1-6–P1-7, P1-8, P1-9, P1-17–P1-18, P3-8–P3-9; support P3-16–P3-17
Student missionary P1-4, P1-7, P3-18
Student movement P3-53
Subsidiarity P5-15, P5-54–P5-56
Substance abuse P2-48
Suicide P1-39, P2-9, P2-50, P3-58, P5-30; after the "cure" P1-41; attempt P1-5, P3-34; gay youth P2-16, P2-27, P2-37; marriage and P1-46; thoughts of P1-33
Suitable helper P4-49
Sullivan, Andrew P5-20
Sunday laws P5-44–P5-48
Swaab, D.F. P3-26
Switzer, David P1-37
Symonds, J.A. P2-24

T

Takoma Park, Maryland. P1-32
Talbot, E.S. P2-24
Task Force on Homosexuality P2-26
Ten Commandments P4-65
Testicles P2-8, P2-25, P3-4, P3-5
Testosterone P2-13–P2-14, P2-27, P3-4
The Twilight Zone P5-30
Theophilus P4-11, P4-35
Therapies P2-3, P3-79; aversion P1-41; behavioral P2-13; castration P2-24; change P3-25, P4-48–P4-49; conversion P2-21, P2-23, P2-47. *See also* Reparative therapy; drug P1-41; electric shock P2-25; electro-convulsive P2-9, P2-25; emetics P2-8, P2-25; radiation P2-8, P2-25; reparative P1-42, P1-44, P2-21, P2-22, P2-23, P2-28; failures of P2-17
Thompson, George P2-9, P2-25
Thumma, S. P3-27
Tibbits-Kleber, Alta L. P5-61
Tillich, Paul P4-59
Tolerance P2-16, P5-56
Tomboys P1-5, P3-5
Torres, Rudy P5-25
Trademark, SDA P3-41, P3-42
Trajectory P4-6, P4-24, P4-69, P4-76, P4-79
Transgender P2-30, P3-7
Transsexual people P1-40
Transvestitism P2-32
Treatment P2-10, P2-31–P2-35; AMA on P2-22; Bieber on P2-26; intersex individuals P1-39; sissies and P2-25, P2-27; social workers on P2-23
Trinity P3-78
Triple minority P2-37
Troiden, R. P2-42
Troilism P5-8
Troy, Owen A. P3-67
Truth P1-4, P1-6, P1-13
Tuskegee Syphilis Study P2-6
Twelve-step program P1-9
Twentieth century P2-5–P2-6, P2-6, P4-22, P5-46
Twenty-first century P2-19
Twins P1-39, P2-14–P2-15, P2-18, P2-47
Tyler, Janet P5-31
Tyner, Mitchell P5-35–P5-49; response to P5-56–P5-58, P5-59

Subject Index

U

U.S. Supreme Court: *Bowers vs. Hardwick* P2-27; gay marriage and P3-52; *Lawrence vs. Texas* P2-11, P2-17, P2-28, P3-44, P5-35; Oregon vs. Smith case P5-43; R.M. King case P5-46; *Romer vs. Evans* P2-15, P2-28; sodomy laws and P3-30
Uncleanness P4-13, P4-19–P4-20, P4-21, P4-26, P4-75, P4-76; ceremonial P4-28
Unitive purpose P5-15
Unnatural P4-15, P4-19, P4-43, P4-54, P4-74, P5-15, P5-17; behavior P4-55; context of P3-21; female sex P4-14; nonprocreative sex P4-74; Paul on P4-65, P4-69; to shameless P4-17; unusual as P4-55

V

Vagina P3-4, P4-65
Variation P2-10, P2-21, P2-24, P2-31
Via, Dan O. P4-40
Vice. *See also* Pauline vice lists; betrayal P5-9; Freud on P2-8, P2-25, P2-31; gentile P4-16, P4-17; nonprocreative sex as P2-30
Violence P2-15, P4-11, P4-52; against homosexuals P3-30; as factor in "cure" P2-17; coming out and P2-38; element in intimacy P4-57; LGBT and P2-40; marriage and P1-46; school and P2-51; sexual coercion P4-11; youth and P2-50–P2-51
Virgin Mary P4-59
Virtue P1-28, P4-7, P4-9
Vomiting P2-8

Von Krafft-Ebing, Richard P2-5, P2-24, P2-31
Voyeurism P5-8

W

Walla Walla College P1-7, P3-49, P3-53
Wallerstein, Judith S. P5-61
Wang, Harry C. P2-43; response to P2-45, P2-49–P2-52
Wanton living P5-28
Watson, James P2-7
Watson, Robin P5-61
Weinrich, J. P2-41
Weiss, Harold P5-24
Westphal, Carl P2-30
Wherry, Ken P2-9, P2-25
White, Ellen P3-31, P3-76, P3-79, P5-24, P5-28, P5-48; mental health P3-32; worst sins P3-81
White, Mel P1-37
Whitehead, Minnie M. P5-61
Whole person P4-44
Wife P4-28; desire for a P3-9, P3-18; dominated by husband P4-48; husband's love P4-49, P5-7, P5-10–P5-11; impotent husband P5-5; Levirate Marriage Law P5-4
Wilde, Oscar P2-6, P2-24
Wilkinson, S. P3-27
Williams, Sheyanne P3-71
Willow, Tessa P3-71
Wilson, Neal P3-33, P3-34, P3-39, P3-40, P3-68, P3-69, P3-70
Wink, Walter P1-37, P4-61, P4-62
Wittschiebe, C.E. P3-68
Witztum, Eliezer P2-28
Wogaman, J. Philip P5-20, P5-21
Wood, Allen W. P5-20
Wood, Kenneth P3-67
Wood, Miriam P3-67
Work, coming out P3-14–P3-15

Subject Index

World Health Organization P2-35
World League for Sexual Reform P2-24
Worthington Foods P1-8
Wrath of God P4-13, P4-76
Wright, Lester P3-74
Wyrick, D. P2-44

Y

Yancey, Philip P1-14, P1-54
Yarhouse, Mark A. P4-39, P4-40
Youth: bias against P2-29; challenges of P2-35; dating P2-36; friends and P2-35; HIV/AIDS P2-38, P2-38–P2-39; psychosocial issues for P2-37; Quest Learning Center P3-81; suicide P2-16, P2-27, P2-37–P2-38

Z

Zucker, K.J. P1-50, P3-5, P3-26